Pandora Hearts

Jun Mochizuki

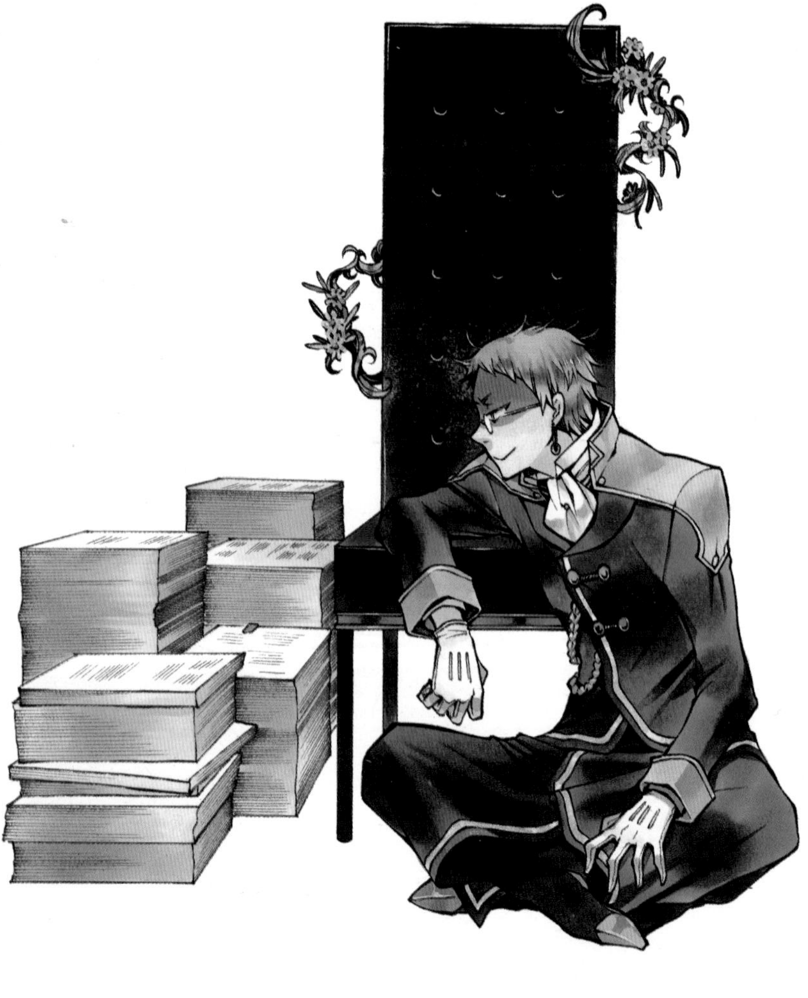

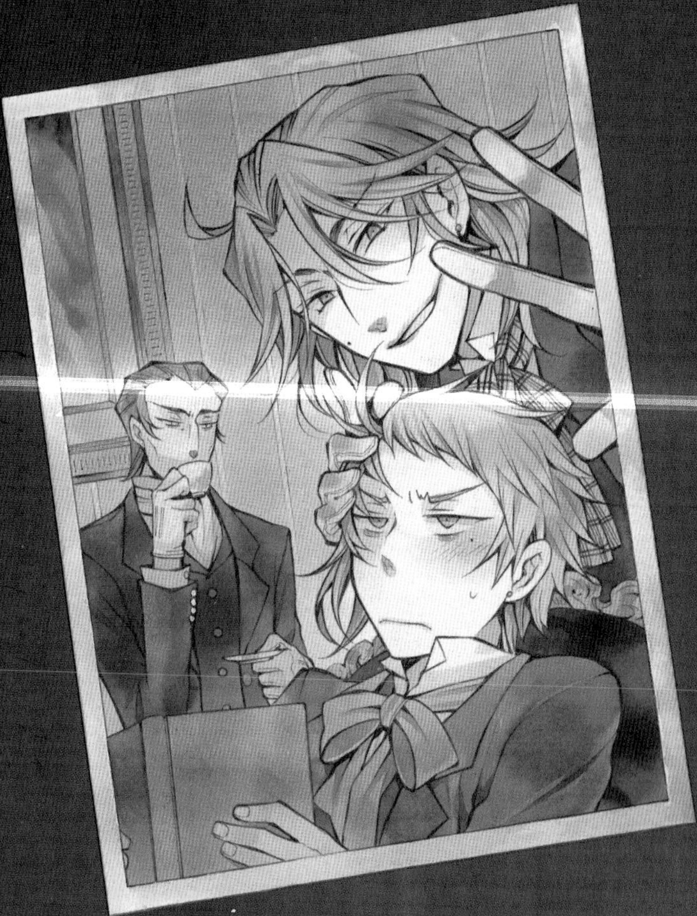

CONTENTS

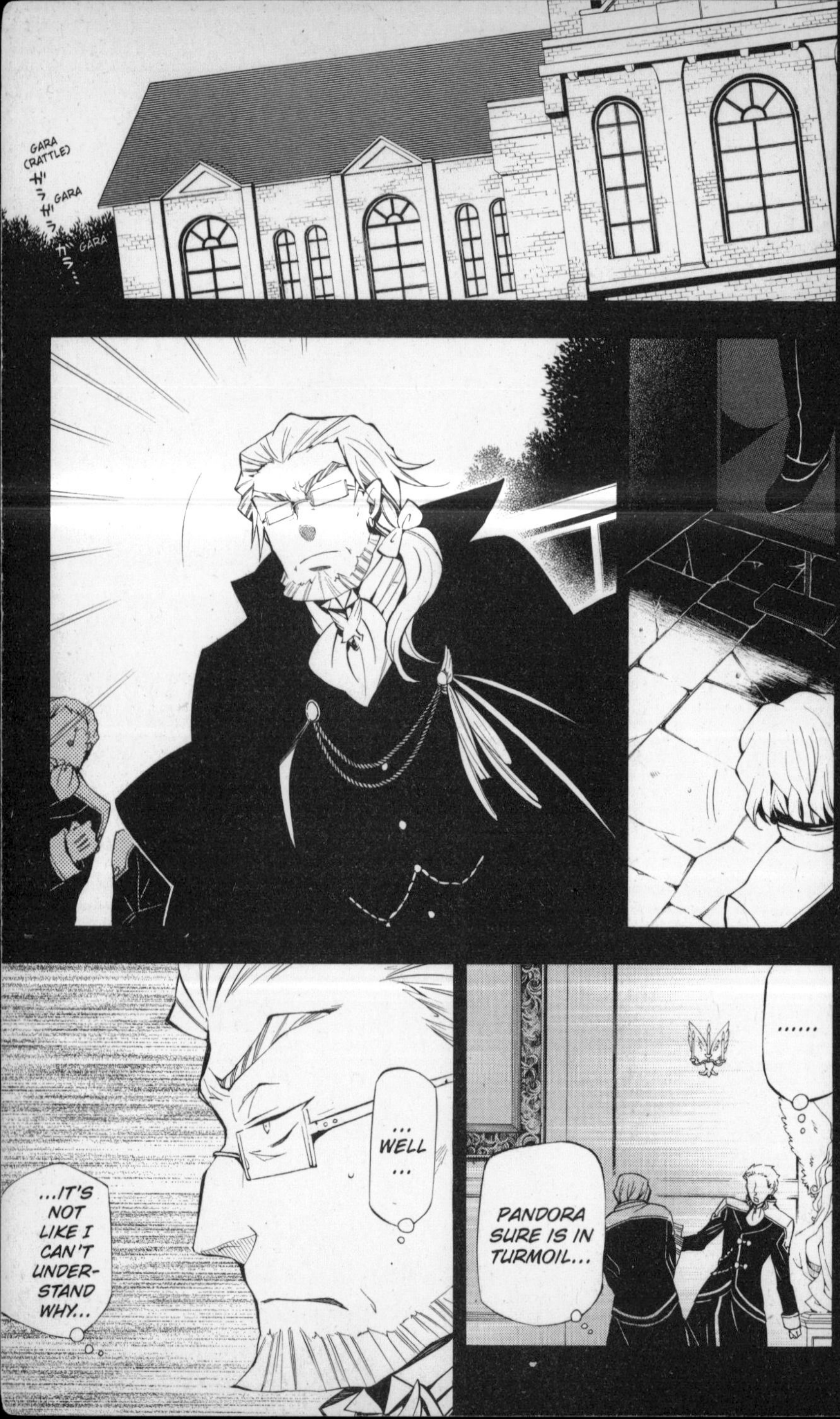
GARA (RATTLE)
ガラ
GARA
ガラ
GARA
ガラ…
......
PANDORA SURE IS IN TURMOIL...
...WELL...
...IT'S NOT LIKE I CAN'T UNDER-STAND WHY...

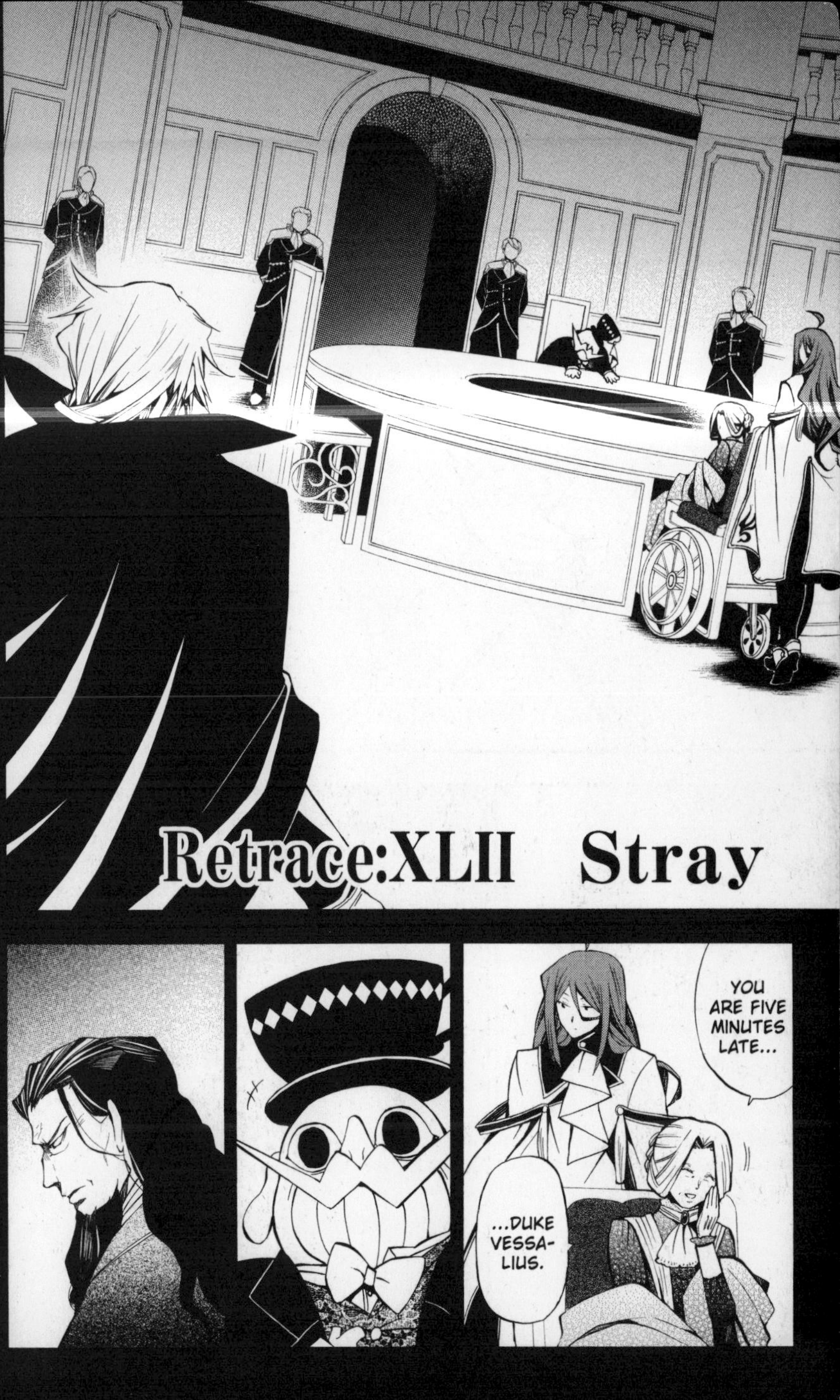
Retrace:XLII Stray
YOU ARE FIVE MINUTES LATE...
...DUKE VESSALIUS.

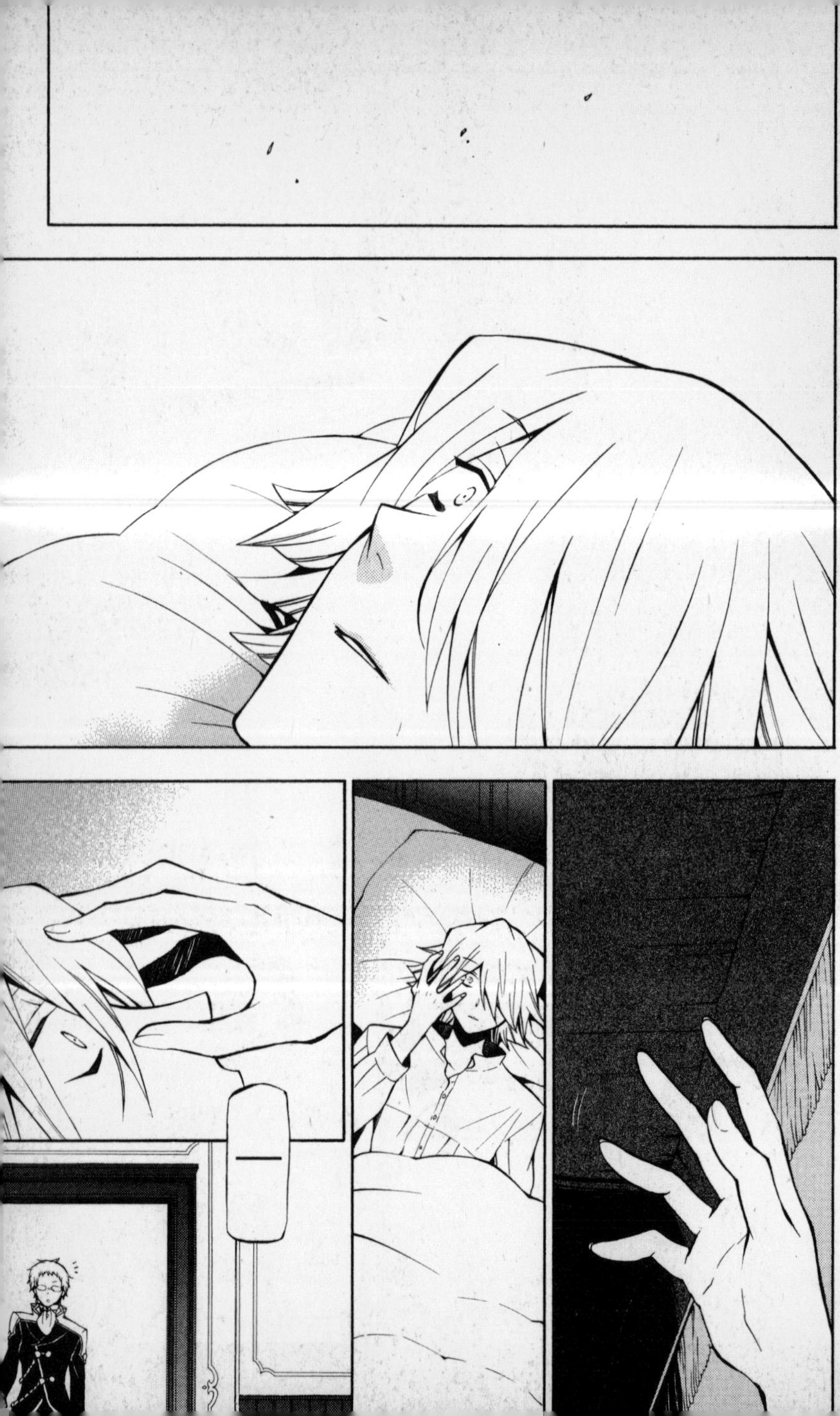

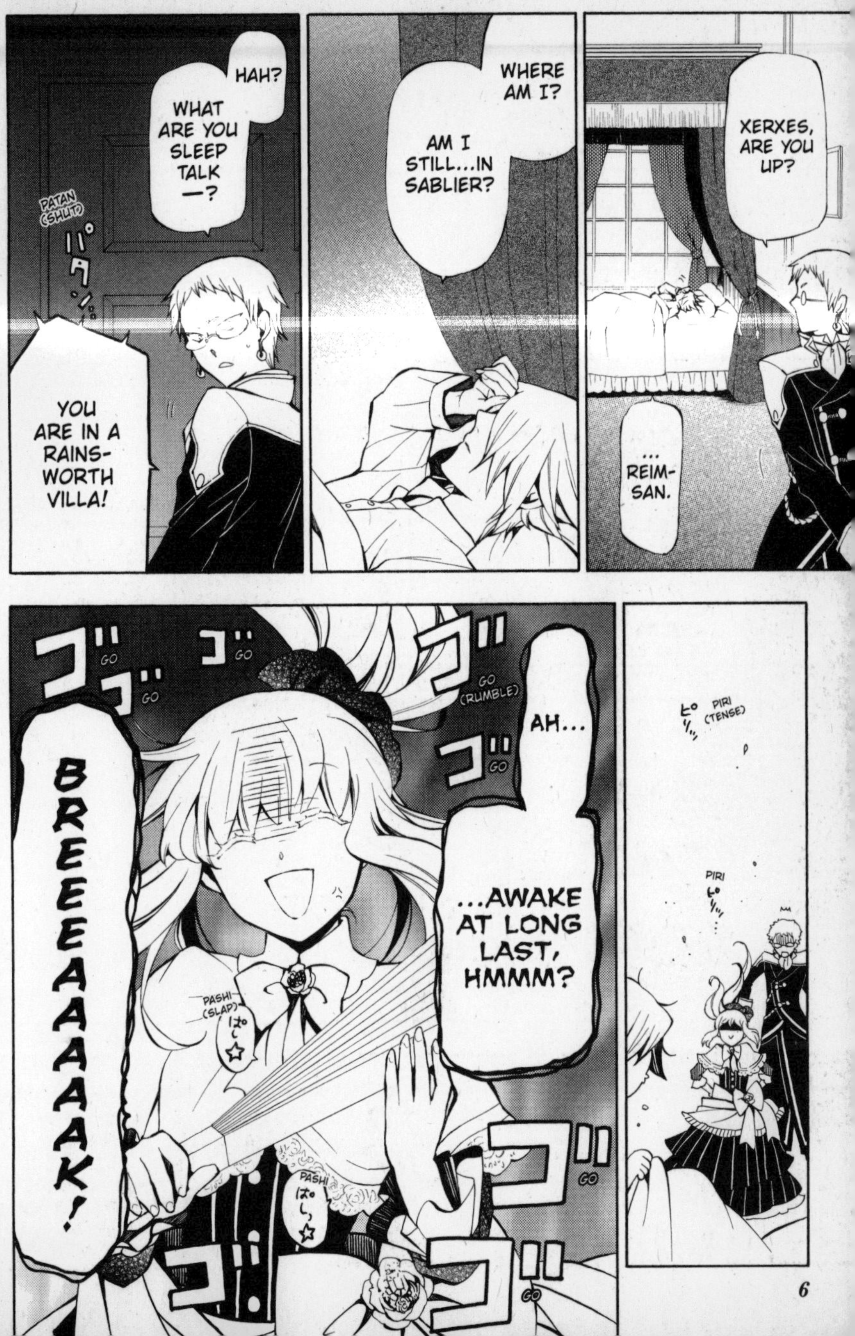
XERXES, ARE YOU UP?
...REIM-SAN.
WHERE AM I?
AM I STILL...IN SABLIER?
HAH?
WHAT ARE YOU SLEEP TALK—?
PATAN (SHUT)
YOU ARE IN A RAINS-WORTH VILLA!
PIRI (TENSE)
PIRI
GO GO GO
GO (RUMBLE)
AH...
GO
...AWAKE AT LONG LAST, HMMM?
BREEEAAAAAK!
PASHI (SLAP)
PASHI
GO
GO

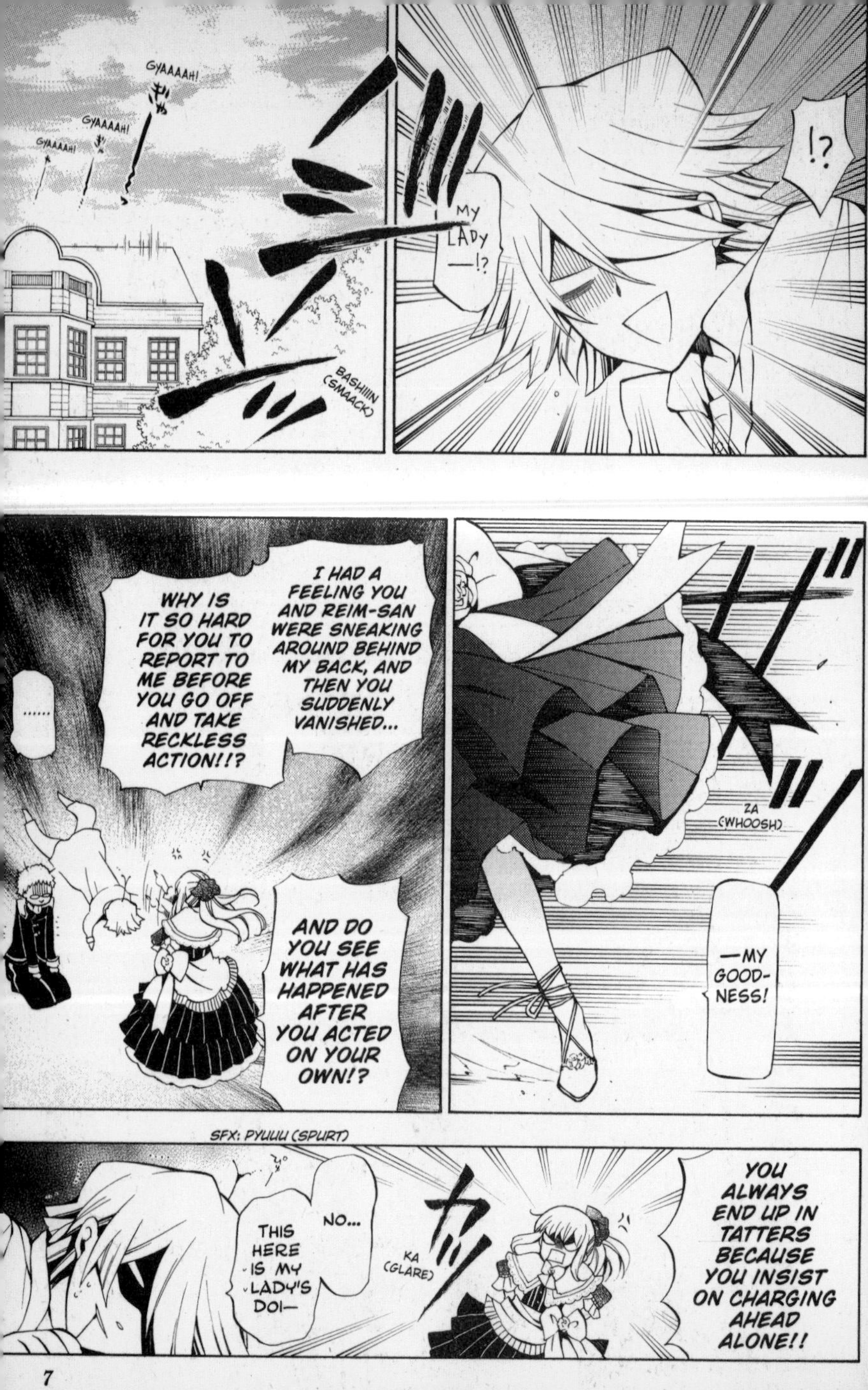
!?
MY LADY—!?
BASHIIN (SMAACK)
GYAAAAH!
GYAAAAH!
GYAAAAH!
—MY GOODNESS!
ZA (WHOOSH)
I HAD A FEELING YOU AND REIM-SAN WERE SNEAKING AROUND BEHIND MY BACK, AND THEN YOU SUDDENLY VANISHED...
WHY IS IT SO HARD FOR YOU TO REPORT TO ME BEFORE YOU GO OFF AND TAKE RECKLESS ACTION!!?
......
AND DO YOU SEE WHAT HAS HAPPENED AFTER YOU ACTED ON YOUR OWN!?
SFX: PYUUU (SPURT)
YOU ALWAYS END UP IN TATTERS BECAUSE YOU INSIST ON CHARGING AHEAD ALONE!!
KA (GLARE)
NO... THIS HERE IS MY LADY'S DOI—

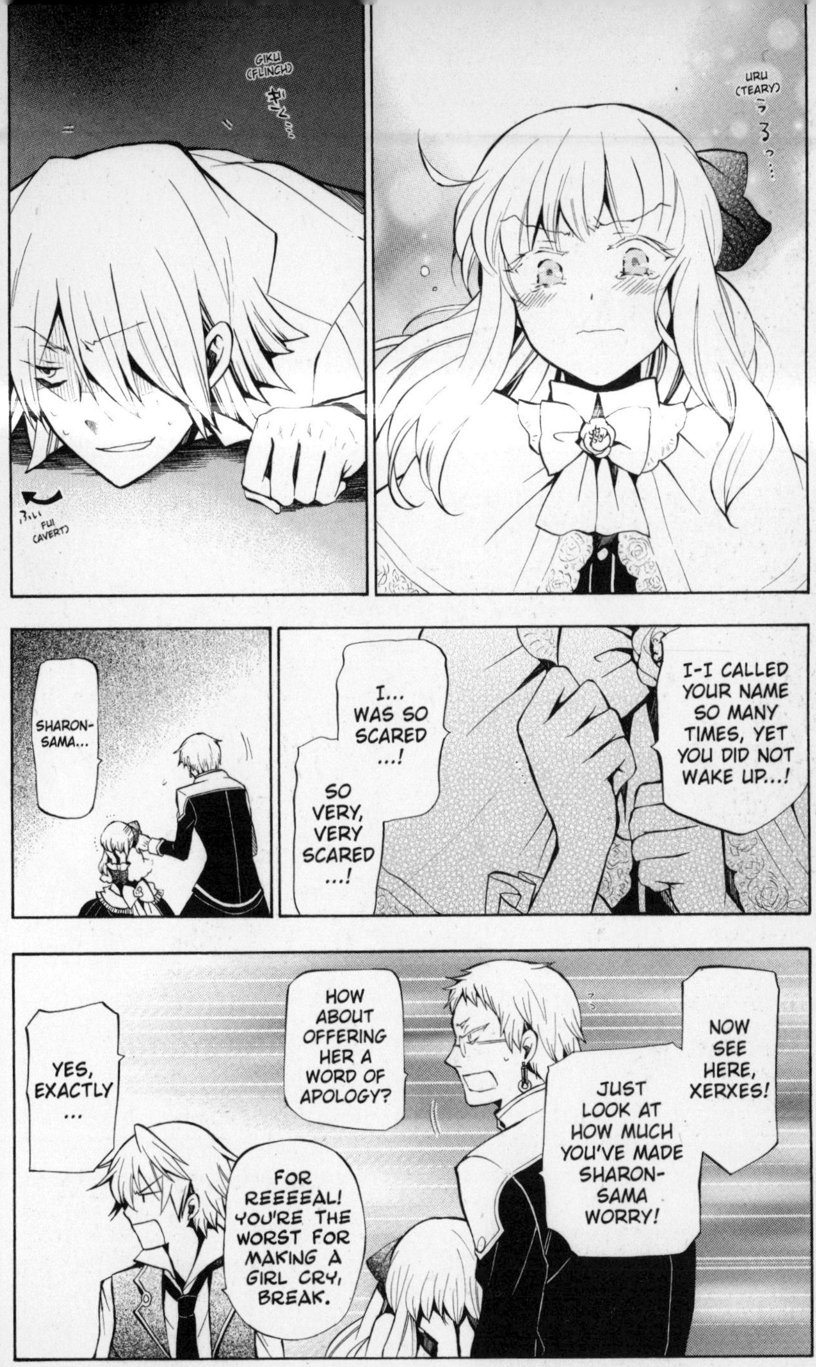
URU (TEARY)
うるっ……
GIKU (FLINCH)
ぎく…
ふい
FUI (AVERT)
I-I CALLED YOUR NAME SO MANY TIMES, YET YOU DID NOT WAKE UP...!
I... WAS SO SCARED ...!
SO VERY, VERY SCARED ...!
SHARON-SAMA...
NOW SEE HERE, XERXES!
JUST LOOK AT HOW MUCH YOU'VE MADE SHARON-SAMA WORRY!
HOW ABOUT OFFERING HER A WORD OF APOLOGY?
FOR REEEEAL! YOU'RE THE WORST FOR MAKING A GIRL CRY, BREAK.
YES, EXACTLY ...

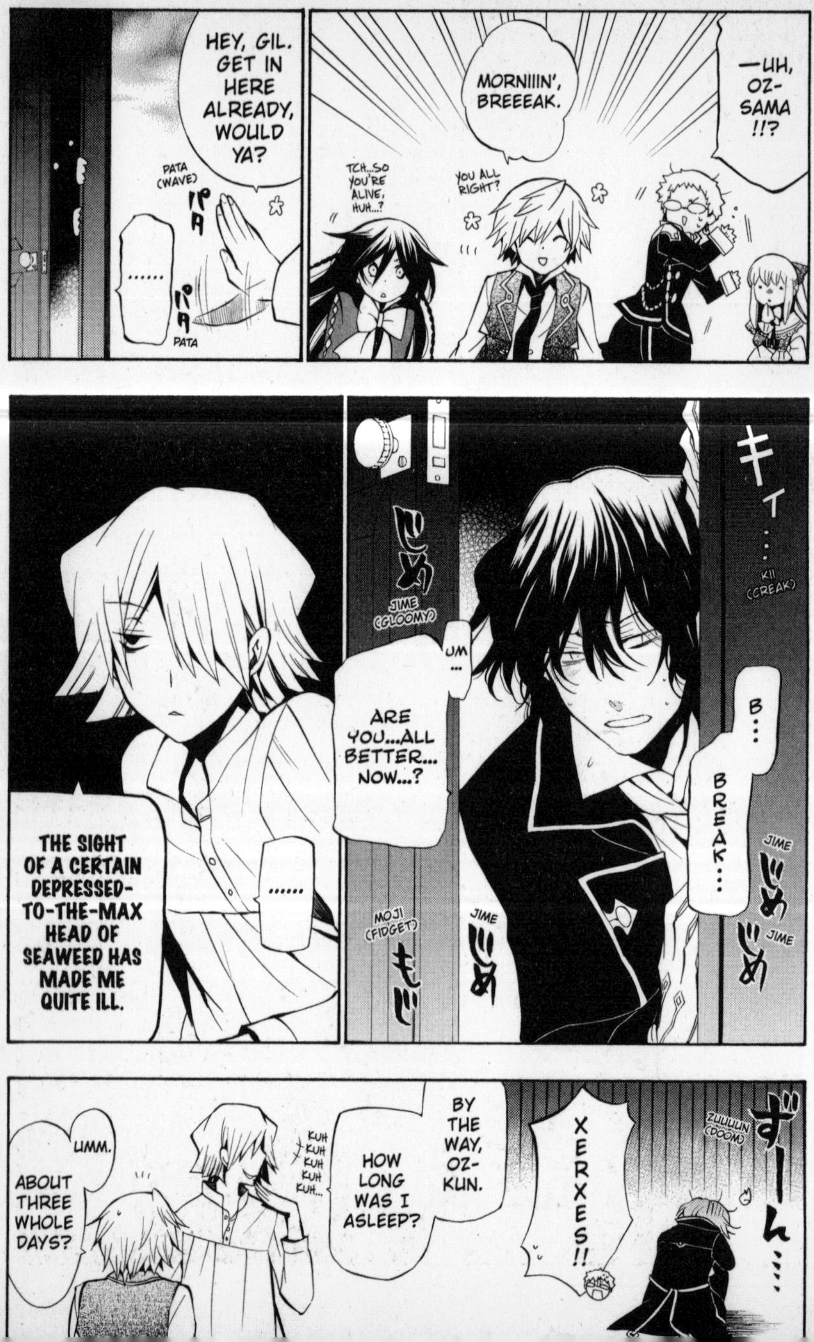
—UH, OZ-SAMA!!?
MORNIIIN', BREEEAK.
YOU ALL RIGHT?
TCH...SO YOU'RE ALIVE, HUH...?
HEY, GIL. GET IN HERE ALREADY, WOULD YA?
PATA (WAVE)
......
PATA
KII (CREAK)
B...
BREAK...
JIME
JIME
UM...
ARE YOU...ALL BETTER... NOW...?
JIME (GLOOMY)
JIME
MOJI (FIDGET)
......
THE SIGHT OF A CERTAIN DEPRESSED-TO-THE-MAX HEAD OF SEAWEED HAS MADE ME QUITE ILL.
ZUUUUN (DOOM)
XERXES!!
BY THE WAY, OZ-KUN.
HOW LONG WAS I ASLEEP?
KUH KUH KUH KUH KUH...
UMM.
ABOUT THREE WHOLE DAYS?

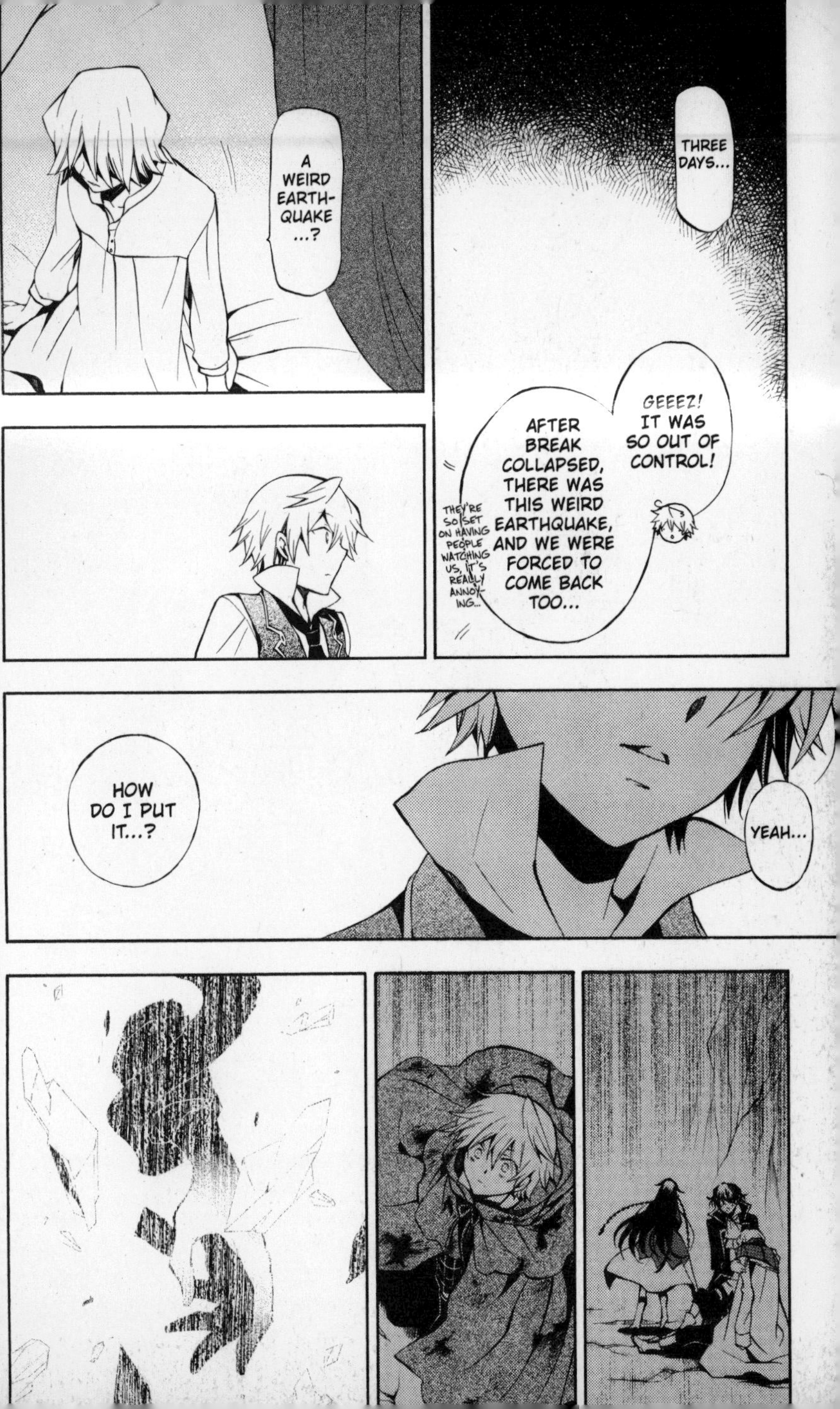
THREE DAYS...
A WEIRD EARTHQUAKE...?
GEEEZ! IT WAS SO OUT OF CONTROL!
AFTER BREAK COLLAPSED, THERE WAS THIS WEIRD EARTHQUAKE, AND WE WERE FORCED TO COME BACK TOO...
THEY'RE SO SET ON HAVING PEOPLE WATCHING US, IT'S REALLY ANNOYING...
YEAH...
HOW DO I PUT IT...?

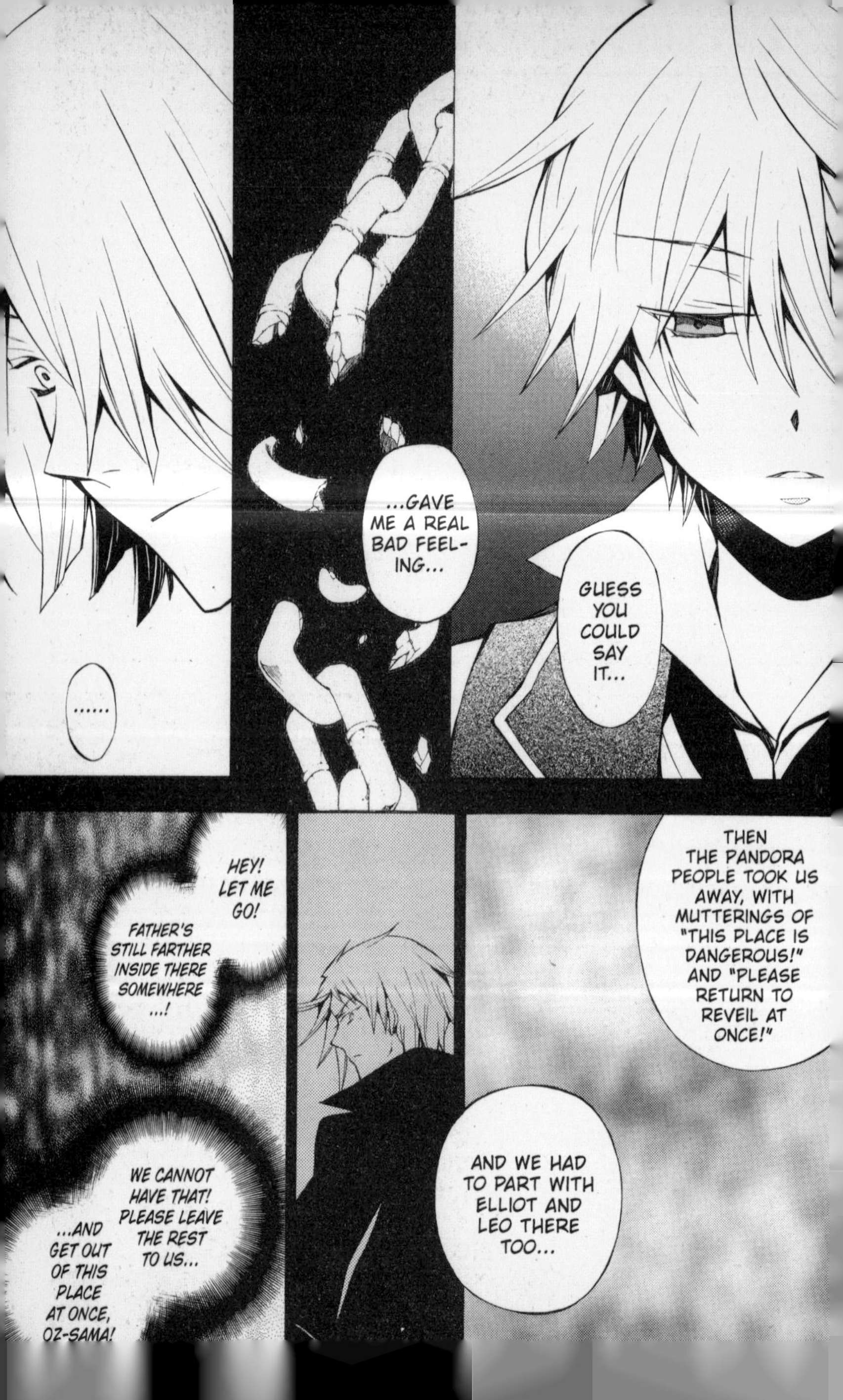
GUESS YOU COULD SAY IT...
...GAVE ME A REAL BAD FEELING...
......
THEN THE PANDORA PEOPLE TOOK US AWAY, WITH MUTTERINGS OF "THIS PLACE IS DANGEROUS!" AND "PLEASE RETURN TO REVEIL AT ONCE!"
AND WE HAD TO PART WITH ELLIOT AND LEO THERE TOO...
HEY! LET ME GO!
FATHER'S STILL FARTHER INSIDE THERE SOMEWHERE...!
WE CANNOT HAVE THAT! PLEASE LEAVE THE REST TO US...
...AND GET OUT OF THIS PLACE AT ONCE, OZ-SAMA!

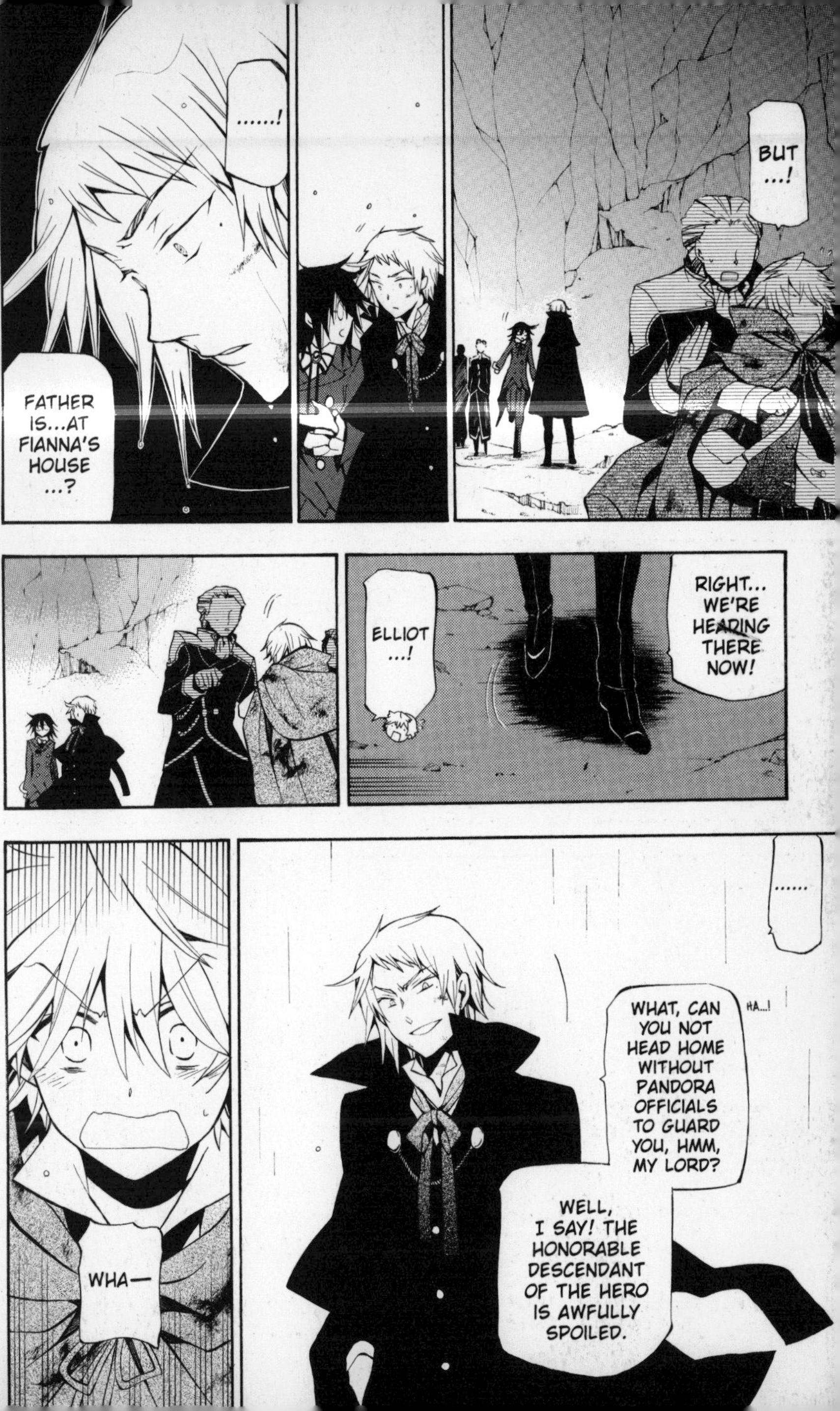
BUT ...!
......!
FATHER IS...AT FIANNA'S HOUSE ...?
RIGHT... WE'RE HEADING THERE NOW!
ELLIOT ...!
......
HA...!
WHAT, CAN YOU NOT HEAD HOME WITHOUT PANDORA OFFICIALS TO GUARD YOU, HMM, MY LORD?
WELL, I SAY! THE HONORABLE DESCENDANT OF THE HERO IS AWFULLY SPOILED.
WHA—

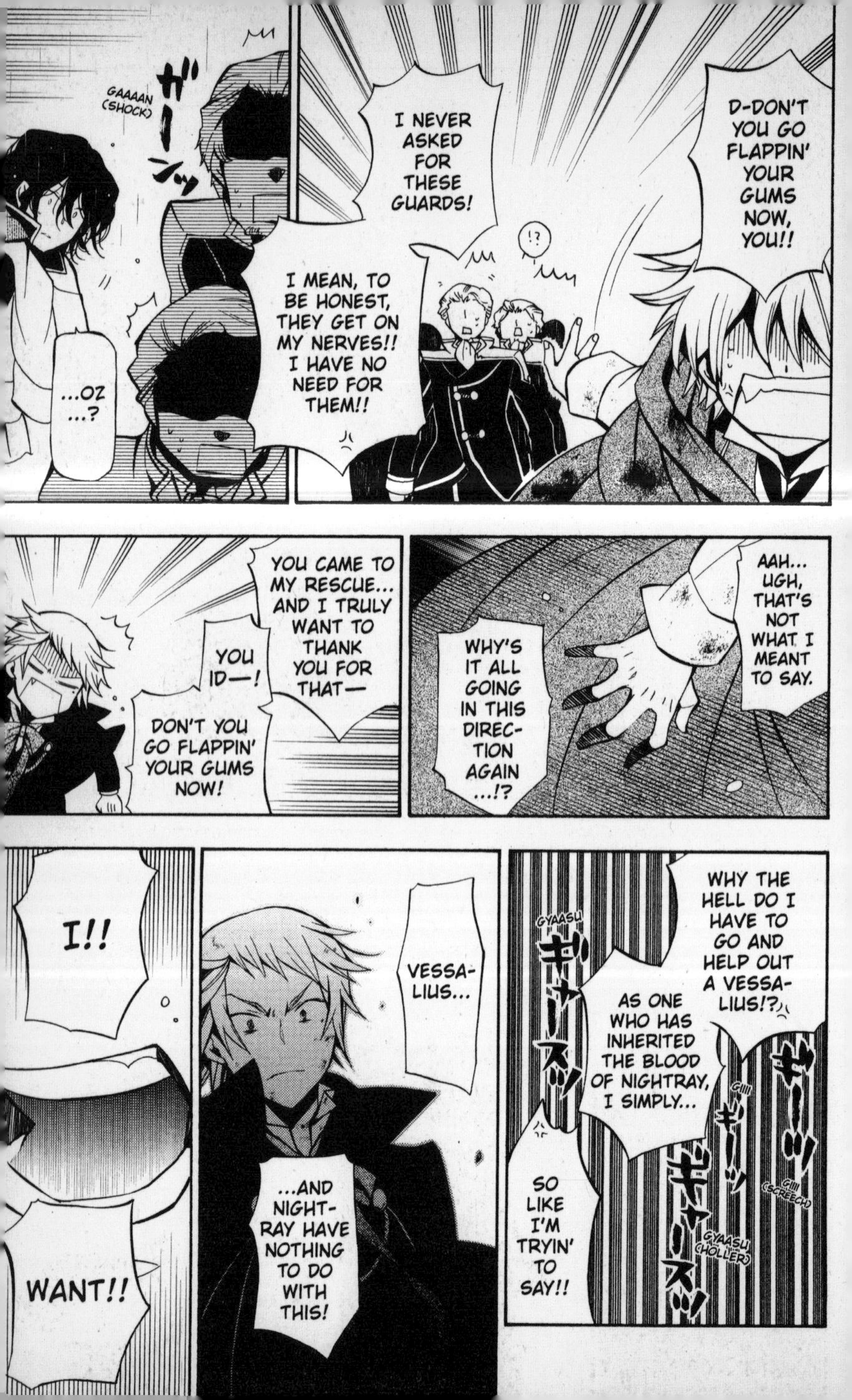
D-DON'T YOU GO FLAPPIN' YOUR GUMS NOW, YOU!!
!?
I NEVER ASKED FOR THESE GUARDS!
I MEAN, TO BE HONEST, THEY GET ON MY NERVES!! I HAVE NO NEED FOR THEM!!
GAAAAN (SHOCK)
...OZ ...?
AAH... UGH, THAT'S NOT WHAT I MEANT TO SAY.
WHY'S IT ALL GOING IN THIS DIRECTION AGAIN ...!?
YOU CAME TO MY RESCUE... AND I TRULY WANT TO THANK YOU FOR THAT—
YOU ID—!
DON'T YOU GO FLAPPIN' YOUR GUMS NOW!
WHY THE HELL DO I HAVE TO GO AND HELP OUT A VESSALIUS!?
GIIII (SCREECH)
GYAASU (HOLLER)
AS ONE WHO HAS INHERITED THE BLOOD OF NIGHTRAY, I SIMPLY...
GYAASU
SO LIKE I'M TRYIN' TO SAY!!
VESSALIUS...
...AND NIGHTRAY HAVE NOTHING TO DO WITH THIS!
I!!
WANT!!

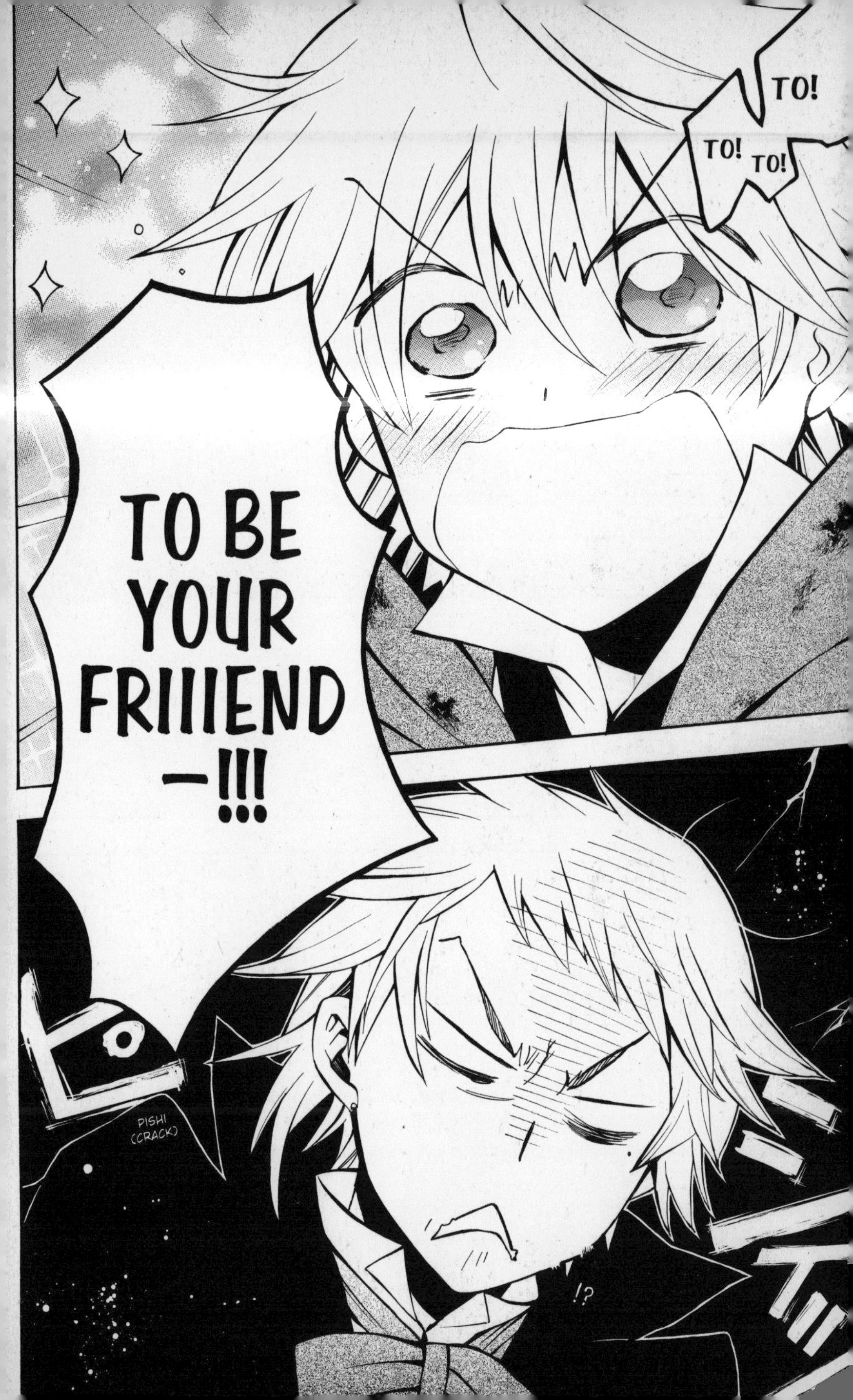
TO! TO! TO!
TO BE YOUR FRIIIEND—!!!
PISHI (CRACK)
!?

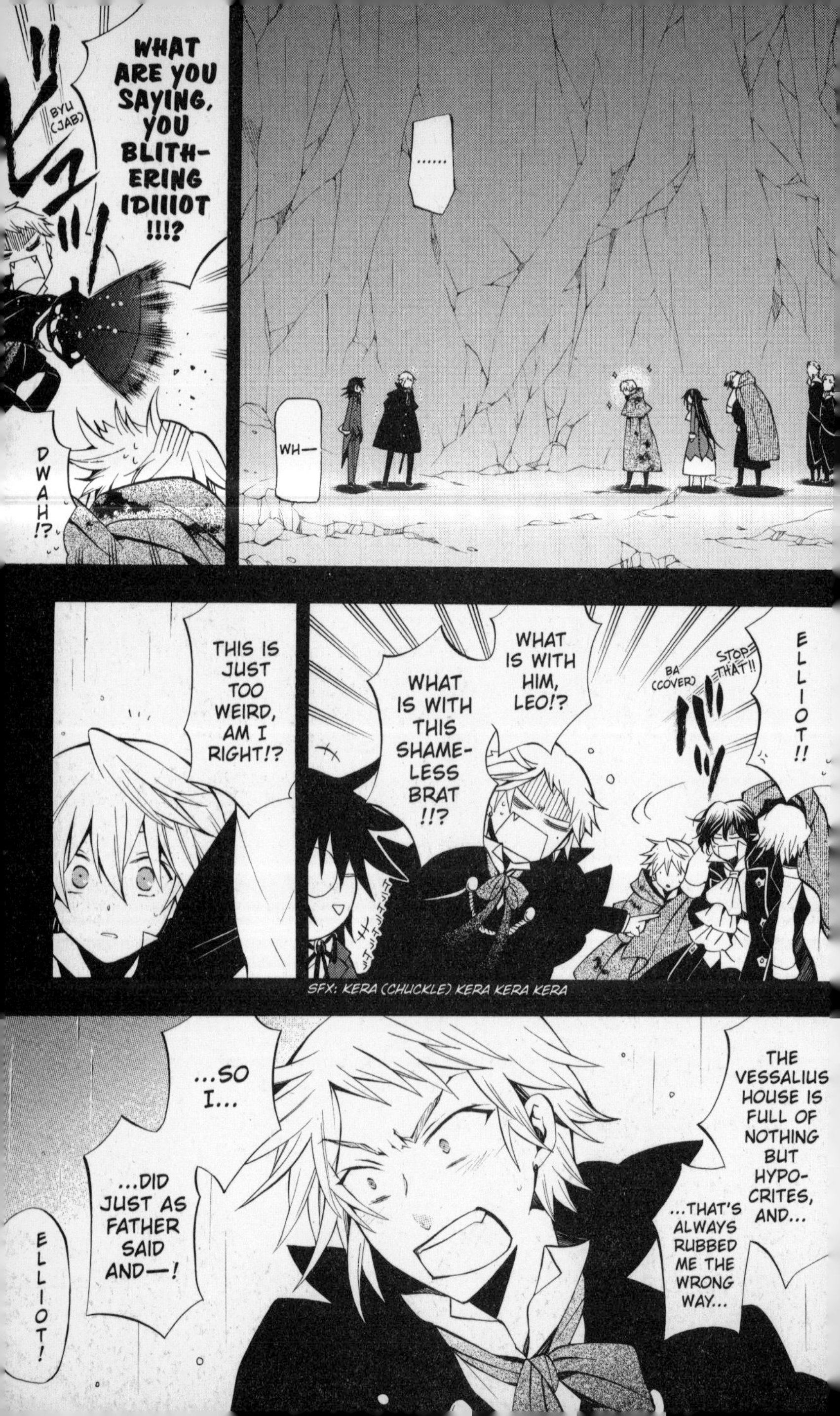
……
WH—
WHAT ARE YOU SAYING, YOU BLITHERING IDIIIOT !!!?
BYU (JAB)
DWAH!?
ELLIOT!!
STOP THAT!!
BA (COVER)
WHAT IS WITH HIM, LEO!?
WHAT IS WITH THIS SHAMELESS BRAT !!?
THIS IS JUST TOO WEIRD, AM I RIGHT!?
SFX: KERA (CHUCKLE) KERA KERA KERA
THE VESSALIUS HOUSE IS FULL OF NOTHING BUT HYPOCRITES, AND...
...THAT'S ALWAYS RUBBED ME THE WRONG WAY...
...SO I...
...DID JUST AS FATHER SAID AND—!
ELLIOT!

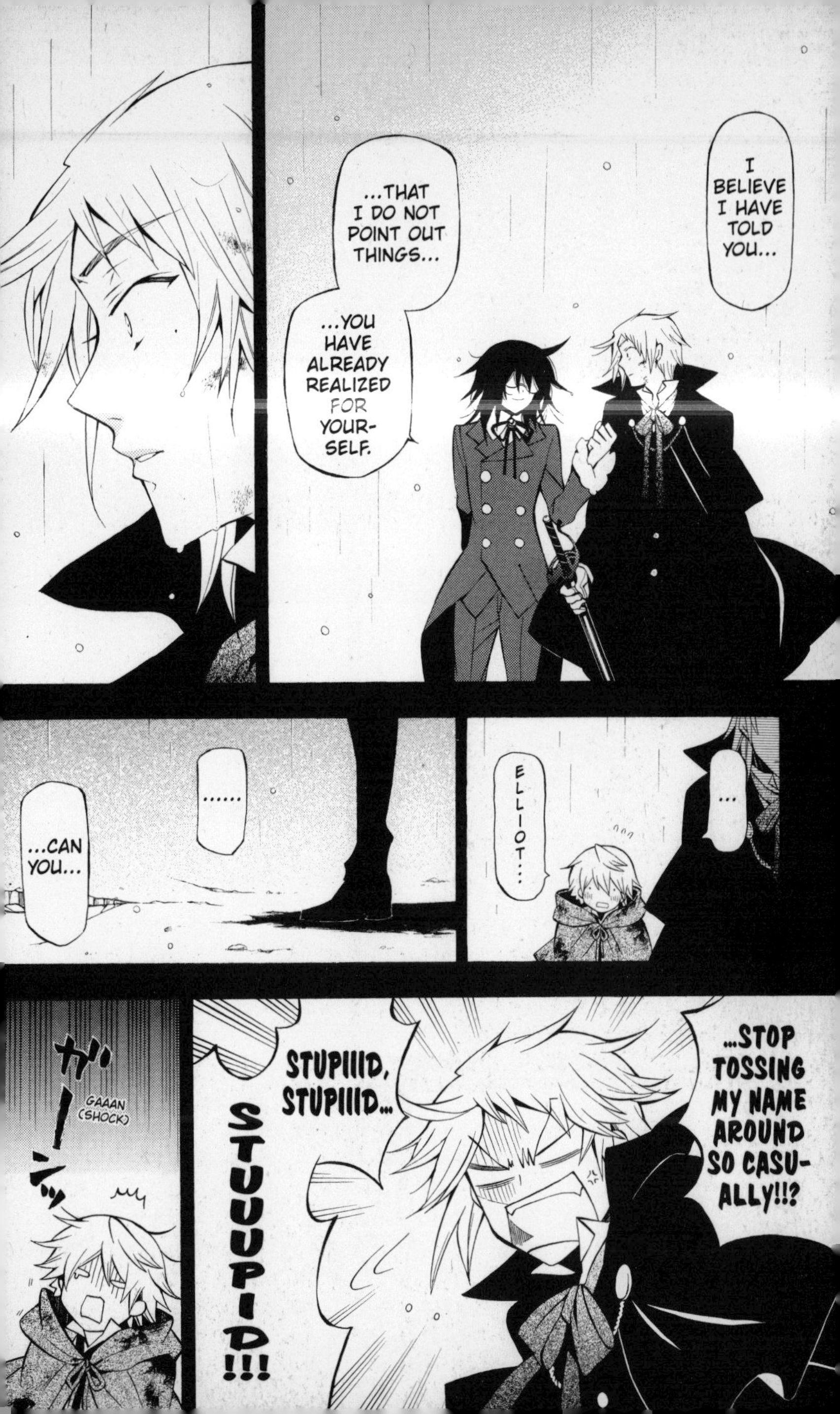
I BELIEVE I HAVE TOLD YOU...
...THAT I DO NOT POINT OUT THINGS...
...YOU HAVE ALREADY REALIZED FOR YOUR-SELF.
...
ELLIOT...
......
...CAN YOU...
...STOP TOSSING MY NAME AROUND SO CASU-ALLY!!?
STUPIIID, STUPIIID...
STUUUPID!!!
GAAAN (SHOCK)

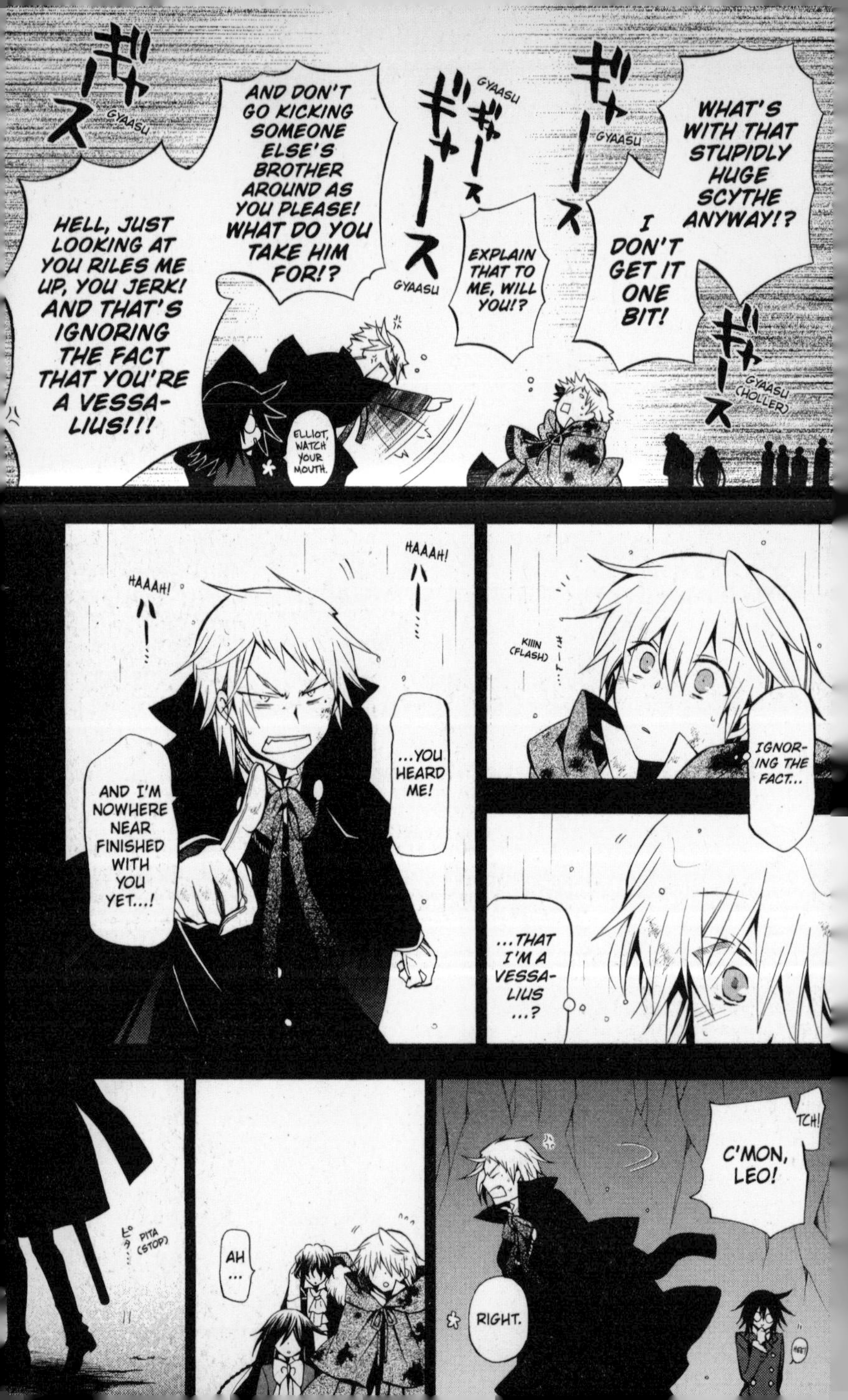
GYAASU (HOLLER)
WHAT'S WITH THAT STUPIDLY HUGE SCYTHE ANYWAY!?
I DON'T GET IT ONE BIT!
GYAASU
GYAASU
EXPLAIN THAT TO ME, WILL YOU!?
GYAASU
AND DON'T GO KICKING SOMEONE ELSE'S BROTHER AROUND AS YOU PLEASE! WHAT DO YOU TAKE HIM FOR!?
GYAASU
HELL, JUST LOOKING AT YOU RILES ME UP, YOU JERK! AND THAT'S IGNORING THE FACT THAT YOU'RE A VESSALIUS!!!
ELLIOT, WATCH YOUR MOUTH.
KIIIN (FLASH)
IGNORING THE FACT...
...THAT I'M A VESSALIUS...?
HAAAH!
HAAAH!
...YOU HEARD ME!
AND I'M NOWHERE NEAR FINISHED WITH YOU YET...!
TCH!
C'MON, LEO!
RIGHT.
AH ...
PITA (STOP)

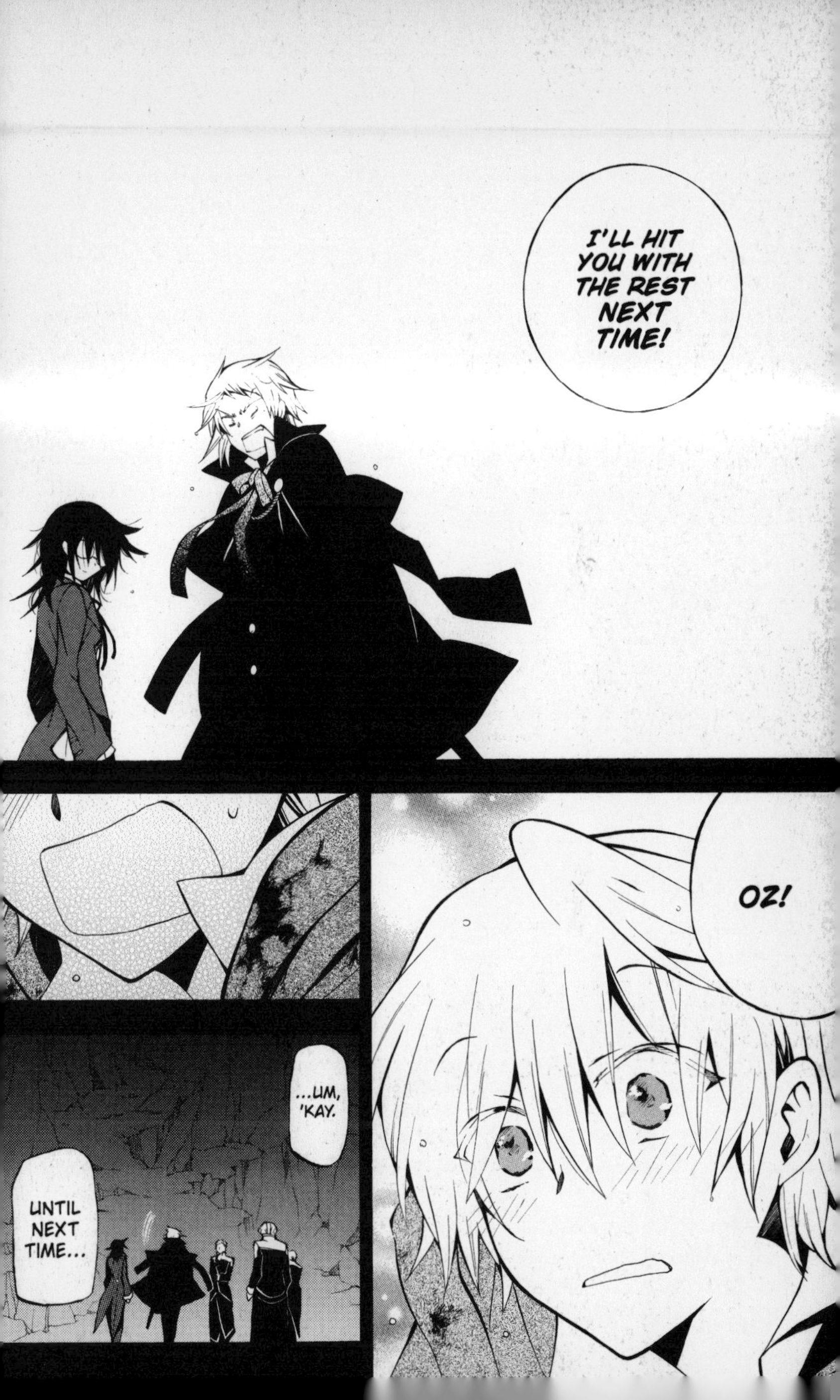
I'LL HIT YOU WITH THE REST NEXT TIME!
OZ!
...UM, 'KAY.
UNTIL NEXT TIME...

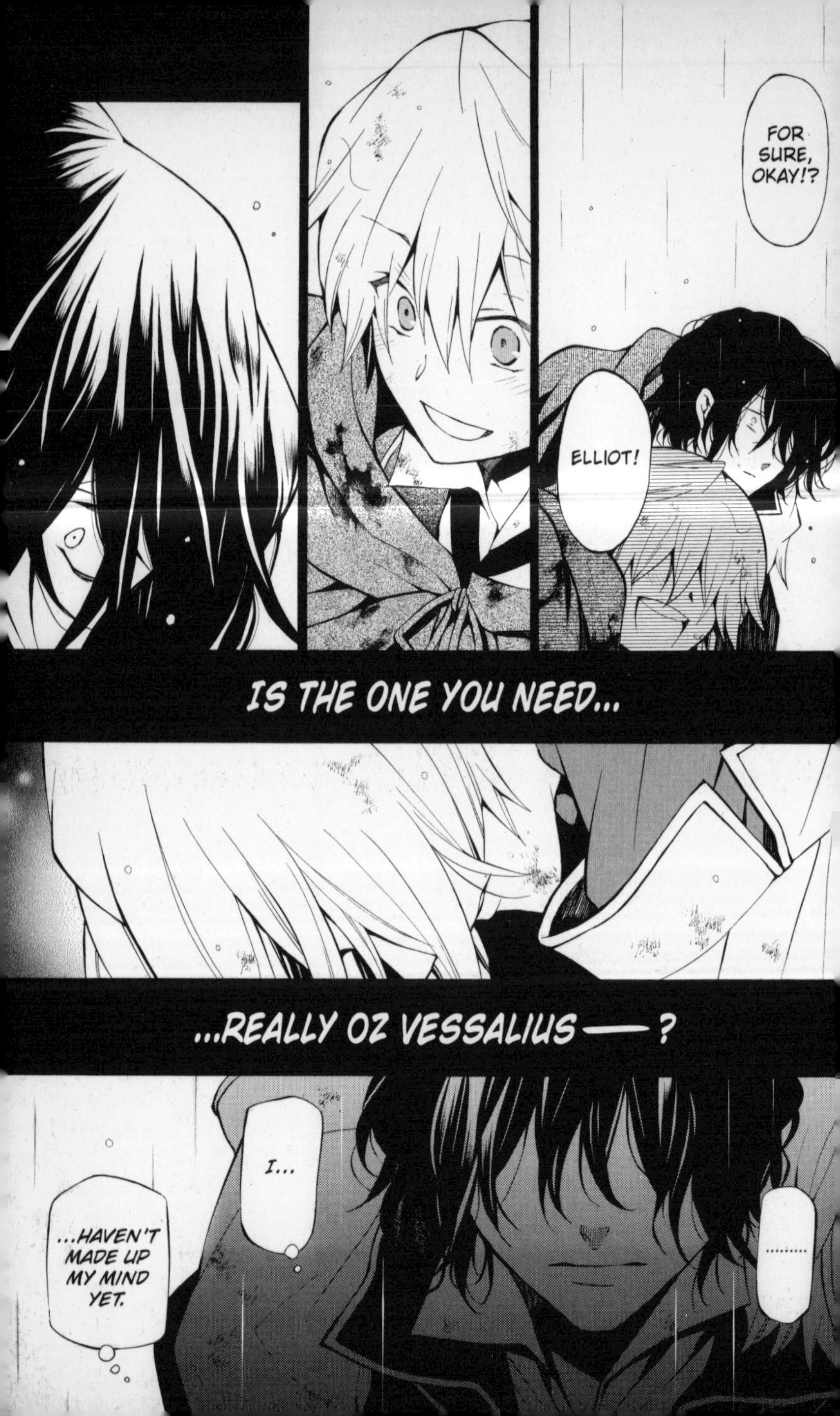
FOR SURE, OKAY!?
ELLIOT!
IS THE ONE YOU NEED...
...REALLY OZ VESSALIUS——?
....
I...
...HAVEN'T MADE UP MY MIND YET.

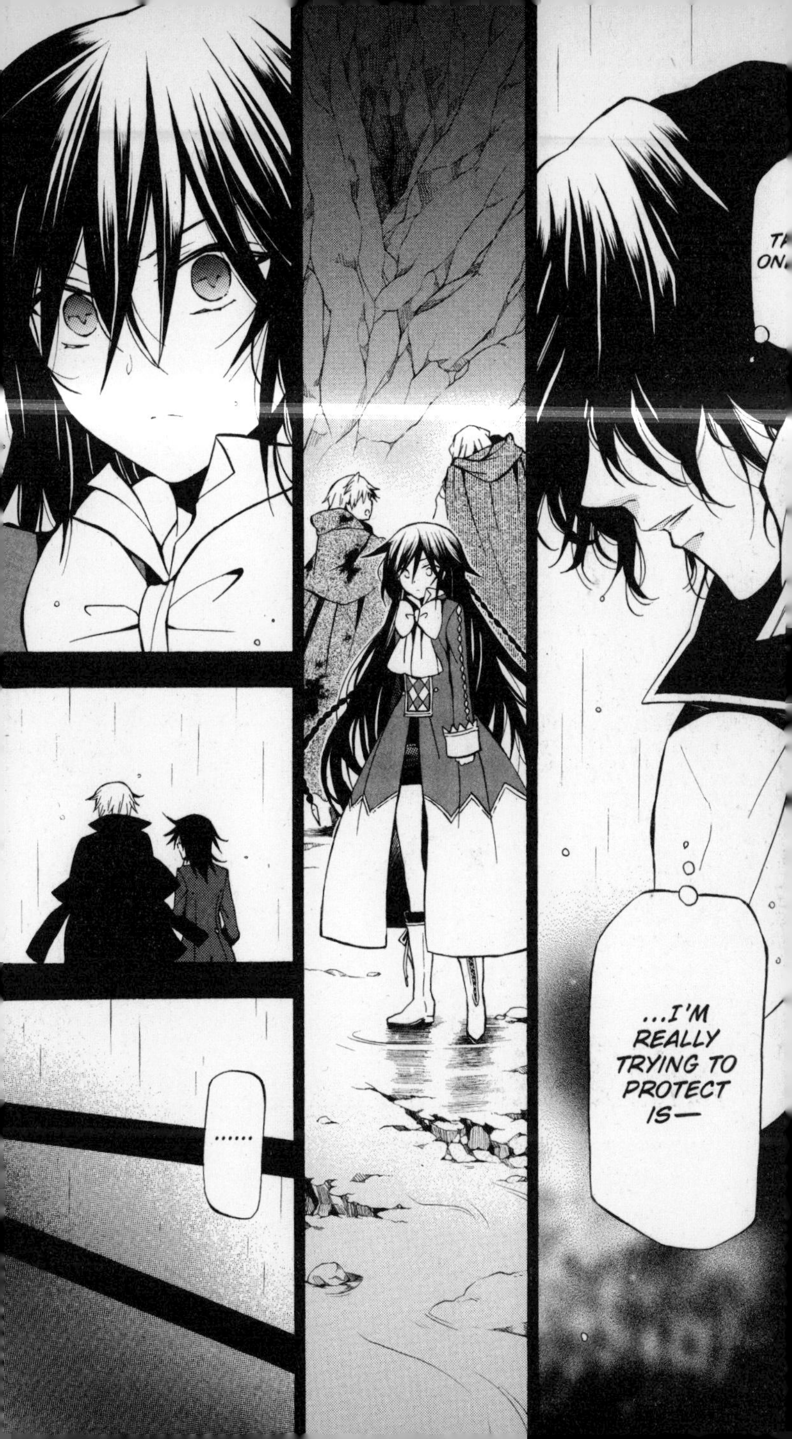
...I'M REALLY TRYING TO PROTECT IS—
......

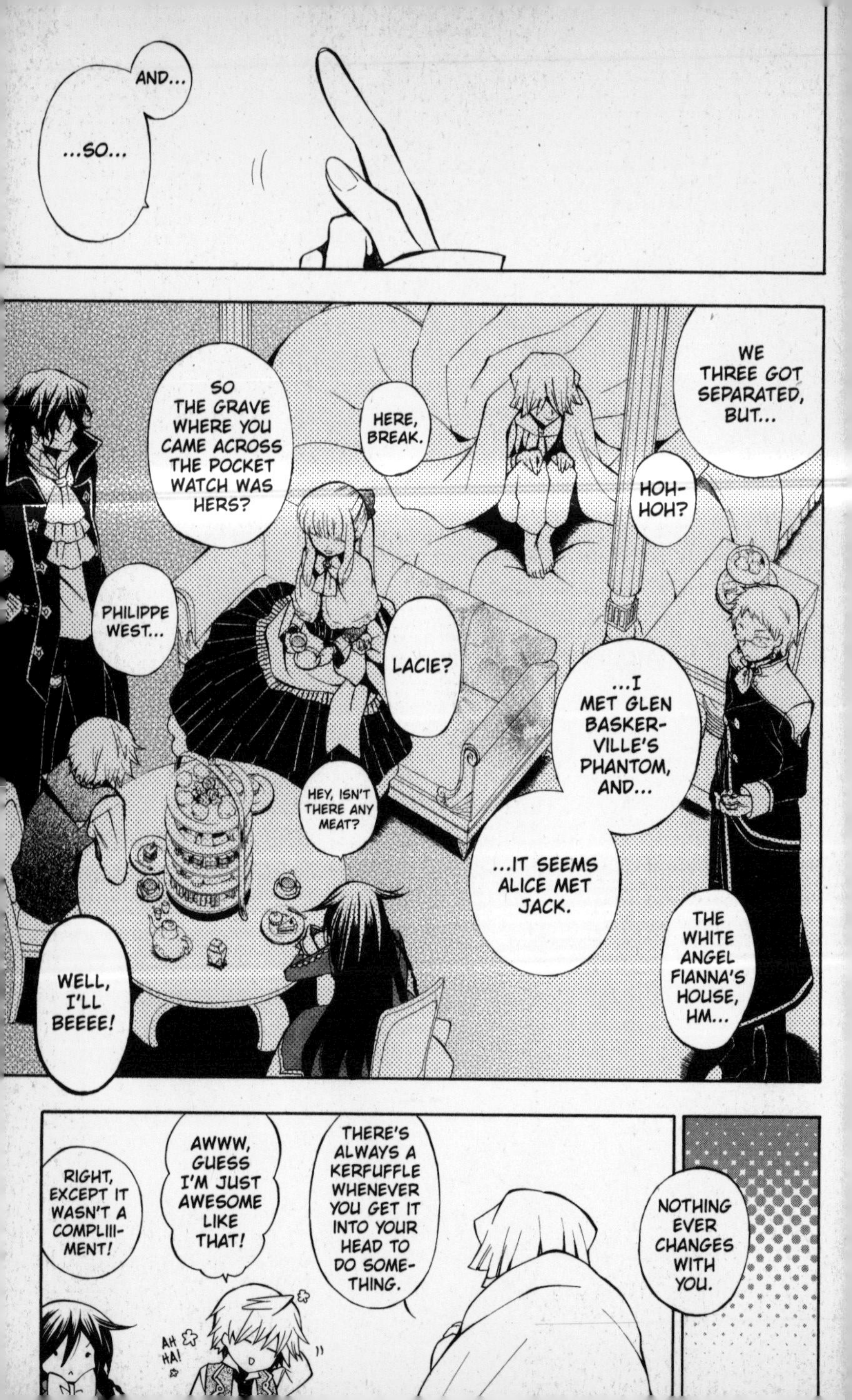
AND...
...SO...
WE THREE GOT SEPARATED, BUT...
HOH-HOH?
HERE, BREAK.
SO THE GRAVE WHERE YOU CAME ACROSS THE POCKET WATCH WAS HERS?
...I MET GLEN BASKER-VILLE'S PHANTOM, AND...
LACIE?
PHILIPPE WEST...
...IT SEEMS ALICE MET JACK.
THE WHITE ANGEL FIANNA'S HOUSE, HM...
HEY, ISN'T THERE ANY MEAT?
WELL, I'LL BEEEE!
NOTHING EVER CHANGES WITH YOU.
THERE'S ALWAYS A KERFUFFLE WHENEVER YOU GET IT INTO YOUR HEAD TO DO SOME-THING.
AWWW, GUESS I'M JUST AWESOME LIKE THAT!
RIGHT, EXCEPT IT WASN'T A COMPLIIII-MENT!
AH HA!

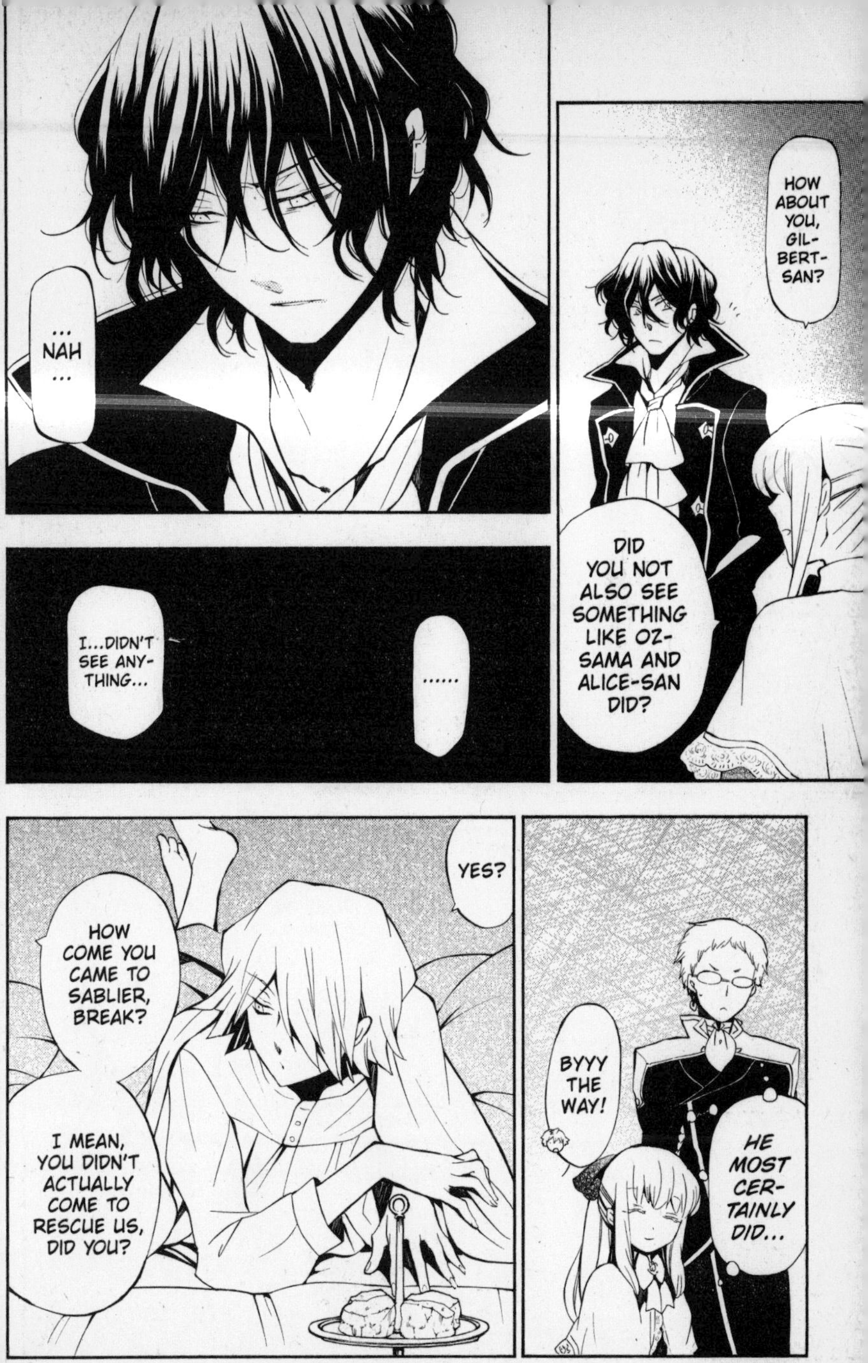
HOW ABOUT YOU, GILBERT-SAN?
DID YOU NOT ALSO SEE SOMETHING LIKE OZ-SAMA AND ALICE-SAN DID?
...NAH...
......
I...DIDN'T SEE ANYTHING...
HE MOST CERTAINLY DID...
BYYY THE WAY!
YES?
HOW COME YOU CAME TO SABLIER, BREAK?
I MEAN, YOU DIDN'T ACTUALLY COME TO RESCUE US, DID YOU?

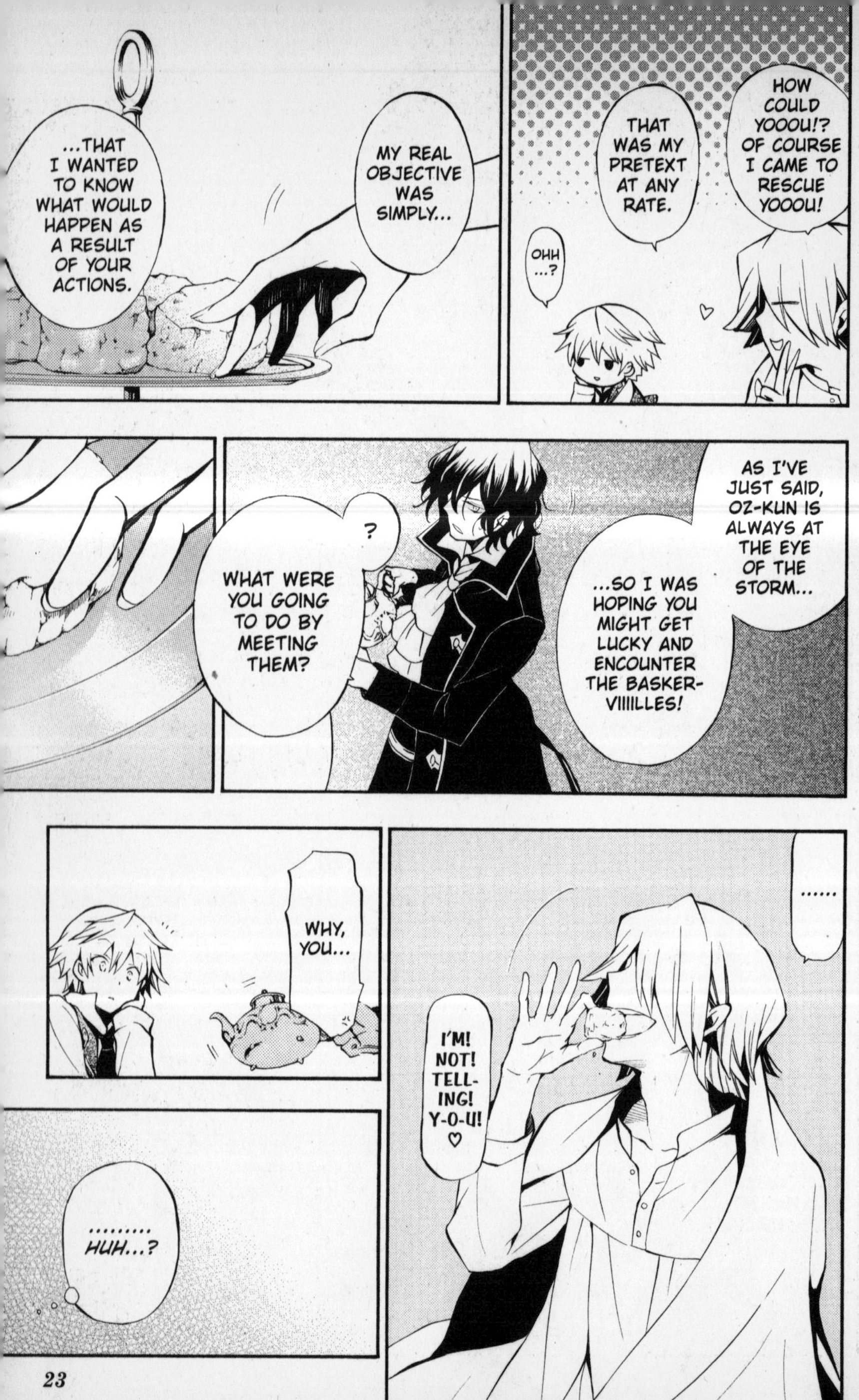
HOW COULD YOOOU!? OF COURSE I CAME TO RESCUE YOOOU!
THAT WAS MY PRETEXT AT ANY RATE.
OHH ...?
MY REAL OBJECTIVE WAS SIMPLY...
...THAT I WANTED TO KNOW WHAT WOULD HAPPEN AS A RESULT OF YOUR ACTIONS.
AS I'VE JUST SAID, OZ-KUN IS ALWAYS AT THE EYE OF THE STORM...
...SO I WAS HOPING YOU MIGHT GET LUCKY AND ENCOUNTER THE BASKER-VIIIILLES!
?
WHAT WERE YOU GOING TO DO BY MEETING THEM?
......
I'M! NOT! TELL-ING! Y-O-U! ♡
WHY, YOU...
.... HUH...?

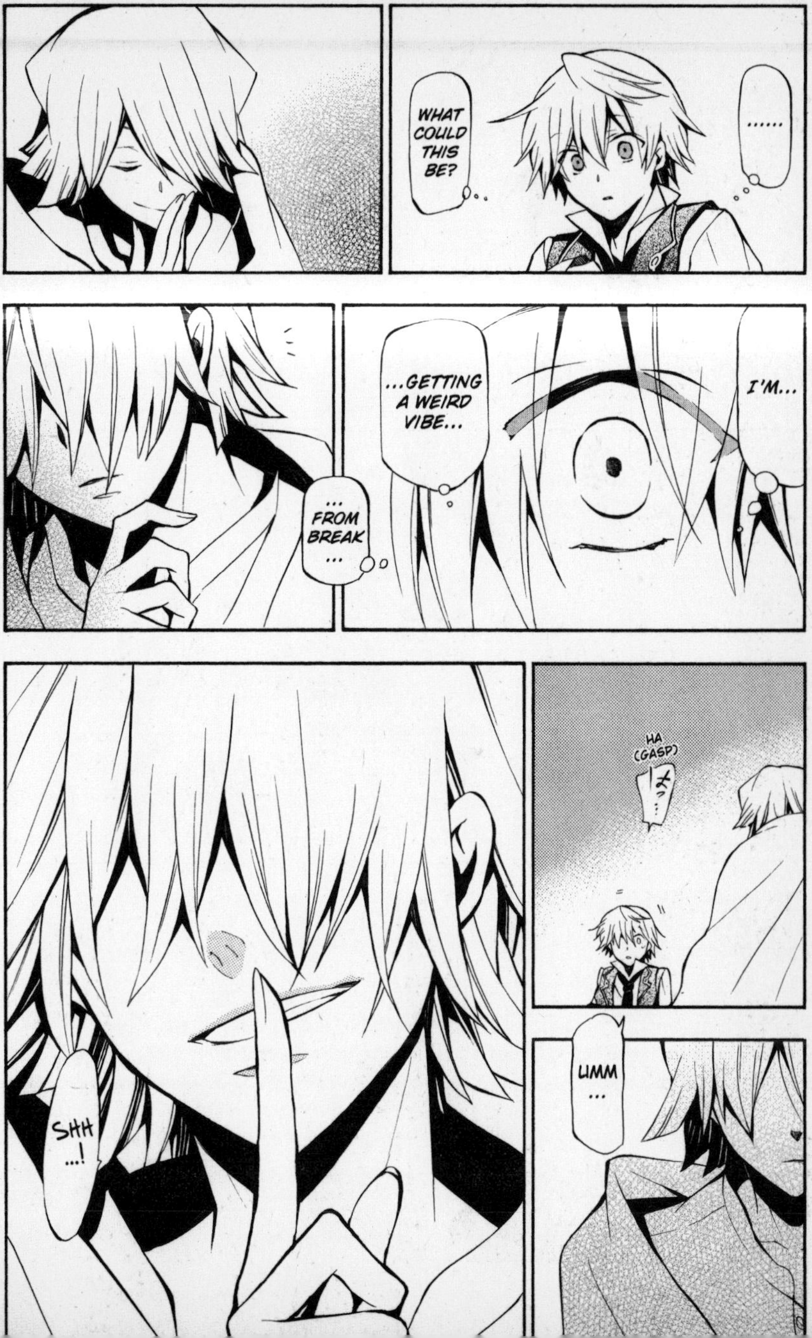
......
WHAT COULD THIS BE?
I'M...
...GETTING A WEIRD VIBE...
... FROM BREAK ...
HA (GASP)
UMM ...
SHH ...!

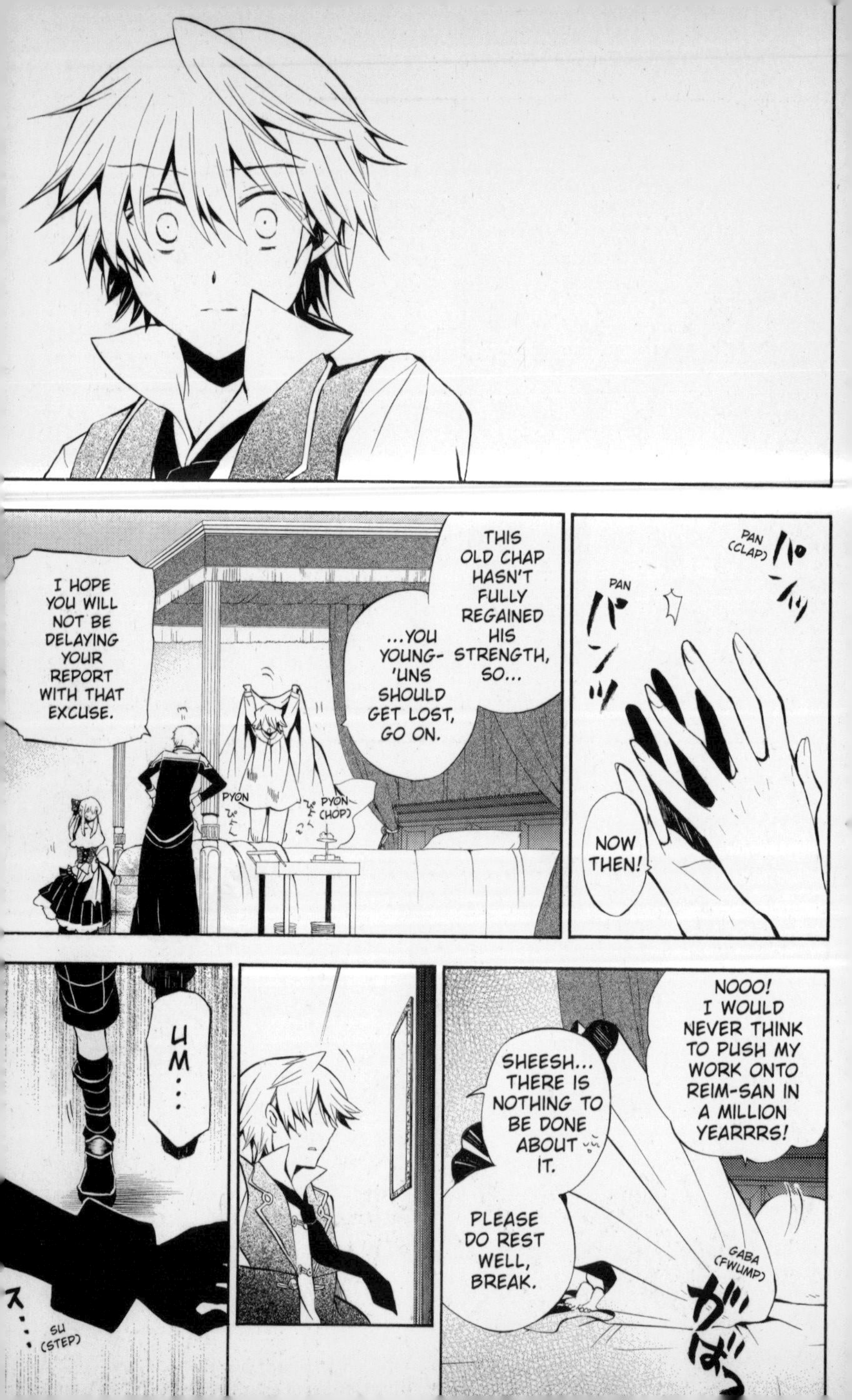

PAN (CLAP)
PAN
NOW THEN!
THIS OLD CHAP HASN'T FULLY REGAINED HIS STRENGTH, SO...
...YOU YOUNG-'UNS SHOULD GET LOST, GO ON.
PYON (HOP)
PYON
I HOPE YOU WILL NOT BE DELAYING YOUR REPORT WITH THAT EXCUSE.
NOOO! I WOULD NEVER THINK TO PUSH MY WORK ONTO REIM-SAN IN A MILLION YEARRRS!
SHEESH... THERE IS NOTHING TO BE DONE ABOUT IT.
PLEASE DO REST WELL, BREAK.
GABA (FWUMP)
UM...
SU (STEP)

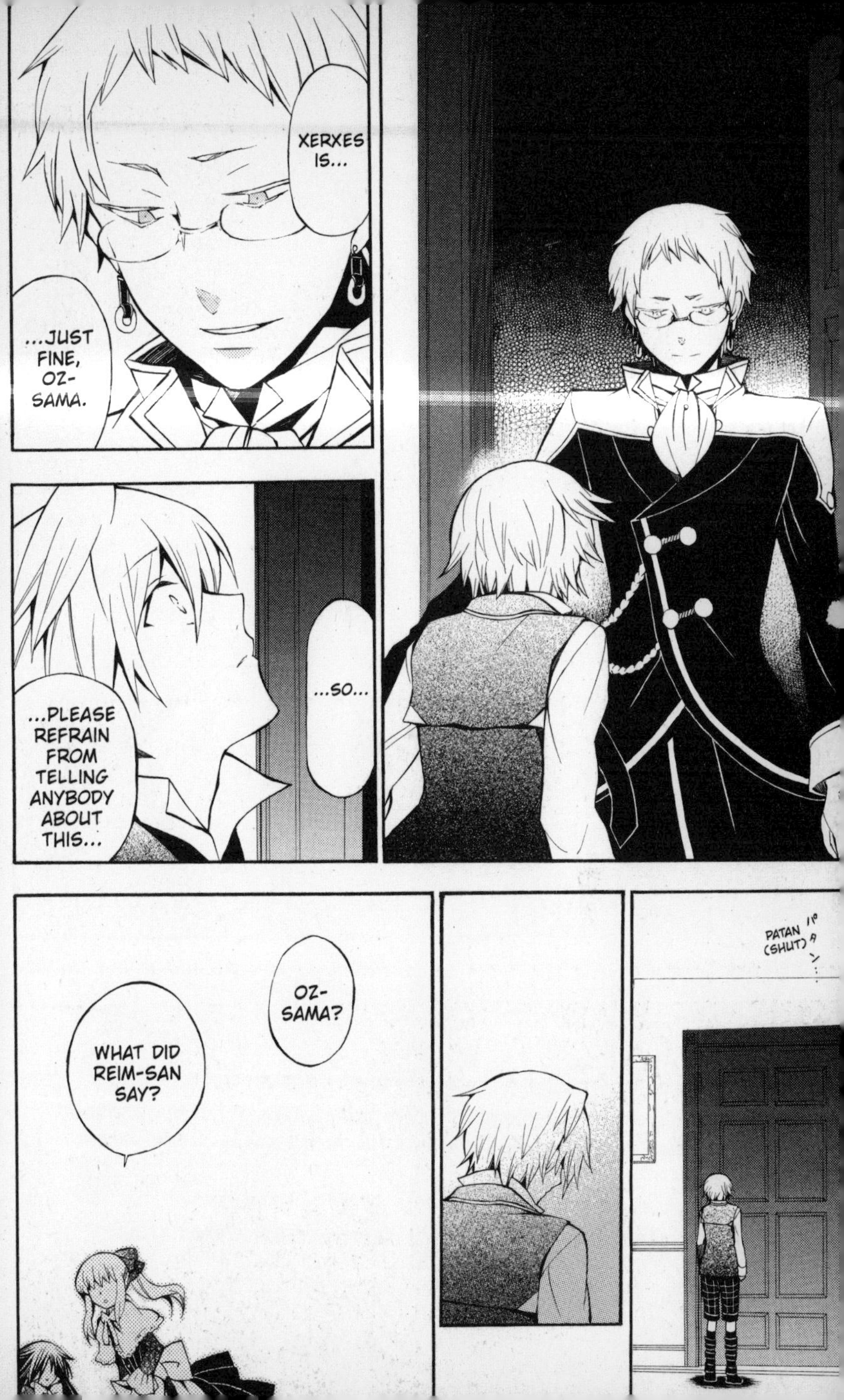
XERXES IS...
...JUST FINE, OZ-SAMA.
...SO...
...PLEASE REFRAIN FROM TELLING ANYBODY ABOUT THIS...
PATAN (SHUT)
パタン…
OZ-SAMA?
WHAT DID REIM-SAN SAY?

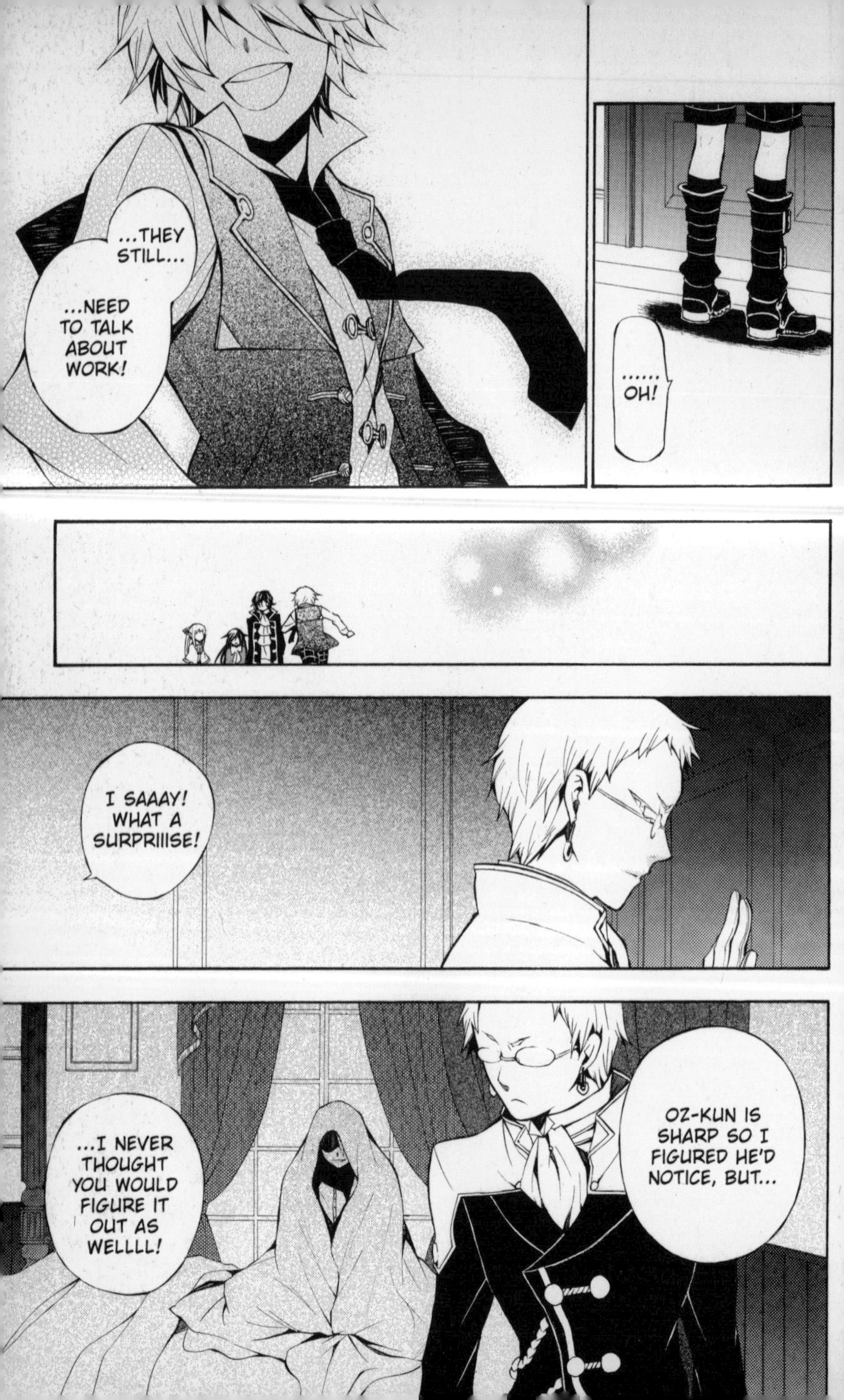
......OH!
...THEY STILL...
...NEED TO TALK ABOUT WORK!
I SAAAY! WHAT A SURPRIIISE!
OZ-KUN IS SHARP SO I FIGURED HE'D NOTICE, BUT...
...I NEVER THOUGHT YOU WOULD FIGURE IT OUT AS WELLLL!

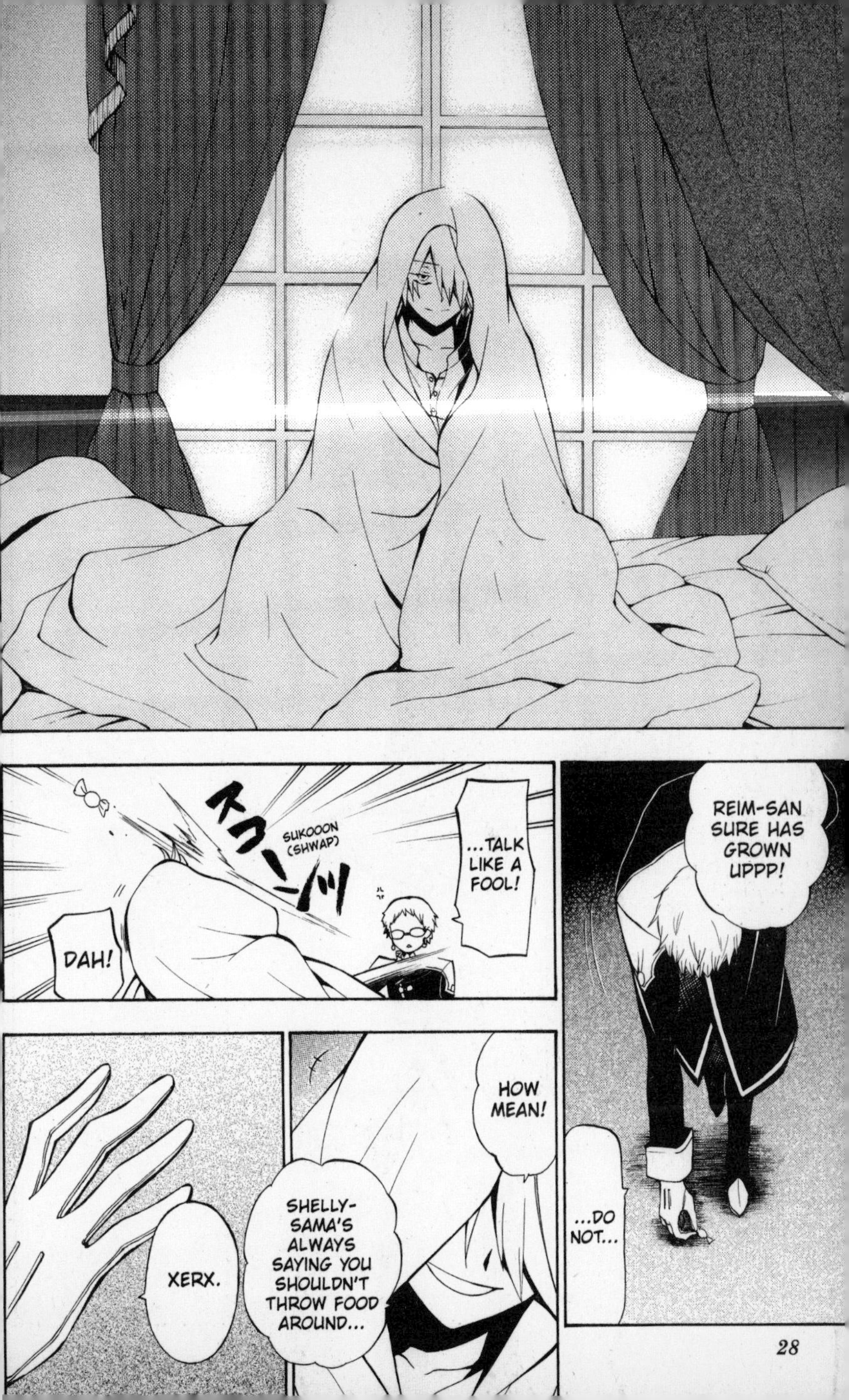
REIM-SAN SURE HAS GROWN UPPP!
...DO NOT...
...TALK LIKE A FOOL!
SUKOOON (SHWAP)
DAH!
HOW MEAN!
SHELLY-SAMA'S ALWAYS SAYING YOU SHOULDN'T THROW FOOD AROUND...
XERX.

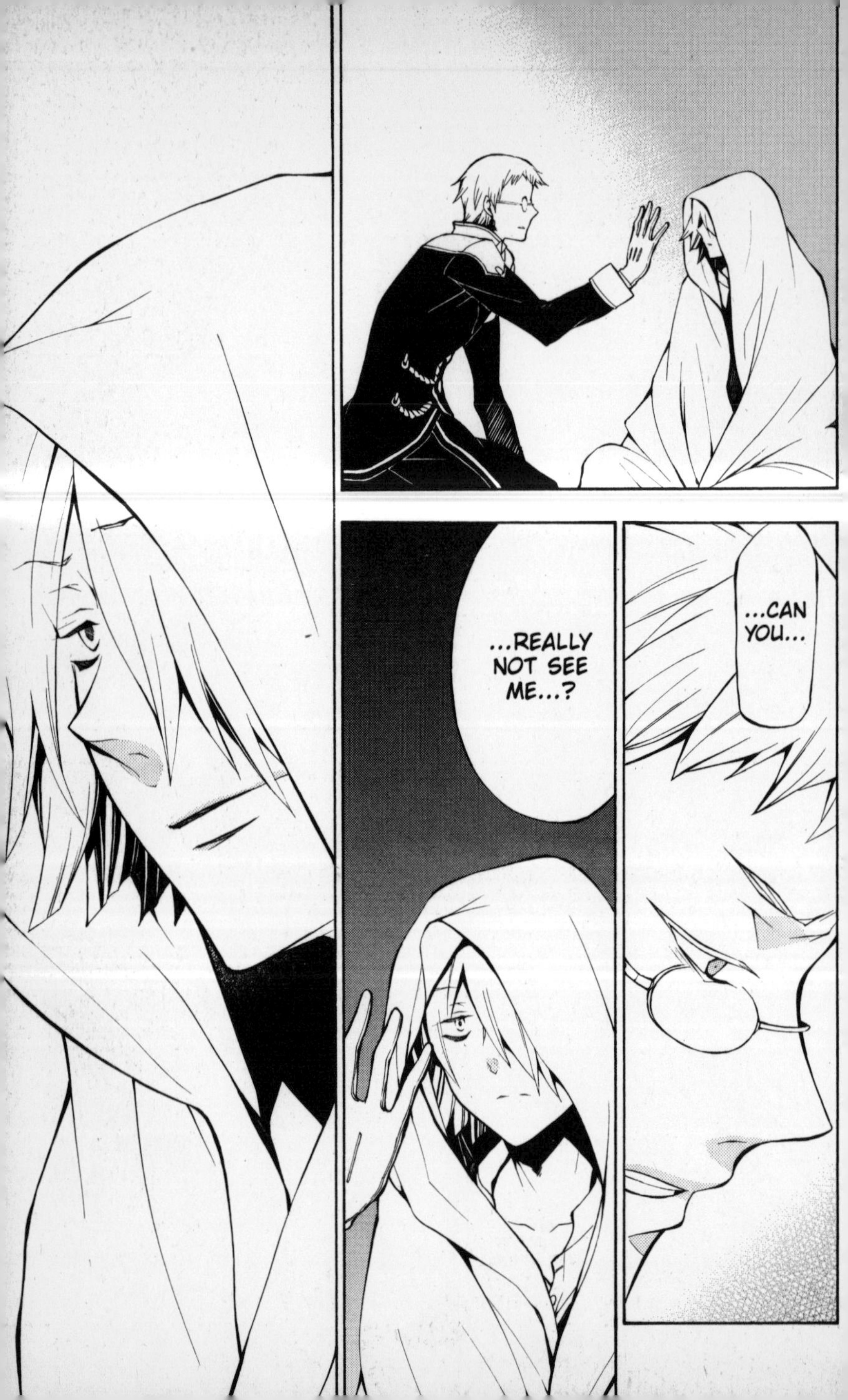
...CAN YOU...
...REALLY NOT SEE ME...?

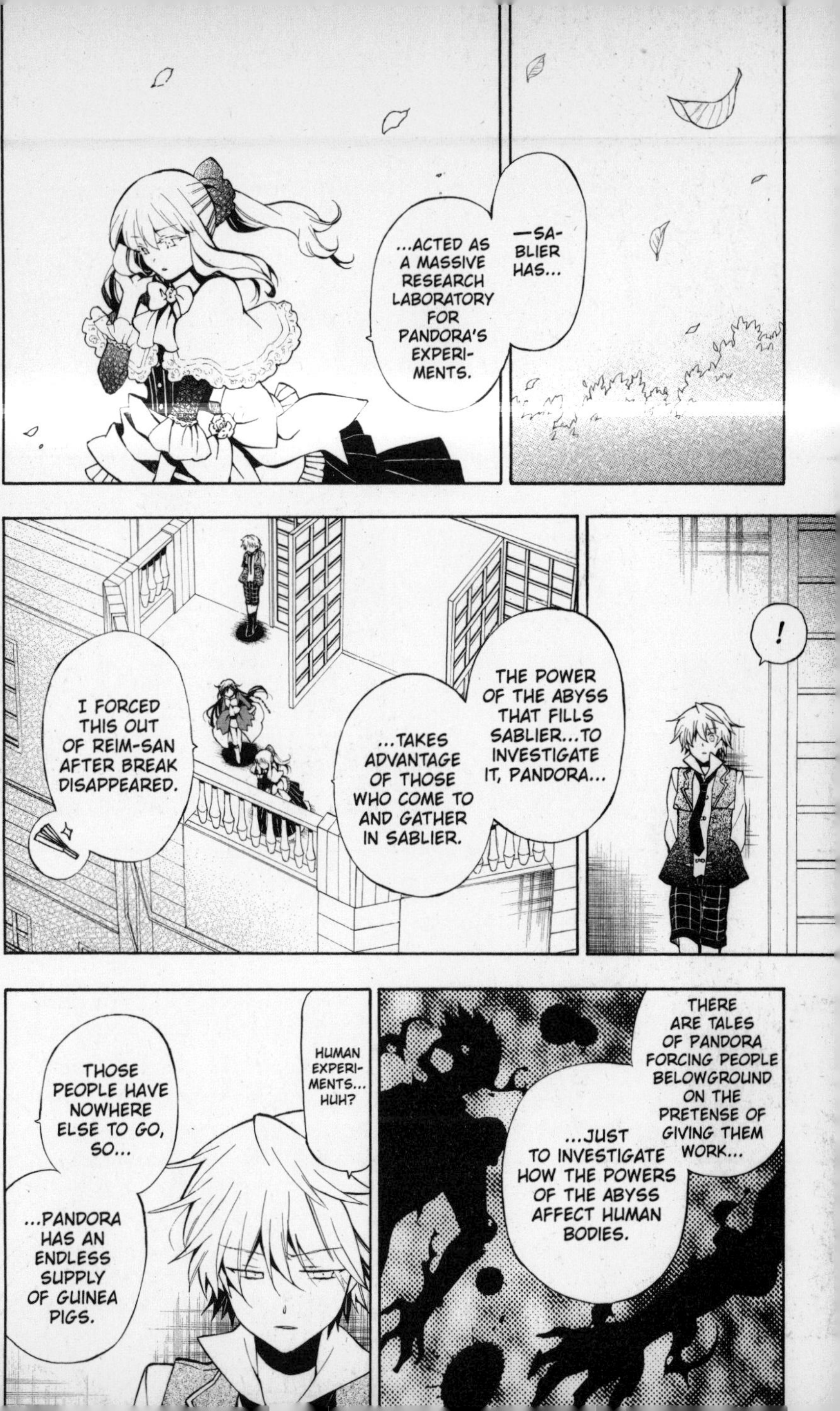
—SABLIER HAS...
...ACTED AS A MASSIVE RESEARCH LABORATORY FOR PANDORA'S EXPERIMENTS.
!
THE POWER OF THE ABYSS THAT FILLS SABLIER...TO INVESTIGATE IT, PANDORA...
...TAKES ADVANTAGE OF THOSE WHO COME TO AND GATHER IN SABLIER.
I FORCED THIS OUT OF REIM-SAN AFTER BREAK DISAPPEARED.
THERE ARE TALES OF PANDORA FORCING PEOPLE BELOWGROUND ON THE PRETENSE OF GIVING THEM WORK...
...JUST TO INVESTIGATE HOW THE POWERS OF THE ABYSS AFFECT HUMAN BODIES.
HUMAN EXPERIMENTS... HUH?
THOSE PEOPLE HAVE NOWHERE ELSE TO GO, SO...
...PANDORA HAS AN ENDLESS SUPPLY OF GUINEA PIGS.

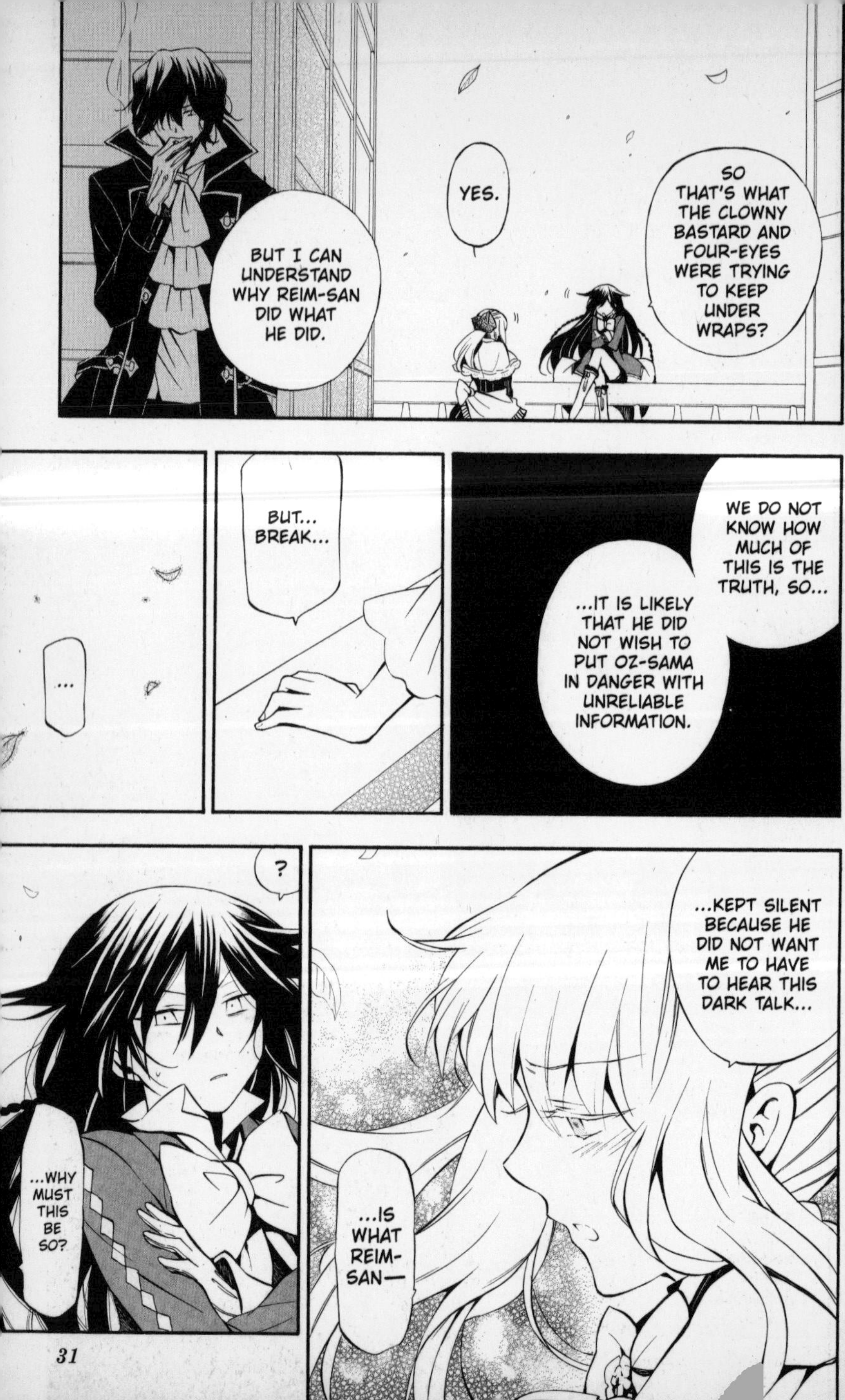
SO THAT'S WHAT THE CLOWNY BASTARD AND FOUR-EYES WERE TRYING TO KEEP UNDER WRAPS?
YES.
BUT I CAN UNDERSTAND WHY REIM-SAN DID WHAT HE DID.
WE DO NOT KNOW HOW MUCH OF THIS IS THE TRUTH, SO...
...IT IS LIKELY THAT HE DID NOT WISH TO PUT OZ-SAMA IN DANGER WITH UNRELIABLE INFORMATION.
BUT... BREAK...
...
...KEPT SILENT BECAUSE HE DID NOT WANT ME TO HAVE TO HEAR THIS DARK TALK...
...IS WHAT REIM-SAN—
?
...WHY MUST THIS BE SO?

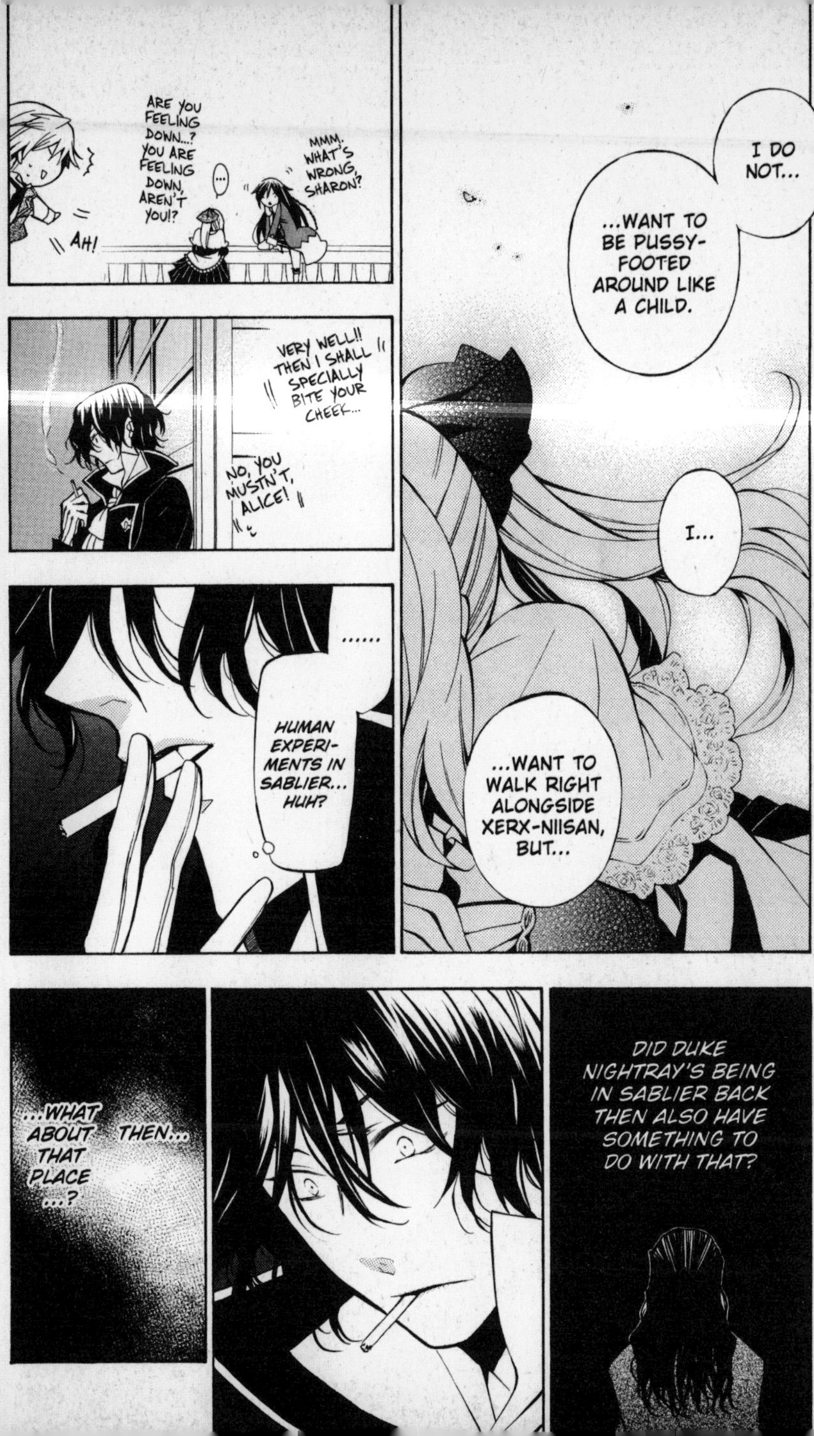
I DO NOT...
...WANT TO BE PUSSY-FOOTED AROUND LIKE A CHILD.
I...
...WANT TO WALK RIGHT ALONGSIDE XERX-NIISAN, BUT...
MMM. WHAT'S WRONG, SHARON?
...
ARE YOU FEELING DOWN...? YOU ARE FEELING DOWN, AREN'T YOU!?
AH!
VERY WELL!! THEN I SHALL SPECIALLY BITE YOUR CHEEK...
NO, YOU MUSTN'T, ALICE!
......
HUMAN EXPERIMENTS IN SABLIER... HUH?
DID DUKE NIGHTRAY'S BEING IN SABLIER BACK THEN ALSO HAVE SOMETHING TO DO WITH THAT?
THEN...
...WHAT ABOUT THAT PLACE...?

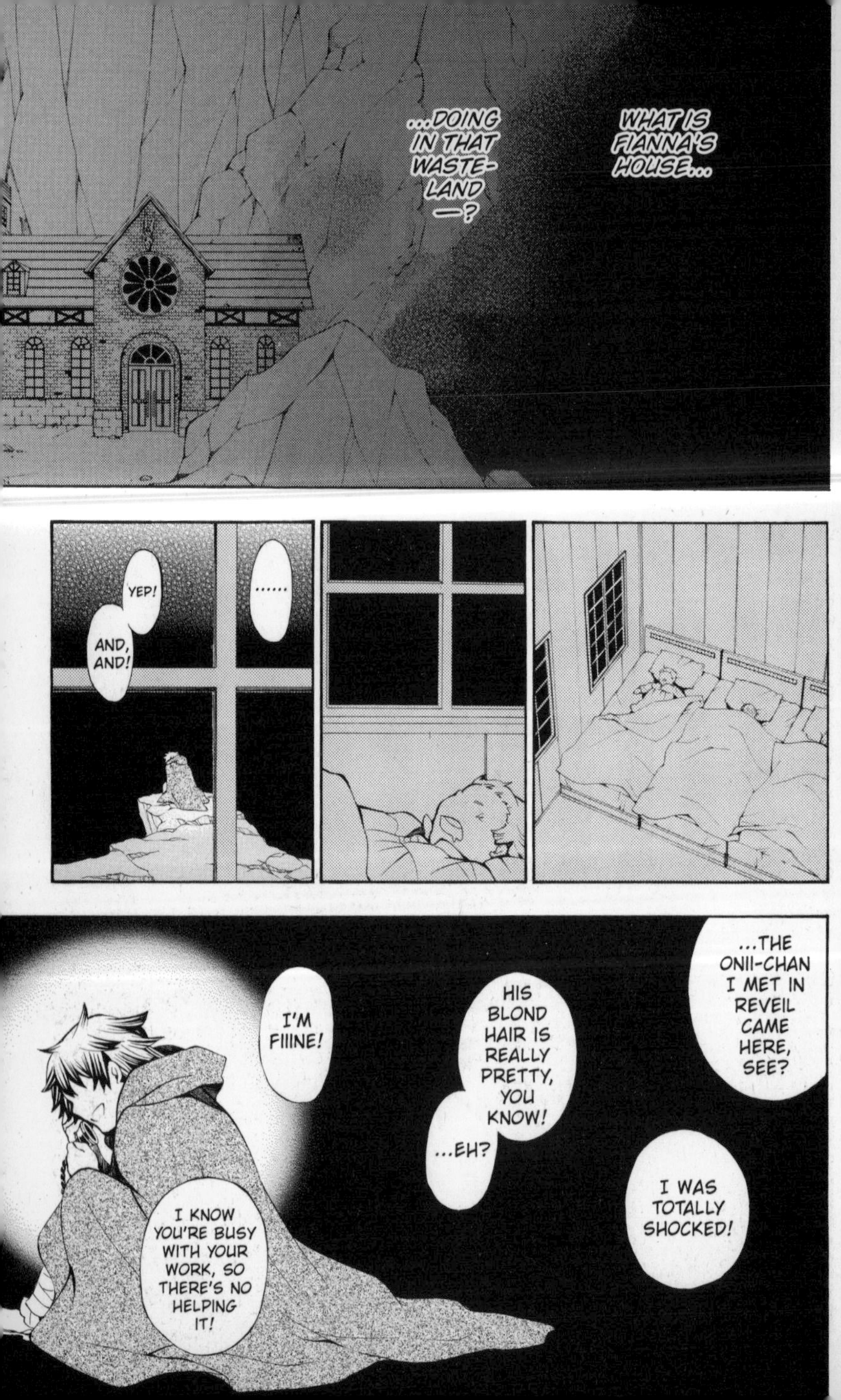
WHAT IS FIANNA'S HOUSE...
...DOING IN THAT WASTE-LAND —?
......
YEP!
AND, AND!
...THE ONII-CHAN I MET IN REVEIL CAME HERE, SEE?
HIS BLOND HAIR IS REALLY PRETTY, YOU KNOW!
I WAS TOTALLY SHOCKED!
...EH?
I'M FIIINE!
I KNOW YOU'RE BUSY WITH YOUR WORK, SO THERE'S NO HELPING IT!

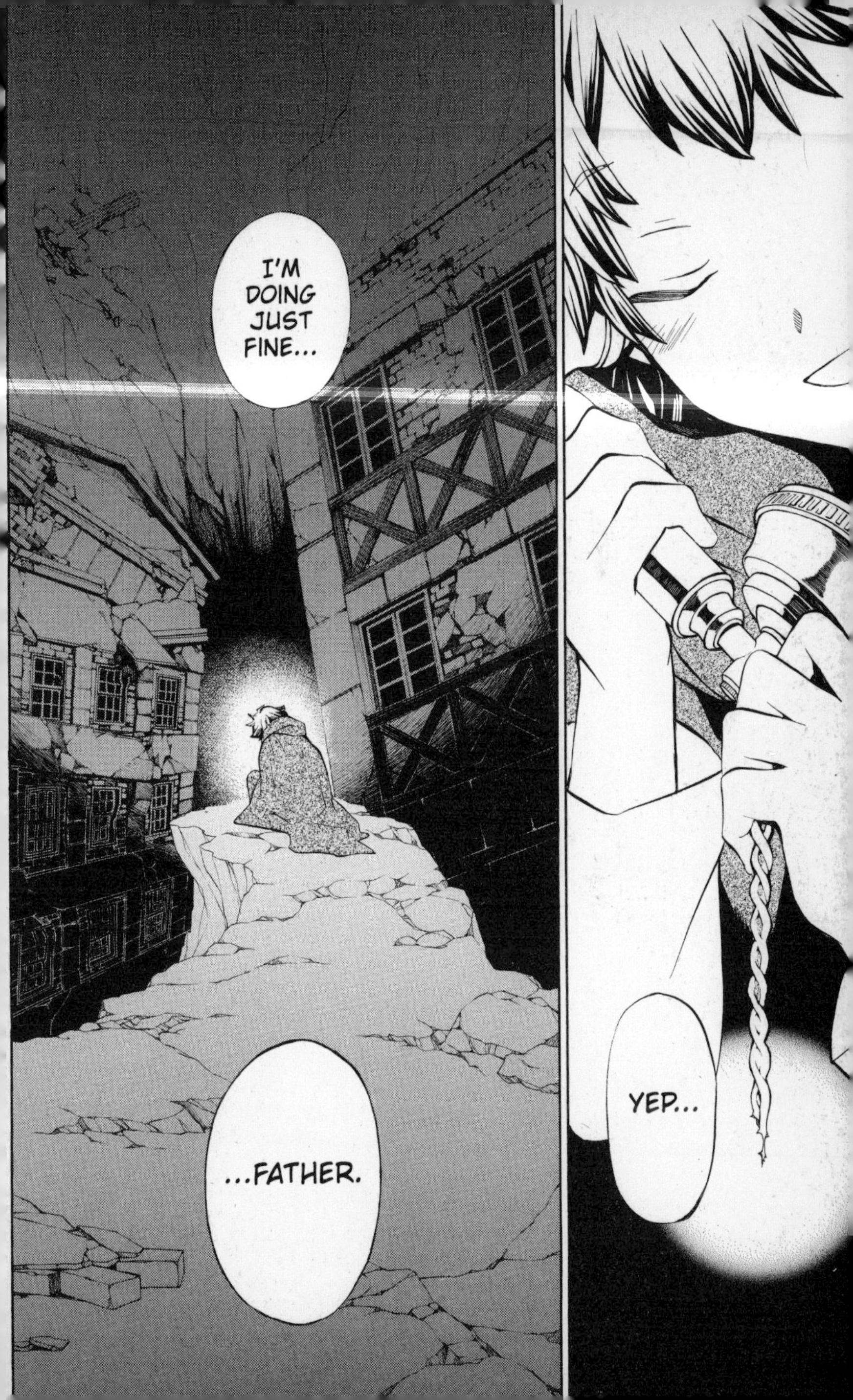
YEP...
I'M DOING JUST FINE...
...FATHER.

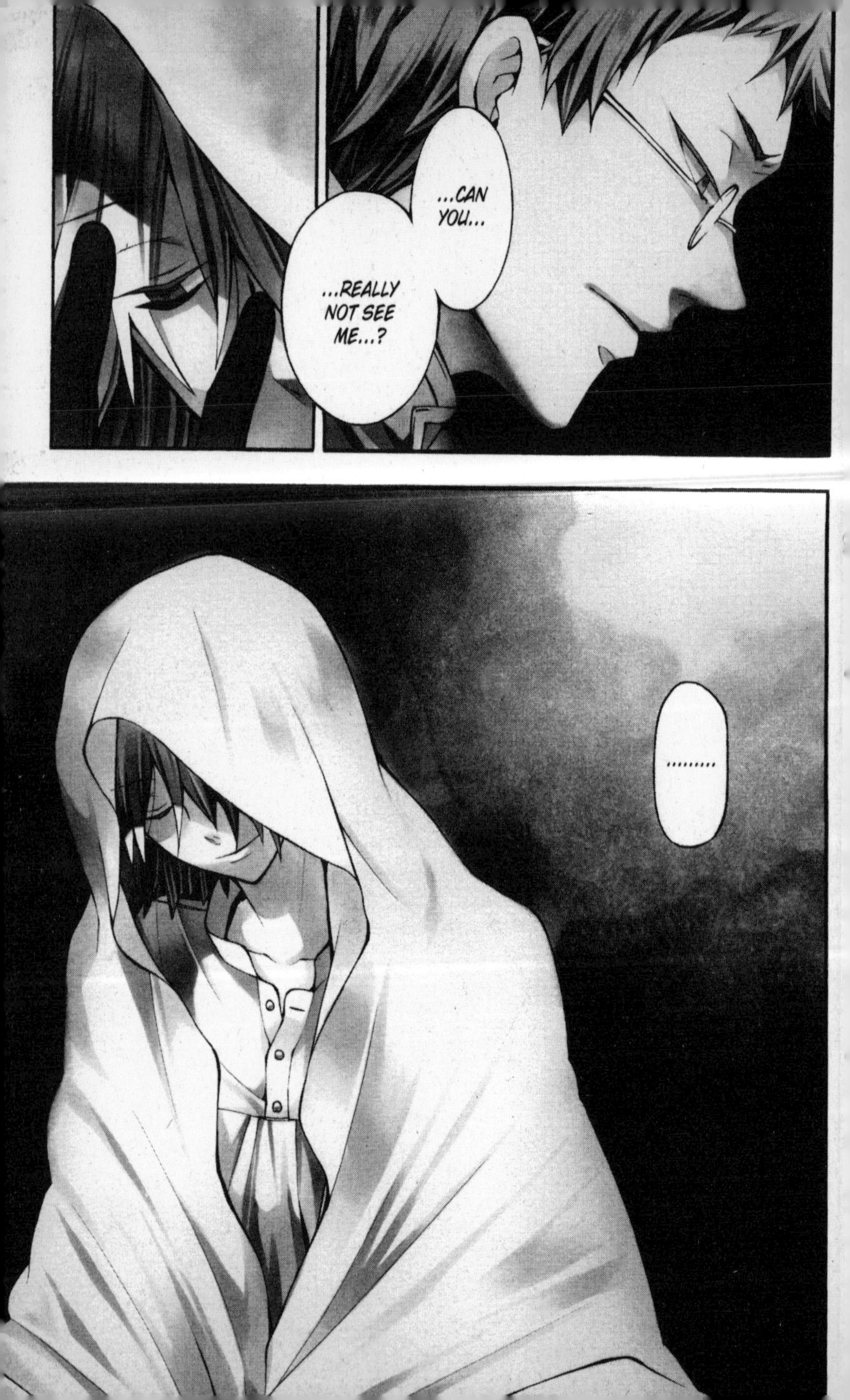
...CAN YOU...
...REALLY NOT SEE ME...?
....

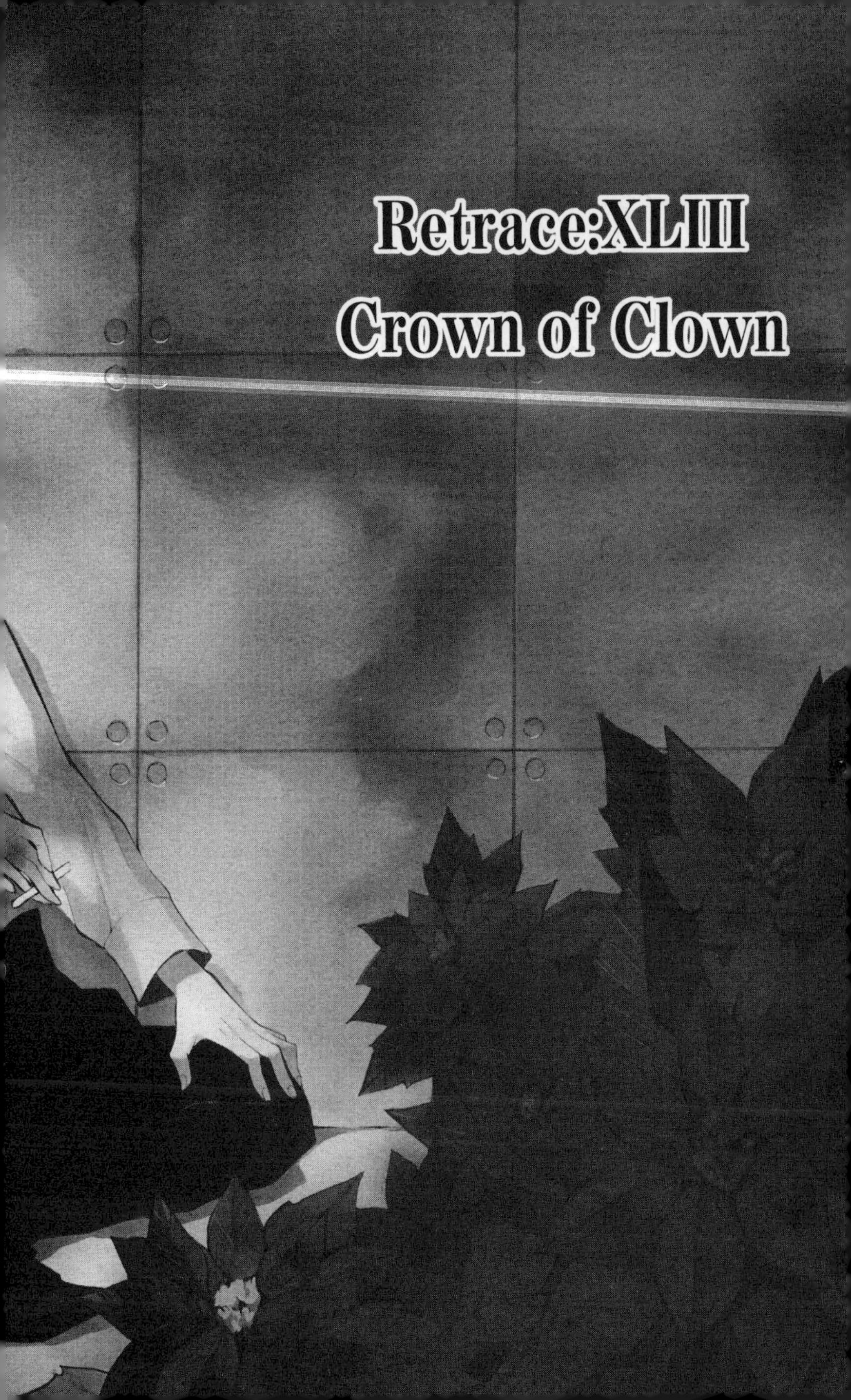
Retrace:XLIII
Crown of Clown

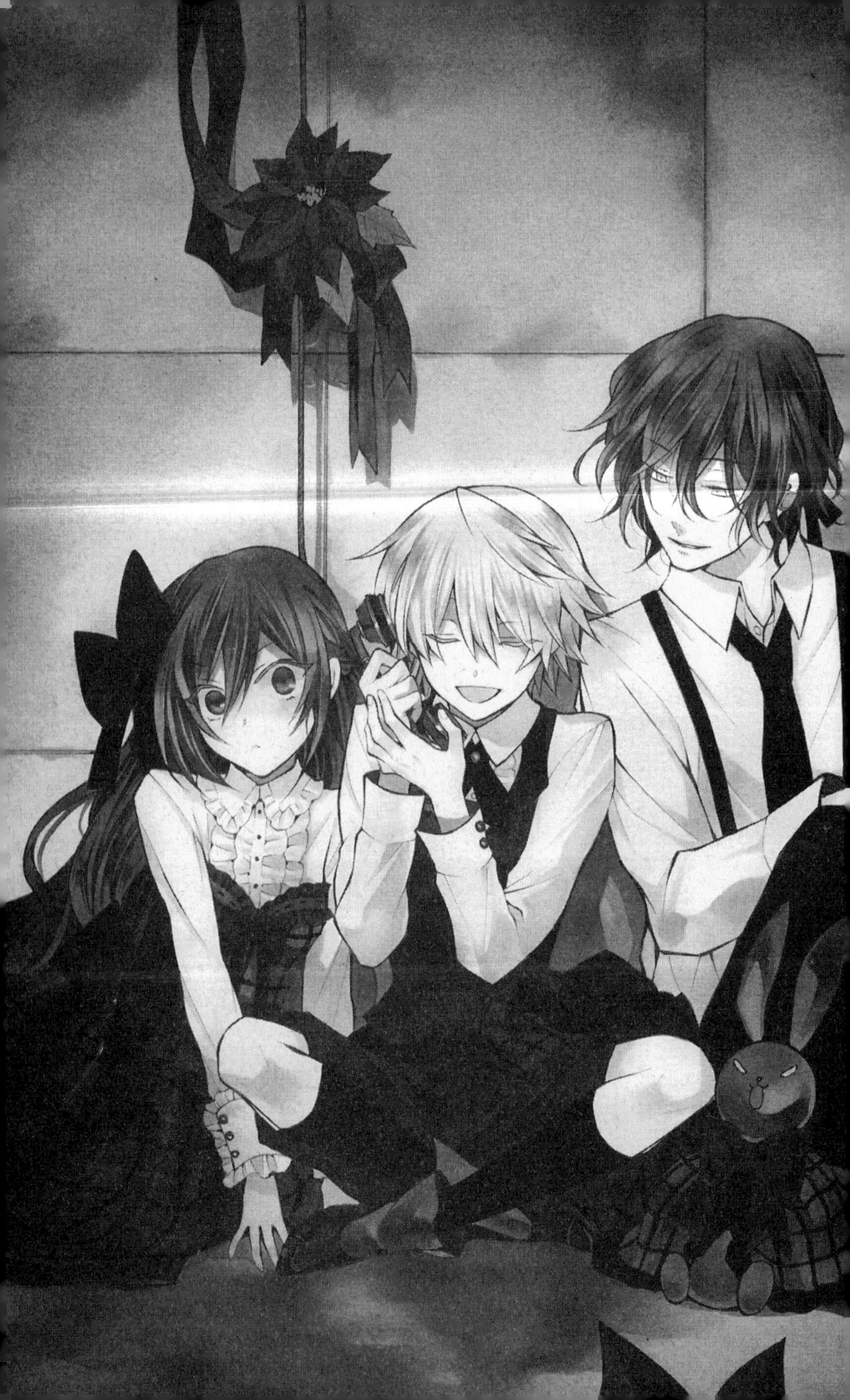

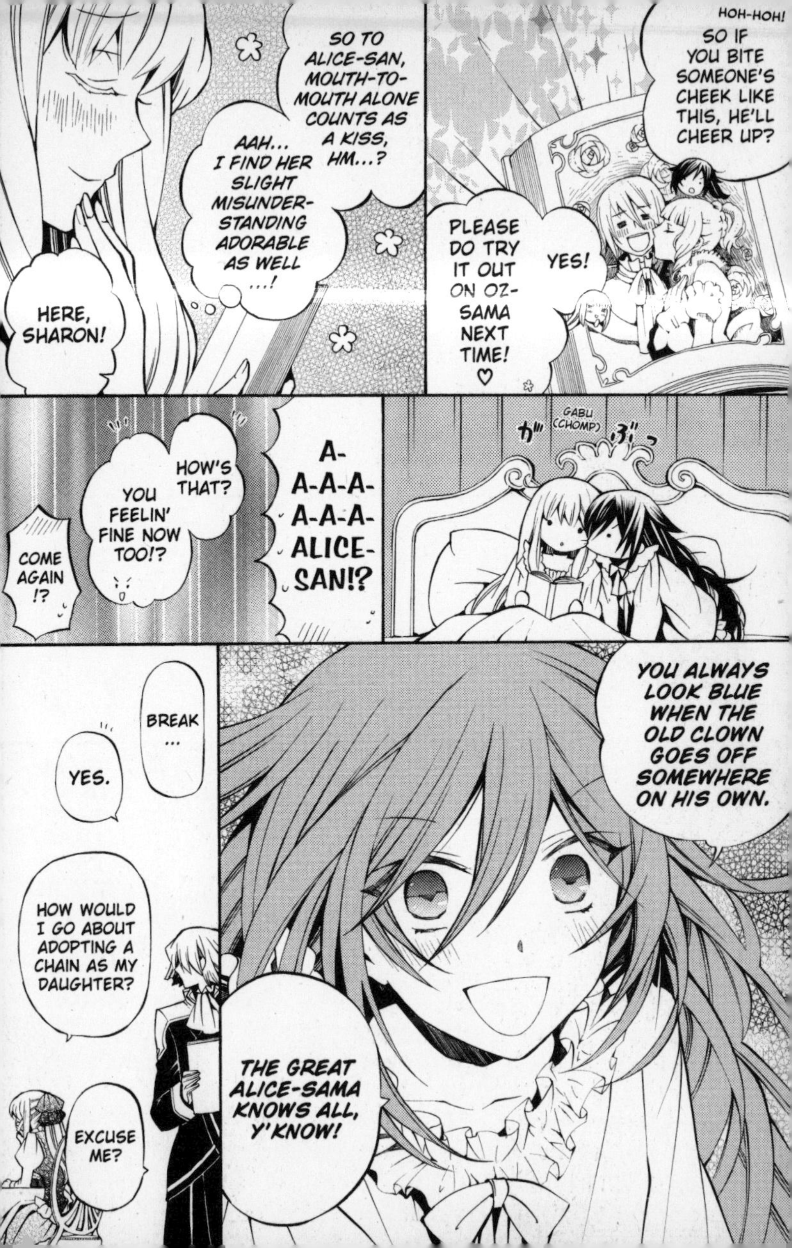
HOH-HOH!
SO IF YOU BITE SOMEONE'S CHEEK LIKE THIS, HE'LL CHEER UP?
YES!
PLEASE DO TRY IT OUT ON OZ-SAMA NEXT TIME! ♡
SO TO ALICE-SAN, MOUTH-TO-MOUTH ALONE COUNTS AS A KISS, HM...?
AAH... I FIND HER SLIGHT MISUNDER-STANDING ADORABLE AS WELL...!
HERE, SHARON!
GABU (CHOMP)
A-A-A-A-A-A-A-ALICE-SAN!?
HOW'S THAT?
YOU FEELIN' FINE NOW TOO!?
COME AGAIN!?
YOU ALWAYS LOOK BLUE WHEN THE OLD CLOWN GOES OFF SOMEWHERE ON HIS OWN.
THE GREAT ALICE-SAMA KNOWS ALL, Y'KNOW!
BREAK...
YES.
HOW WOULD I GO ABOUT ADOPTING A CHAIN AS MY DAUGHTER?
EXCUSE ME?

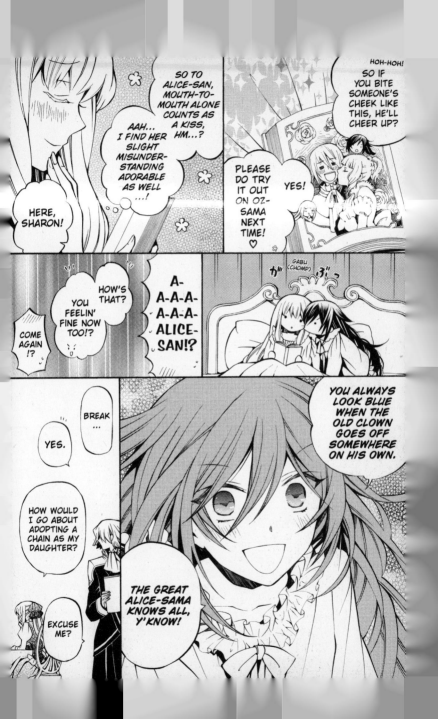

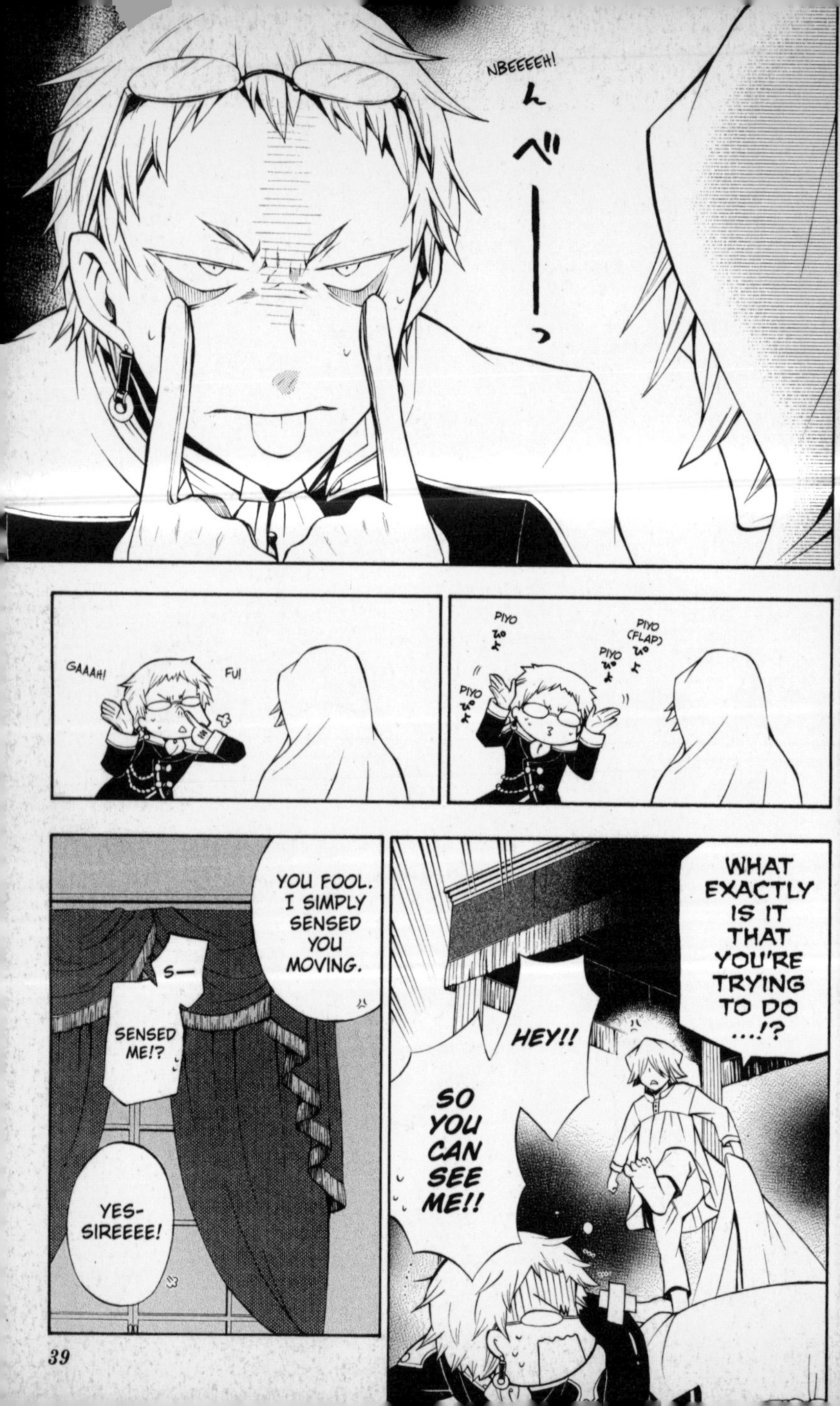
NBEEEEH!
んべーっ
PIYO
ぴよ
PIYO (FLAP)
ぴよ
PIYO
ぴよ
PIYO
ぴよ
FU!
GAAAH!
WHAT EXACTLY IS IT THAT YOU'RE TRYING TO DO ...!?
HEY!!
SO YOU CAN SEE ME!!
YOU FOOL. I SIMPLY SENSED YOU MOVING.
S—
SENSED ME!?
YES-SIREEEE!

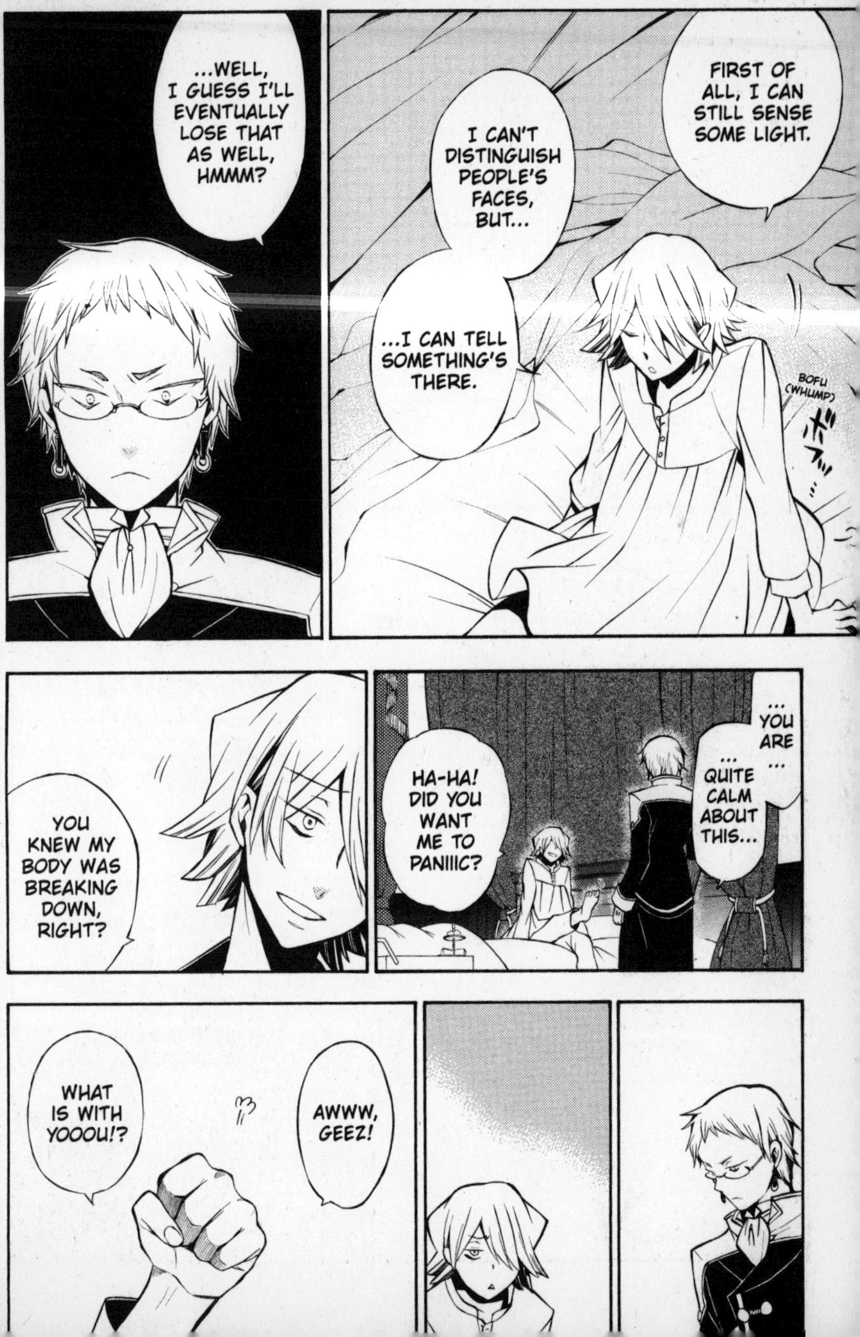
FIRST OF ALL, I CAN STILL SENSE SOME LIGHT.
I CAN'T DISTINGUISH PEOPLE'S FACES, BUT...
...I CAN TELL SOMETHING'S THERE.
BOFU (WHUMP)
...WELL, I GUESS I'LL EVENTUALLY LOSE THAT AS WELL, HMMM?
... YOU ARE ... ... QUITE CALM ABOUT THIS...
HA-HA! DID YOU WANT ME TO PANIIIC?
YOU KNEW MY BODY WAS BREAKING DOWN, RIGHT?
AWWW, GEEZ!
WHAT IS WITH YOOOU!?

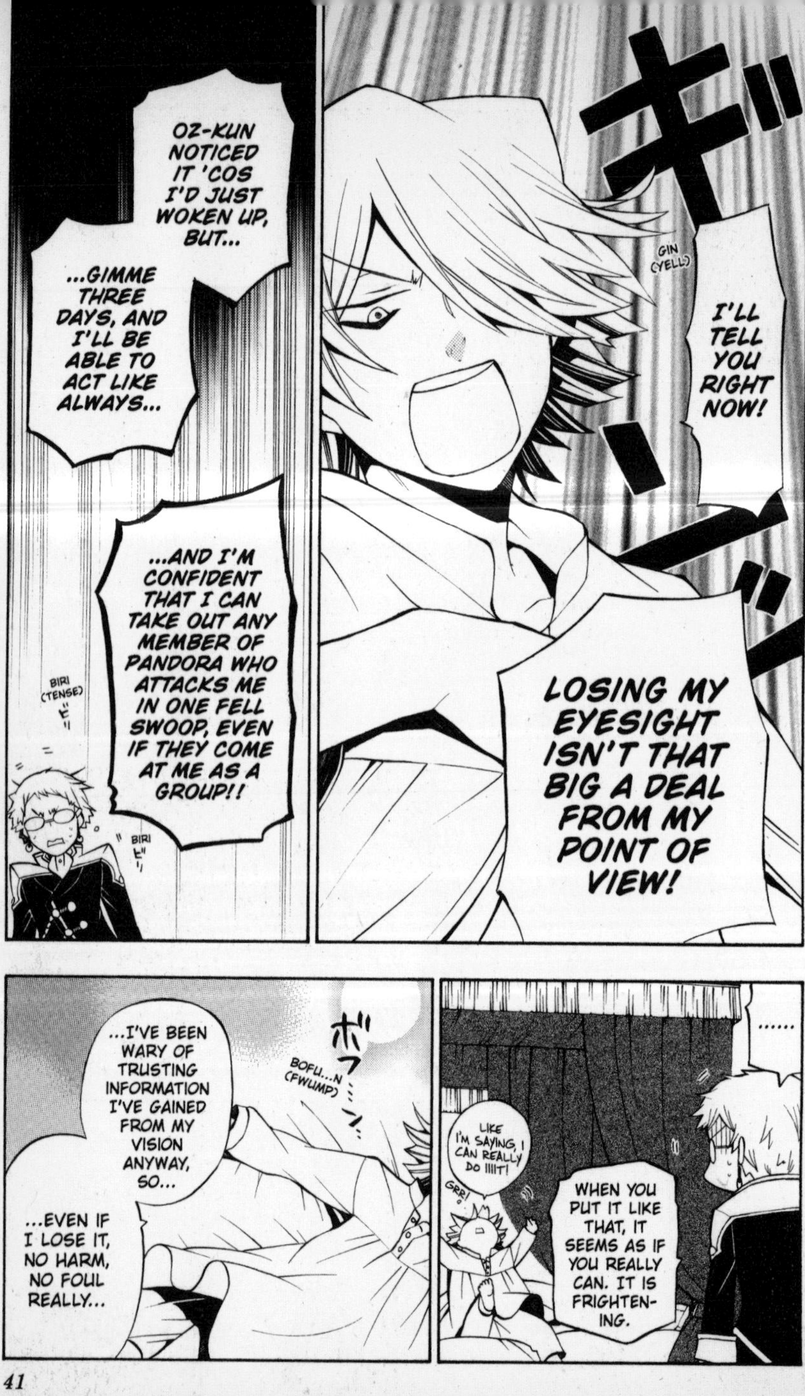
GIN (YELL)
I'LL TELL YOU RIGHT NOW!
LOSING MY EYESIGHT ISN'T THAT BIG A DEAL FROM MY POINT OF VIEW!
OZ-KUN NOTICED IT 'COS I'D JUST WOKEN UP, BUT...
...GIMME THREE DAYS, AND I'LL BE ABLE TO ACT LIKE ALWAYS...
...AND I'M CONFIDENT THAT I CAN TAKE OUT ANY MEMBER OF PANDORA WHO ATTACKS ME IN ONE FELL SWOOP, EVEN IF THEY COME AT ME AS A GROUP!!
BIRI (TENSE)
BIRI
......
LIKE I'M SAYING, I CAN REALLY DO IIIIT!
GRR!
WHEN YOU PUT IT LIKE THAT, IT SEEMS AS IF YOU REALLY CAN. IT IS FRIGHTEN-ING.
BOFU...N (FWUMP)
...I'VE BEEN WARY OF TRUSTING INFORMATION I'VE GAINED FROM MY VISION ANYWAY, SO...
...EVEN IF I LOSE IT, NO HARM, NO FOUL REALLY...

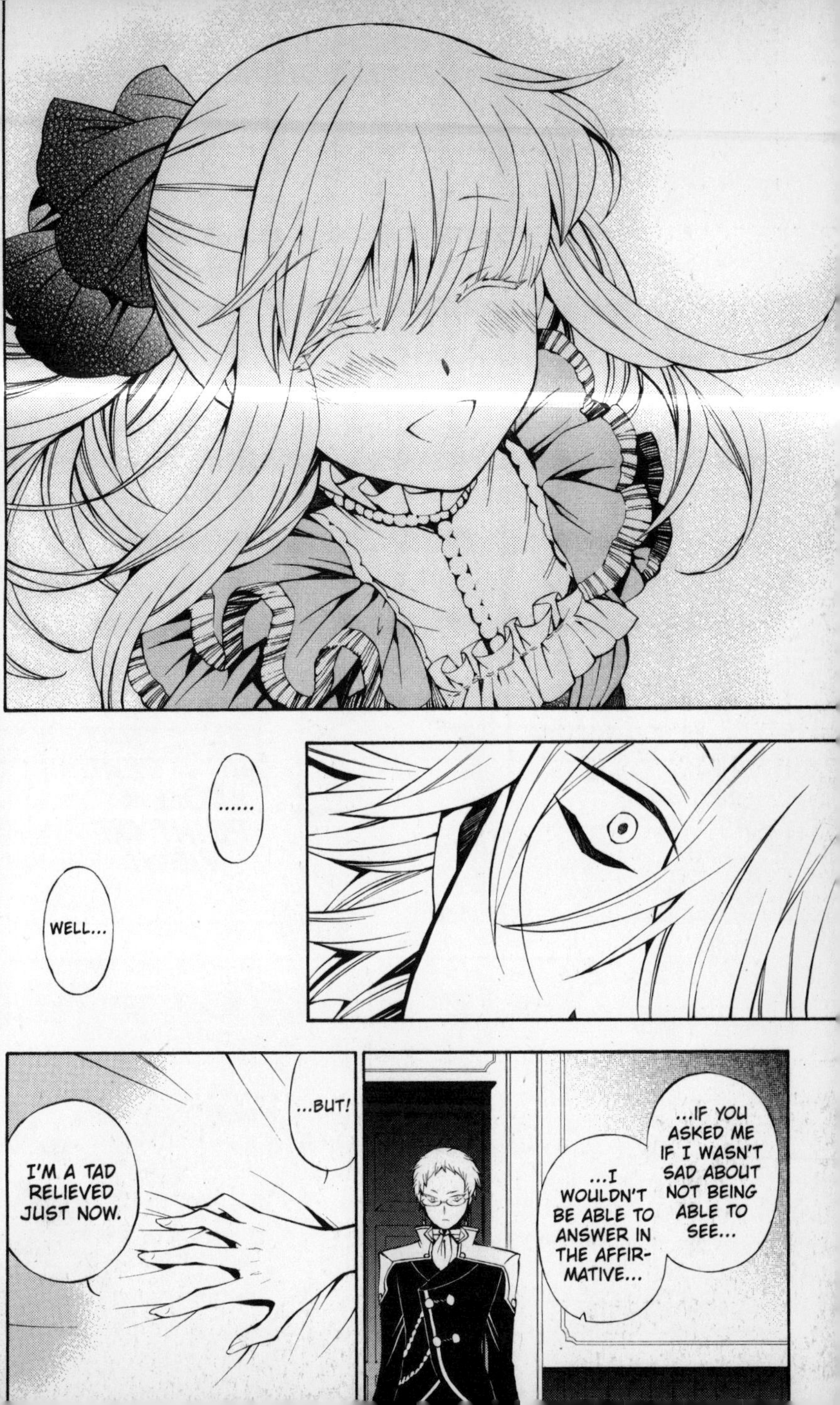
......
WELL...
...IF YOU ASKED ME IF I WASN'T SAD ABOUT NOT BEING ABLE TO SEE...
...I WOULDN'T BE ABLE TO ANSWER IN THE AFFIRMATIVE...
...BUT!
I'M A TAD RELIEVED JUST NOW.

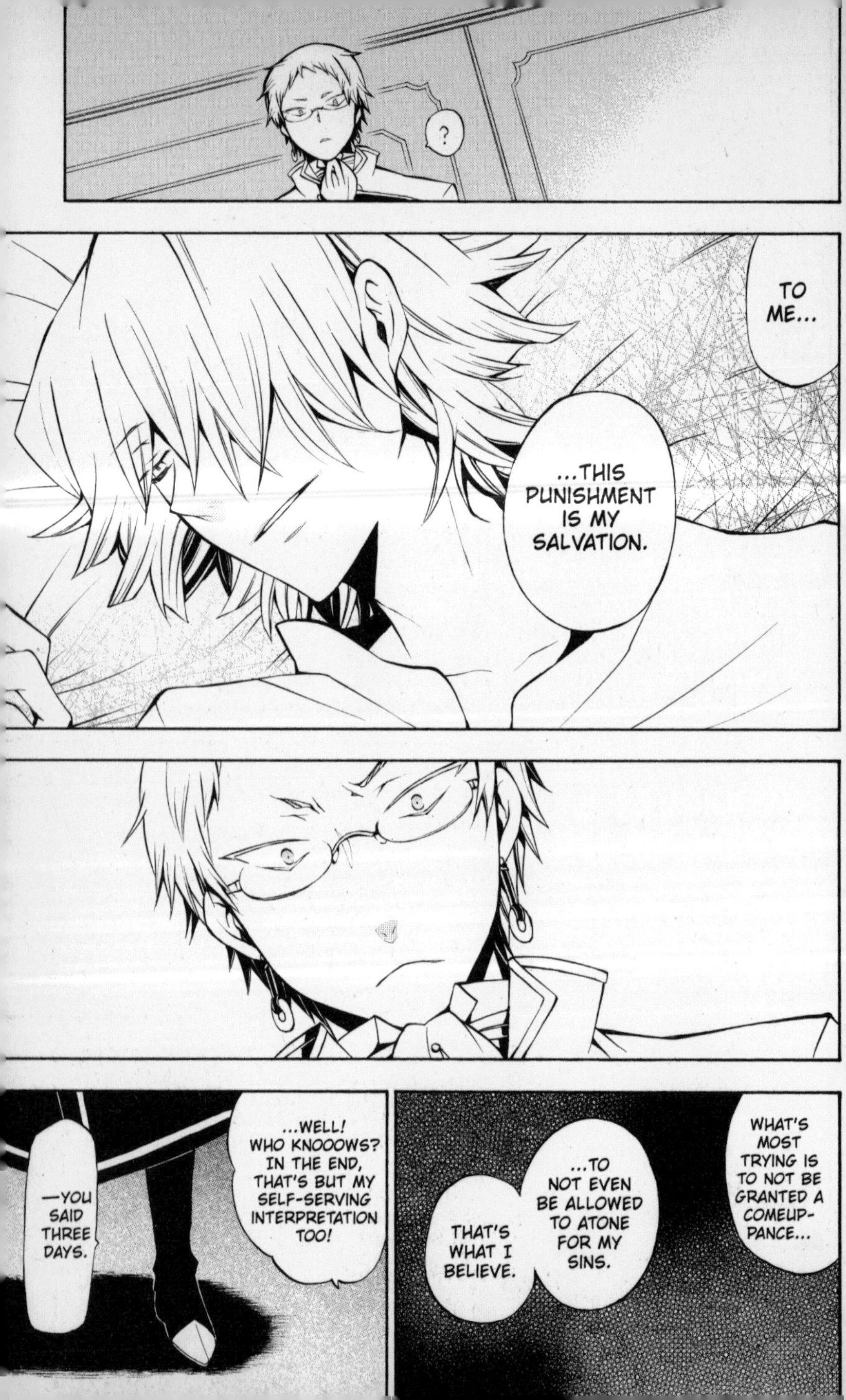
?
TO ME...
...THIS PUNISHMENT IS MY SALVATION.
WHAT'S MOST TRYING IS TO NOT BE GRANTED A COMEUP-PANCE...
...TO NOT EVEN BE ALLOWED TO ATONE FOR MY SINS.
THAT'S WHAT I BELIEVE.
...WELL! WHO KNOOOWS? IN THE END, THAT'S BUT MY SELF-SERVING INTERPRETATION TOO!
—YOU SAID THREE DAYS.

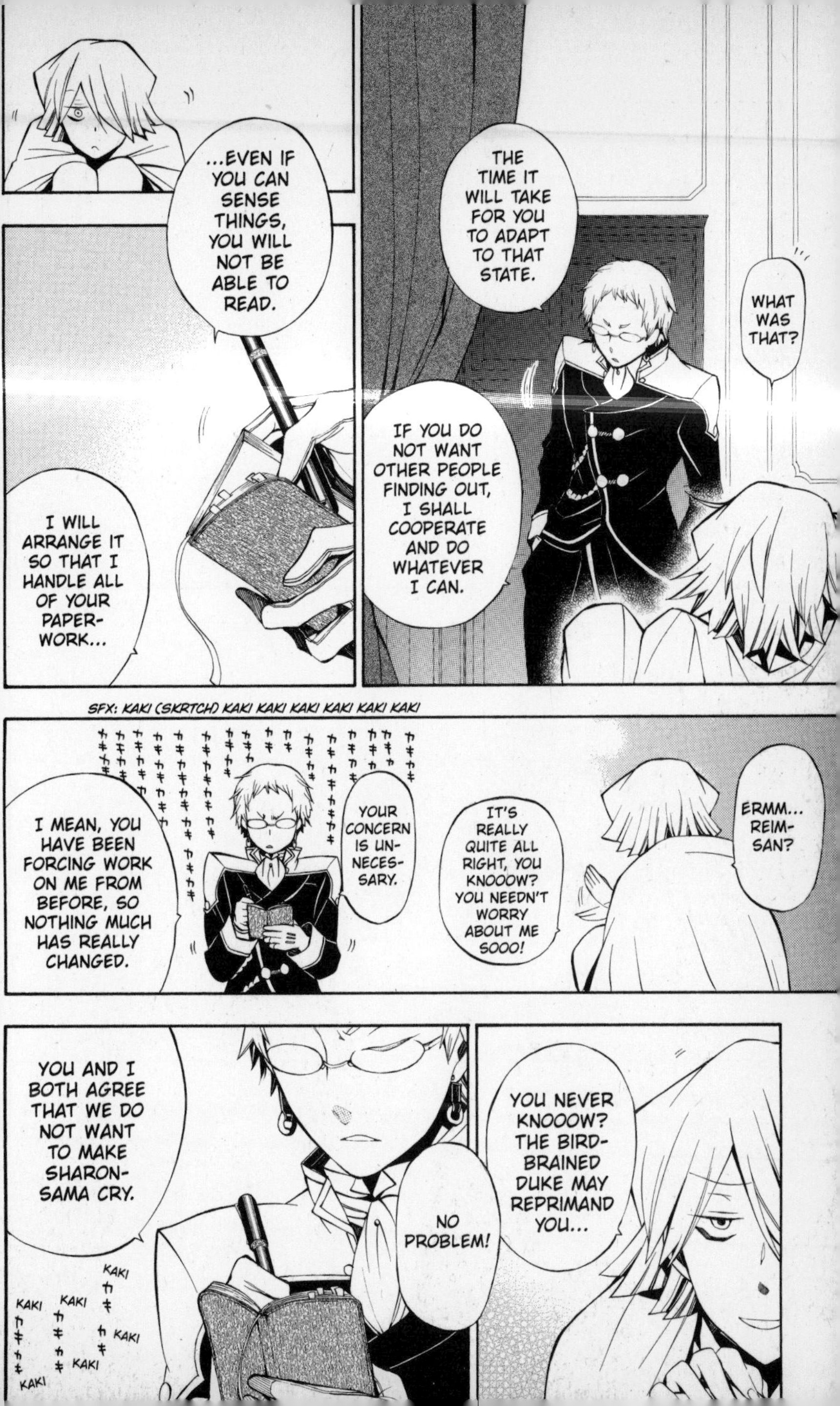
THE TIME IT WILL TAKE FOR YOU TO ADAPT TO THAT STATE.
WHAT WAS THAT?
IF YOU DO NOT WANT OTHER PEOPLE FINDING OUT, I SHALL COOPERATE AND DO WHATEVER I CAN.
...EVEN IF YOU CAN SENSE THINGS, YOU WILL NOT BE ABLE TO READ.
I WILL ARRANGE IT SO THAT I HANDLE ALL OF YOUR PAPER-WORK...
SFX: KAKI (SKRTCH) KAKI KAKI KAKI KAKI KAKI KAKI
ERMM... REIM-SAN?
IT'S REALLY QUITE ALL RIGHT, YOU KNOOOW? YOU NEEDN'T WORRY ABOUT ME SOOO!
YOUR CONCERN IS UN-NECES-SARY.
I MEAN, YOU HAVE BEEN FORCING WORK ON ME FROM BEFORE, SO NOTHING MUCH HAS REALLY CHANGED.
YOU NEVER KNOOOW? THE BIRD-BRAINED DUKE MAY REPRIMAND YOU...
NO PROBLEM!
YOU AND I BOTH AGREE THAT WE DO NOT WANT TO MAKE SHARON-SAMA CRY.
KAKI
KAKI
KAKI
KAKI
KAKI
KAKI

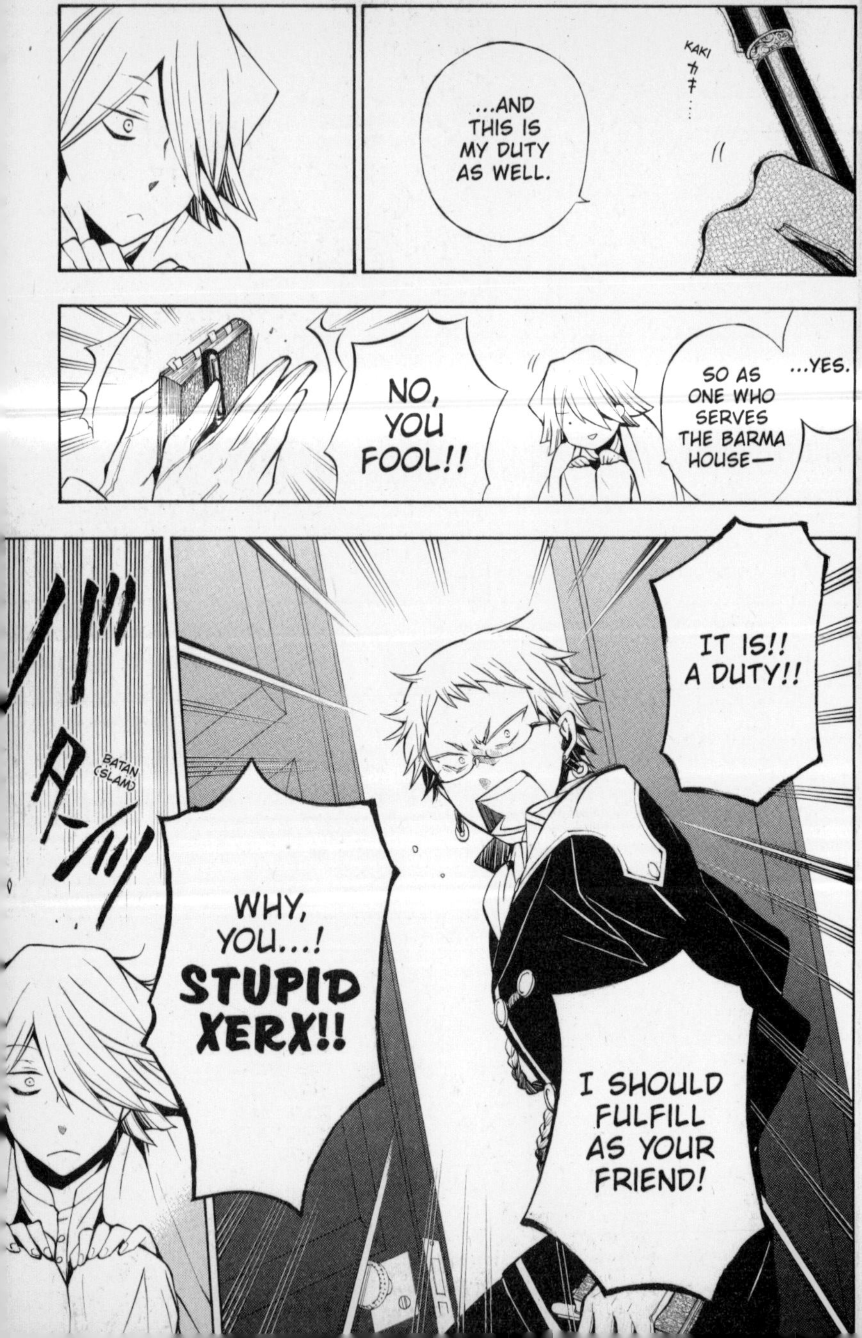
KAKI
カキ…
...AND THIS IS MY DUTY AS WELL.
...YES.
SO AS ONE WHO SERVES THE BARMA HOUSE—
NO, YOU FOOL!!
IT IS!! A DUTY!!
I SHOULD FULFILL AS YOUR FRIEND!
WHY, YOU...! STUPID XERX!!
BATAN (SLAM)

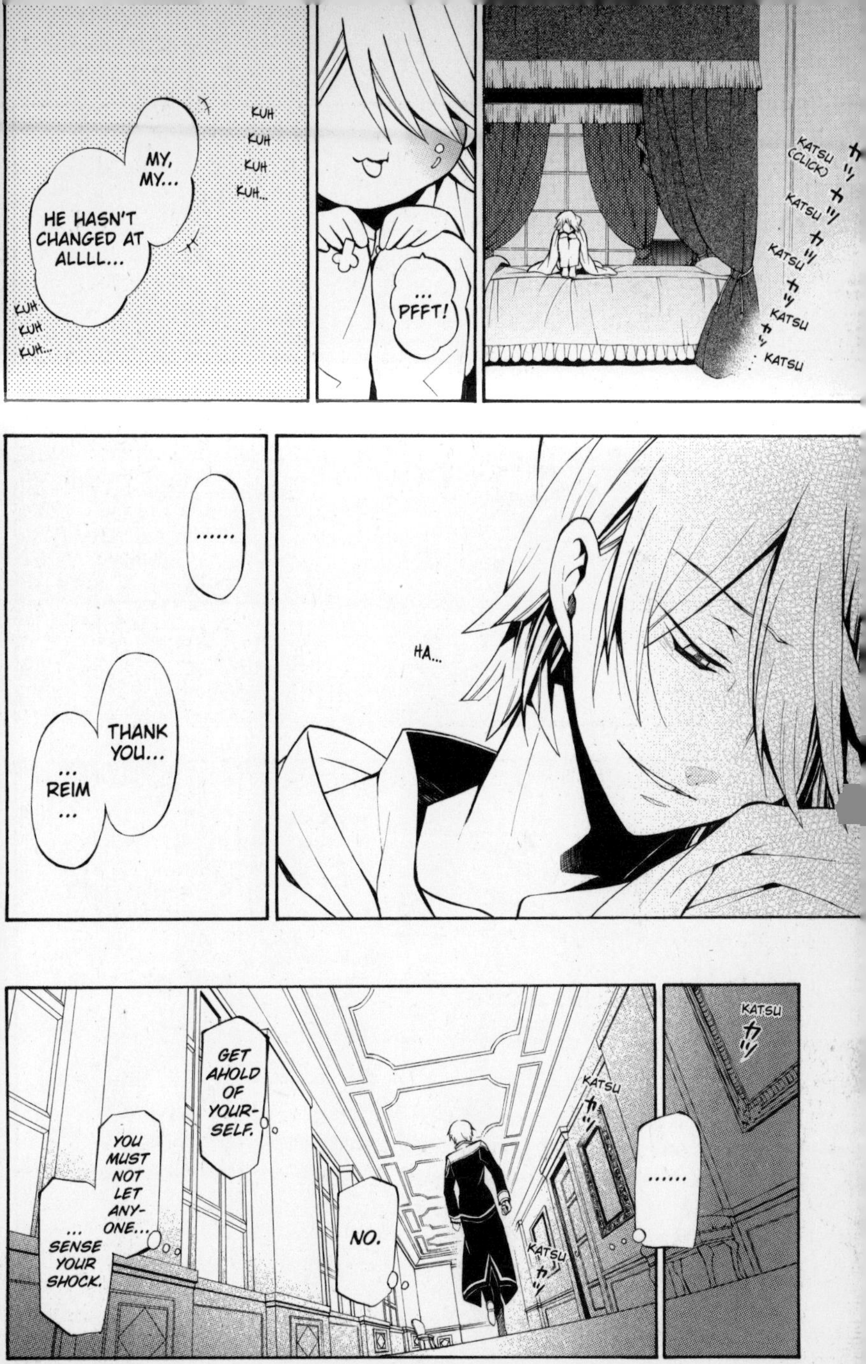
KATSU (CLICK)
KATSU
KATSU
KATSU
KATSU
...PFFT!
KUH KUH KUH KUH...
MY, MY...
HE HASN'T CHANGED AT ALLLL...
KUH KUH KUH...
HA...
......
THANK YOU...
...REIM...
KATSU
......
KATSU
GET AHOLD OF YOURSELF.
YOU MUST NOT LET ANYONE...
...SENSE YOUR SHOCK.
NO.
KATSU

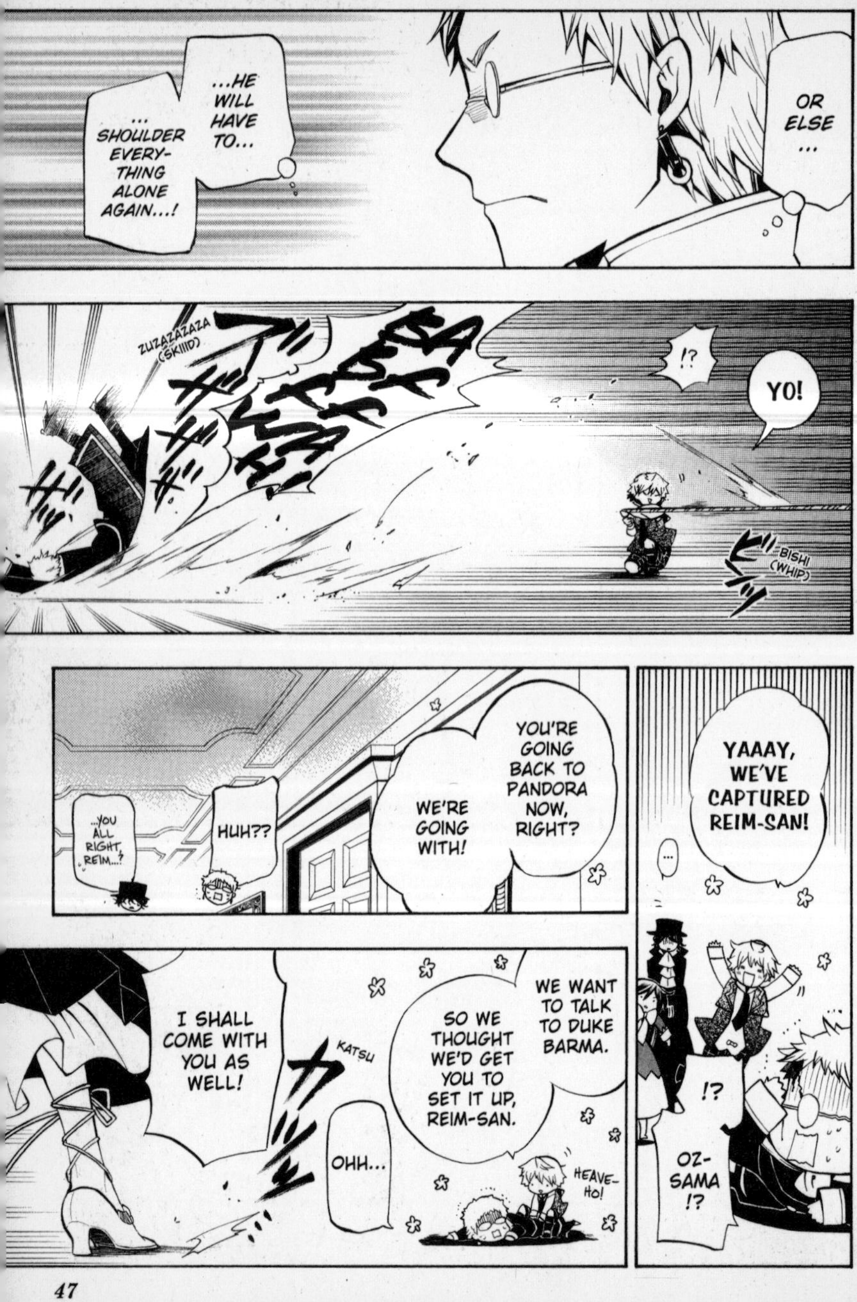
OR ELSE ...
...HE WILL HAVE TO...
... SHOULDER EVERY-THING ALONE AGAIN...!
YO!
!?
BISHI (WHIP)
ZUZAZAZAZA (SKIIID)
YAAAY, WE'VE CAPTURED REIM-SAN!
...
!?
OZ-SAMA !?
YOU'RE GOING BACK TO PANDORA NOW, RIGHT?
WE'RE GOING WITH!
HUH??
...YOU ALL RIGHT, REIM...?
WE WANT TO TALK TO DUKE BARMA.
SO WE THOUGHT WE'D GET YOU TO SET IT UP, REIM-SAN.
HEAVE-HO!
OHH...
KATSU
I SHALL COME WITH YOU AS WELL!

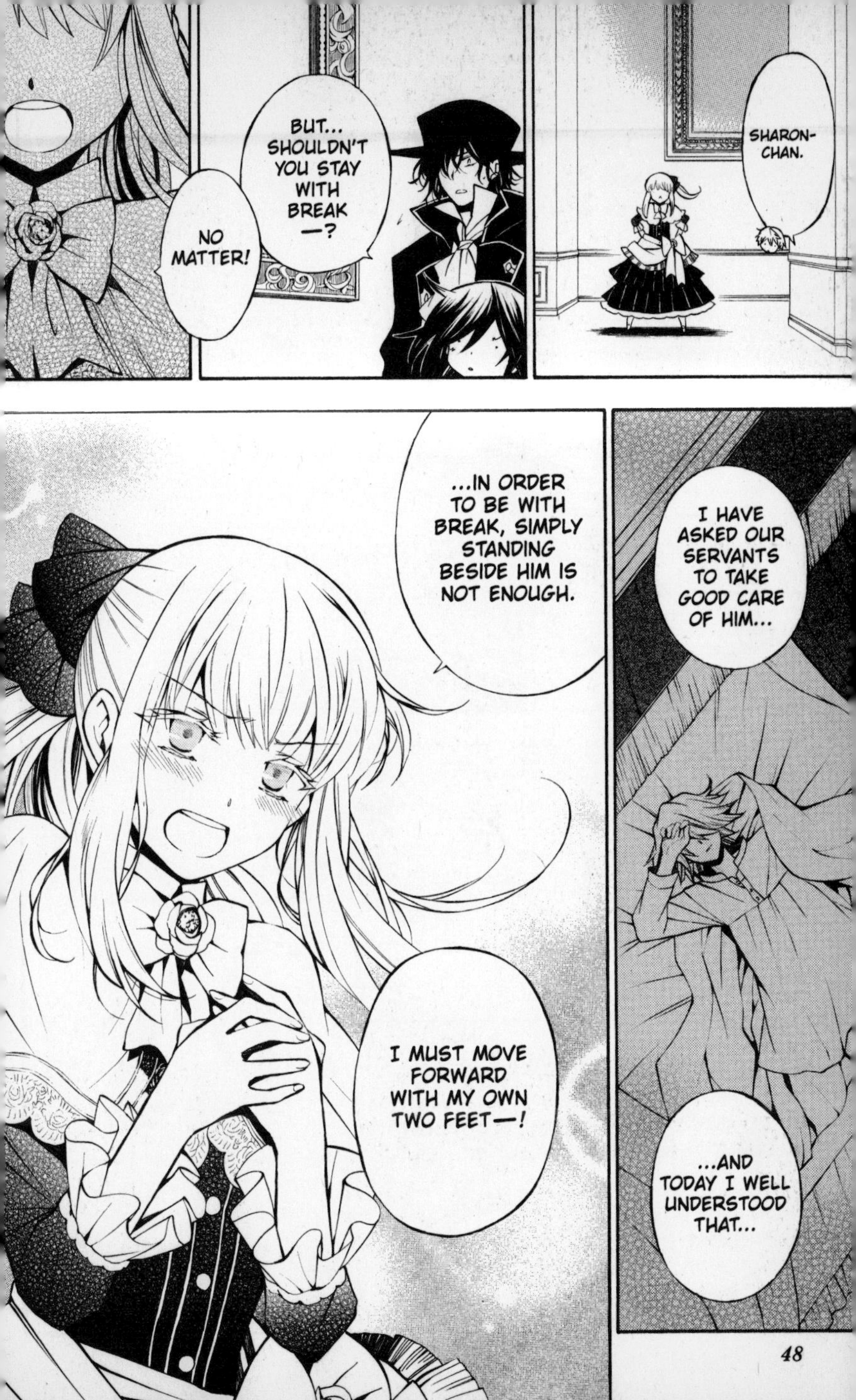
SHARON-CHAN.
BUT... SHOULDN'T YOU STAY WITH BREAK—?
NO MATTER!
I HAVE ASKED OUR SERVANTS TO TAKE GOOD CARE OF HIM...
...AND TODAY I WELL UNDERSTOOD THAT...
...IN ORDER TO BE WITH BREAK, SIMPLY STANDING BESIDE HIM IS NOT ENOUGH.
I MUST MOVE FORWARD WITH MY OWN TWO FEET—!

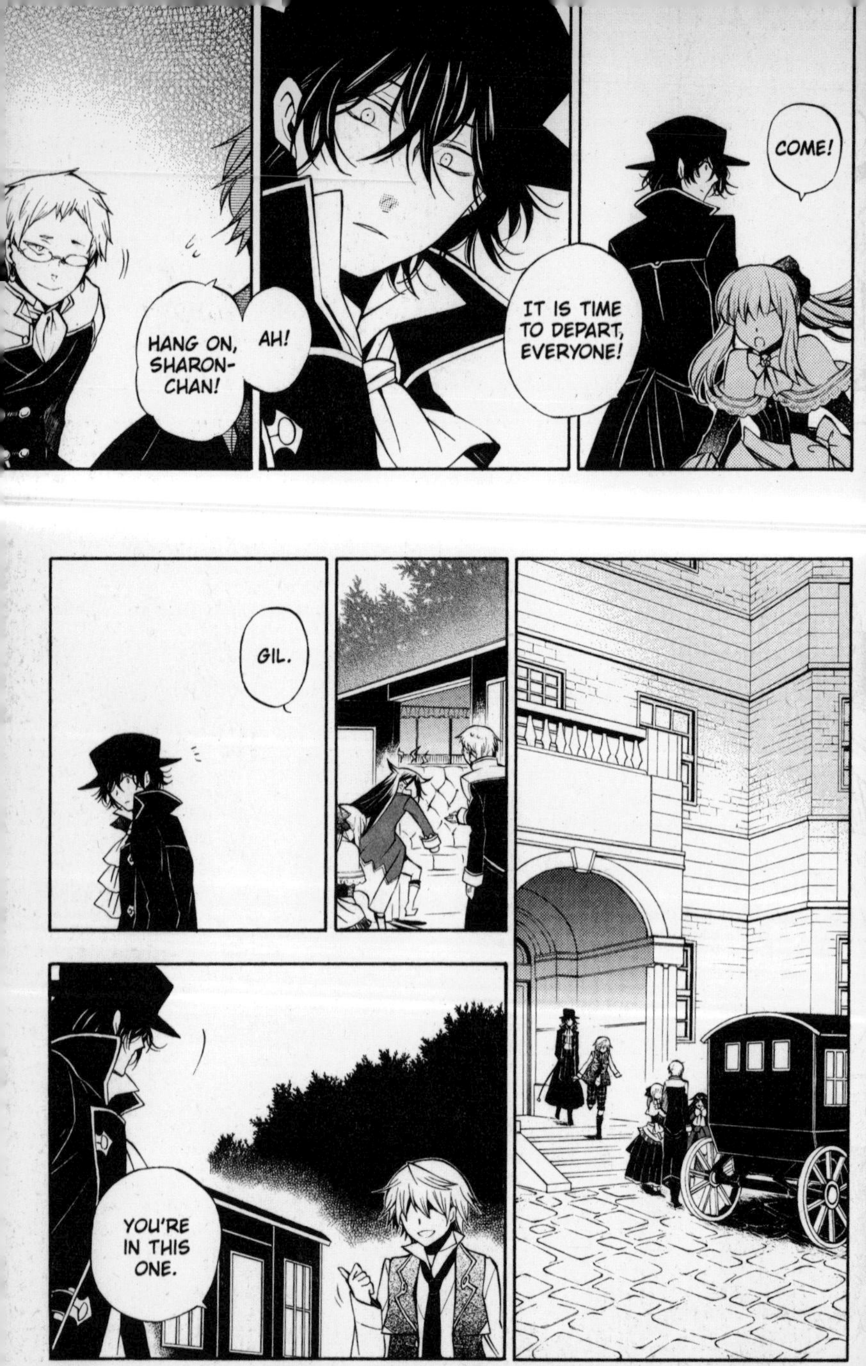
COME!
IT IS TIME TO DEPART, EVERYONE!
AH!
HANG ON, SHARON-CHAN!
GIL.
YOU'RE IN THIS ONE.

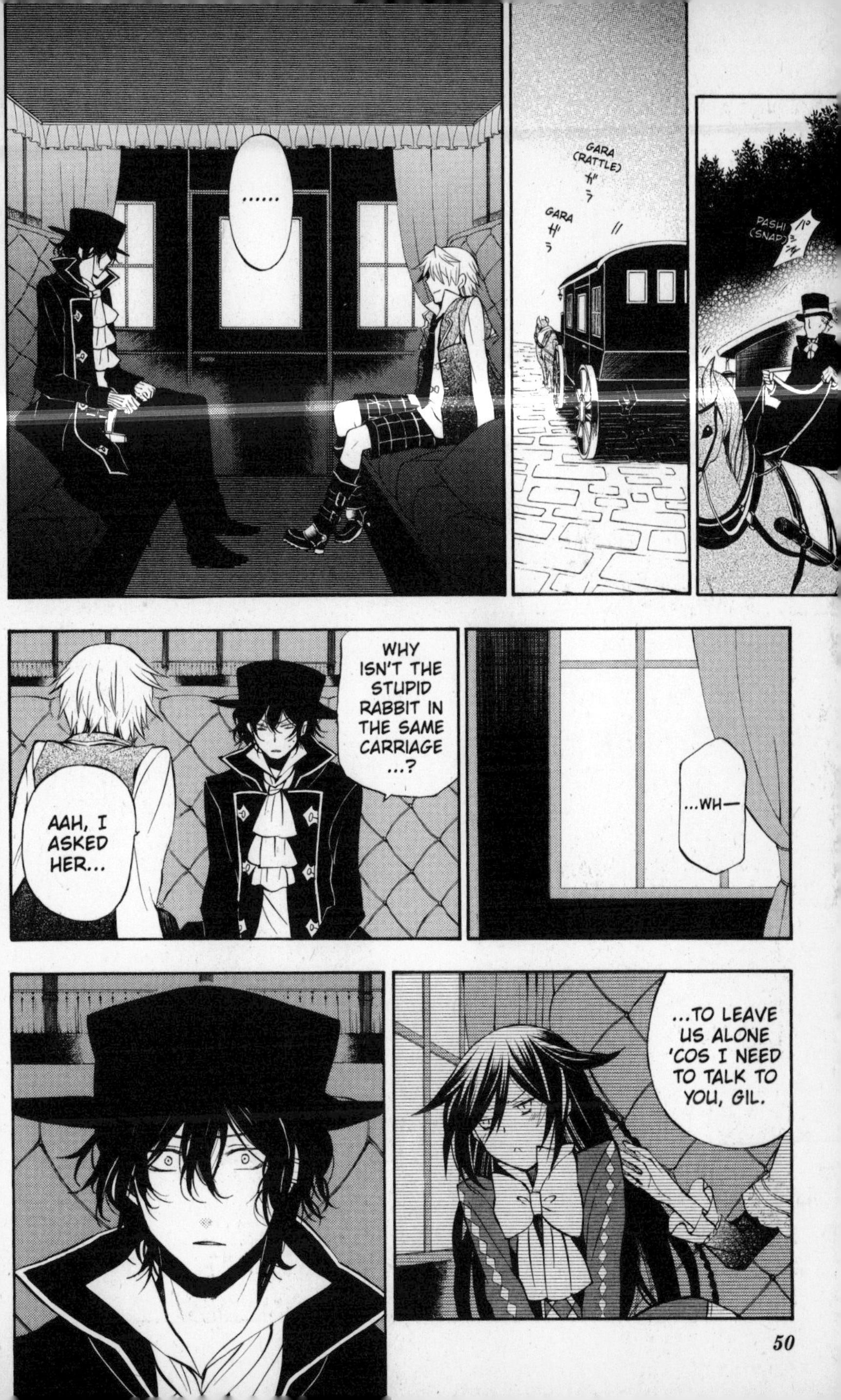
PASHI (SNAP)
GARA (RATTLE)
GARA
......
...WH—
WHY ISN'T THE STUPID RABBIT IN THE SAME CARRIAGE ...?
AAH, I ASKED HER...
...TO LEAVE US ALONE 'COS I NEED TO TALK TO YOU, GIL.

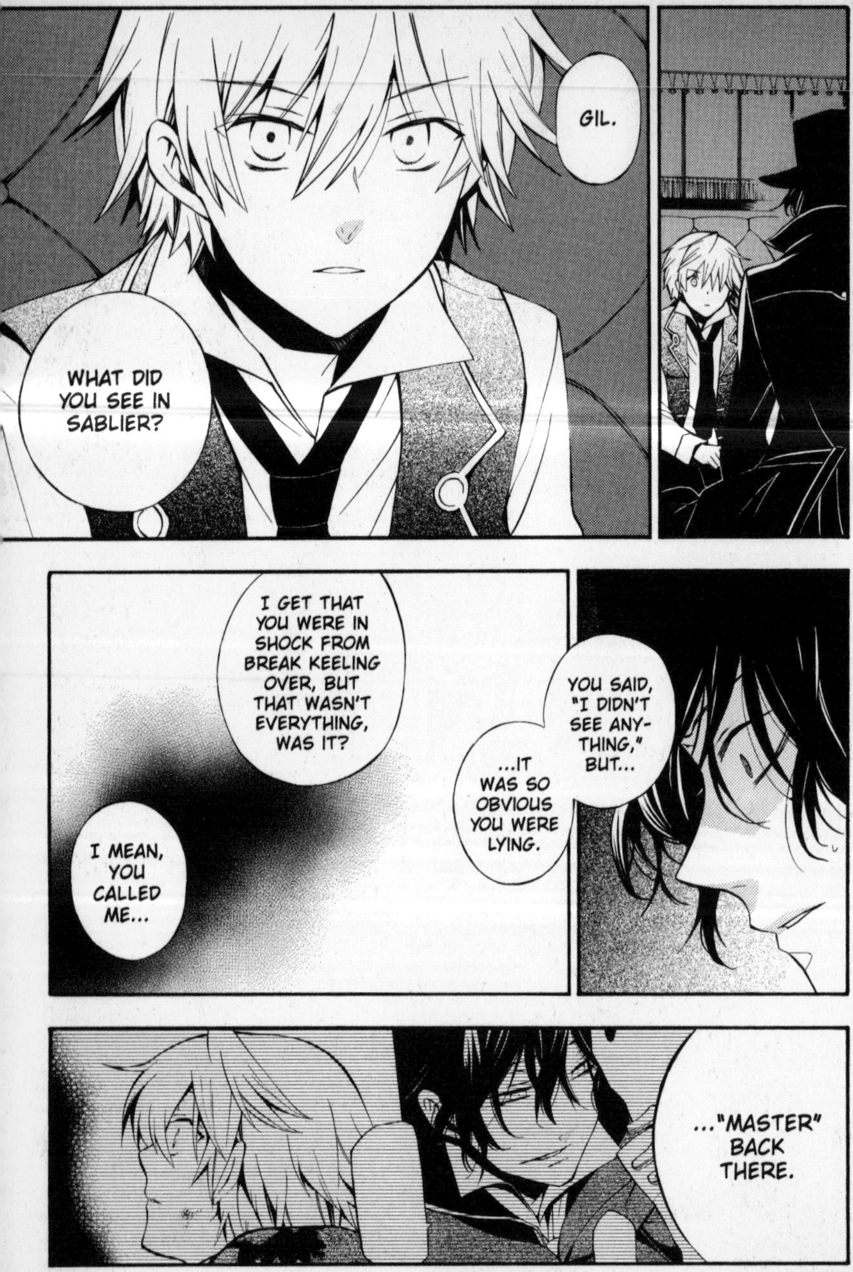
GIL.
WHAT DID YOU SEE IN SABLIER?
YOU SAID, "I DIDN'T SEE ANY-THING," BUT...
...IT WAS SO OBVIOUS YOU WERE LYING.
I GET THAT YOU WERE IN SHOCK FROM BREAK KEELING OVER, BUT THAT WASN'T EVERYTHING, WAS IT?
I MEAN, YOU CALLED ME...
..."MASTER" BACK THERE.

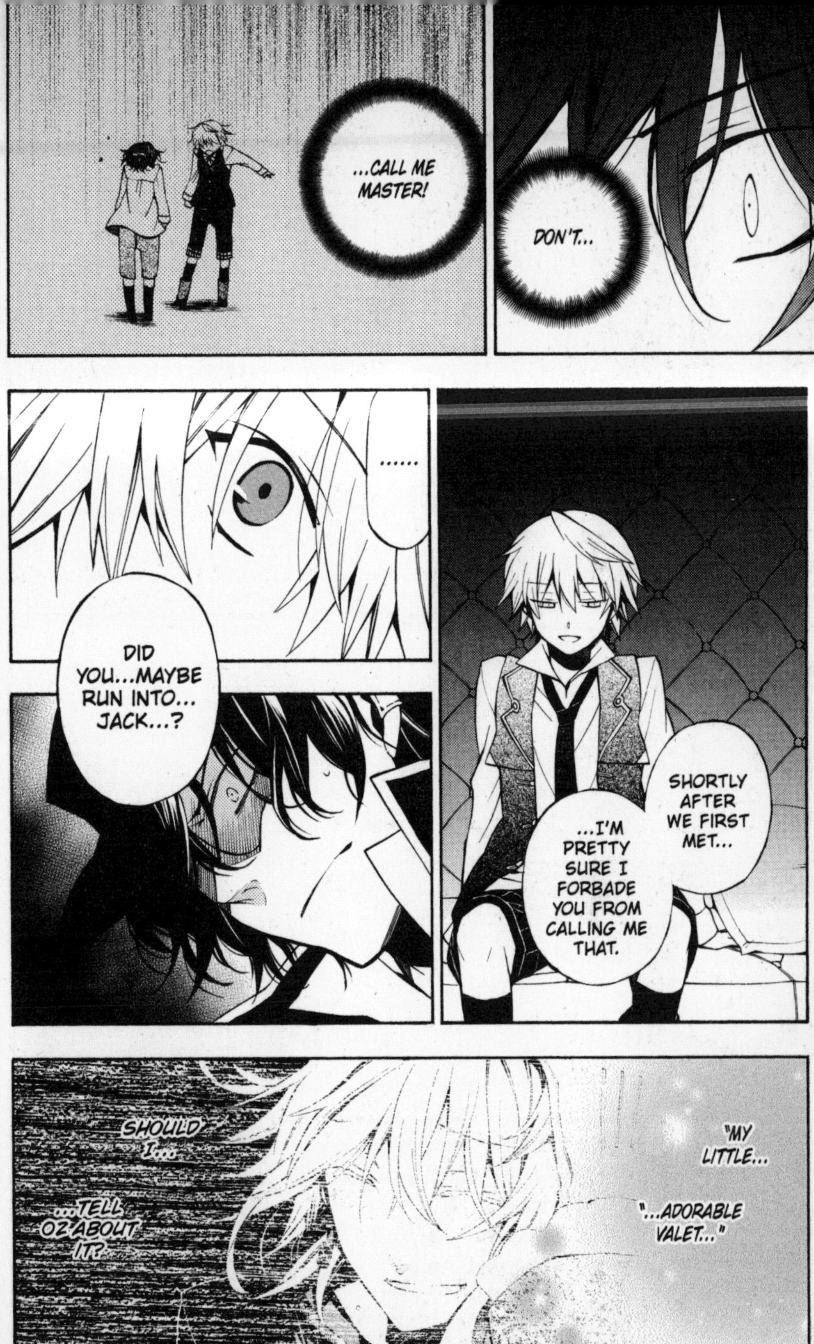
DON'T...
...CALL ME MASTER!
SHORTLY AFTER WE FIRST MET...
...I'M PRETTY SURE I FORBADE YOU FROM CALLING ME THAT.
......
DID YOU...MAYBE RUN INTO... JACK...?
"MY LITTLE...
"...ADORABLE VALET..."
SHOULD I...
...TELL OZ ABOUT IT?

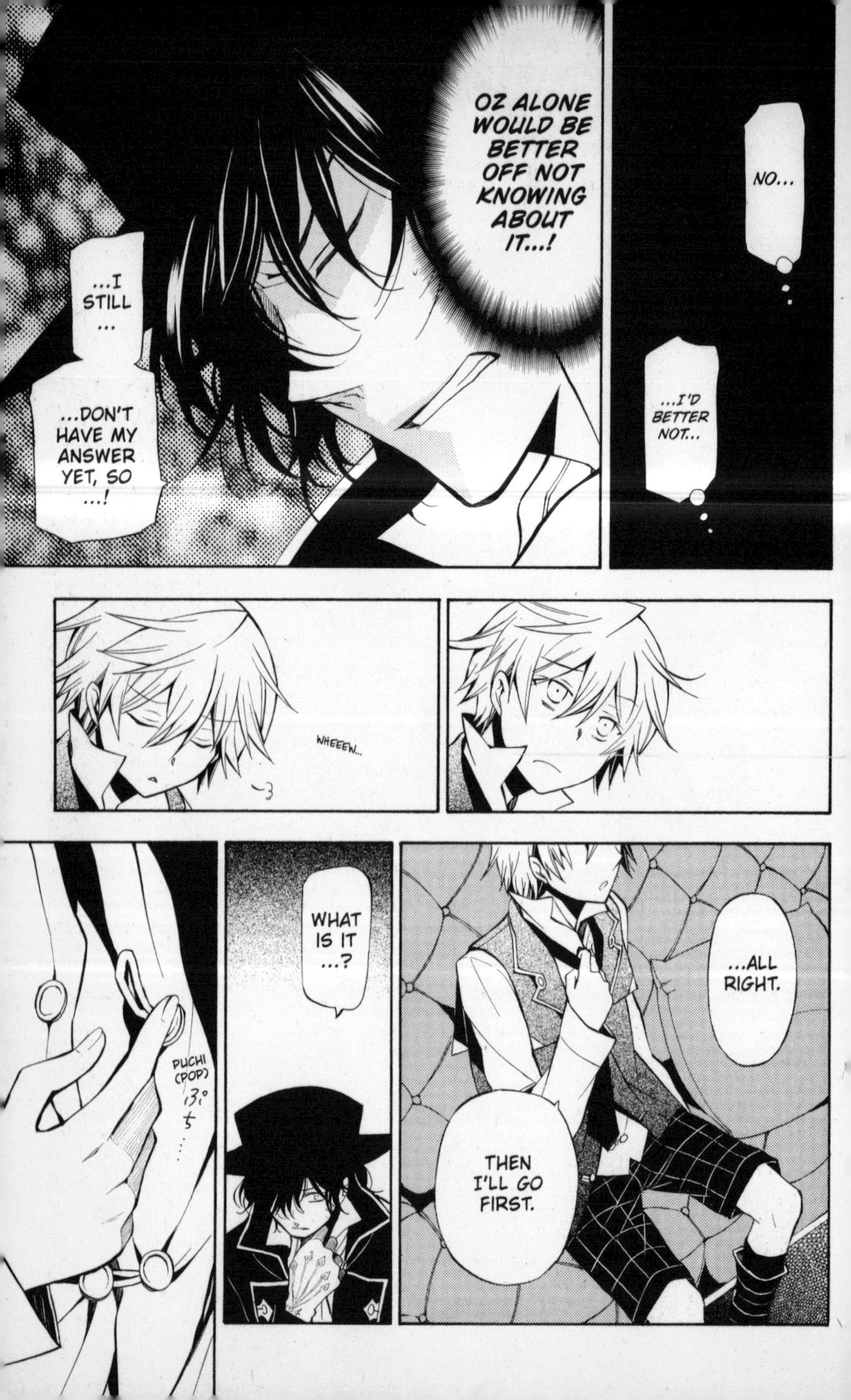
NO...
...I'D BETTER NOT...
OZ ALONE WOULD BE BETTER OFF NOT KNOWING ABOUT IT...!
...I STILL ...
...DON'T HAVE MY ANSWER YET, SO ...!
WHEEEW...
...ALL RIGHT.
THEN I'LL GO FIRST.
WHAT IS IT ...?
PUCHI (POP)
ぷち...

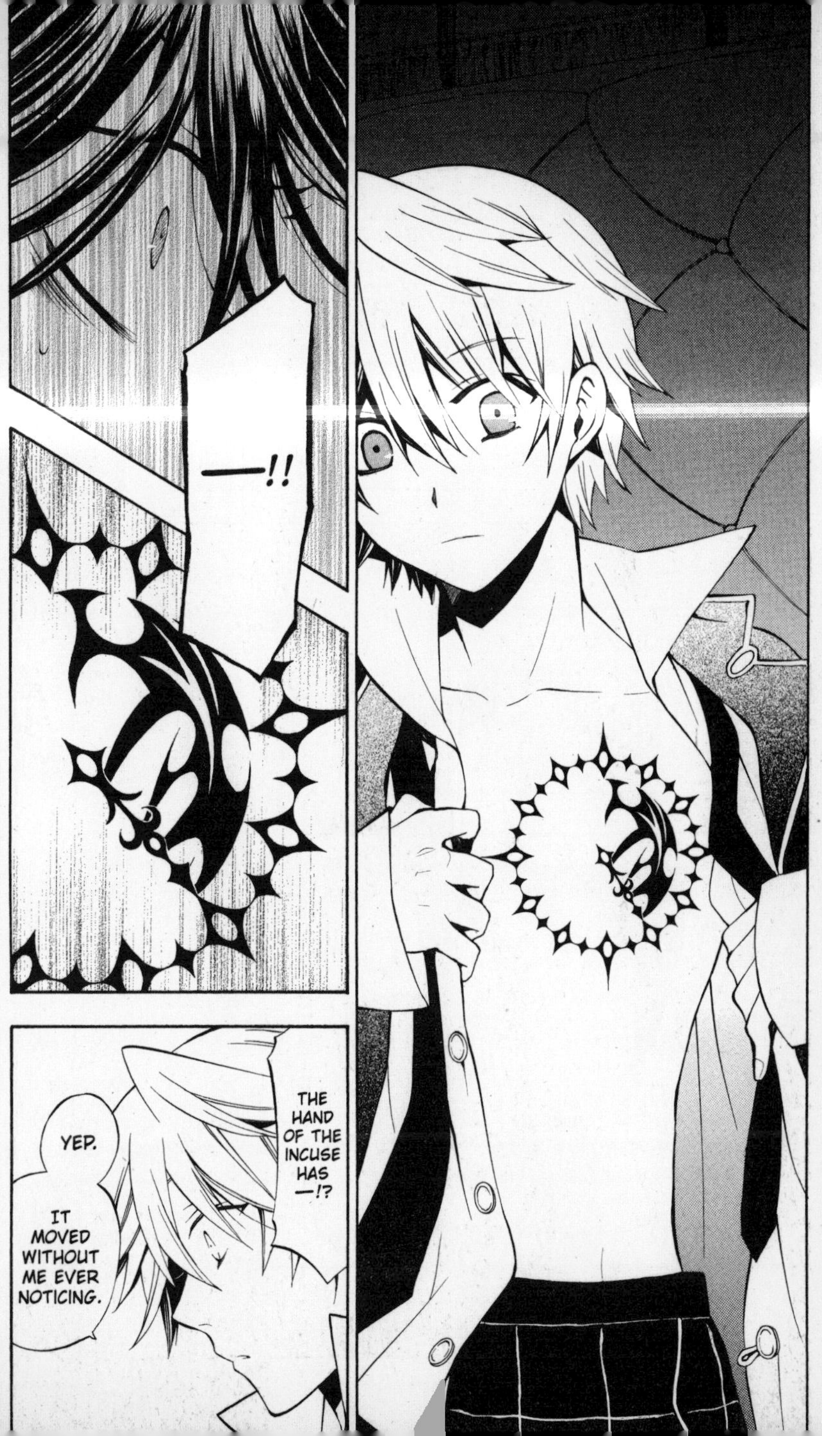
—!!
THE HAND OF THE INCUSE HAS—!?
YEP.
IT MOVED WITHOUT ME EVER NOTICING.

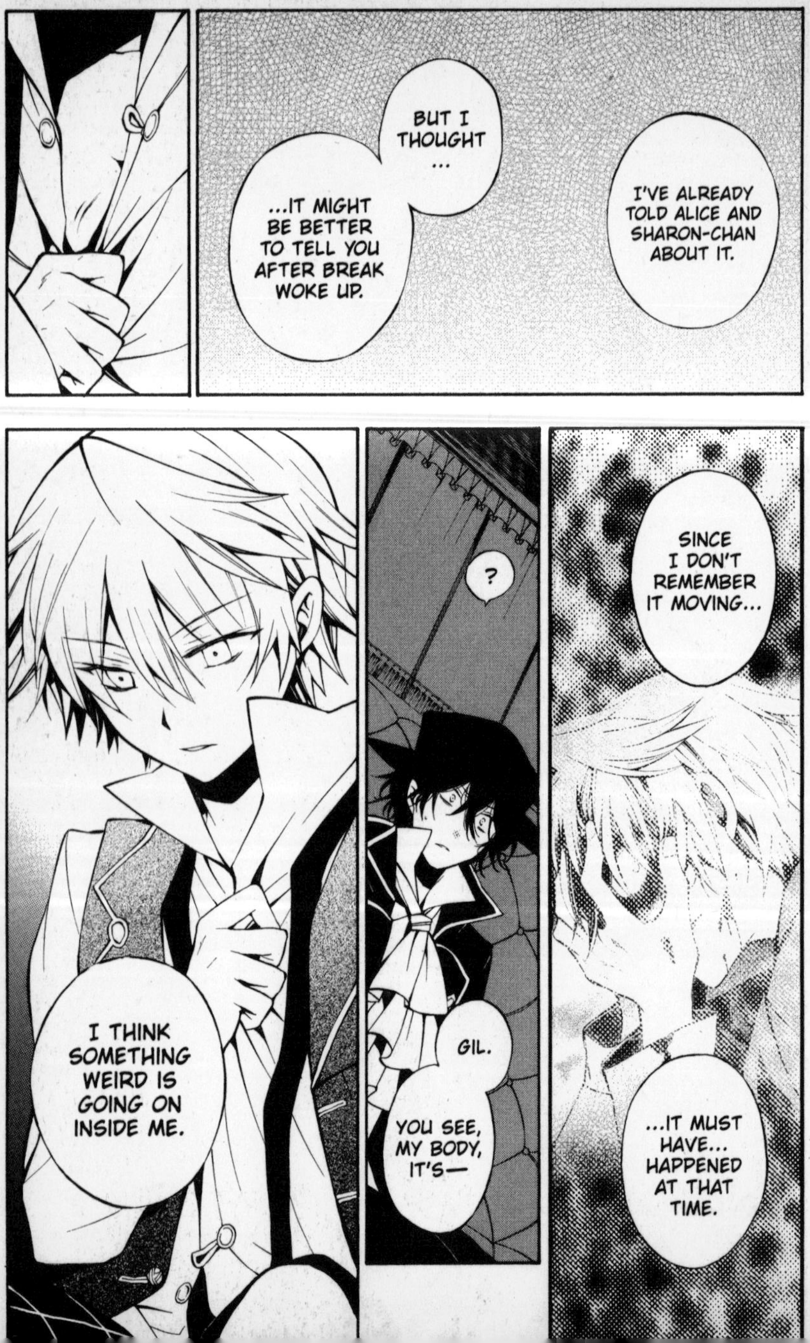
I'VE ALREADY TOLD ALICE AND SHARON-CHAN ABOUT IT.
BUT I THOUGHT...
...IT MIGHT BE BETTER TO TELL YOU AFTER BREAK WOKE UP.
SINCE I DON'T REMEMBER IT MOVING...
...IT MUST HAVE... HAPPENED AT THAT TIME.
?
GIL.
YOU SEE, MY BODY, IT'S—
I THINK SOMETHING WEIRD IS GOING ON INSIDE ME.

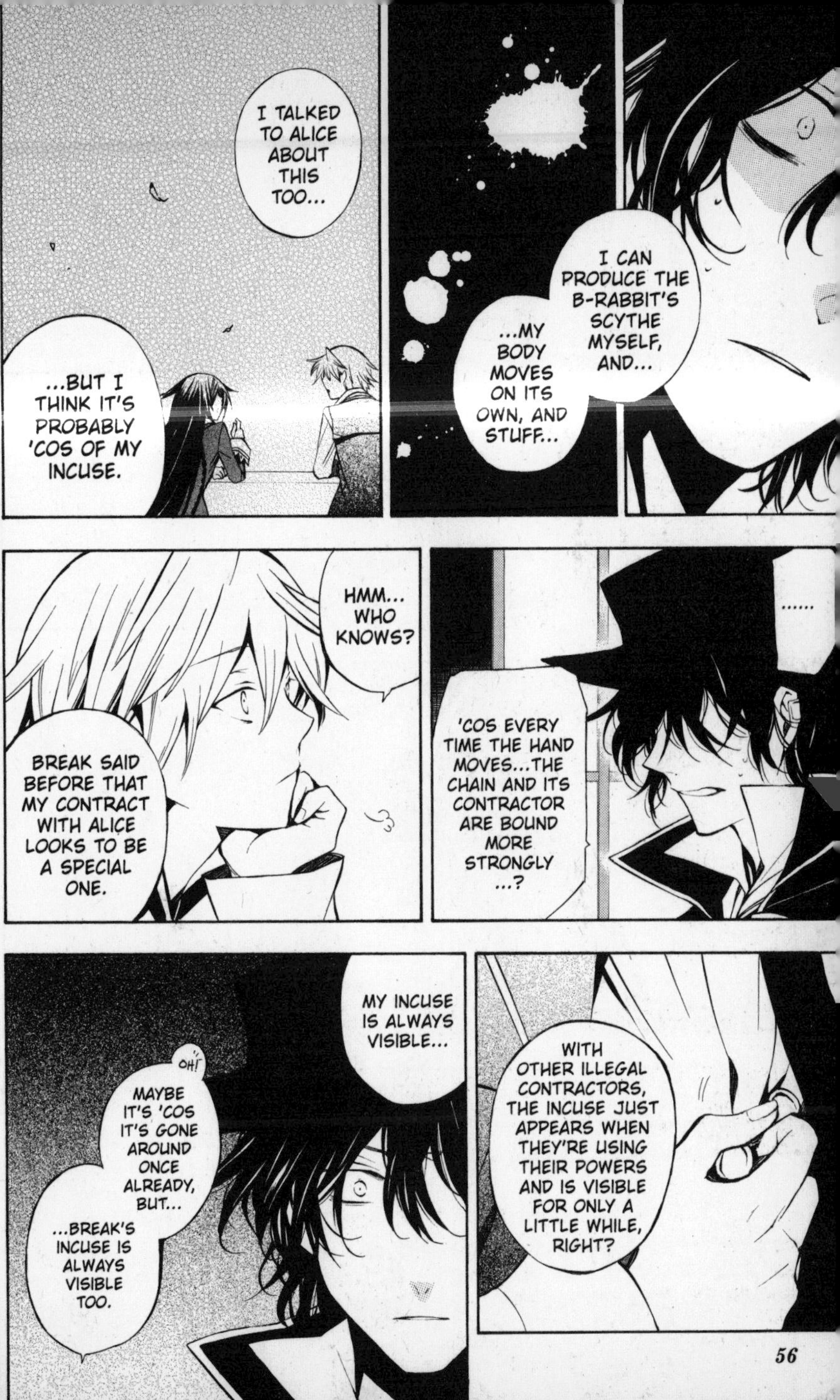
I CAN PRODUCE THE B-RABBIT'S SCYTHE MYSELF, AND...
...MY BODY MOVES ON ITS OWN, AND STUFF...
I TALKED TO ALICE ABOUT THIS TOO...
...BUT I THINK IT'S PROBABLY 'COS OF MY INCUSE.
......
'COS EVERY TIME THE HAND MOVES...THE CHAIN AND ITS CONTRACTOR ARE BOUND MORE STRONGLY ...?
HMM... WHO KNOWS?
BREAK SAID BEFORE THAT MY CONTRACT WITH ALICE LOOKS TO BE A SPECIAL ONE.
WITH OTHER ILLEGAL CONTRACTORS, THE INCUSE JUST APPEARS WHEN THEY'RE USING THEIR POWERS AND IS VISIBLE FOR ONLY A LITTLE WHILE, RIGHT?
MY INCUSE IS ALWAYS VISIBLE...
OH!
MAYBE IT'S 'COS IT'S GONE AROUND ONCE ALREADY, BUT...
...BREAK'S INCUSE IS ALWAYS VISIBLE TOO.

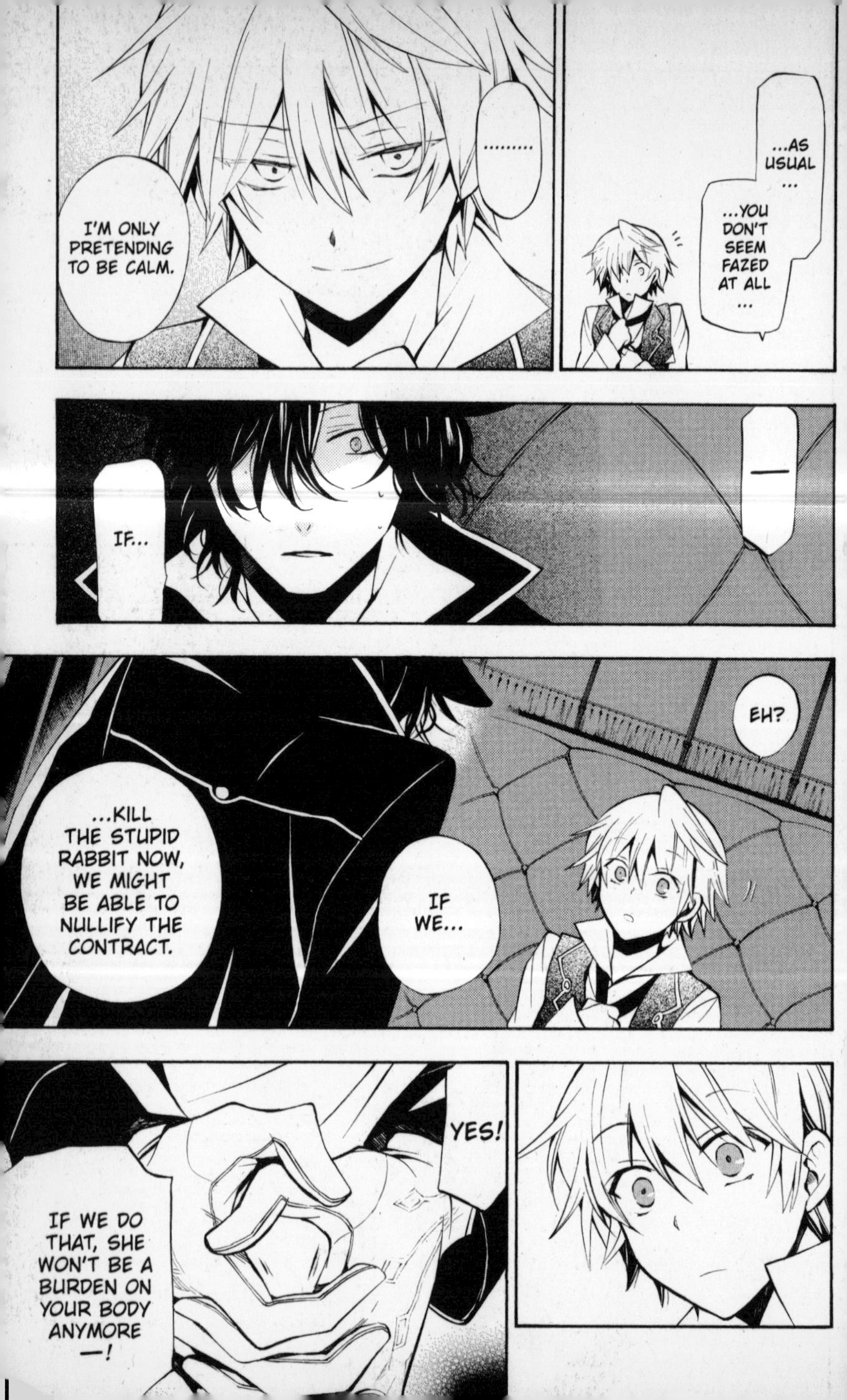
...AS USUAL ...
...YOU DON'T SEEM FAZED AT ALL ...
....
I'M ONLY PRETENDING TO BE CALM.
—
IF...
EH?
IF WE...
...KILL THE STUPID RABBIT NOW, WE MIGHT BE ABLE TO NULLIFY THE CONTRACT.
YES!
IF WE DO THAT, SHE WON'T BE A BURDEN ON YOUR BODY ANYMORE —!

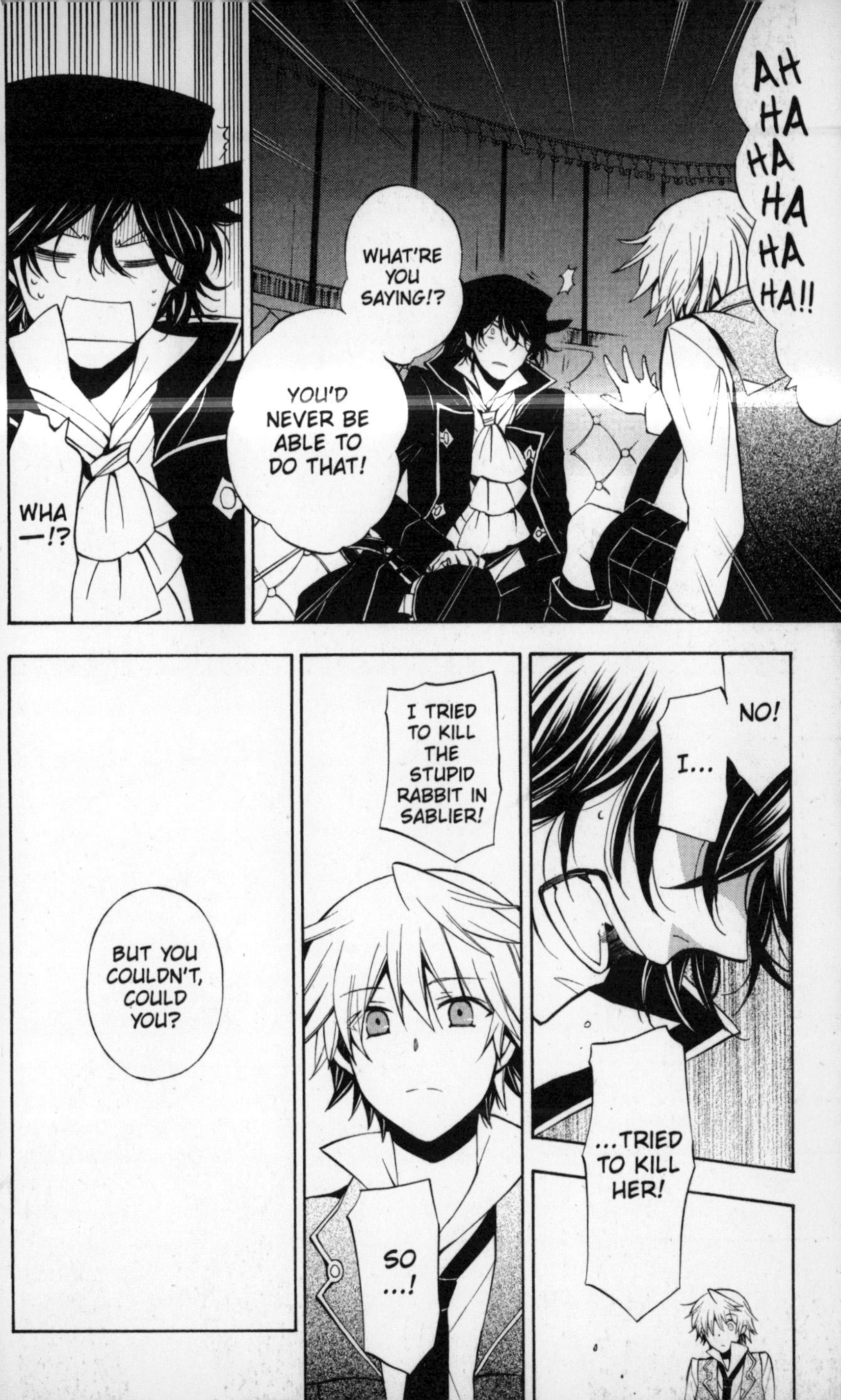
AH HA HA HA HA HA HA!!
WHAT'RE YOU SAYING!?
YOU'D NEVER BE ABLE TO DO THAT!
WHA—!?
NO!
I...
...TRIED TO KILL HER!
I TRIED TO KILL THE STUPID RABBIT IN SABLIER!
SO ...!
BUT YOU COULDN'T, COULD YOU?

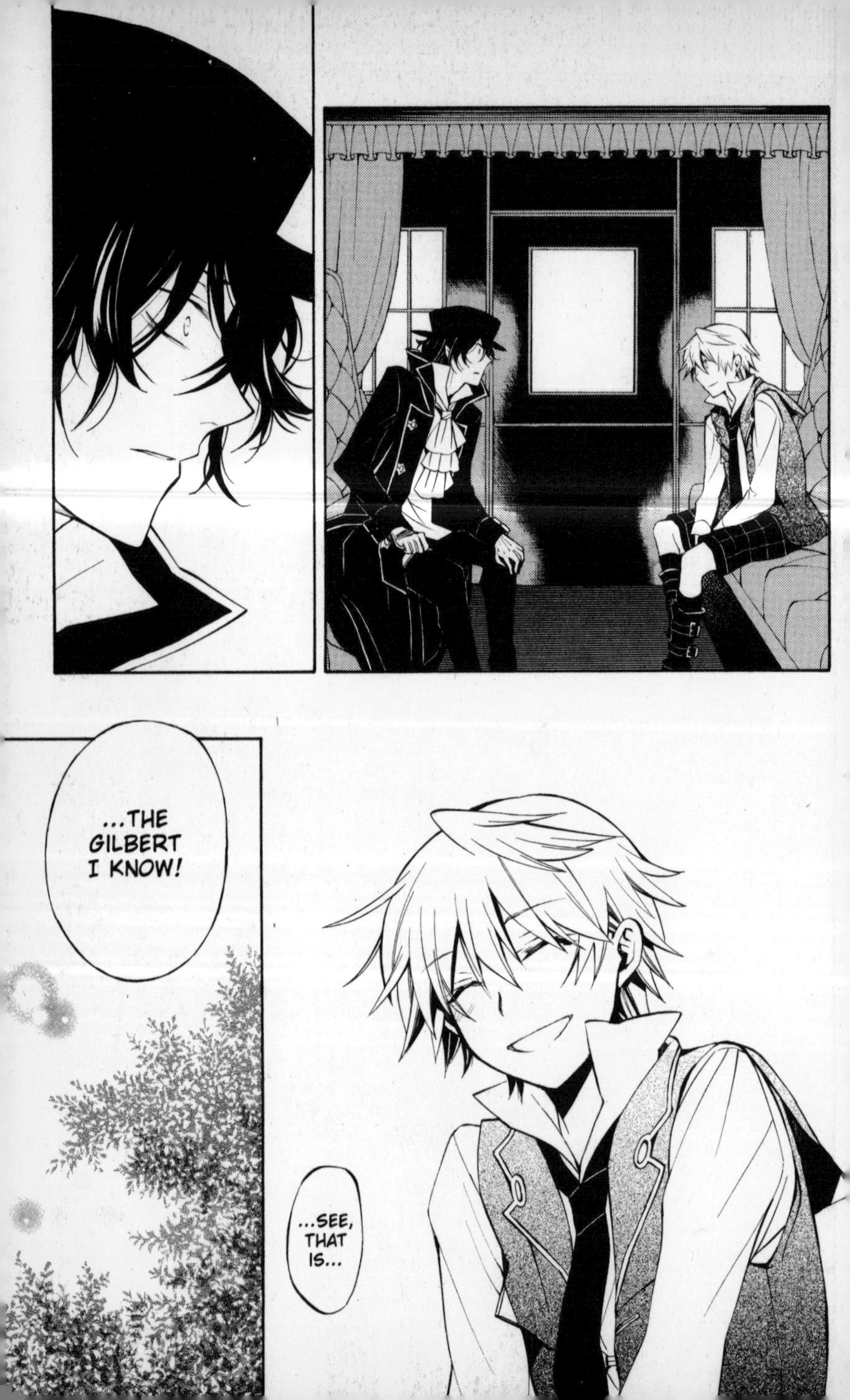
...SEE, THAT IS...
...THE GILBERT I KNOW!

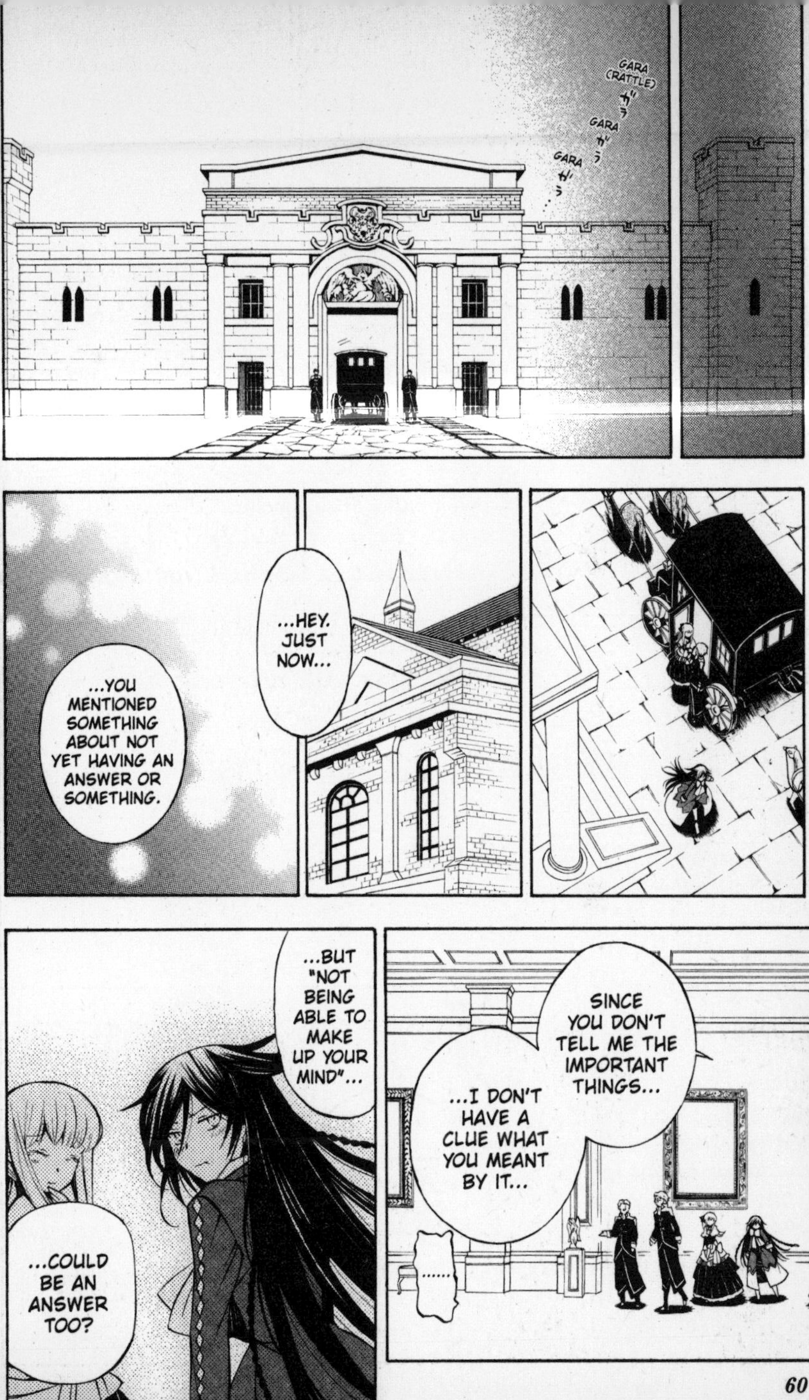
GARA (RATTLE)
GARA
GARA
...HEY. JUST NOW...
...YOU MENTIONED SOMETHING ABOUT NOT YET HAVING AN ANSWER OR SOMETHING.
SINCE YOU DON'T TELL ME THE IMPORTANT THINGS...
...I DON'T HAVE A CLUE WHAT YOU MEANT BY IT...
......
...BUT "NOT BEING ABLE TO MAKE UP YOUR MIND"...
...COULD BE AN ANSWER TOO?

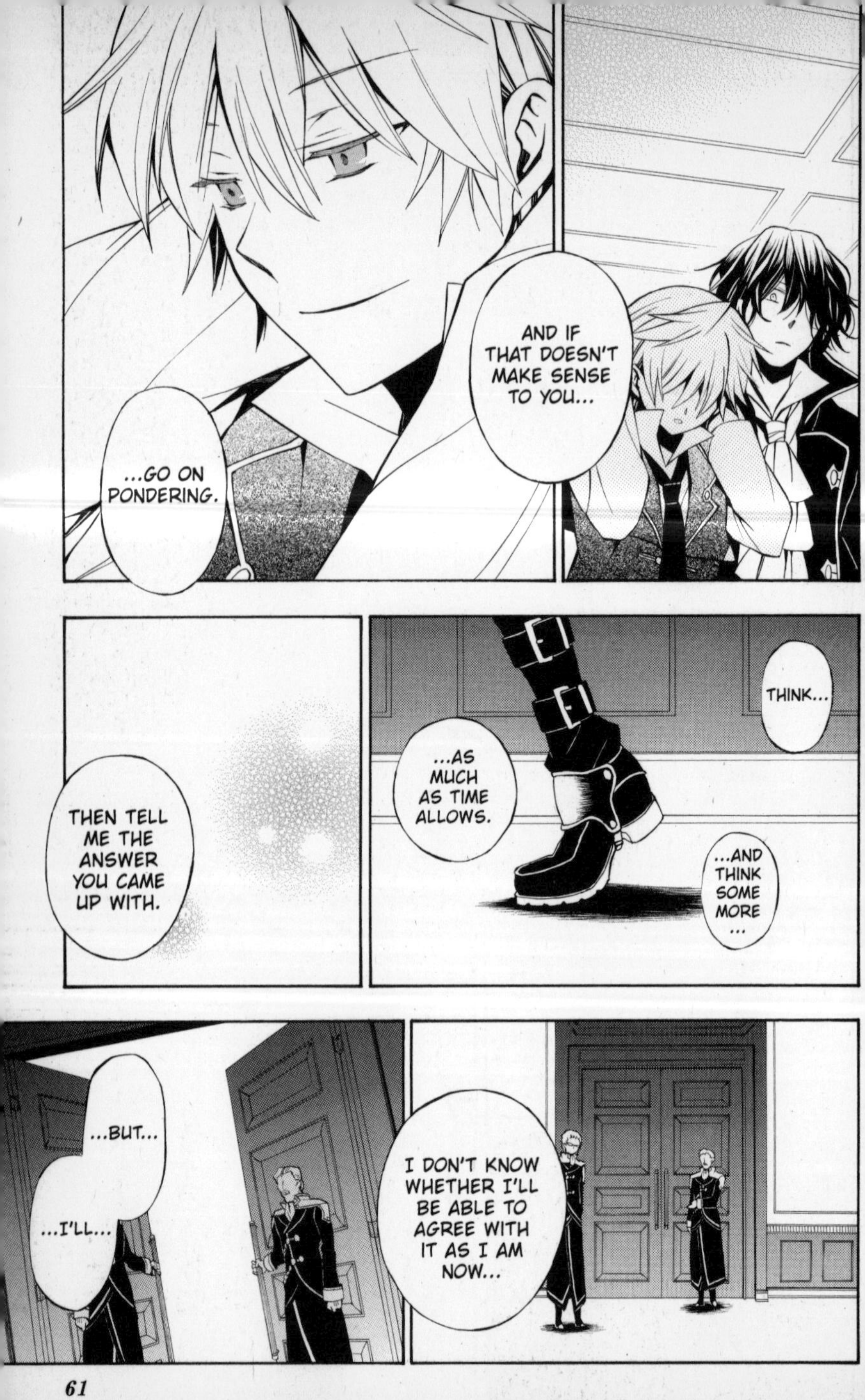
AND IF THAT DOESN'T MAKE SENSE TO YOU...
...GO ON PONDERING.
THINK...
...AS MUCH AS TIME ALLOWS.
...AND THINK SOME MORE ...
THEN TELL ME THE ANSWER YOU CAME UP WITH.
I DON'T KNOW WHETHER I'LL BE ABLE TO AGREE WITH IT AS I AM NOW...
...BUT...
...I'LL...

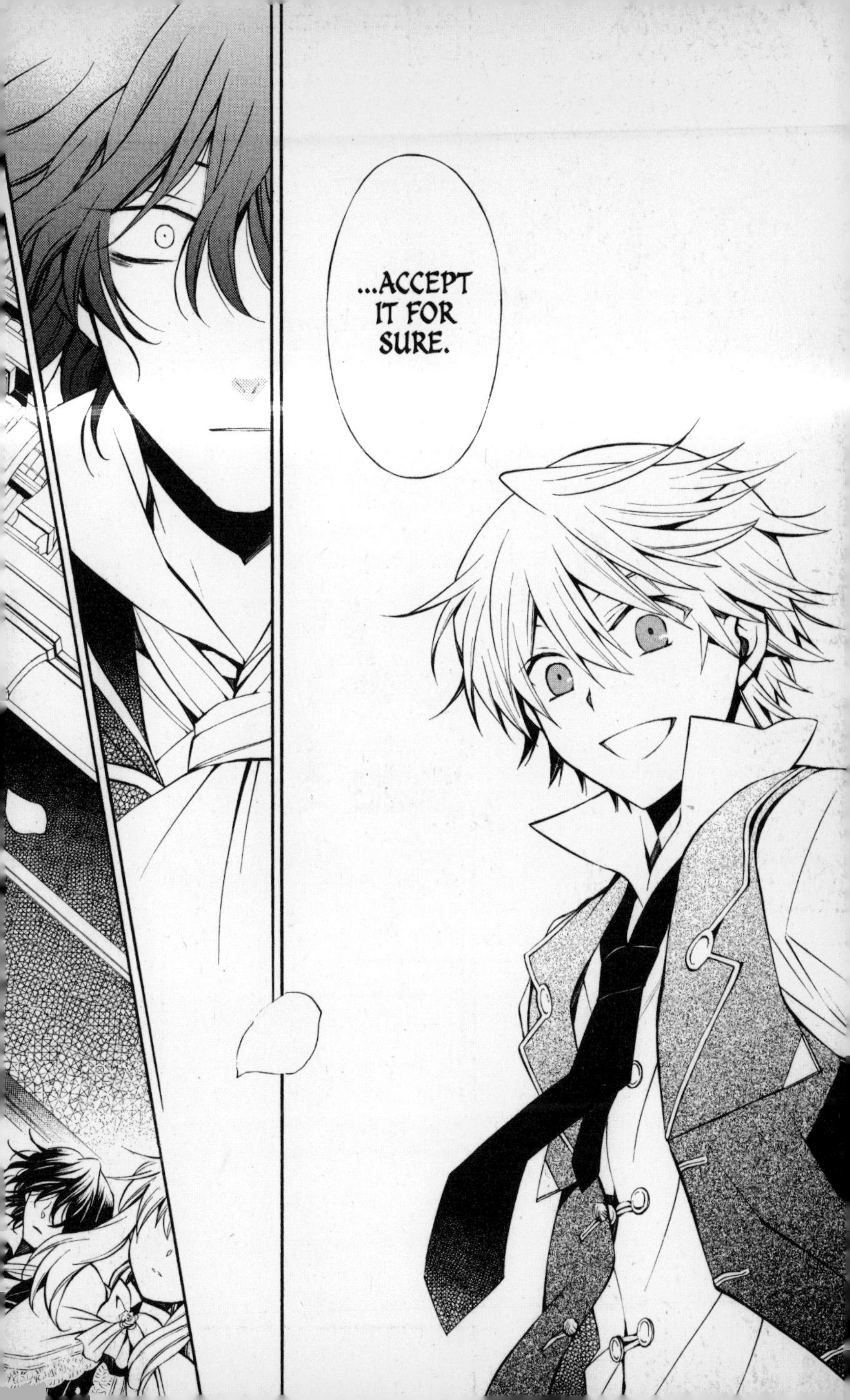
...ACCEPT IT FOR SURE.

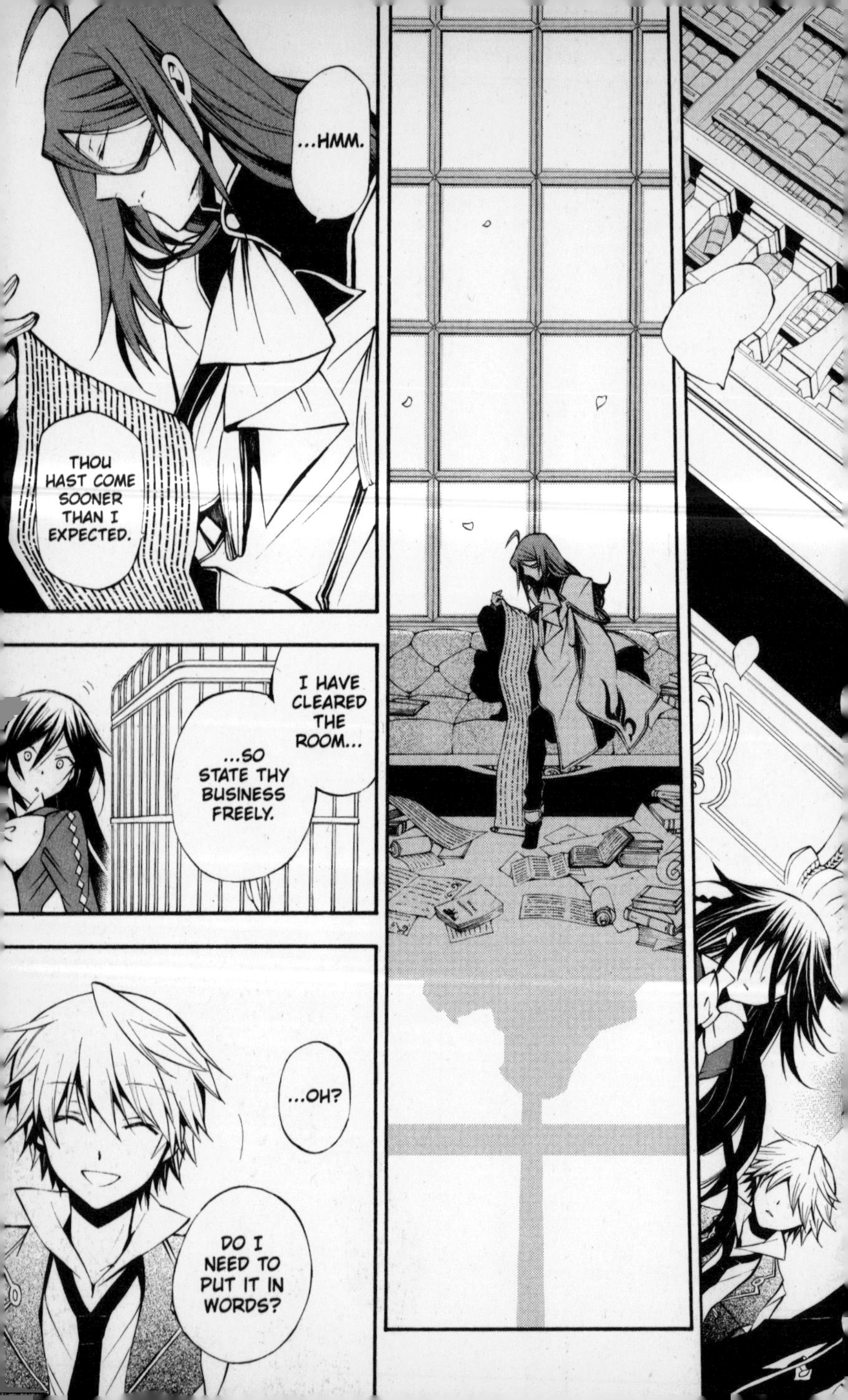
...HMM.
THOU HAST COME SOONER THAN I EXPECTED.
I HAVE CLEARED THE ROOM...
...SO STATE THY BUSINESS FREELY.
...OH?
DO I NEED TO PUT IT IN WORDS?

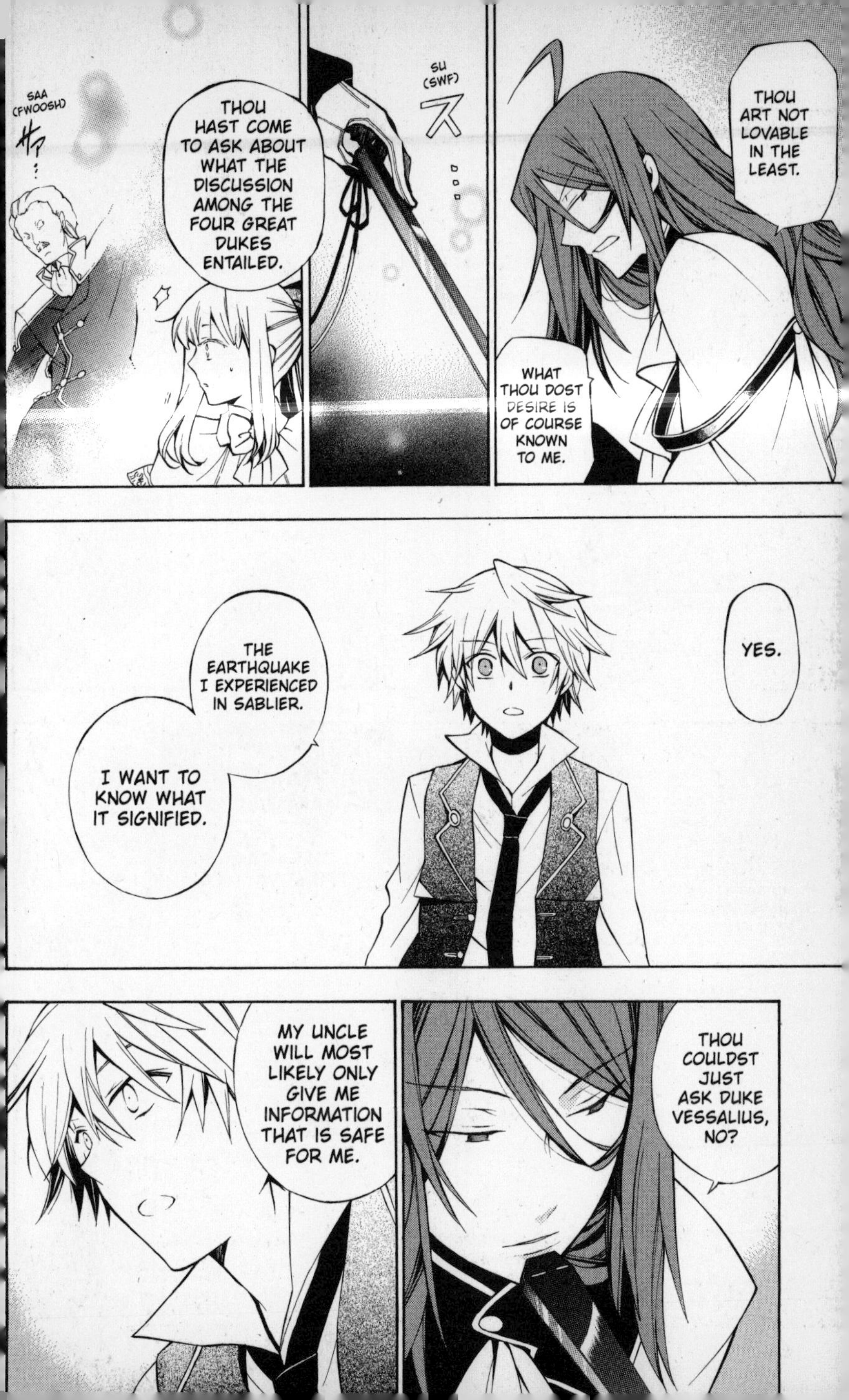
THOU ART NOT LOVABLE IN THE LEAST.
WHAT THOU DOST DESIRE IS OF COURSE KNOWN TO ME.
SU (SWF)
ス
THOU HAST COME TO ASK ABOUT WHAT THE DISCUSSION AMONG THE FOUR GREAT DUKES ENTAILED.
SAA (FWOOSH)
サァ
YES.
THE EARTHQUAKE I EXPERIENCED IN SABLIER.
I WANT TO KNOW WHAT IT SIGNIFIED.
THOU COULDST JUST ASK DUKE VESSALIUS, NO?
MY UNCLE WILL MOST LIKELY ONLY GIVE ME INFORMATION THAT IS SAFE FOR ME.

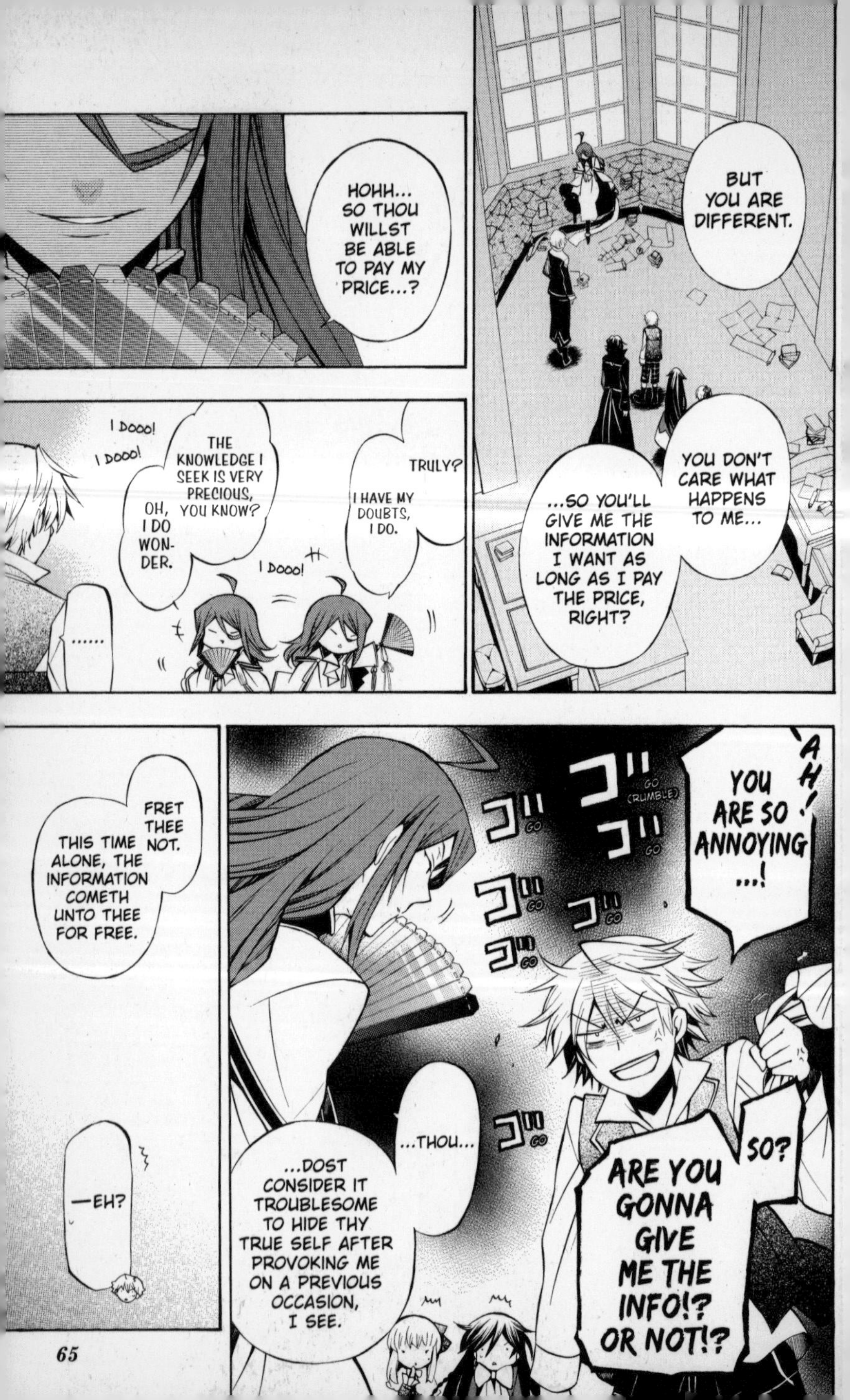
BUT YOU ARE DIFFERENT.
YOU DON'T CARE WHAT HAPPENS TO ME...
...SO YOU'LL GIVE ME THE INFORMATION I WANT AS LONG AS I PAY THE PRICE, RIGHT?
HOHH... SO THOU WILLST BE ABLE TO PAY MY PRICE...?
TRULY?
I HAVE MY DOUBTS, I DO.
I DOOO!
THE KNOWLEDGE I SEEK IS VERY PRECIOUS, YOU KNOW?
OH, I DO WONDER.
I DOOO!
I DOOO!
......
AH!
YOU ARE SO ANNOYING...!
GO (RUMBLE)
GO
GO
GO
GO
GO
GO
SO?
ARE YOU GONNA GIVE ME THE INFO!? OR NOT!?
...THOU...
...DOST CONSIDER IT TROUBLESOME TO HIDE THY TRUE SELF AFTER PROVOKING ME ON A PREVIOUS OCCASION, I SEE.
FRET THEE NOT.
THIS TIME ALONE, THE INFORMATION COMETH UNTO THEE FOR FREE.
—EH?

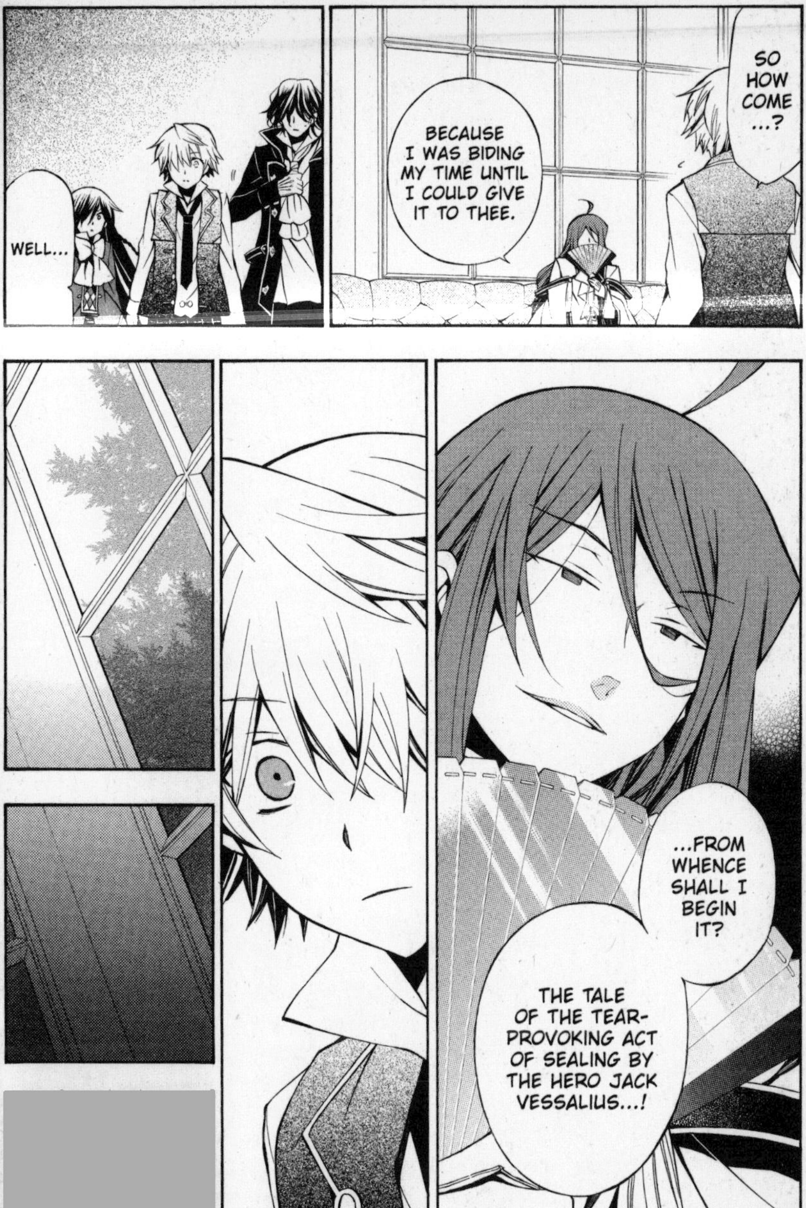
SO HOW COME ...?
BECAUSE I WAS BIDING MY TIME UNTIL I COULD GIVE IT TO THEE.
WELL...
...FROM WHENCE SHALL I BEGIN IT?
THE TALE OF THE TEAR-PROVOKING ACT OF SEALING BY THE HERO JACK VESSALIUS...!

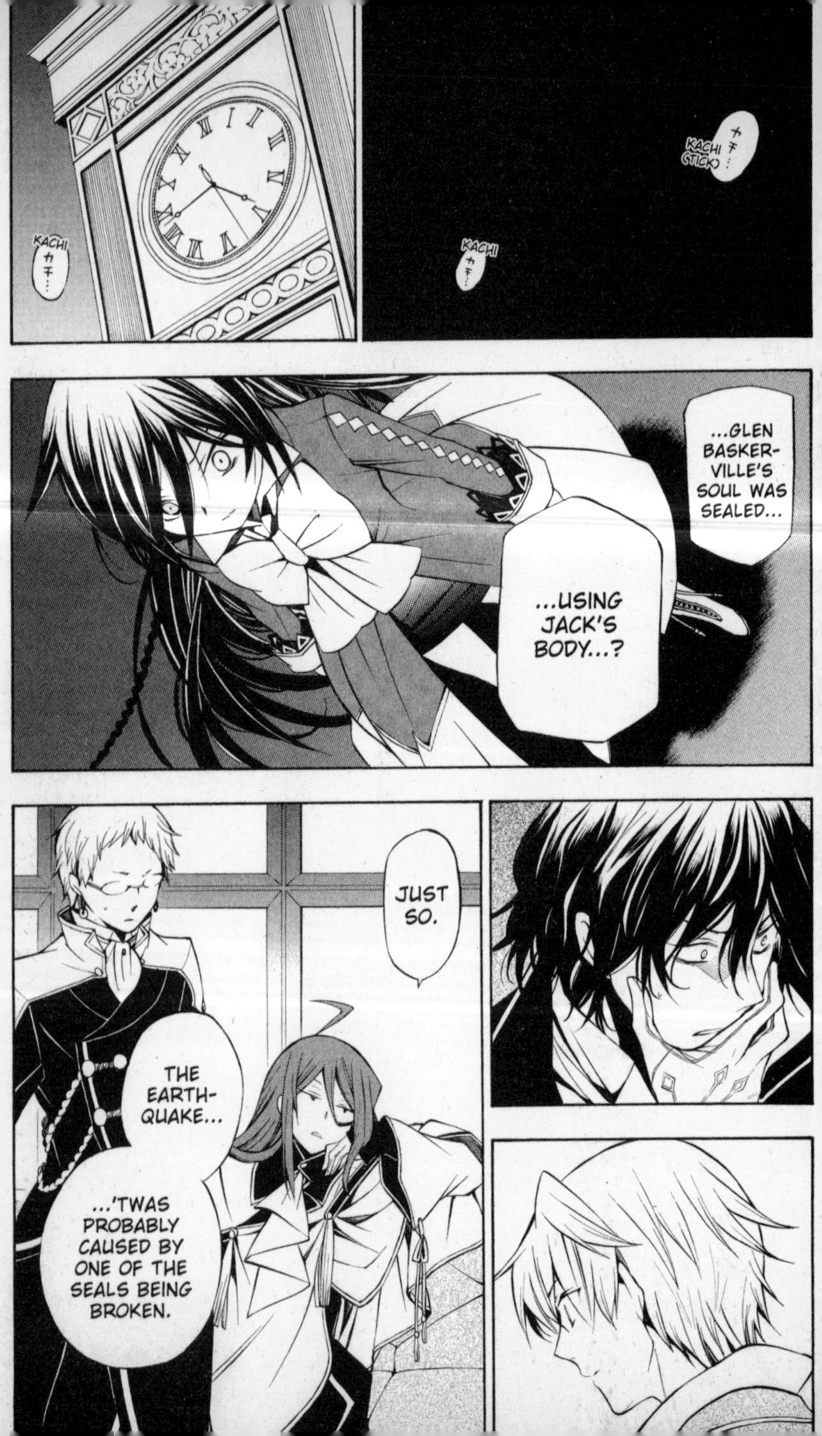
カチ… KACHI (TICK)
KACHI カチ…
KACHI カチ…
...GLEN BASKER-VILLE'S SOUL WAS SEALED...
...USING JACK'S BODY...?
JUST SO.
THE EARTH-QUAKE...
...'TWAS PROBABLY CAUSED BY ONE OF THE SEALS BEING BROKEN.

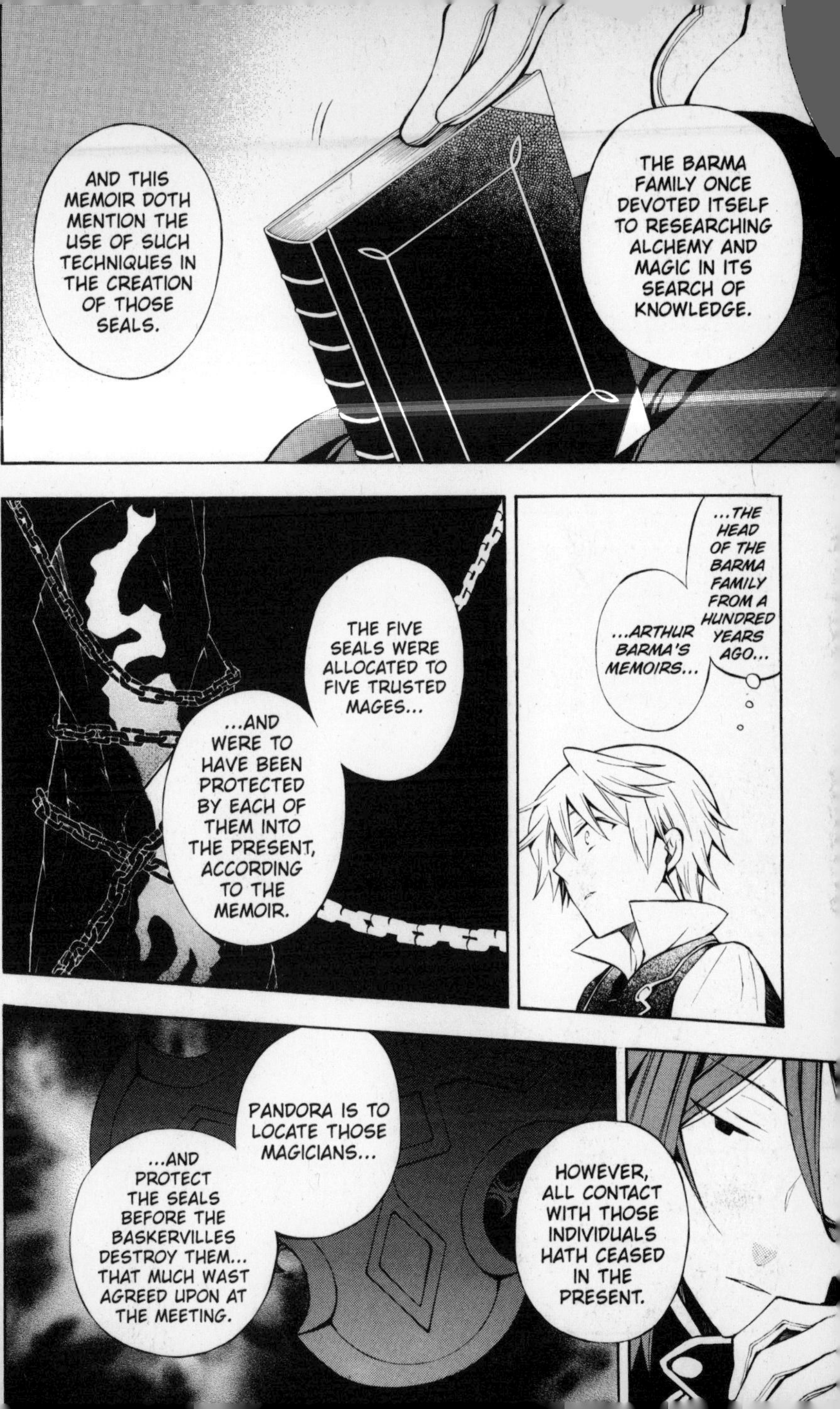
THE BARMA FAMILY ONCE DEVOTED ITSELF TO RESEARCHING ALCHEMY AND MAGIC IN ITS SEARCH OF KNOWLEDGE.
AND THIS MEMOIR DOTH MENTION THE USE OF SUCH TECHNIQUES IN THE CREATION OF THOSE SEALS.
...THE HEAD OF THE BARMA FAMILY FROM A HUNDRED YEARS AGO...
...ARTHUR BARMA'S MEMOIRS...
THE FIVE SEALS WERE ALLOCATED TO FIVE TRUSTED MAGES...
...AND WERE TO HAVE BEEN PROTECTED BY EACH OF THEM INTO THE PRESENT, ACCORDING TO THE MEMOIR.
PANDORA IS TO LOCATE THOSE MAGICIANS...
...AND PROTECT THE SEALS BEFORE THE BASKERVILLES DESTROY THEM... THAT MUCH WAST AGREED UPON AT THE MEETING.
HOWEVER, ALL CONTACT WITH THOSE INDIVIDUALS HATH CEASED IN THE PRESENT.

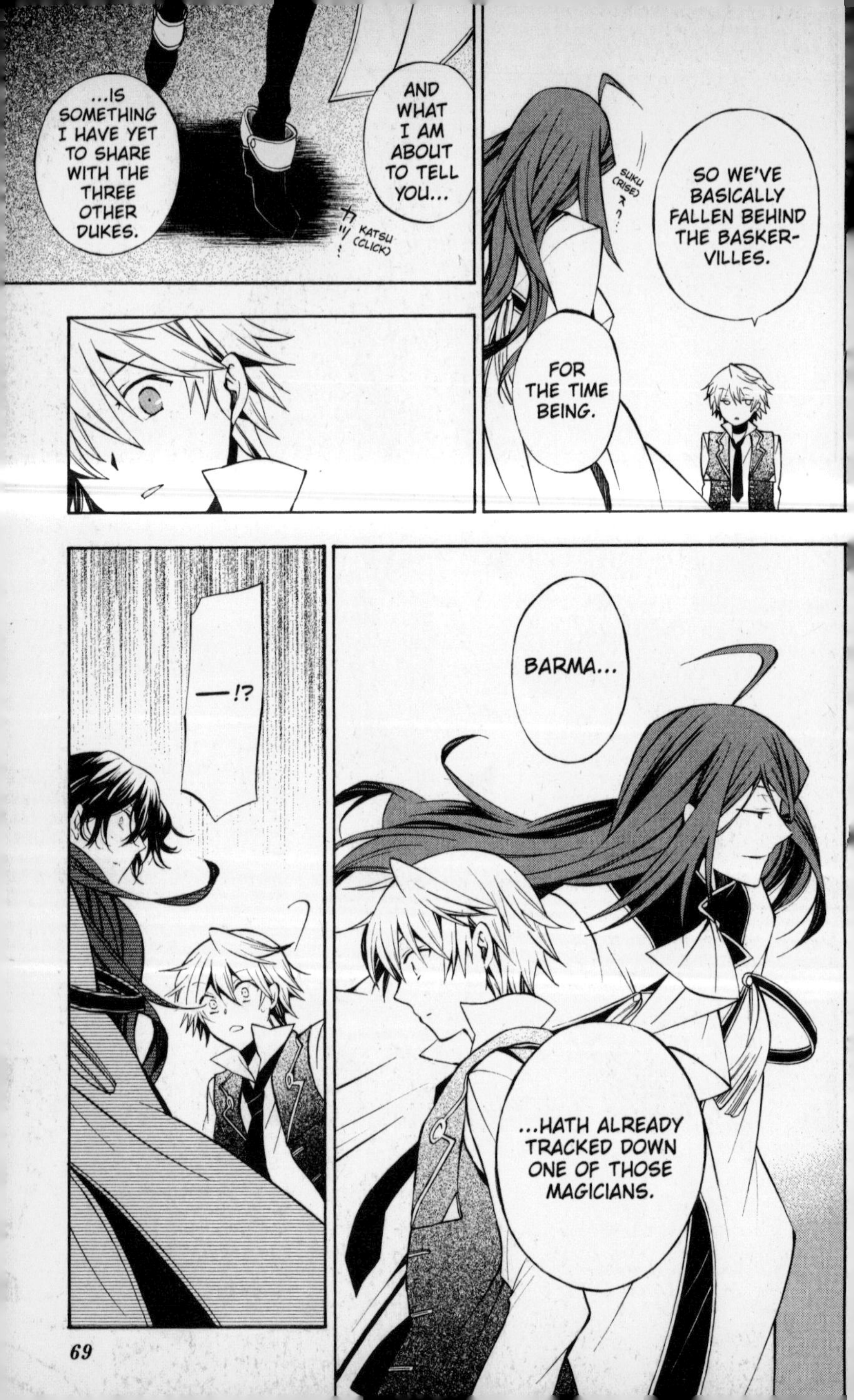
SUKU (RISE)
SO WE'VE BASICALLY FALLEN BEHIND THE BASKER-VILLES.
FOR THE TIME BEING.
AND WHAT I AM ABOUT TO TELL YOU...
...IS SOMETHING I HAVE YET TO SHARE WITH THE THREE OTHER DUKES.
KATSU (CLICK)
BARMA...
...HATH ALREADY TRACKED DOWN ONE OF THOSE MAGICIANS.
—!?

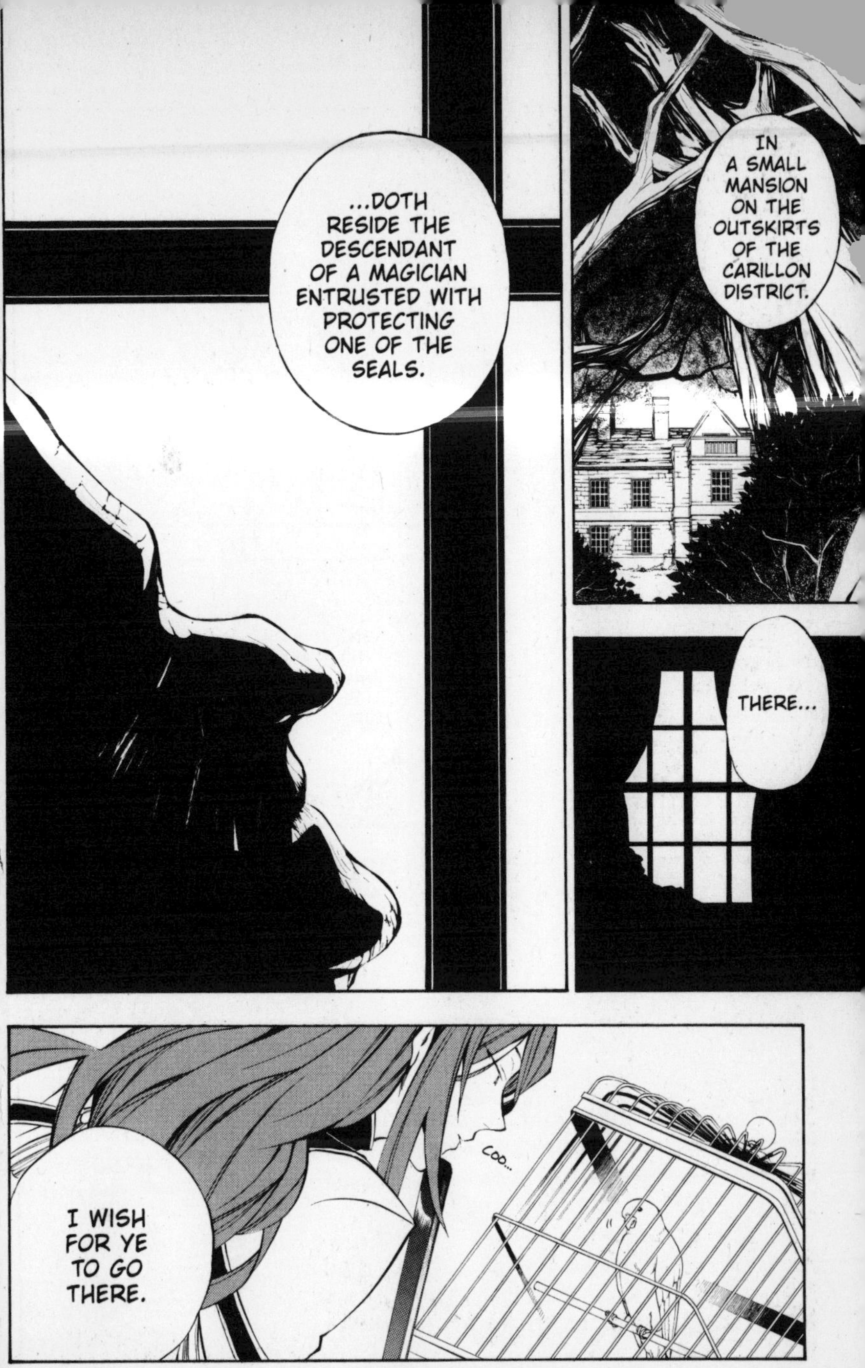
IN A SMALL MANSION ON THE OUTSKIRTS OF THE CARILLON DISTRICT.
THERE...
...DOTH RESIDE THE DESCENDANT OF A MAGICIAN ENTRUSTED WITH PROTECTING ONE OF THE SEALS.
COO...
I WISH FOR YE TO GO THERE.

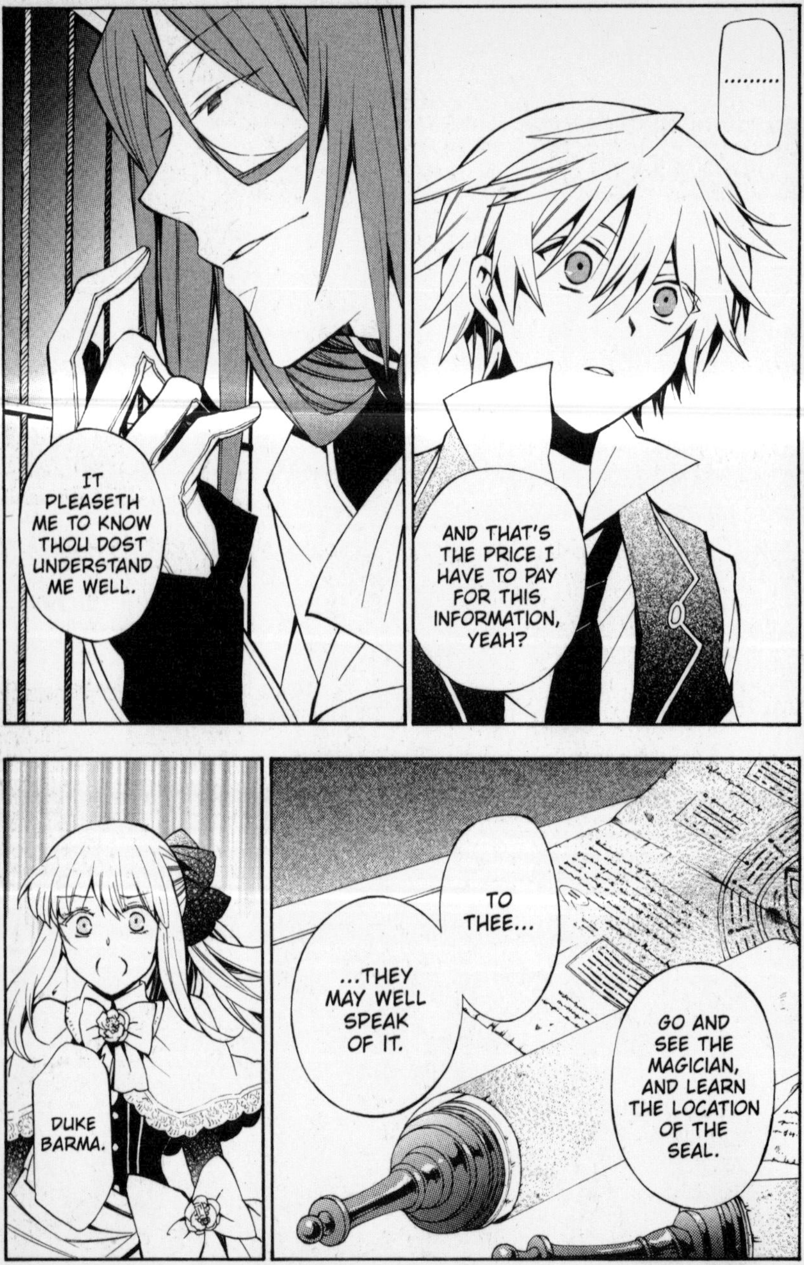
....
AND THAT'S THE PRICE I HAVE TO PAY FOR THIS INFORMATION, YEAH?
IT PLEASETH ME TO KNOW THOU DOST UNDERSTAND ME WELL.
GO AND SEE THE MAGICIAN, AND LEARN THE LOCATION OF THE SEAL.
TO THEE...
...THEY MAY WELL SPEAK OF IT.
DUKE BARMA.

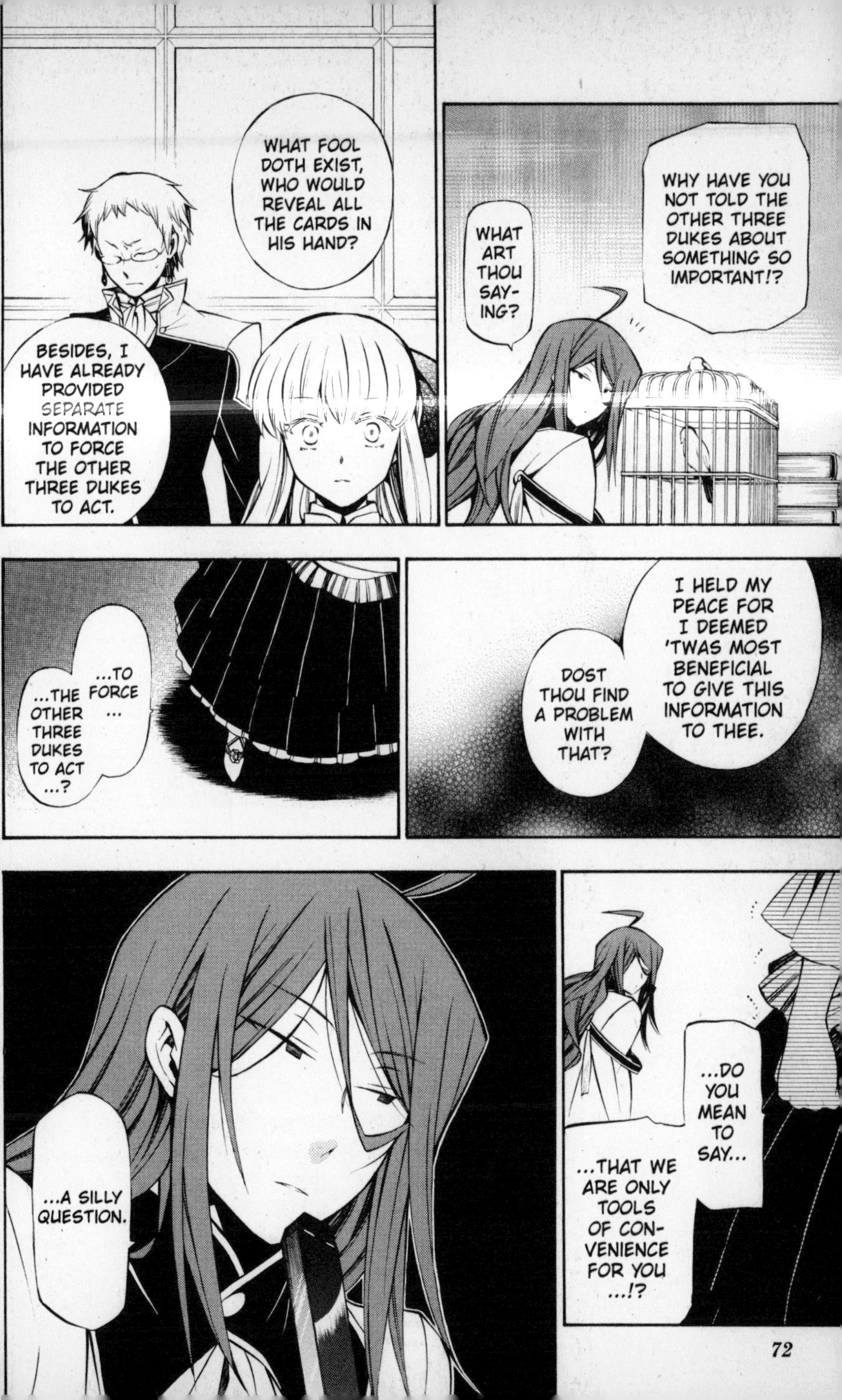
WHY HAVE YOU NOT TOLD THE OTHER THREE DUKES ABOUT SOMETHING SO IMPORTANT!?
WHAT ART THOU SAYING?
WHAT FOOL DOTH EXIST, WHO WOULD REVEAL ALL THE CARDS IN HIS HAND?
BESIDES, I HAVE ALREADY PROVIDED SEPARATE INFORMATION TO FORCE THE OTHER THREE DUKES TO ACT.
I HELD MY PEACE FOR I DEEMED 'TWAS MOST BENEFICIAL TO GIVE THIS INFORMATION TO THEE.
DOST THOU FIND A PROBLEM WITH THAT?
...TO FORCE...
...THE OTHER THREE DUKES TO ACT...?
...DO YOU MEAN TO SAY...
...THAT WE ARE ONLY TOOLS OF CONVENIENCE FOR YOU...!?
...A SILLY QUESTION.

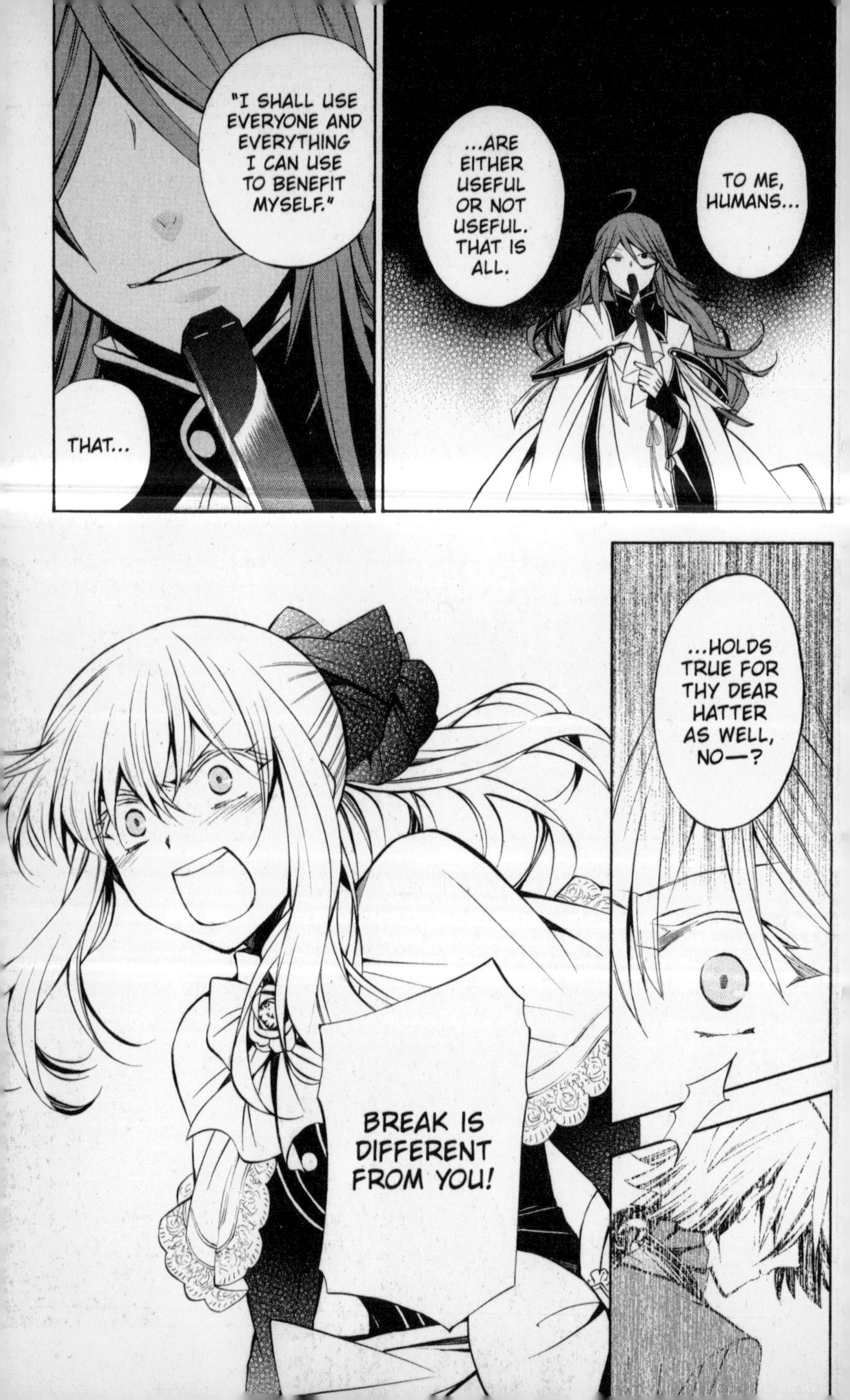
TO ME, HUMANS...
...ARE EITHER USEFUL OR NOT USEFUL. THAT IS ALL.
"I SHALL USE EVERYONE AND EVERYTHING I CAN USE TO BENEFIT MYSELF."
THAT...
...HOLDS TRUE FOR THY DEAR HATTER AS WELL, NO—?
BREAK IS DIFFERENT FROM YOU!

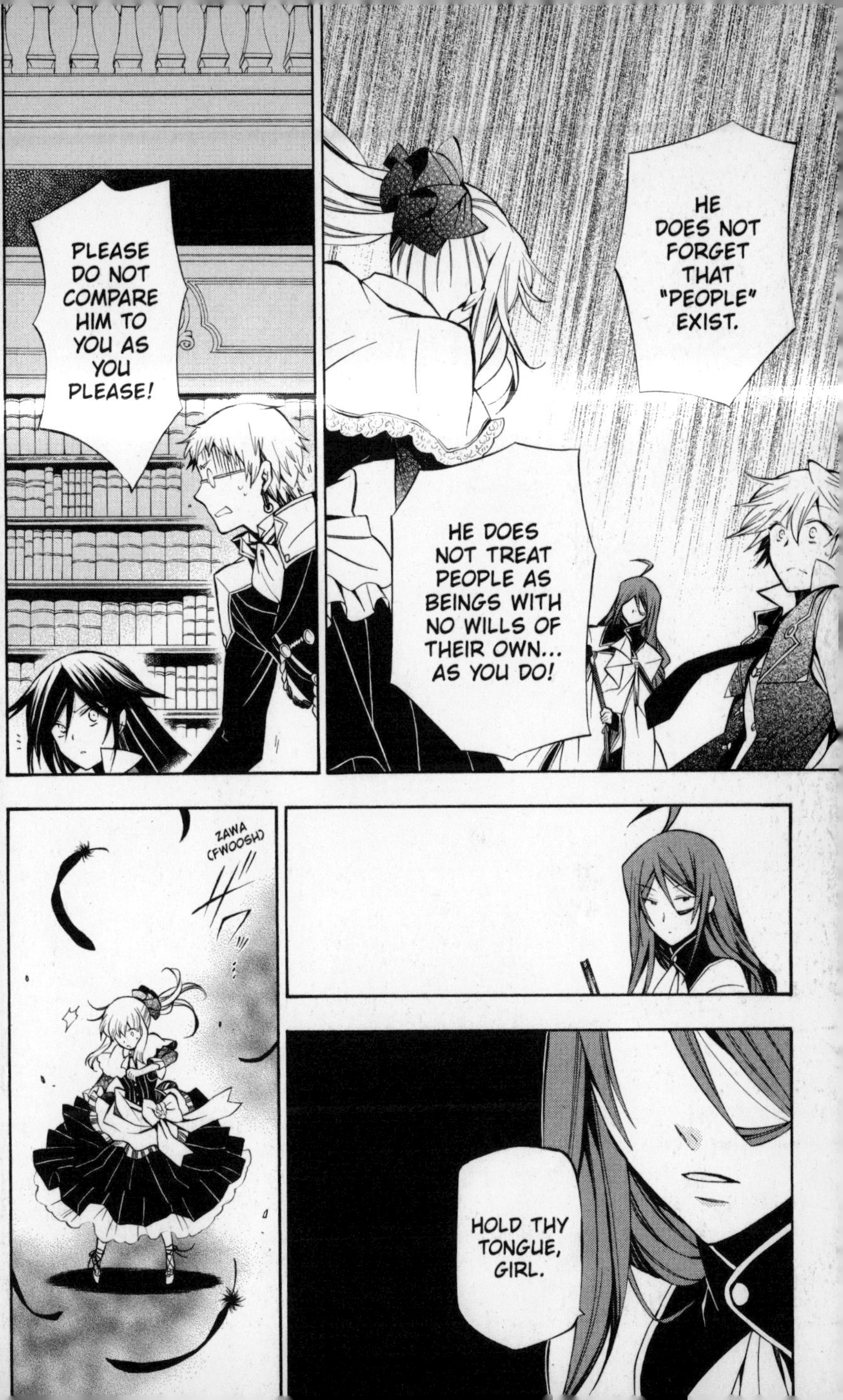
HE DOES NOT FORGET THAT "PEOPLE" EXIST.
HE DOES NOT TREAT PEOPLE AS BEINGS WITH NO WILLS OF THEIR OWN... AS YOU DO!
PLEASE DO NOT COMPARE HIM TO YOU AS YOU PLEASE!
HOLD THY TONGUE, GIRL.
ZAWA (FWOOSH)

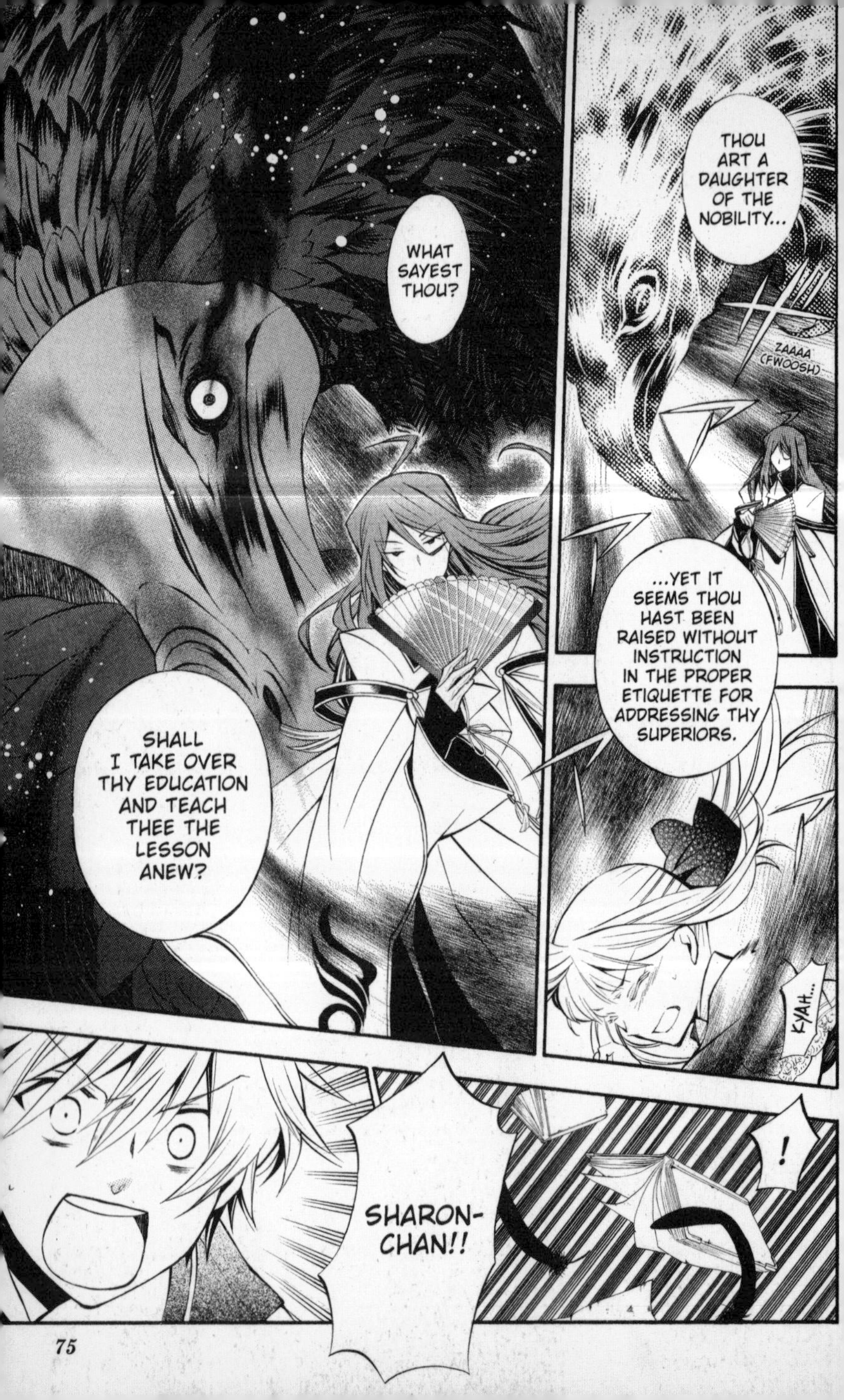
THOU ART A DAUGHTER OF THE NOBILITY...
ZAAAA (FWOOSH)
...YET IT SEEMS THOU HAST BEEN RAISED WITHOUT INSTRUCTION IN THE PROPER ETIQUETTE FOR ADDRESSING THY SUPERIORS.
KYAH...
WHAT SAYEST THOU?
SHALL I TAKE OVER THY EDUCATION AND TEACH THEE THE LESSON ANEW?
!
SHARON-CHAN!!

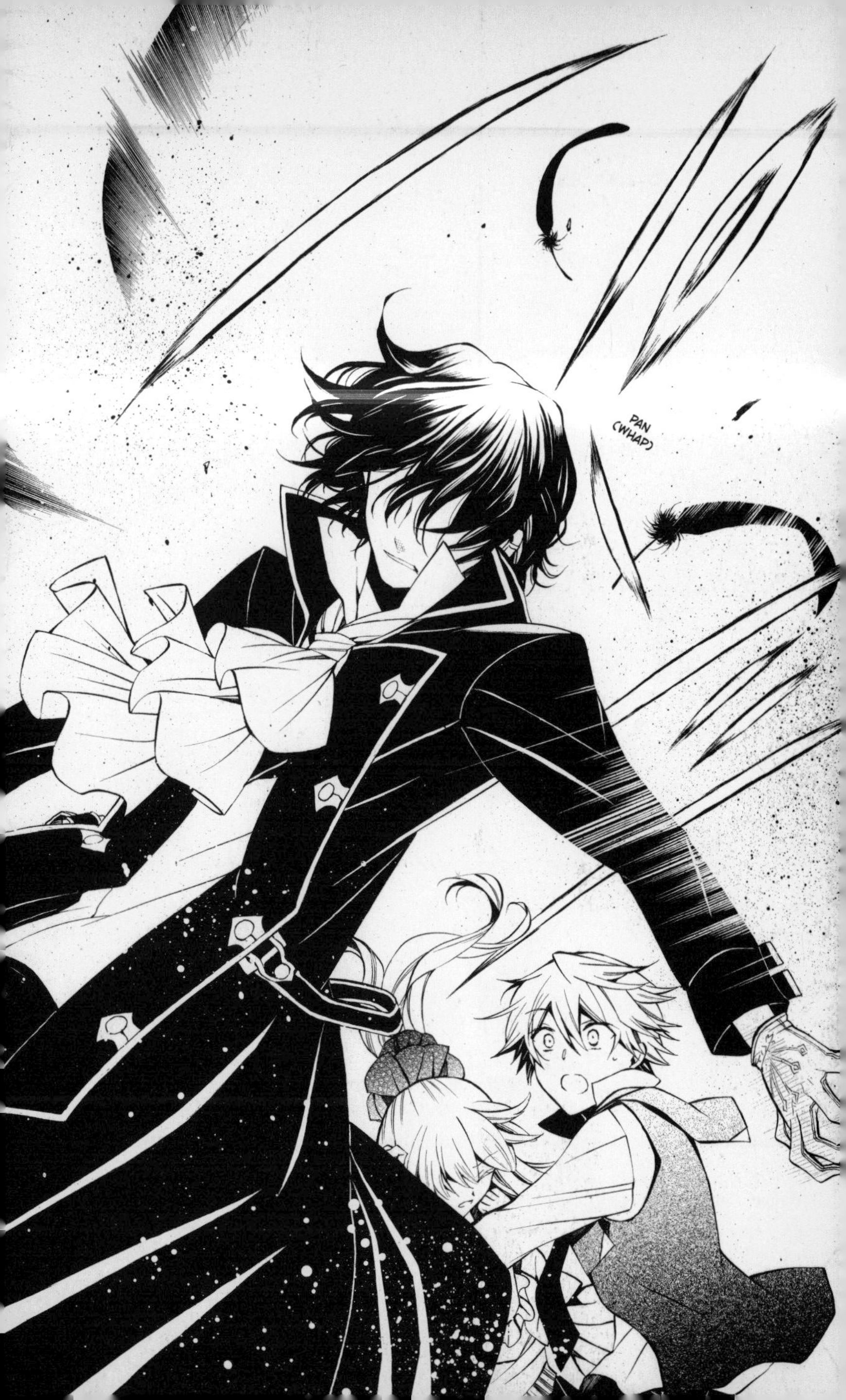
PAN
(WHAP)

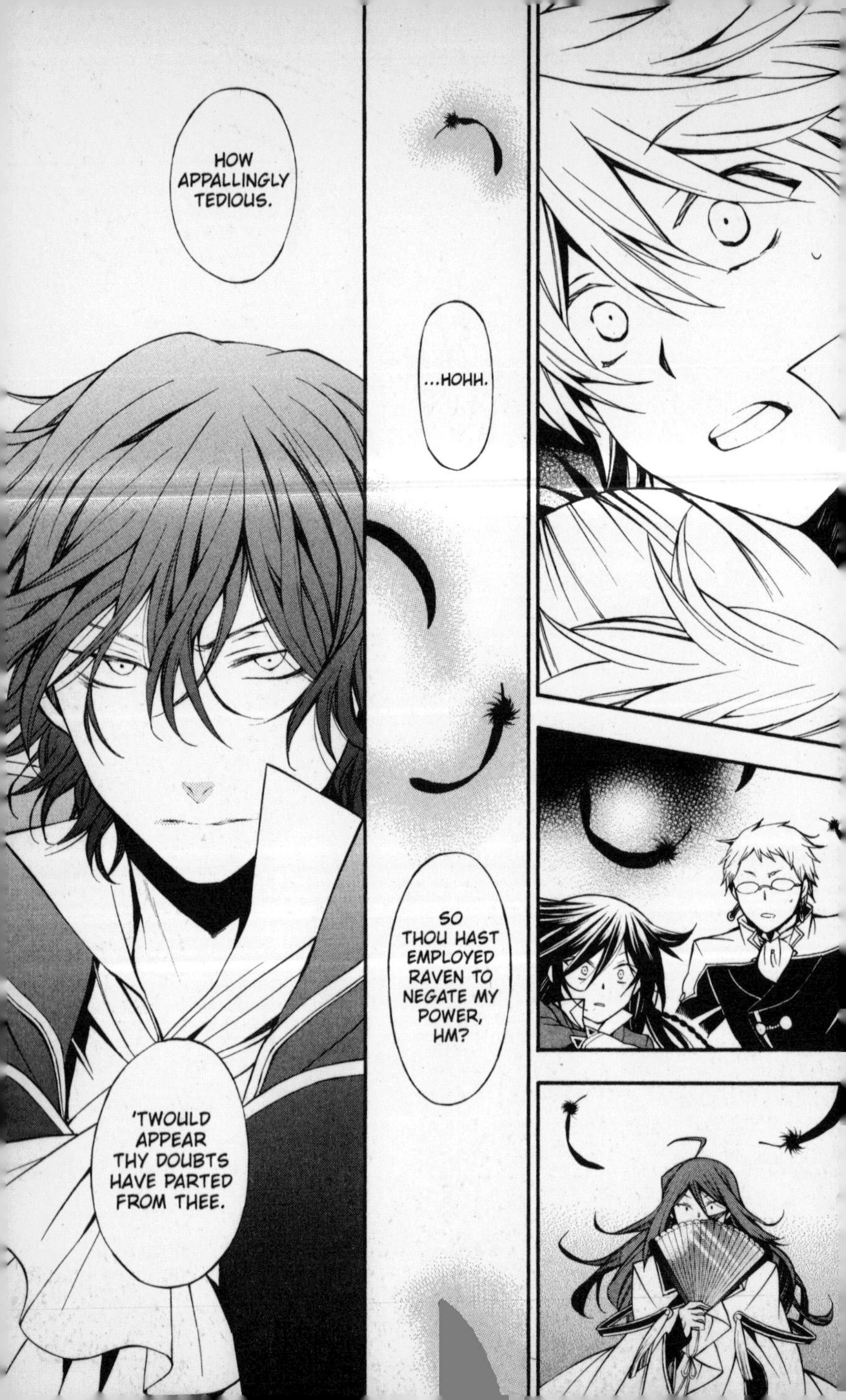
...HOHH.
SO THOU HAST EMPLOYED RAVEN TO NEGATE MY POWER, HM?
HOW APPALLINGLY TEDIOUS.
'TWOULD APPEAR THY DOUBTS HAVE PARTED FROM THEE.

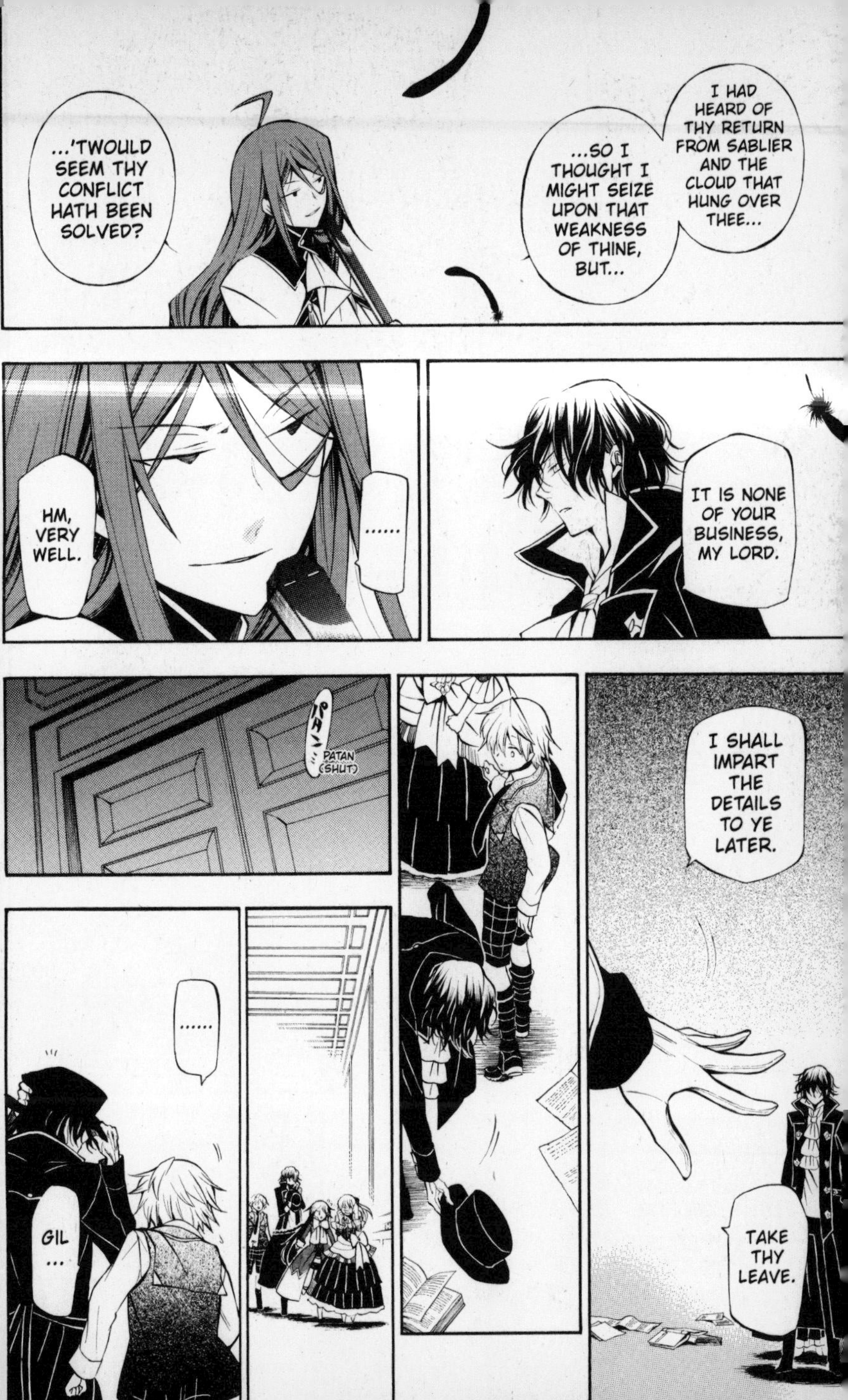
I HAD HEARD OF THY RETURN FROM SABLIER AND THE CLOUD THAT HUNG OVER THEE...
...SO I THOUGHT I MIGHT SEIZE UPON THAT WEAKNESS OF THINE, BUT...
...'TWOULD SEEM THY CONFLICT HATH BEEN SOLVED?
IT IS NONE OF YOUR BUSINESS, MY LORD.
......
HM, VERY WELL.
I SHALL IMPART THE DETAILS TO YE LATER.
TAKE THY LEAVE.
PATAN (SHUT)
......
GIL ...

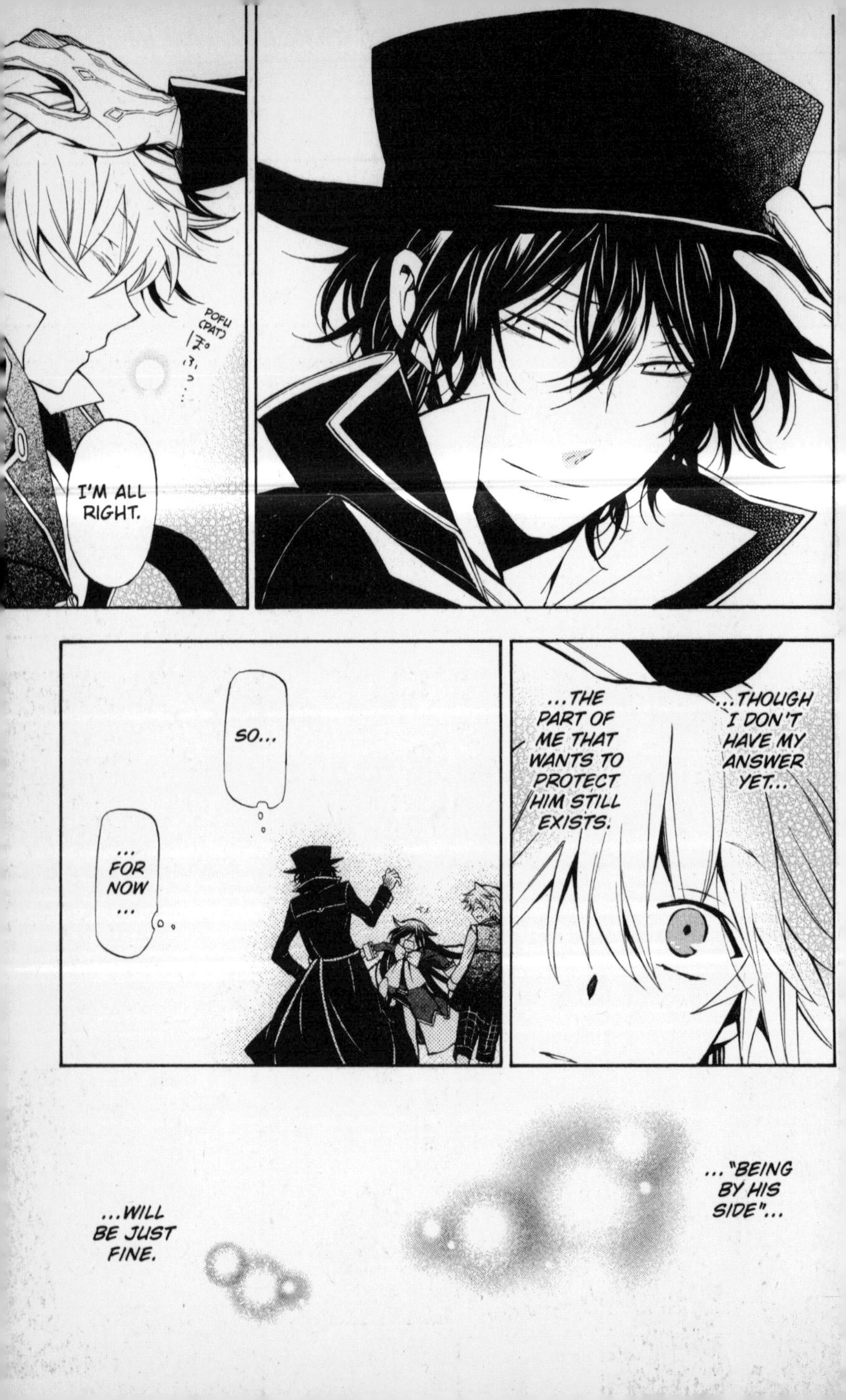
POFU (PAT) ぽふっ…
I'M ALL RIGHT.
...THOUGH I DON'T HAVE MY ANSWER YET...
...THE PART OF ME THAT WANTS TO PROTECT HIM STILL EXISTS.
SO...
...FOR NOW...
..."BEING BY HIS SIDE"...
...WILL BE JUST FINE.

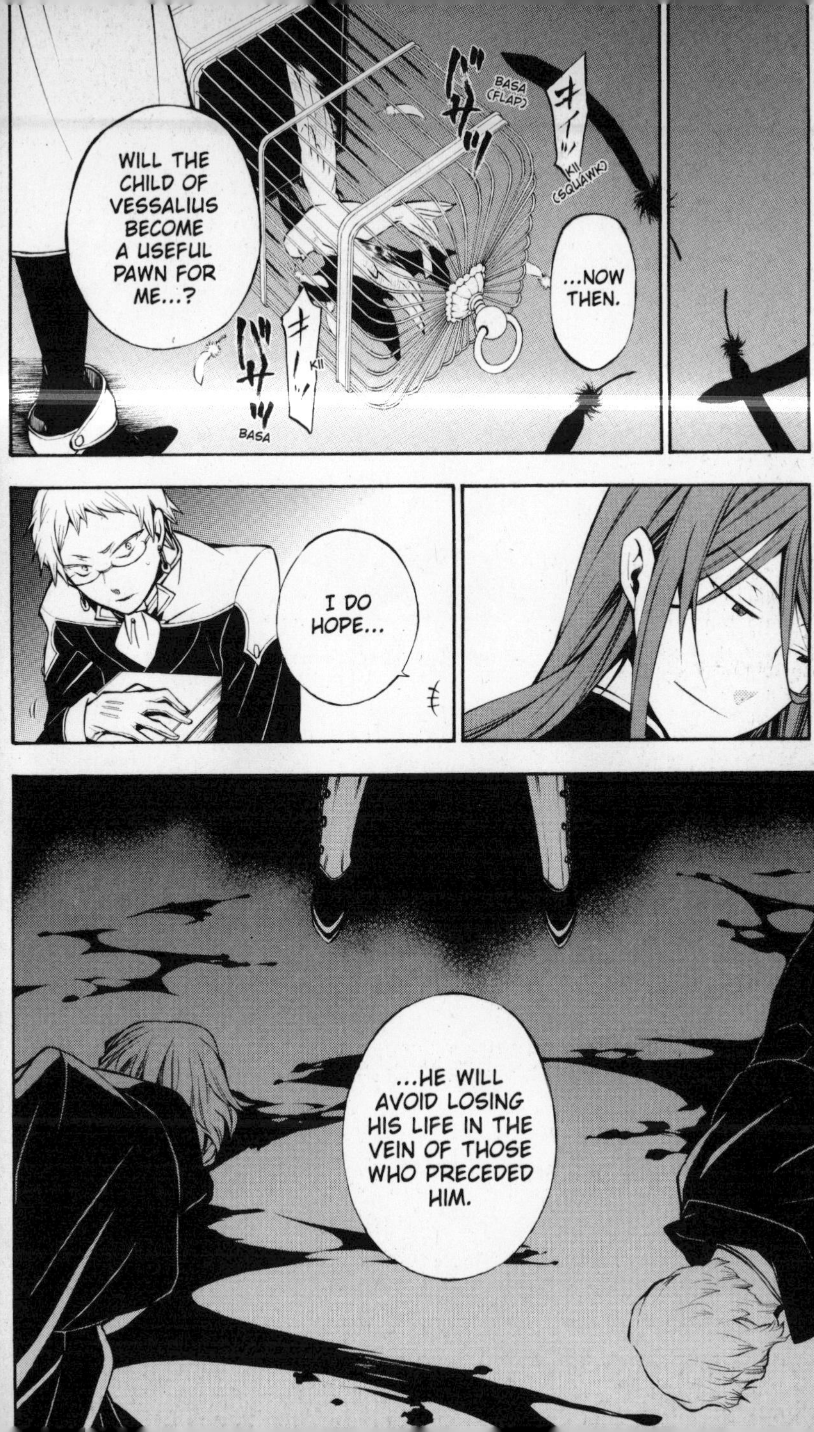

KII (SQUAWK)
BASA (FLAP)
...NOW THEN.
WILL THE CHILD OF VESSALIUS BECOME A USEFUL PAWN FOR ME...?
KII
BASA
I DO HOPE...
...HE WILL AVOID LOSING HIS LIFE IN THE VEIN OF THOSE WHO PRECEDED HIM.

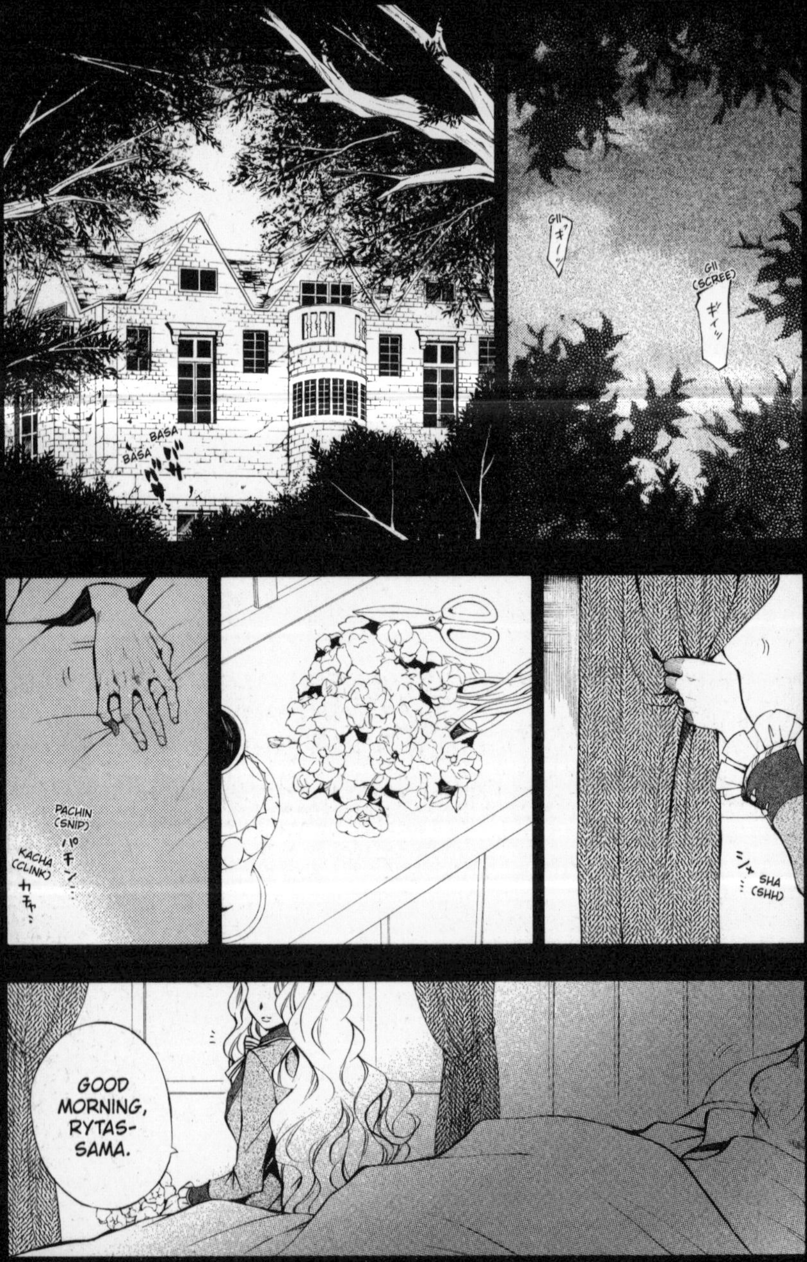
GII
GII (SCREE)
BASA BASA
SHA (SHH)
PACHIN (SNIP)
KACHA (CLINK)
GOOD MORNING, RYTAS-SAMA.

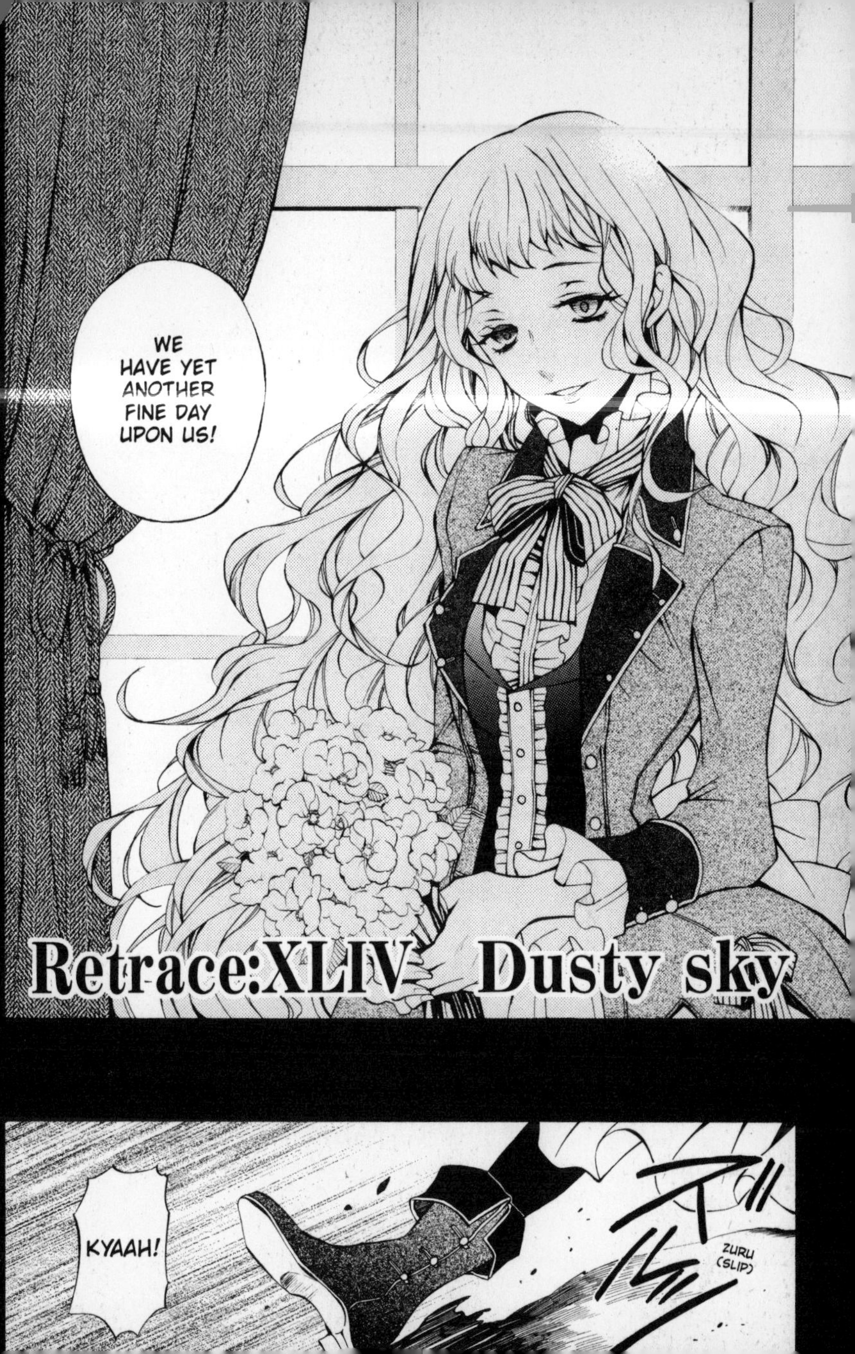
WE HAVE YET ANOTHER FINE DAY UPON US!
Retrace:XLIV Dusty sky
ZURU (SLIP)
KYAAH!

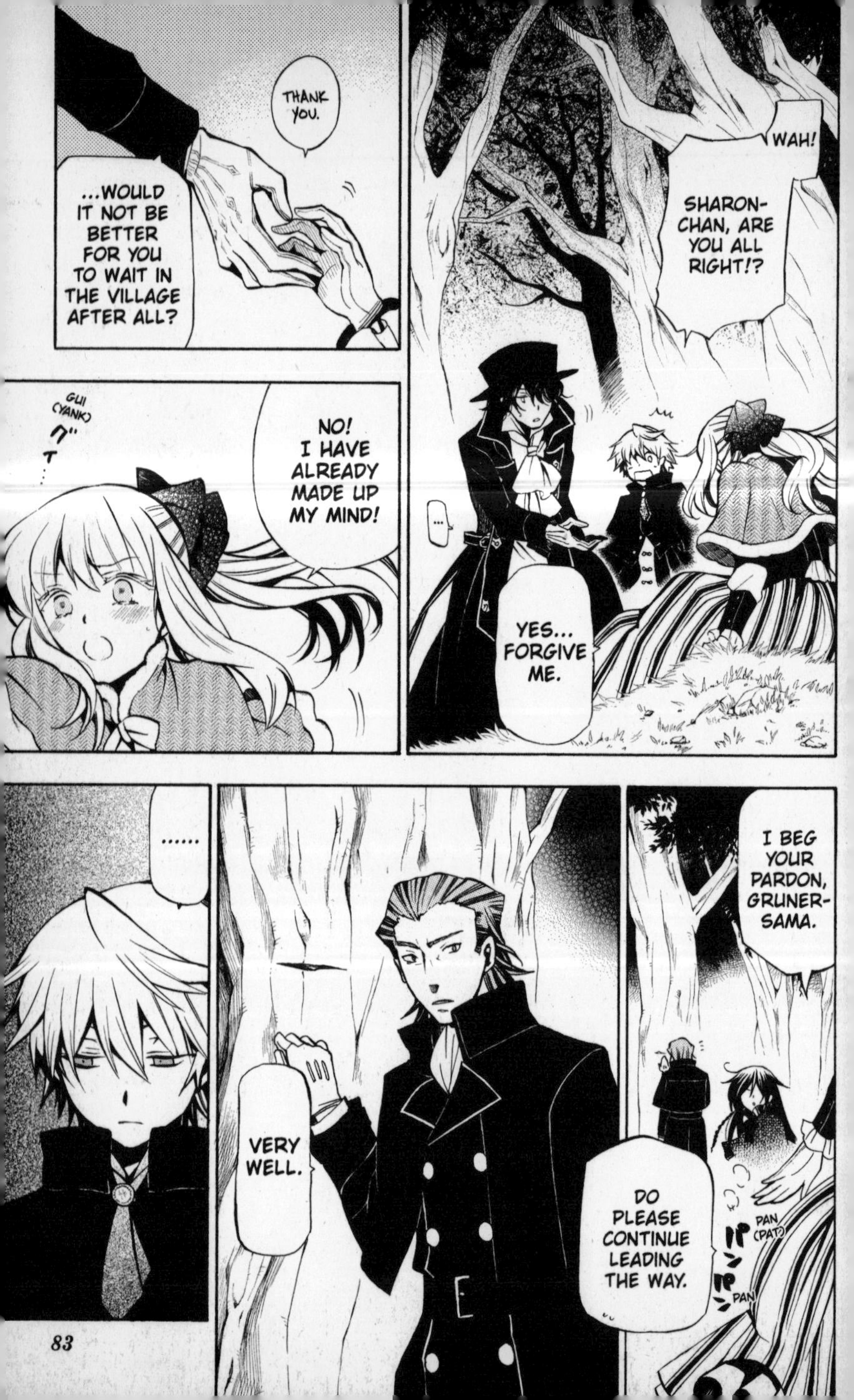
WAH!
SHARON-CHAN, ARE YOU ALL RIGHT!?
...
YES... FORGIVE ME.
THANK YOU.
...WOULD IT NOT BE BETTER FOR YOU TO WAIT IN THE VILLAGE AFTER ALL?
GUI (YANK)
NO! I HAVE ALREADY MADE UP MY MIND!
I BEG YOUR PARDON, GRUNER-SAMA.
PAN (PAT)
PAN
DO PLEASE CONTINUE LEADING THE WAY.
VERY WELL.
......

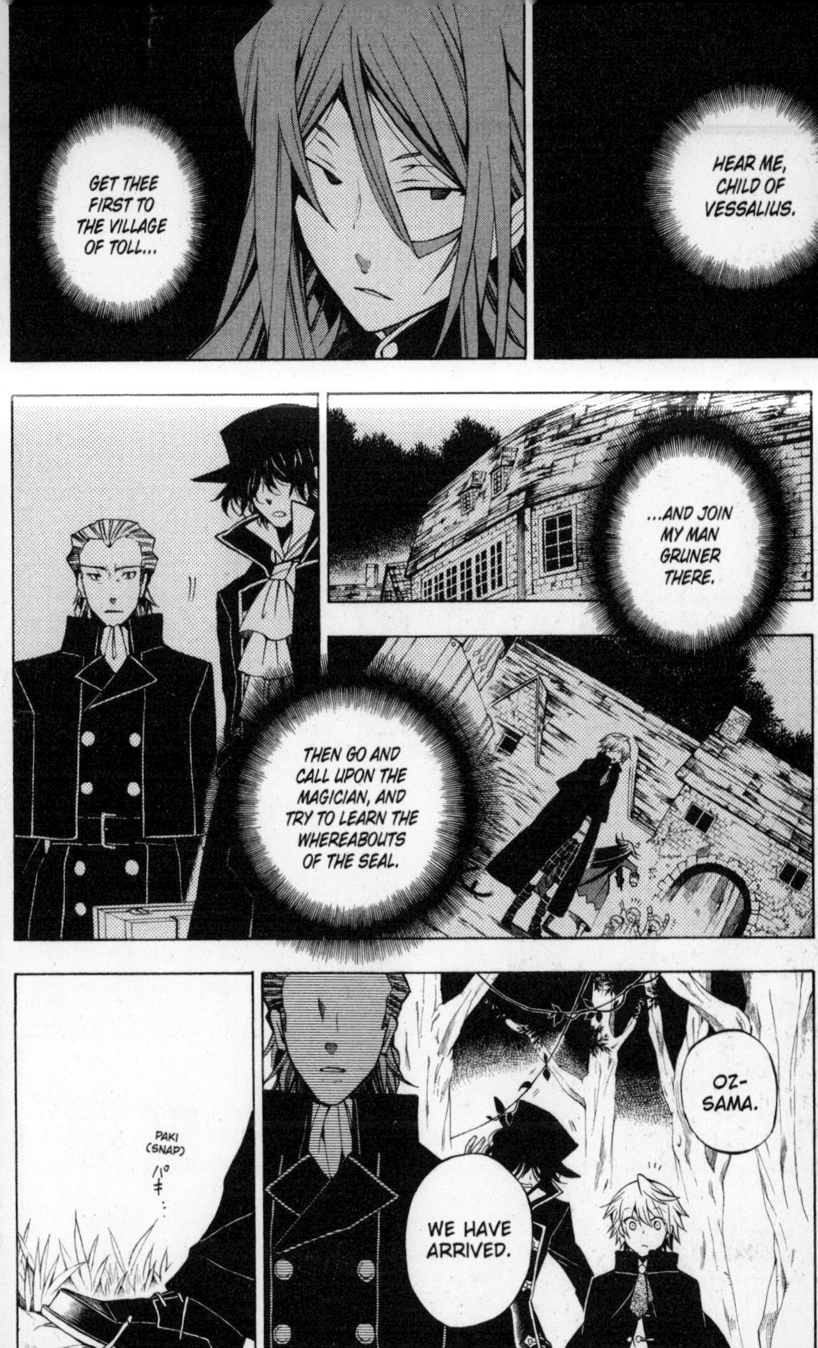
HEAR ME, CHILD OF VESSALIUS.
GET THEE FIRST TO THE VILLAGE OF TOLL...
...AND JOIN MY MAN GRUNER THERE.
THEN GO AND CALL UPON THE MAGICIAN, AND TRY TO LEARN THE WHEREABOUTS OF THE SEAL.
OZ-SAMA.
WE HAVE ARRIVED.
PAKI (SNAP)
パキ

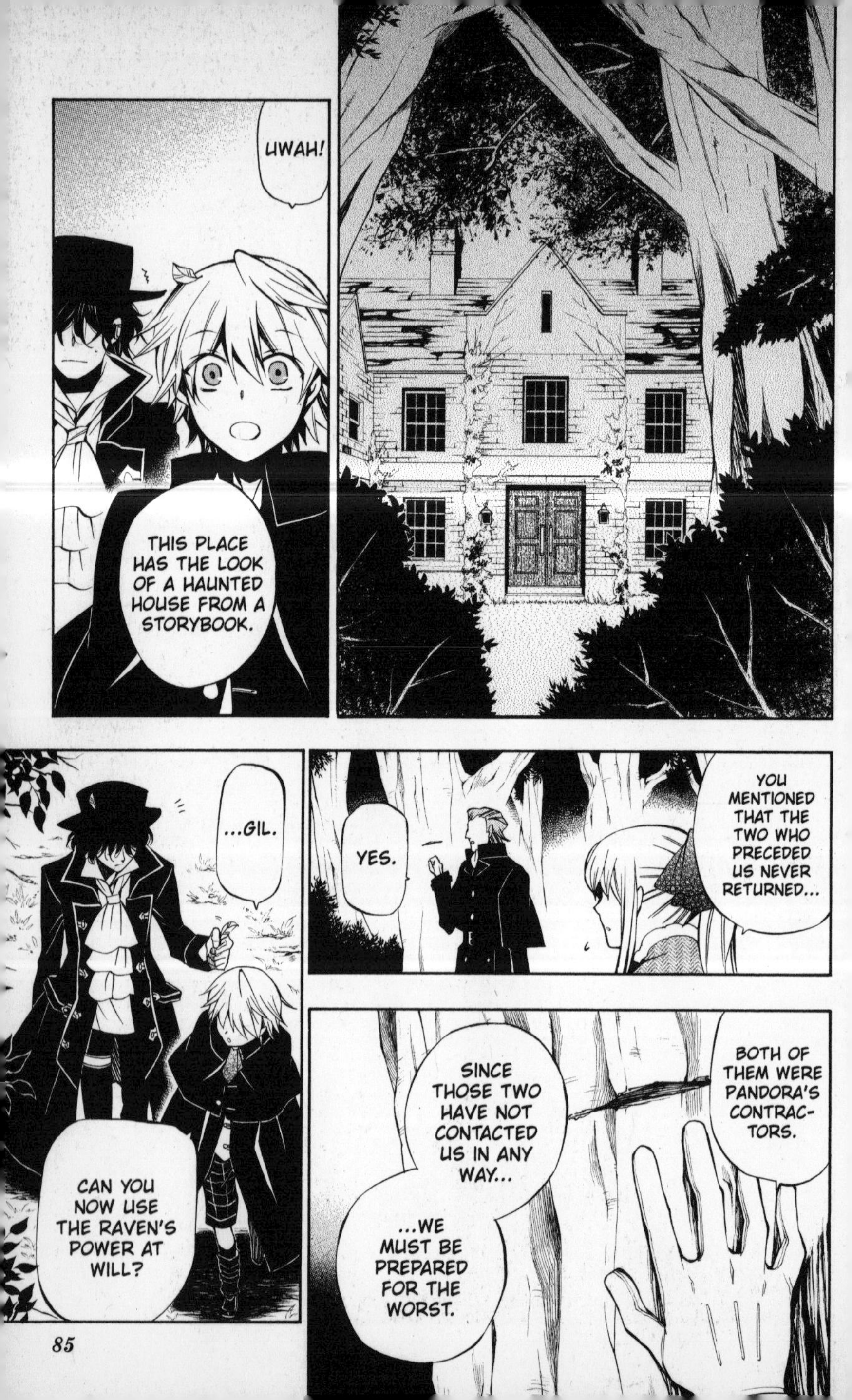
UWAH!
THIS PLACE HAS THE LOOK OF A HAUNTED HOUSE FROM A STORYBOOK.
YOU MENTIONED THAT THE TWO WHO PRECEDED US NEVER RETURNED...
YES.
BOTH OF THEM WERE PANDORA'S CONTRAC-TORS.
SINCE THOSE TWO HAVE NOT CONTACTED US IN ANY WAY...
...WE MUST BE PREPARED FOR THE WORST.
...GIL.
CAN YOU NOW USE THE RAVEN'S POWER AT WILL?

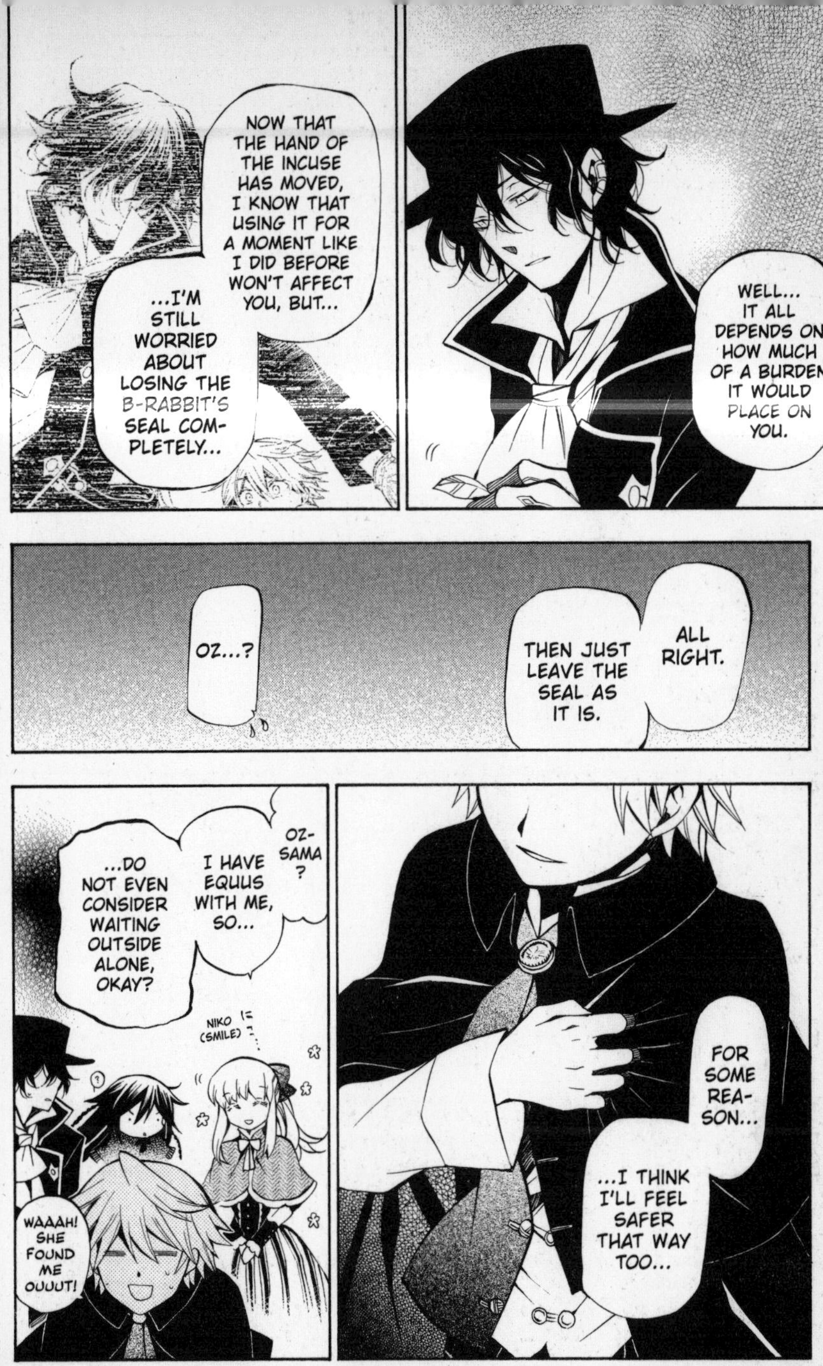
WELL... IT ALL DEPENDS ON HOW MUCH OF A BURDEN IT WOULD PLACE ON YOU.
NOW THAT THE HAND OF THE INCUSE HAS MOVED, I KNOW THAT USING IT FOR A MOMENT LIKE I DID BEFORE WON'T AFFECT YOU, BUT...
...I'M STILL WORRIED ABOUT LOSING THE B-RABBIT'S SEAL COMPLETELY...
ALL RIGHT.
THEN JUST LEAVE THE SEAL AS IT IS.
OZ...?
FOR SOME REASON...
...I THINK I'LL FEEL SAFER THAT WAY TOO...
OZ-SAMA?
I HAVE EQUUS WITH ME, SO...
...DO NOT EVEN CONSIDER WAITING OUTSIDE ALONE, OKAY?
NIKO (SMILE)
WAAAH! SHE FOUND ME OUUUT!

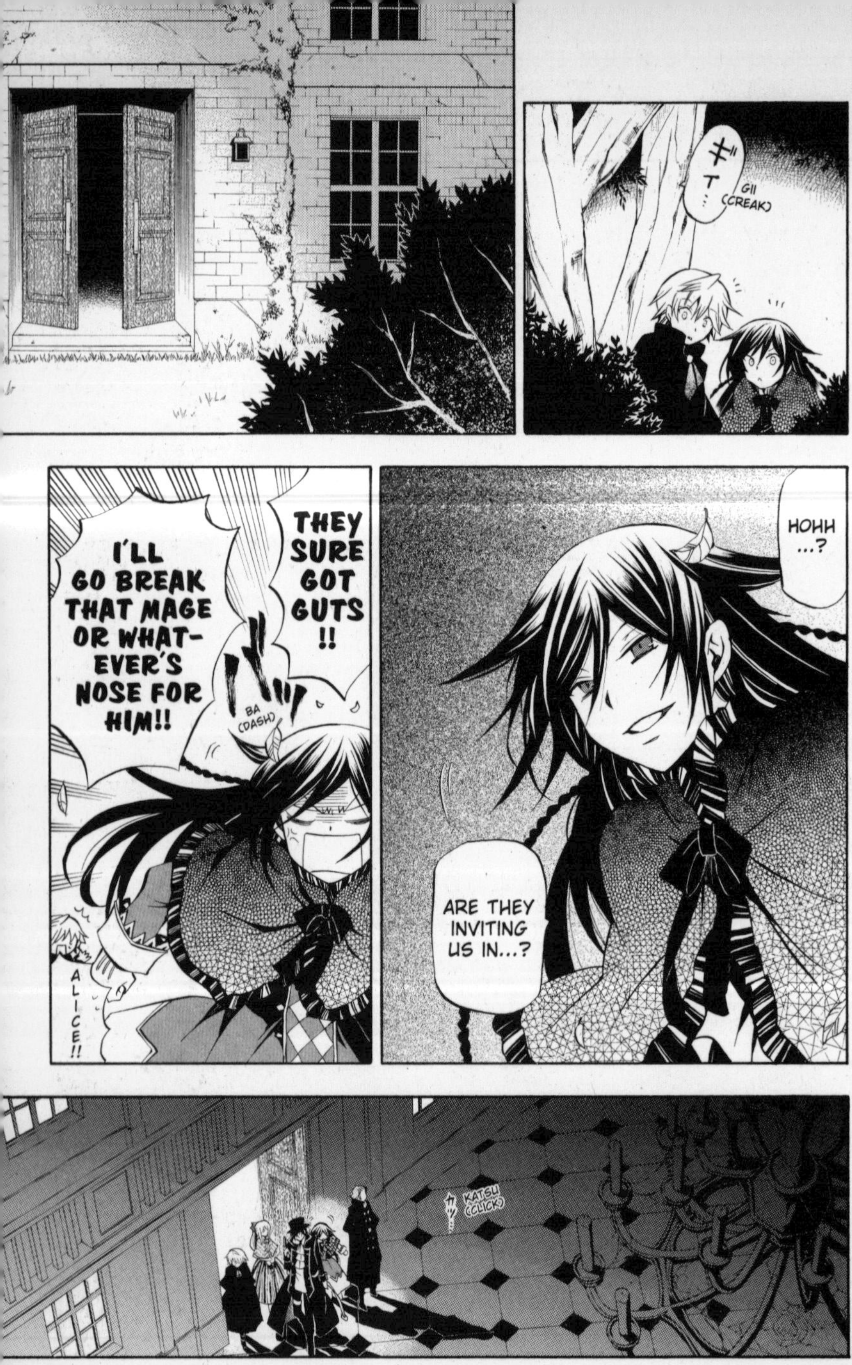
ギィ…
GII (CREAK)
HOHH ...?
ARE THEY INVITING US IN...?
THEY SURE GOT GUTS!!
I'LL GO BREAK THAT MAGE OR WHAT-EVER'S NOSE FOR HIM!!
BA (DASH)
ALICE!!
カッ…
KATSU (CLICK)

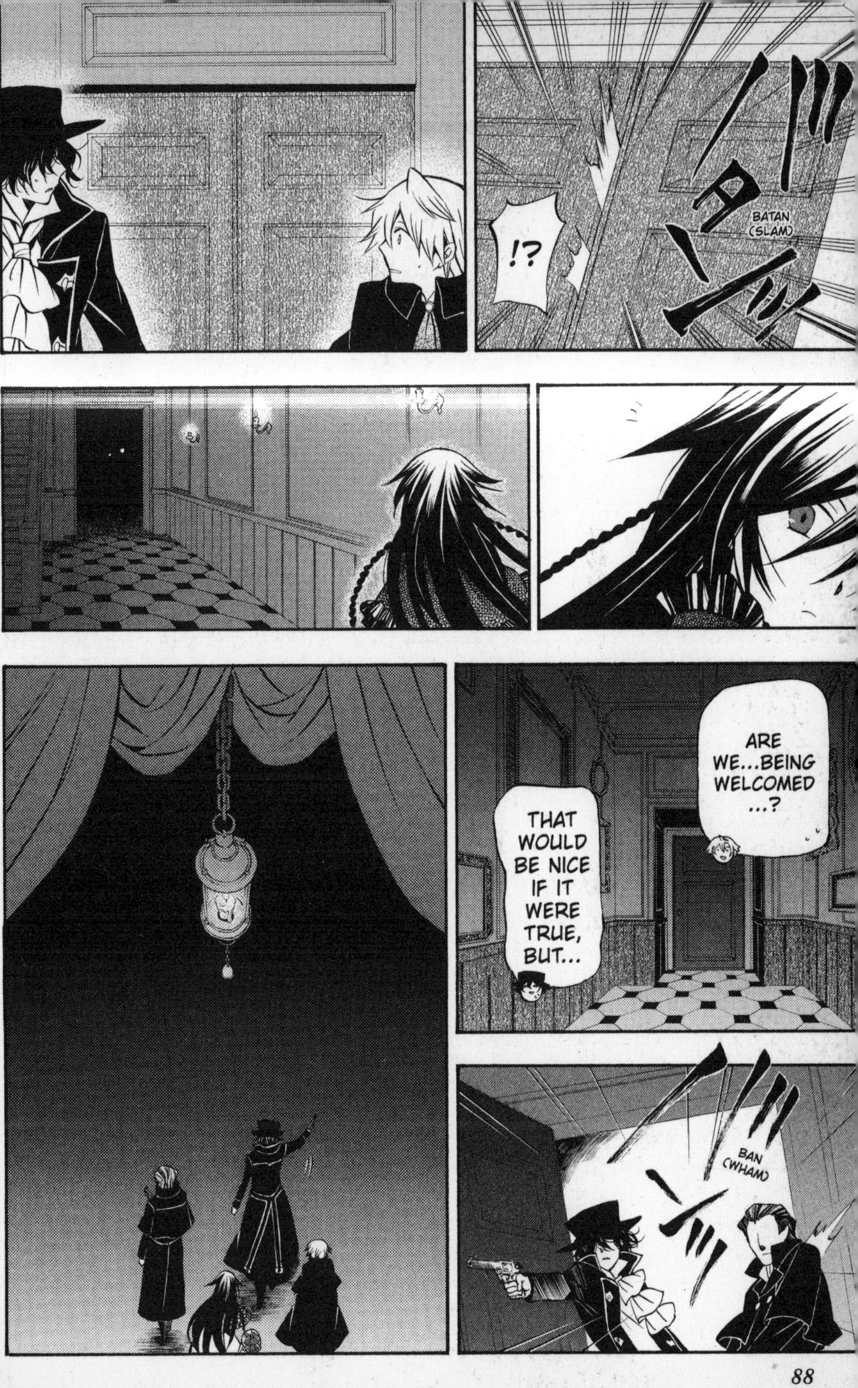
BATAN (SLAM)
!?
ARE WE...BEING WELCOMED...?
THAT WOULD BE NICE IF IT WERE TRUE, BUT...
BAN (WHAM)

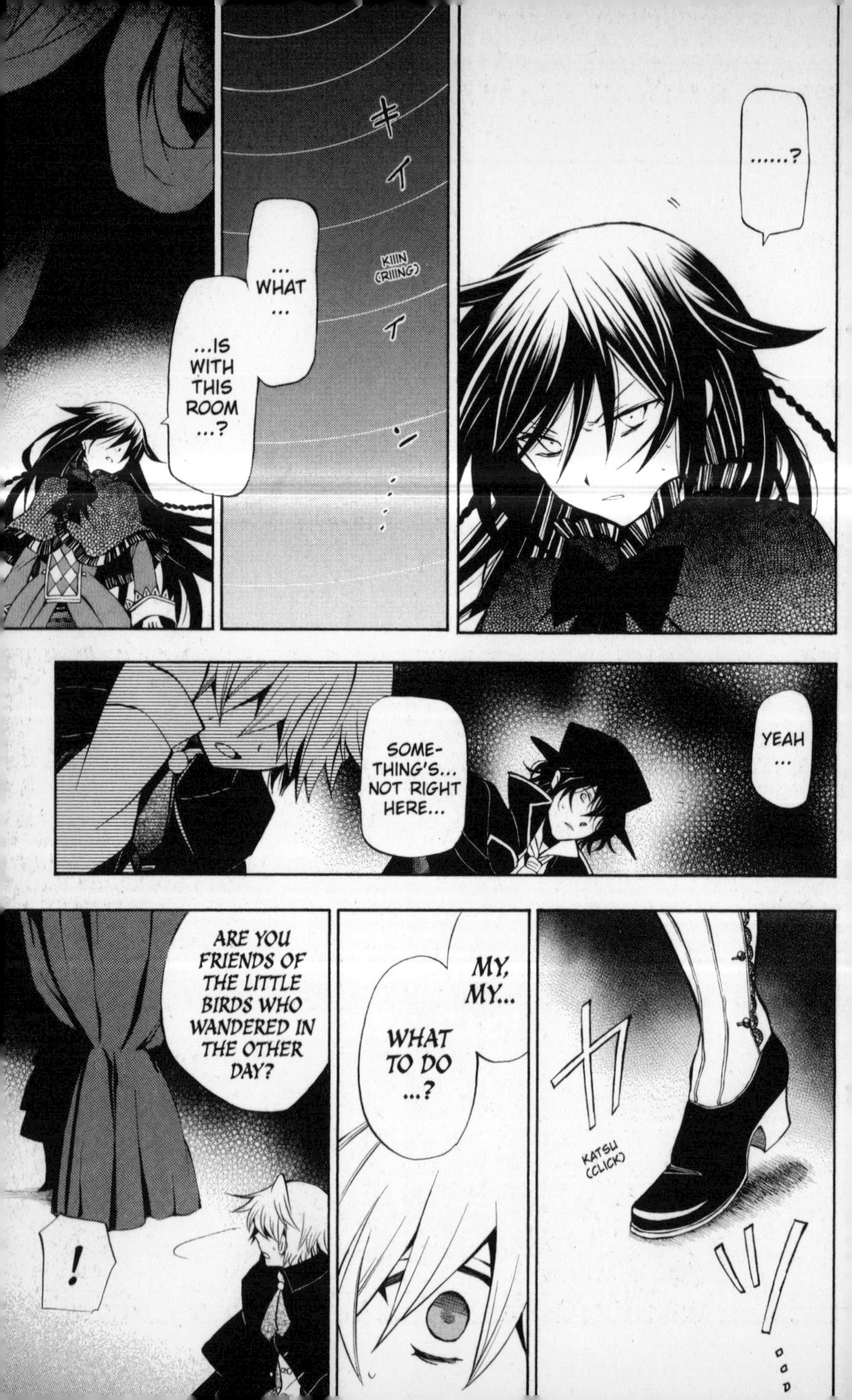
......?
KIIN (RIIING)
... WHAT ...
...IS WITH THIS ROOM ...?
YEAH ...
SOME-THING'S... NOT RIGHT HERE...
KATSU (CLICK)
MY, MY...
WHAT TO DO ...?
ARE YOU FRIENDS OF THE LITTLE BIRDS WHO WANDERED IN THE OTHER DAY?
!

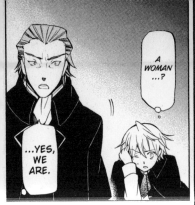

A WOMAN ...?

...YES, WE ARE.

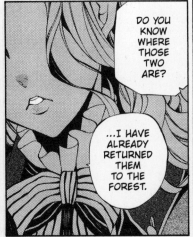

DO YOU KNOW WHERE THOSE TWO ARE?

...I HAVE ALREADY RETURNED THEM TO THE FOREST.

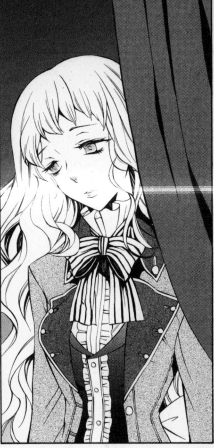

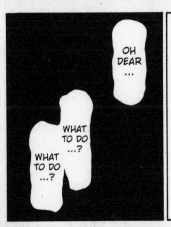

OH DEAR ...

WHAT TO DO ...?

WHAT TO DO ...?

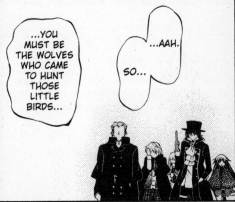

...YOU MUST BE THE WOLVES WHO CAME TO HUNT THOSE LITTLE BIRDS...

...AAH.

SO...

90

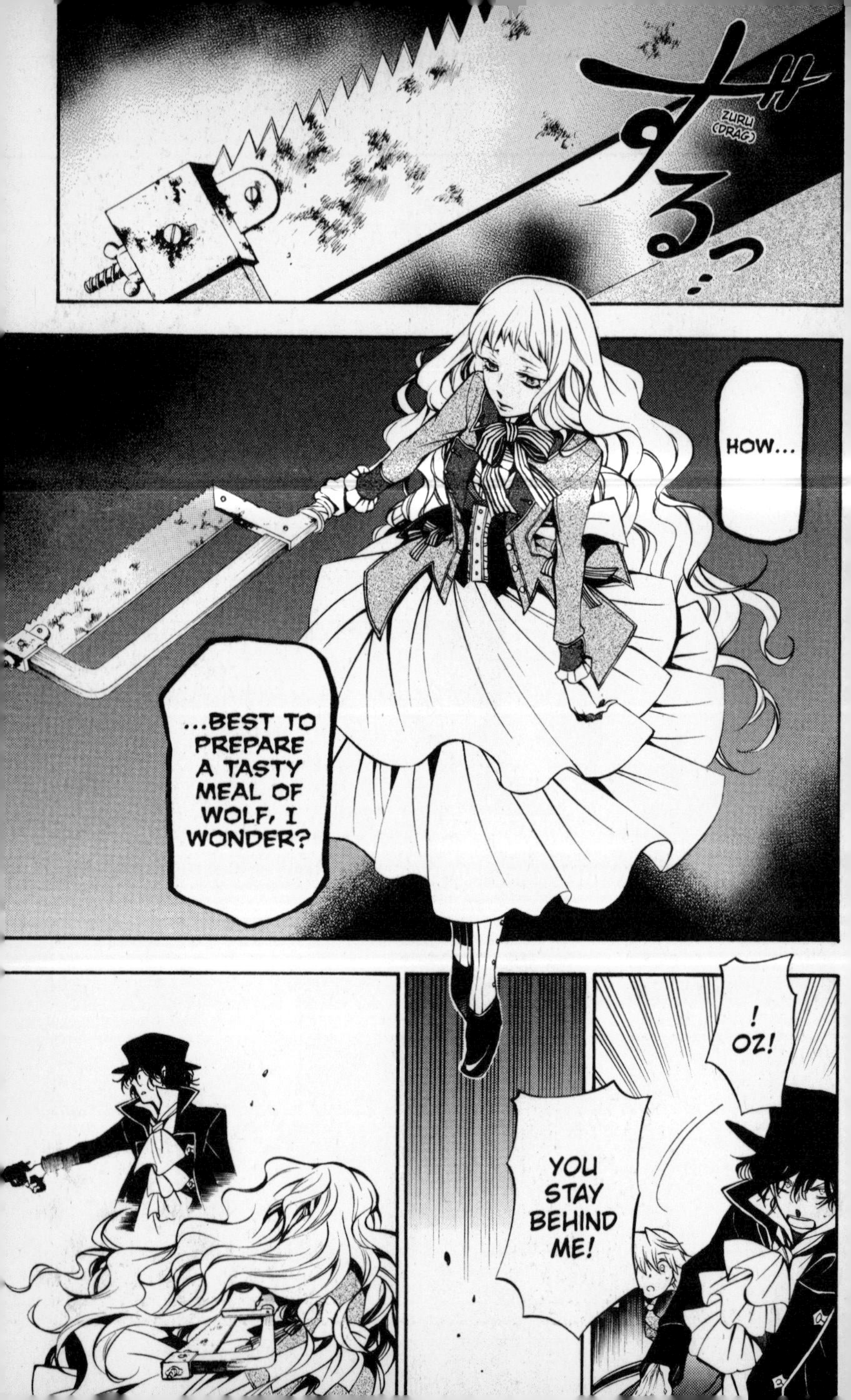

ずるっ
ZURU (DRAG)
HOW...
...BEST TO PREPARE A TASTY MEAL OF WOLF, I WONDER?
! OZ!
YOU STAY BEHIND ME!

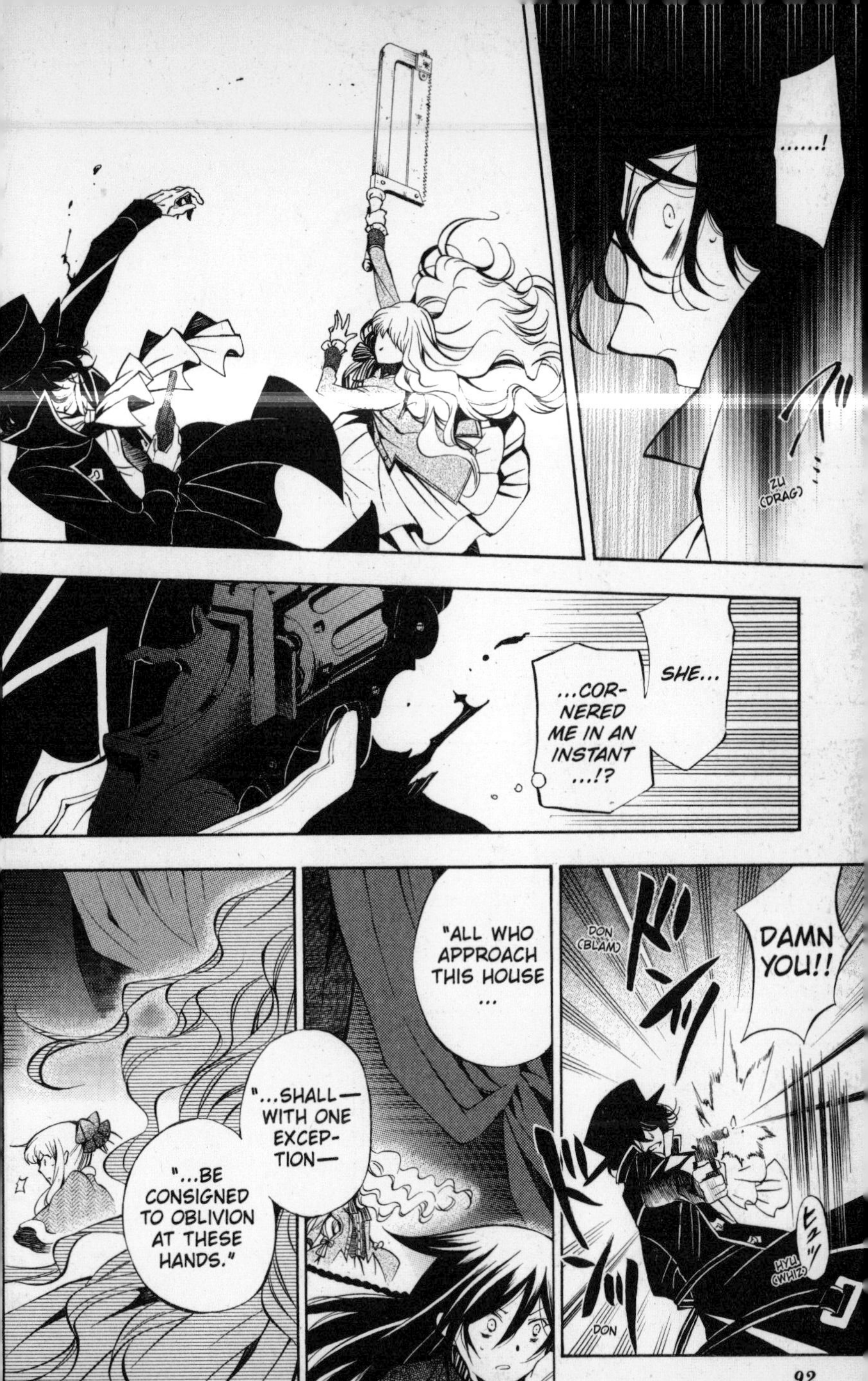
......!
ZU (DRAG)
SHE...
...COR-NERED ME IN AN INSTANT ...!?
DAMN YOU!!
DON (BLAM)
HYU (WHIZ)
DON
"ALL WHO APPROACH THIS HOUSE ...
"...SHALL— WITH ONE EXCEP-TION—
"...BE CONSIGNED TO OBLIVION AT THESE HANDS."

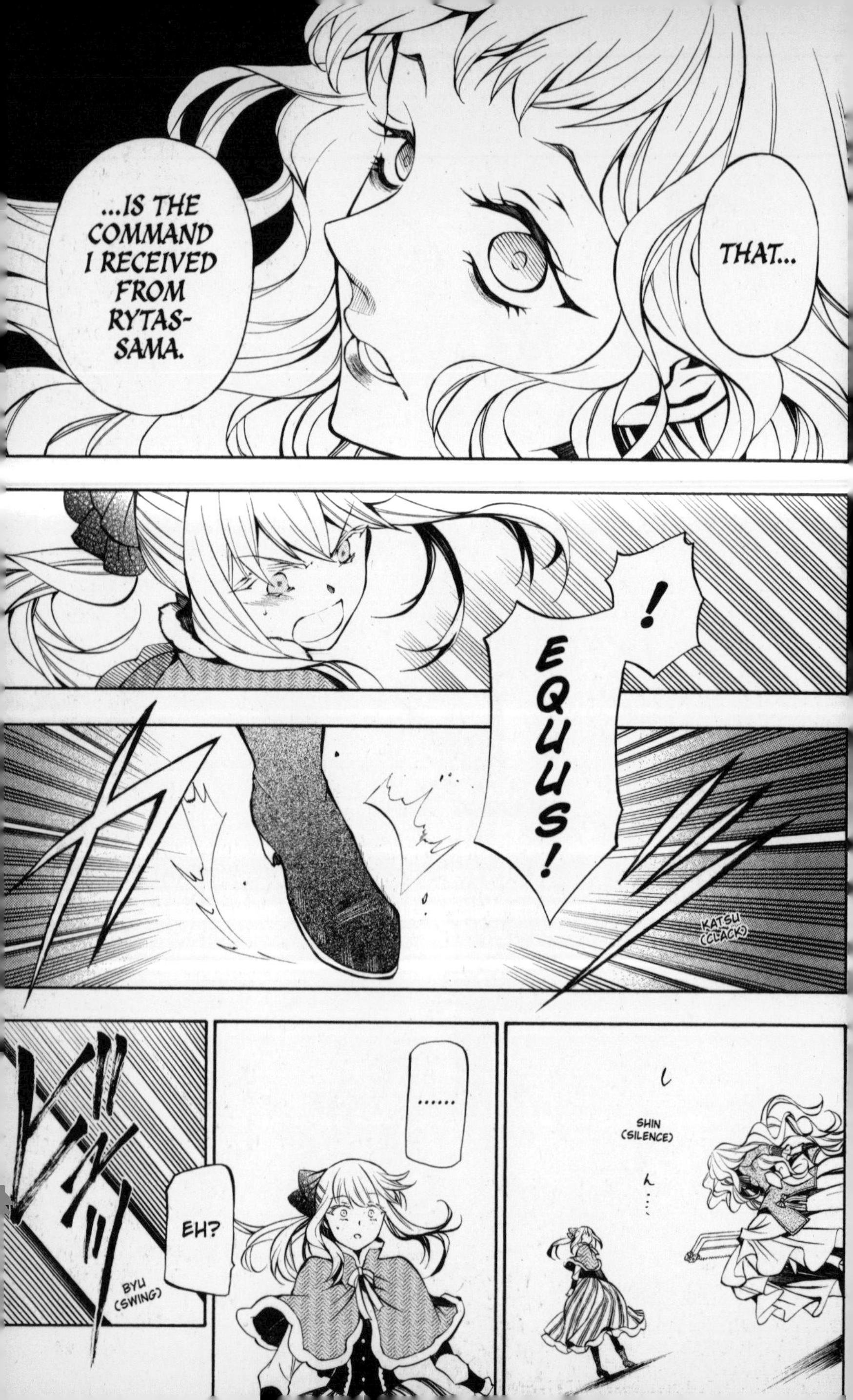
THAT...
...IS THE COMMAND I RECEIVED FROM RYTAS-SAMA.
!
EQUUS!
KATSU (CLACK)
し
ん…
SHIN (SILENCE)
......
EH?
BYU (SWING)

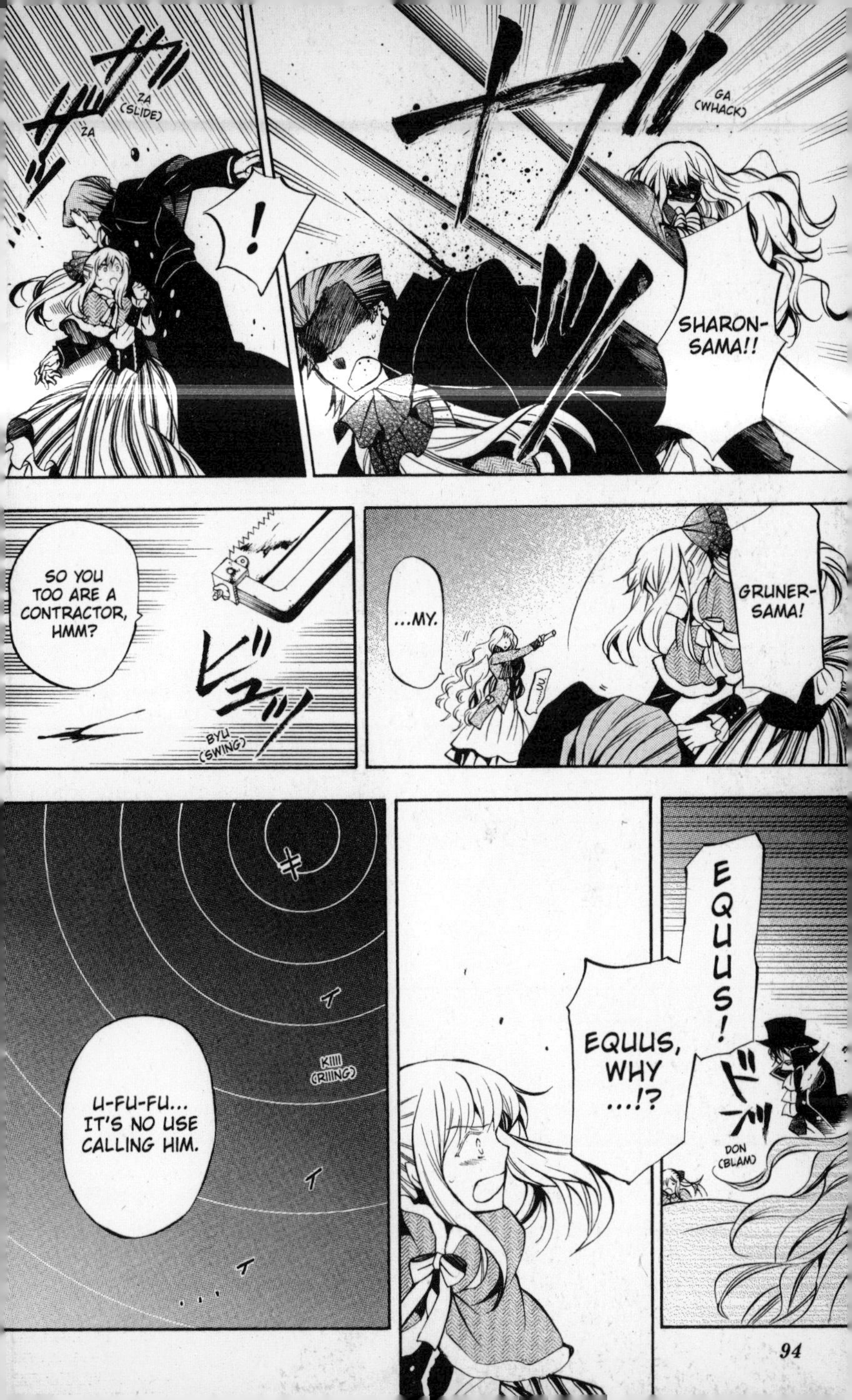
GA (WHACK)
SHARON-SAMA!!
ZA ZA (SLIDE)
!
GRUNER-SAMA!
...UU.
...MY.
SO YOU TOO ARE A CONTRACTOR, HMM?
BYU (SWING)
EQUUS!
DON (BLAM)
EQUUS, WHY ...!?
KIIII (RIIING)
U-FU-FU... IT'S NO USE CALLING HIM.

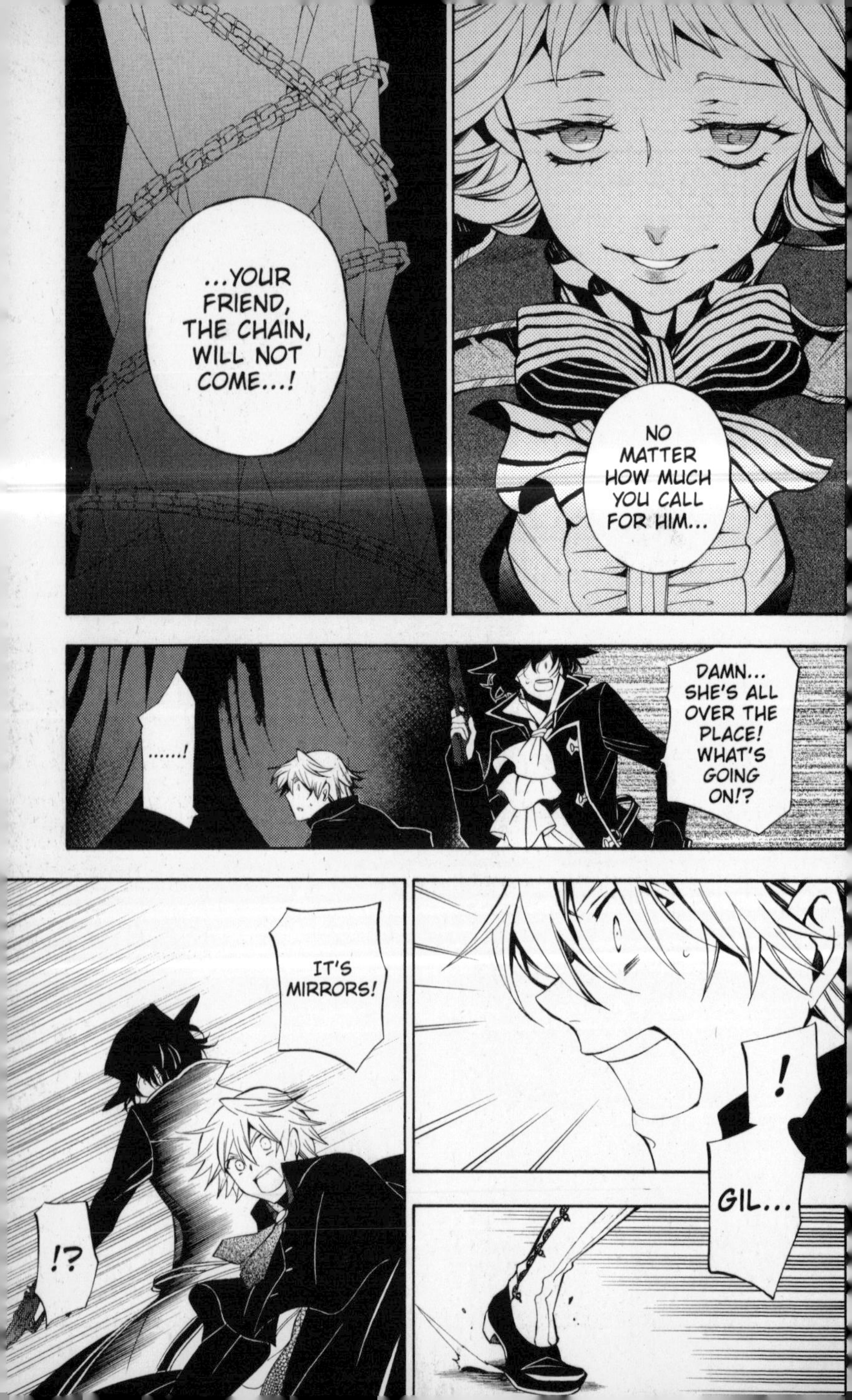
NO MATTER HOW MUCH YOU CALL FOR HIM...
...YOUR FRIEND, THE CHAIN, WILL NOT COME...!
DAMN... SHE'S ALL OVER THE PLACE! WHAT'S GOING ON!?
......!
!
GIL...
IT'S MIRRORS!
!?

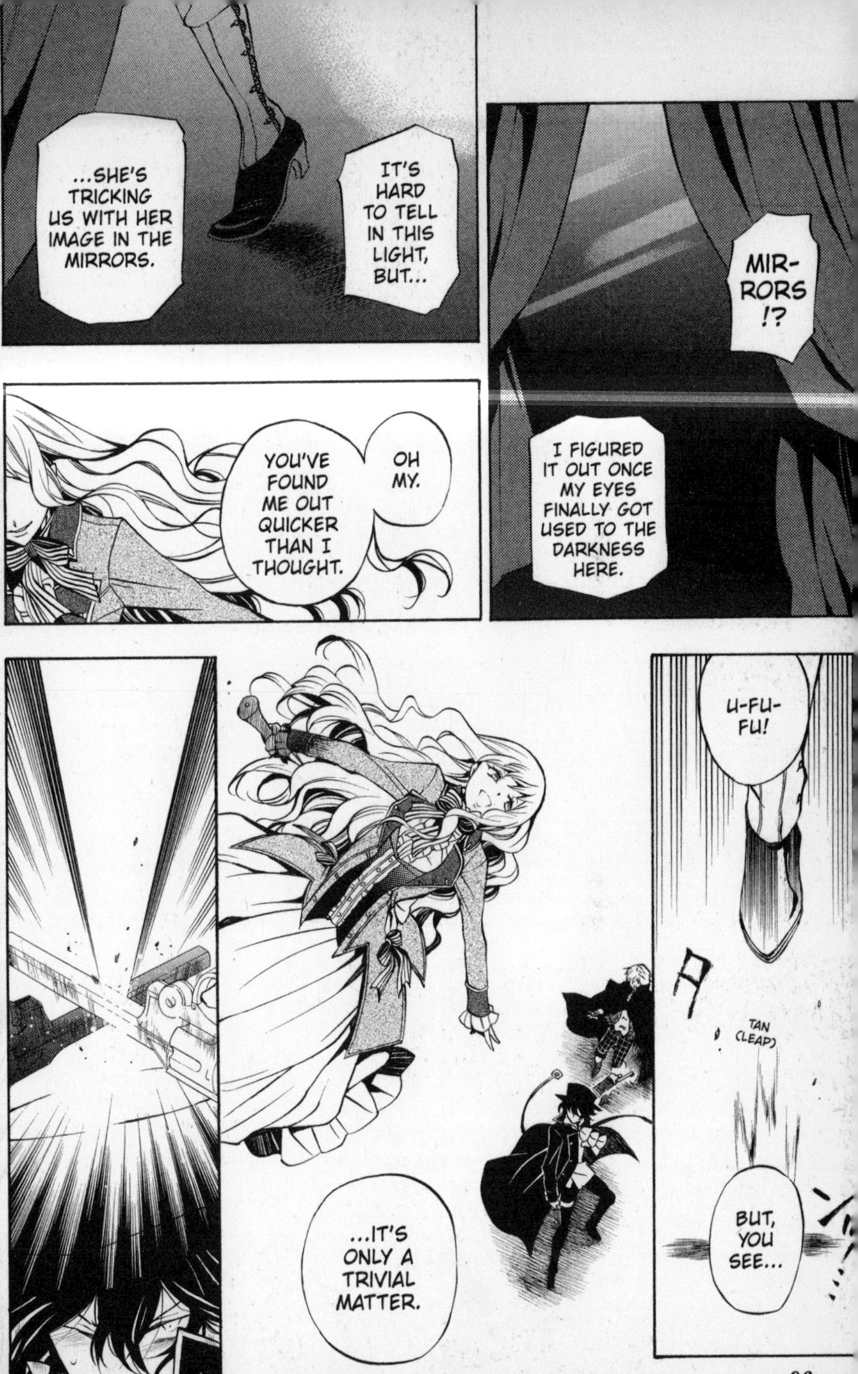
IT'S HARD TO TELL IN THIS LIGHT, BUT...
...SHE'S TRICKING US WITH HER IMAGE IN THE MIRRORS.
MIR-RORS!?
I FIGURED IT OUT ONCE MY EYES FINALLY GOT USED TO THE DARKNESS HERE.
OH MY.
YOU'VE FOUND ME OUT QUICKER THAN I THOUGHT.
U-FU-FU!
TAN (LEAP)
BUT, YOU SEE...
...IT'S ONLY A TRIVIAL MATTER.

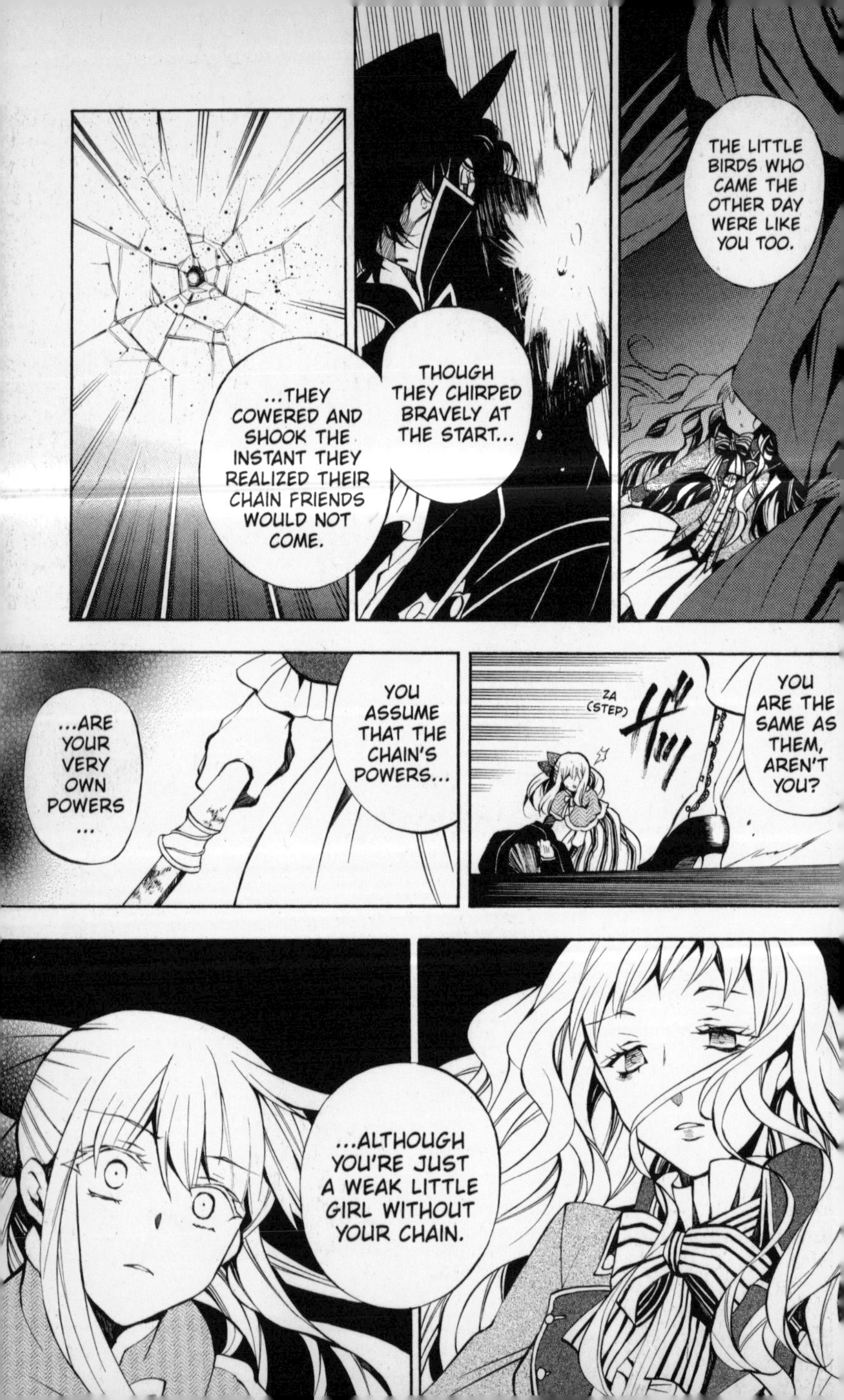
THE LITTLE BIRDS WHO CAME THE OTHER DAY WERE LIKE YOU TOO.
THOUGH THEY CHIRPED BRAVELY AT THE START...
...THEY COWERED AND SHOOK THE INSTANT THEY REALIZED THEIR CHAIN FRIENDS WOULD NOT COME.
YOU ARE THE SAME AS THEM, AREN'T YOU?
ZA (STEP)
YOU ASSUME THAT THE CHAIN'S POWERS...
...ARE YOUR VERY OWN POWERS...
...ALTHOUGH YOU'RE JUST A WEAK LITTLE GIRL WITHOUT YOUR CHAIN.

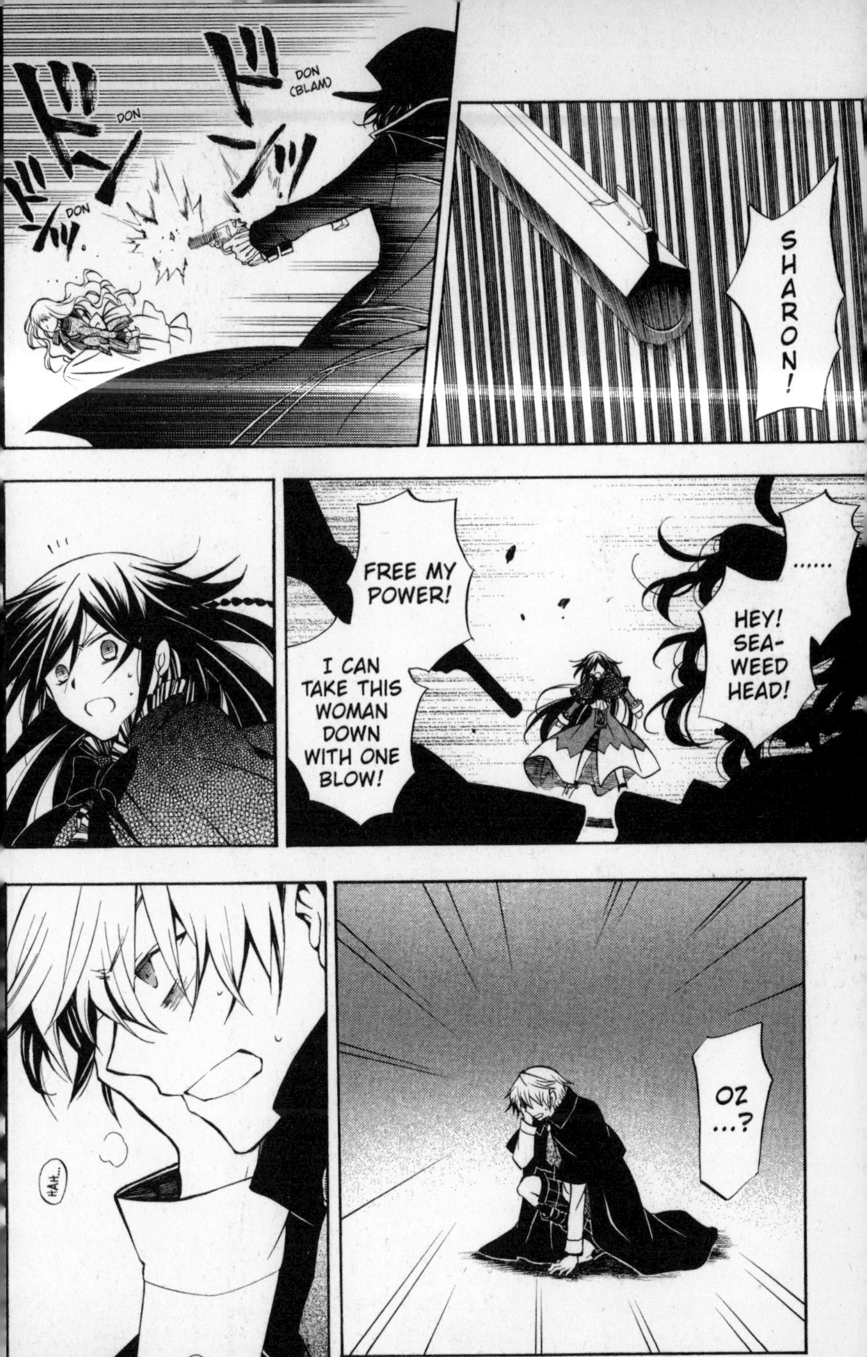
SHARON!
DON (BLAM)
DON
DON
......
HEY! SEA-WEED HEAD!
FREE MY POWER!
I CAN TAKE THIS WOMAN DOWN WITH ONE BLOW!
OZ ...?
HAH...
HAH...

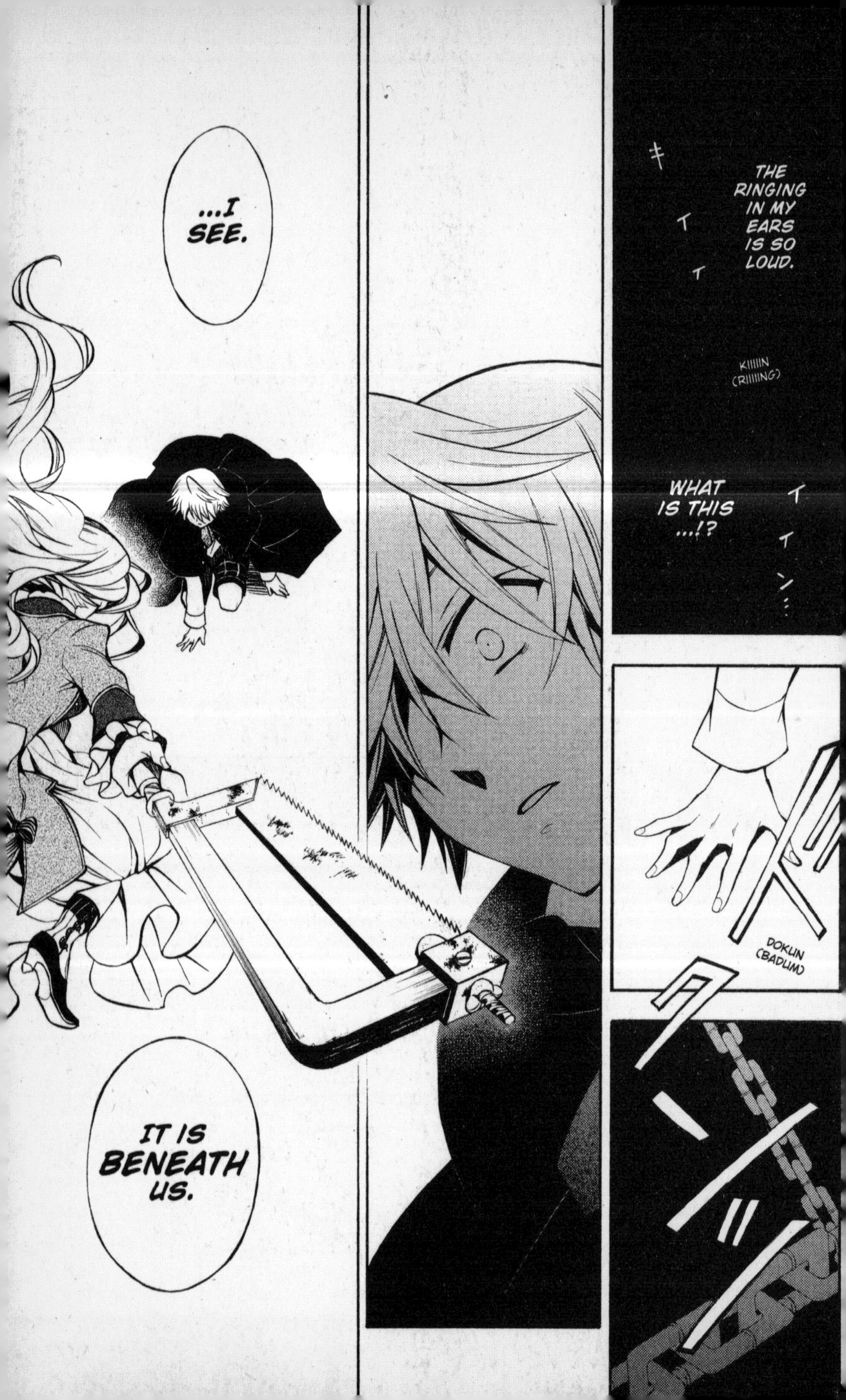
THE RINGING IN MY EARS IS SO LOUD.
KIIIIN (RIIIING)
WHAT IS THIS ...!?
DOKUN (BADUM)
...I SEE.
IT IS BENEATH US.

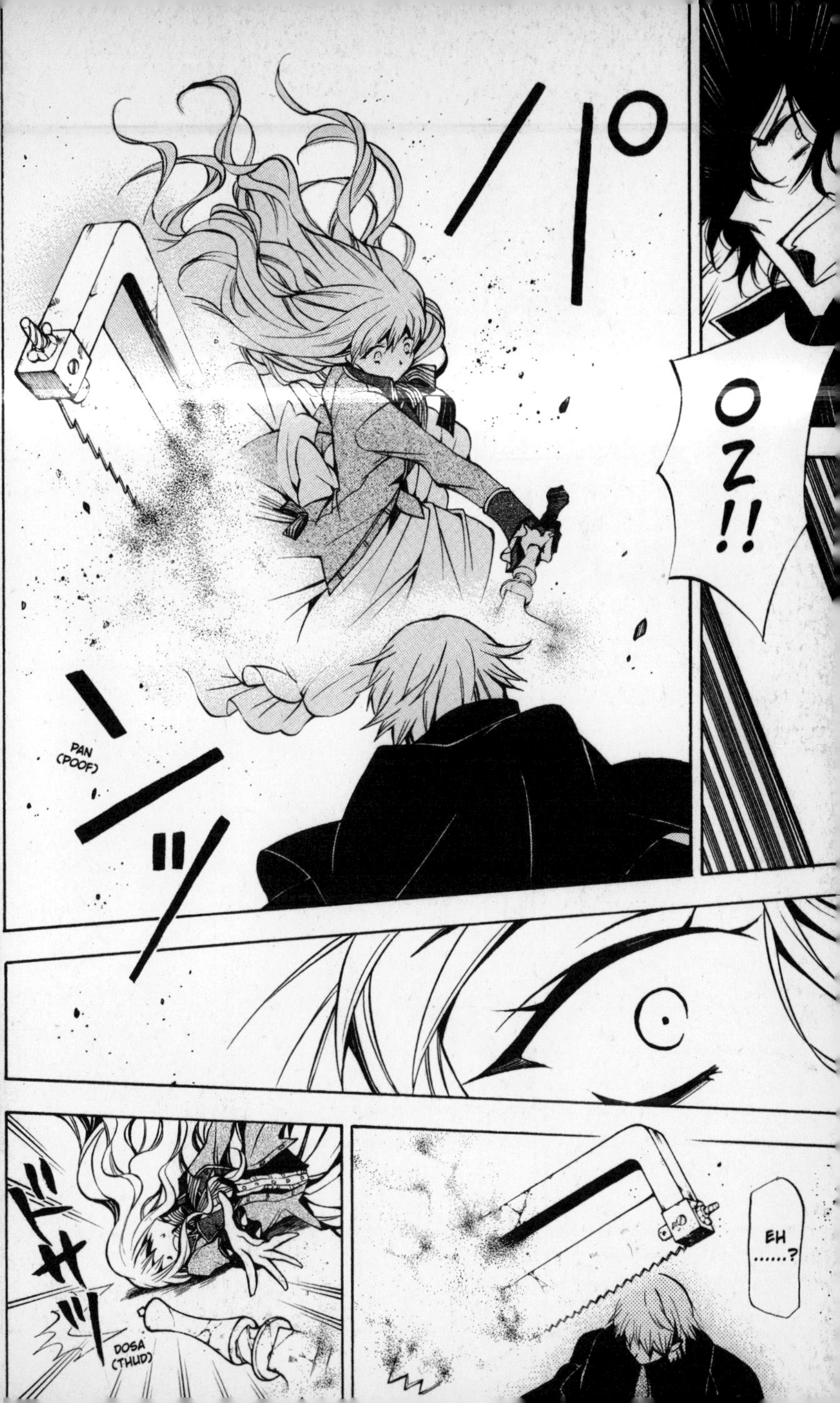
OZ!!
PAN (POOF)
EH ......?
DOSA (THUD)

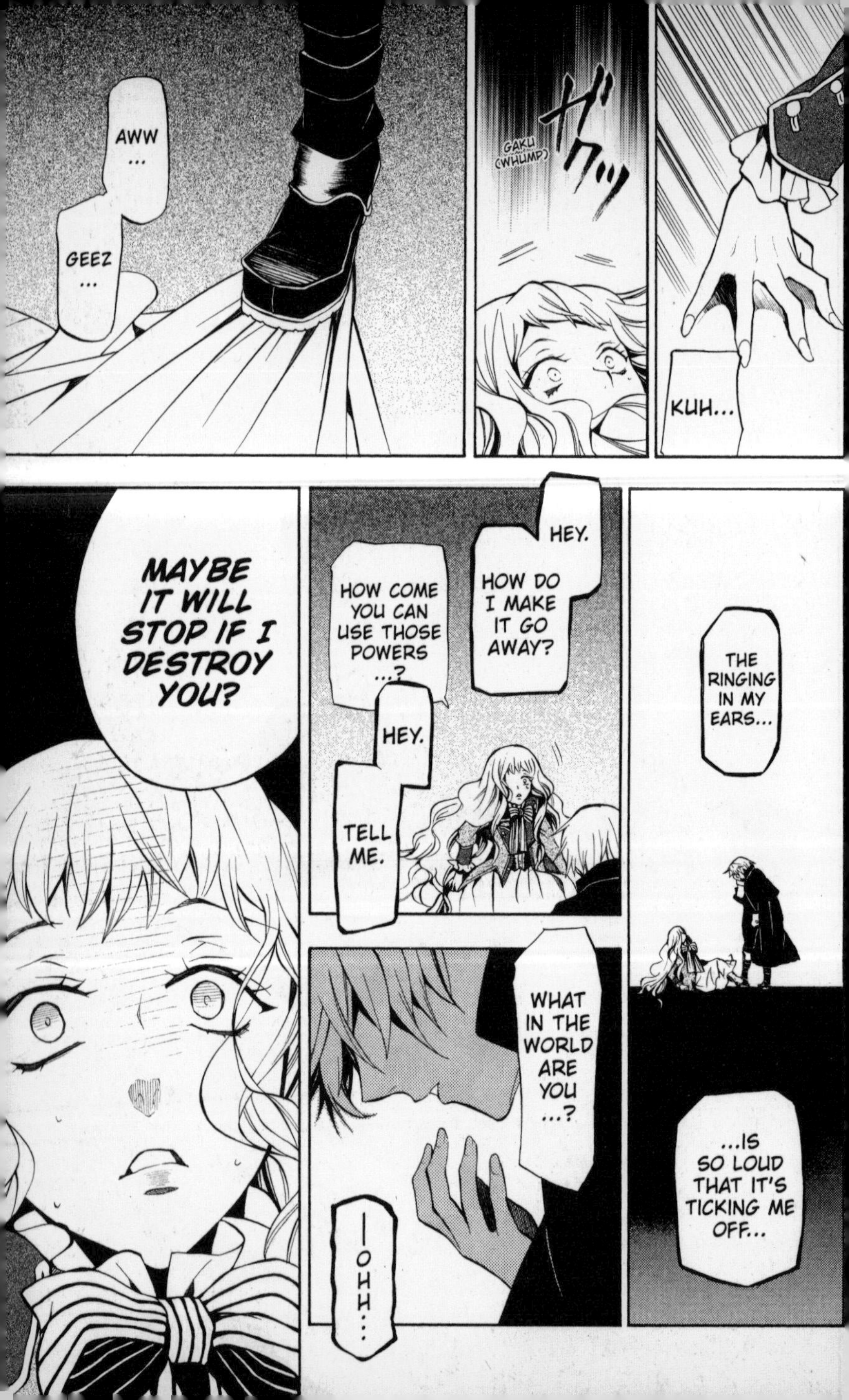
KUH...
GAKU (WHUMP)
AWW ...
GEEZ ...
THE RINGING IN MY EARS...
...IS SO LOUD THAT IT'S TICKING ME OFF...
HEY.
HOW DO I MAKE IT GO AWAY?
HOW COME YOU CAN USE THOSE POWERS ...?
HEY.
TELL ME.
WHAT IN THE WORLD ARE YOU ...?
OHH...
MAYBE IT WILL STOP IF I DESTROY YOU?

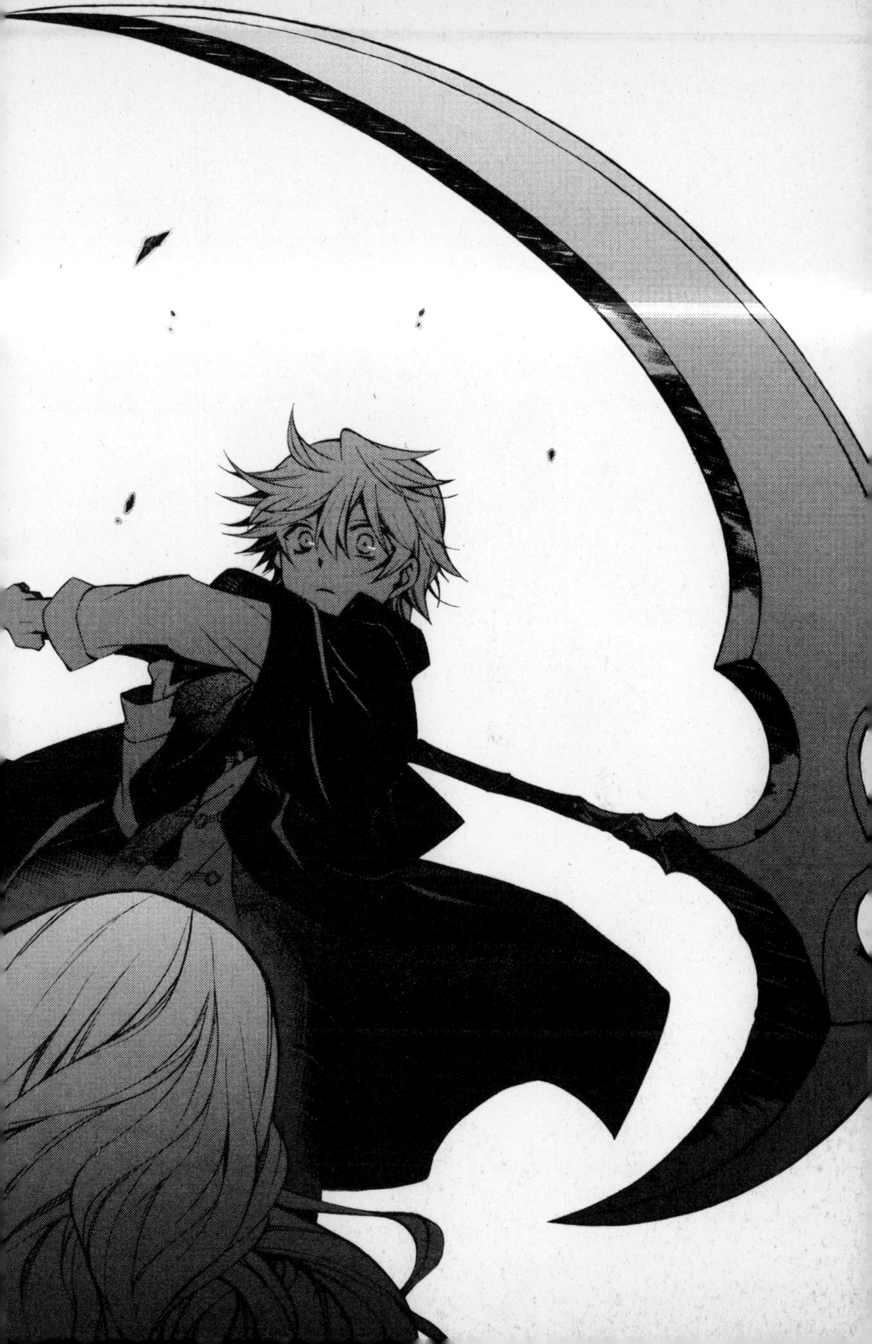

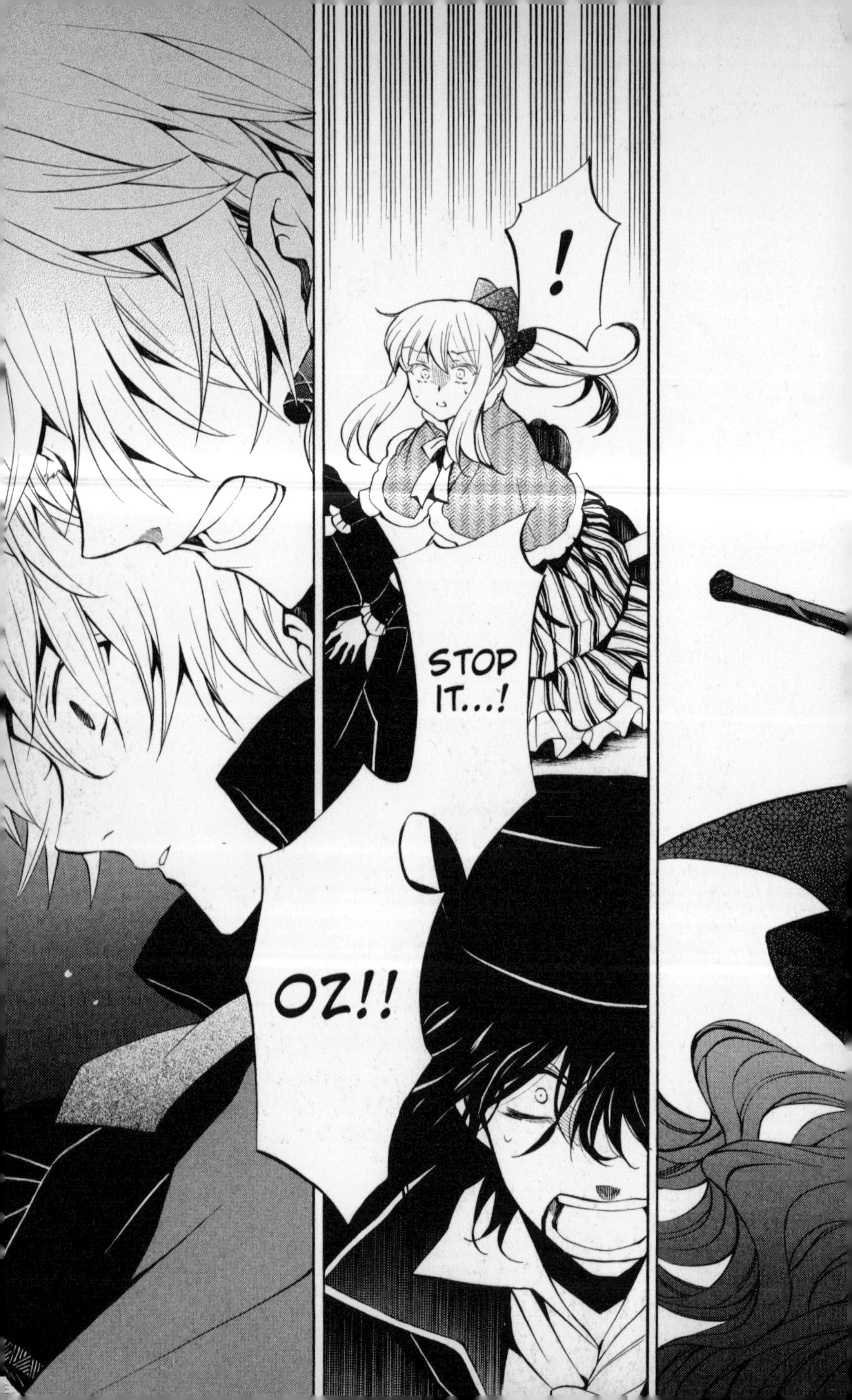
!
STOP IT...!
OZ!!

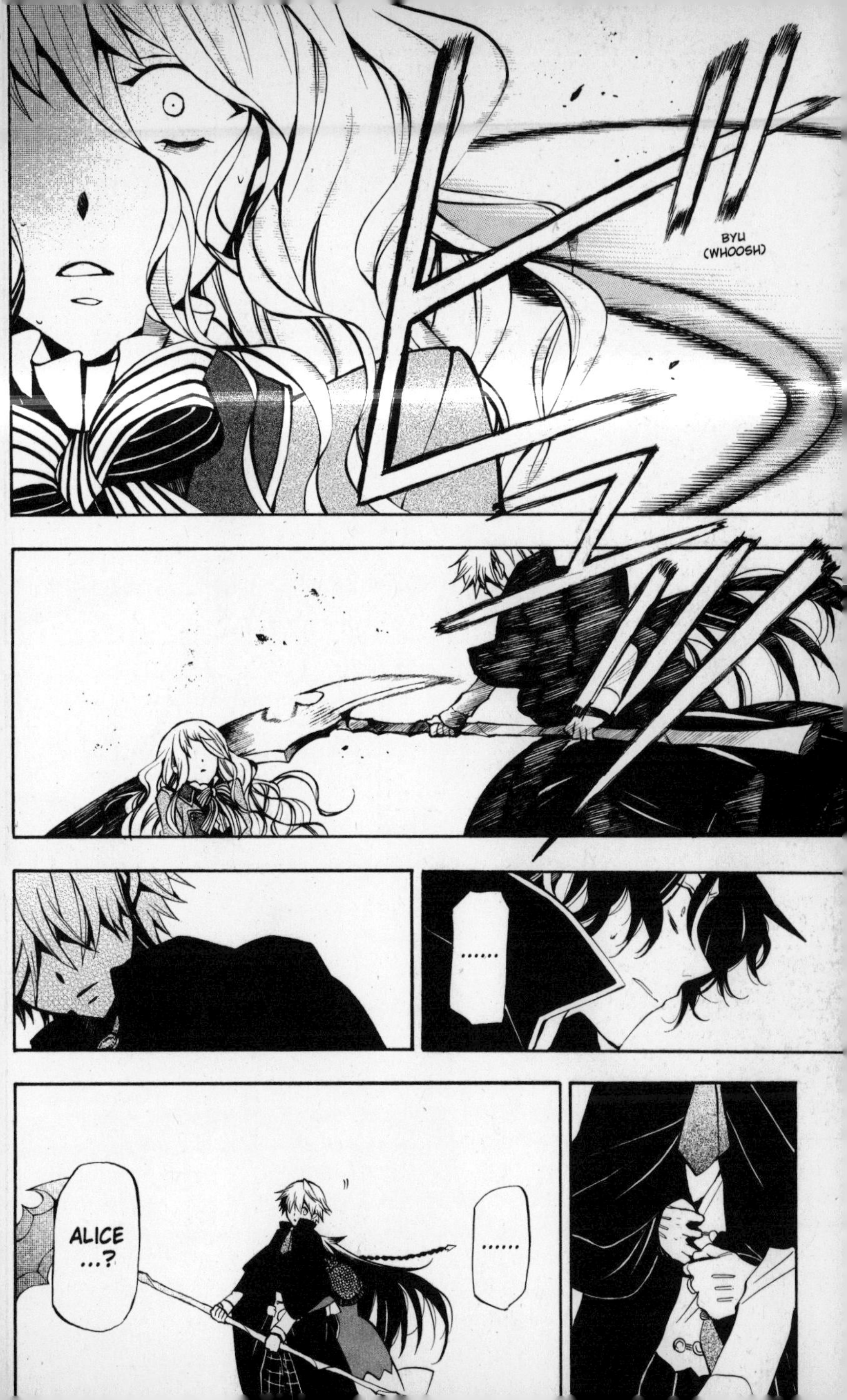
BYU
(WHOOSH)
......
......
ALICE
...?

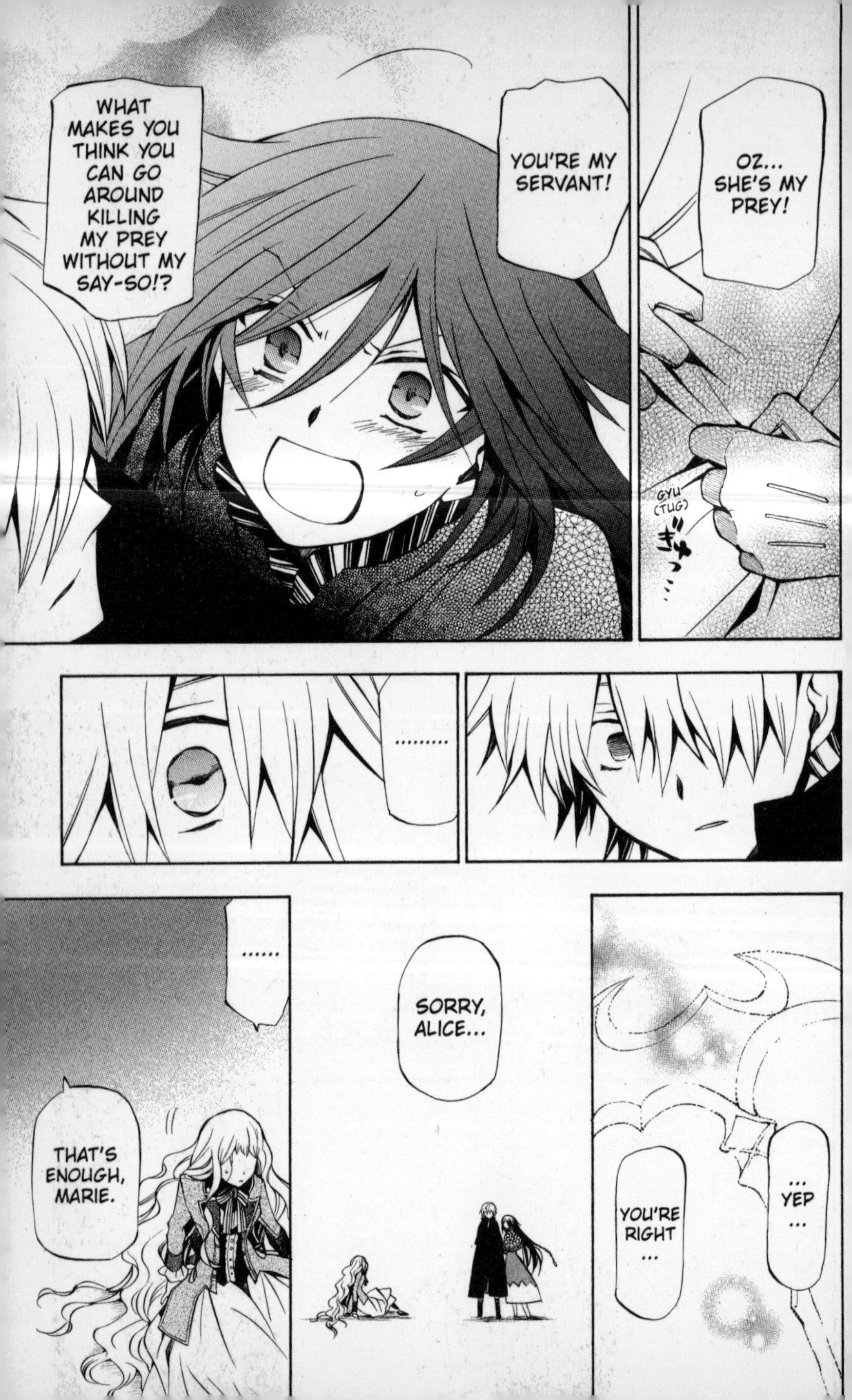
OZ... SHE'S MY PREY!
GYU (TUG)
ぎゅっ
YOU'RE MY SERVANT!
WHAT MAKES YOU THINK YOU CAN GO AROUND KILLING MY PREY WITHOUT MY SAY-SO!?
....
... YEP ...
YOU'RE RIGHT ...
SORRY, ALICE...
......
THAT'S ENOUGH, MARIE.

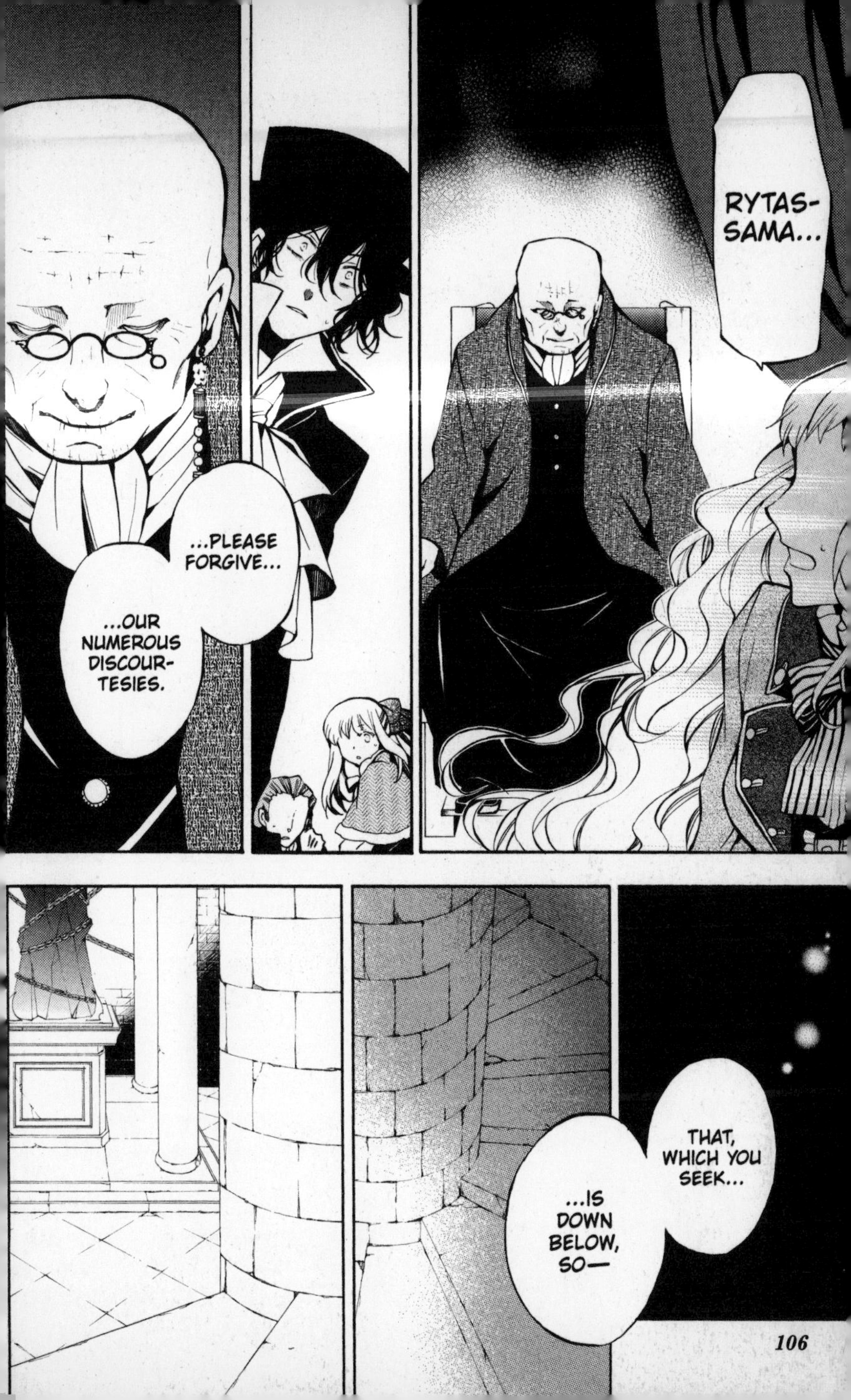
RYTAS-SAMA...
...PLEASE FORGIVE...
...OUR NUMEROUS DISCOURTESIES.
THAT, WHICH YOU SEEK...
...IS DOWN BELOW, SO—

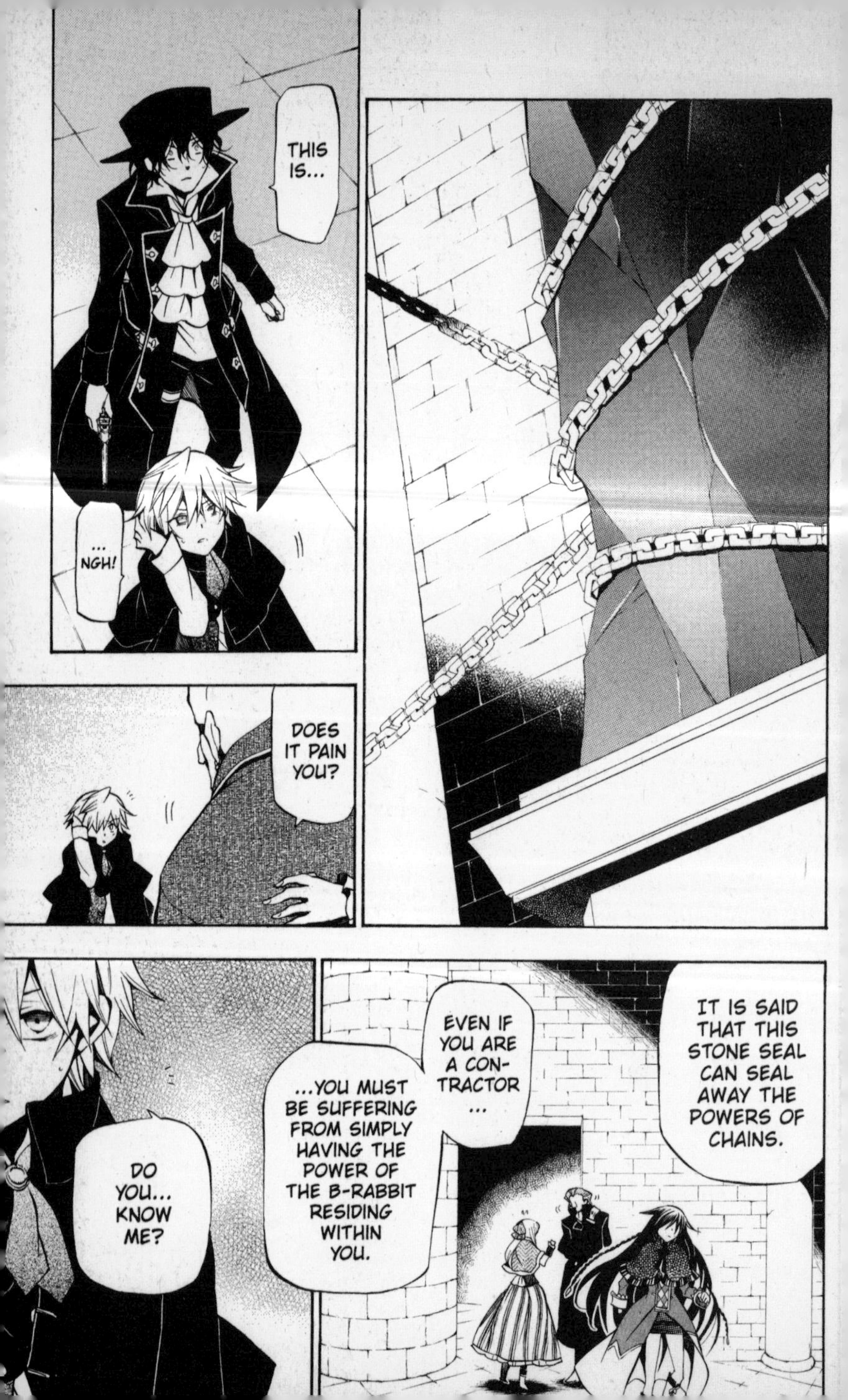
THIS IS...
...NGH!
DOES IT PAIN YOU?
IT IS SAID THAT THIS STONE SEAL CAN SEAL AWAY THE POWERS OF CHAINS.
EVEN IF YOU ARE A CON-TRACTOR...
...YOU MUST BE SUFFERING FROM SIMPLY HAVING THE POWER OF THE B-RABBIT RESIDING WITHIN YOU.
DO YOU... KNOW ME?

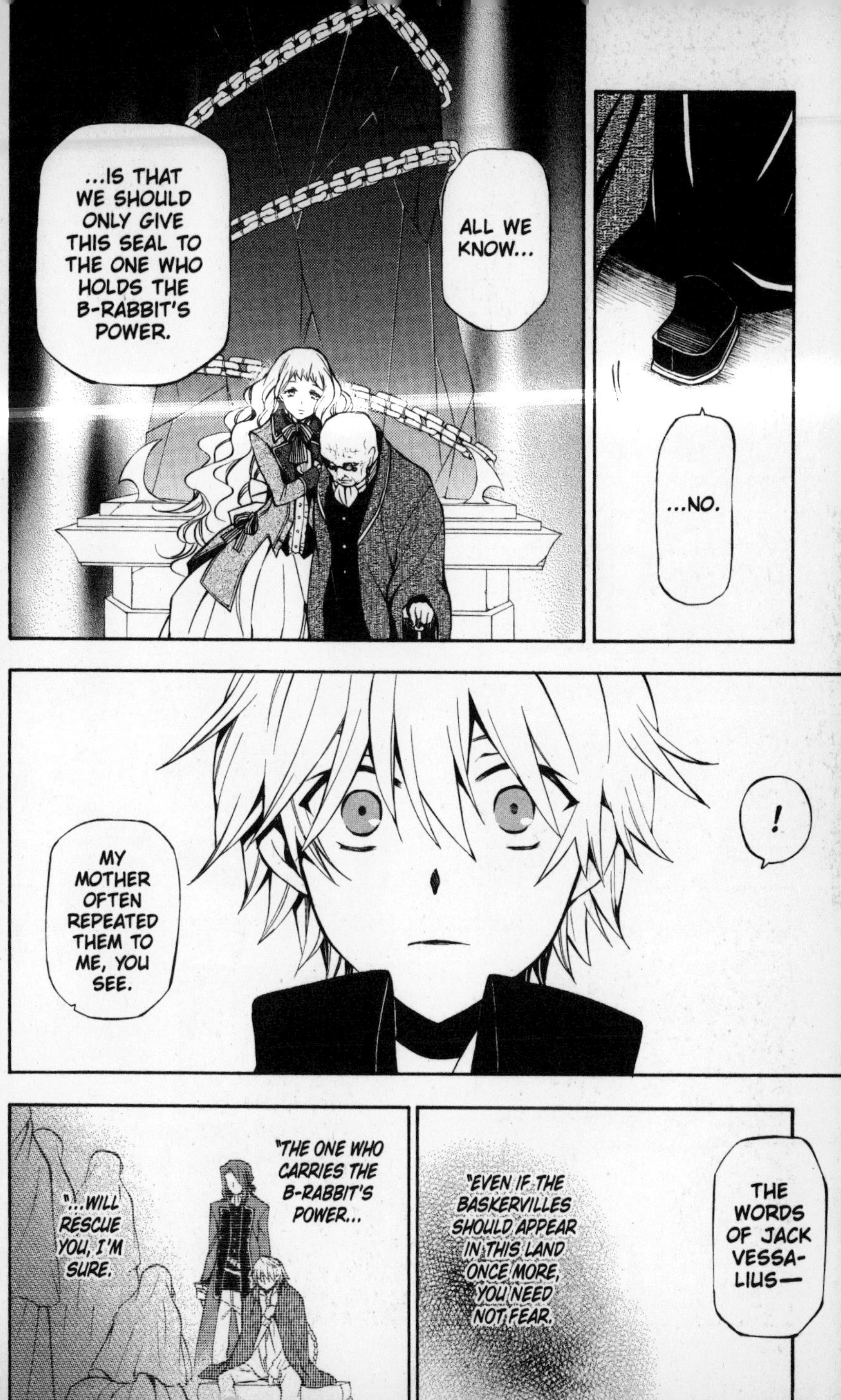
...NO.
ALL WE KNOW...
...IS THAT WE SHOULD ONLY GIVE THIS SEAL TO THE ONE WHO HOLDS THE B-RABBIT'S POWER.
!
MY MOTHER OFTEN REPEATED THEM TO ME, YOU SEE.
THE WORDS OF JACK VESSA-LIUS—
"EVEN IF THE BASKERVILLES SHOULD APPEAR IN THIS LAND ONCE MORE, YOU NEED NOT FEAR.
"THE ONE WHO CARRIES THE B-RABBIT'S POWER...
"...WILL RESCUE YOU, I'M SURE.

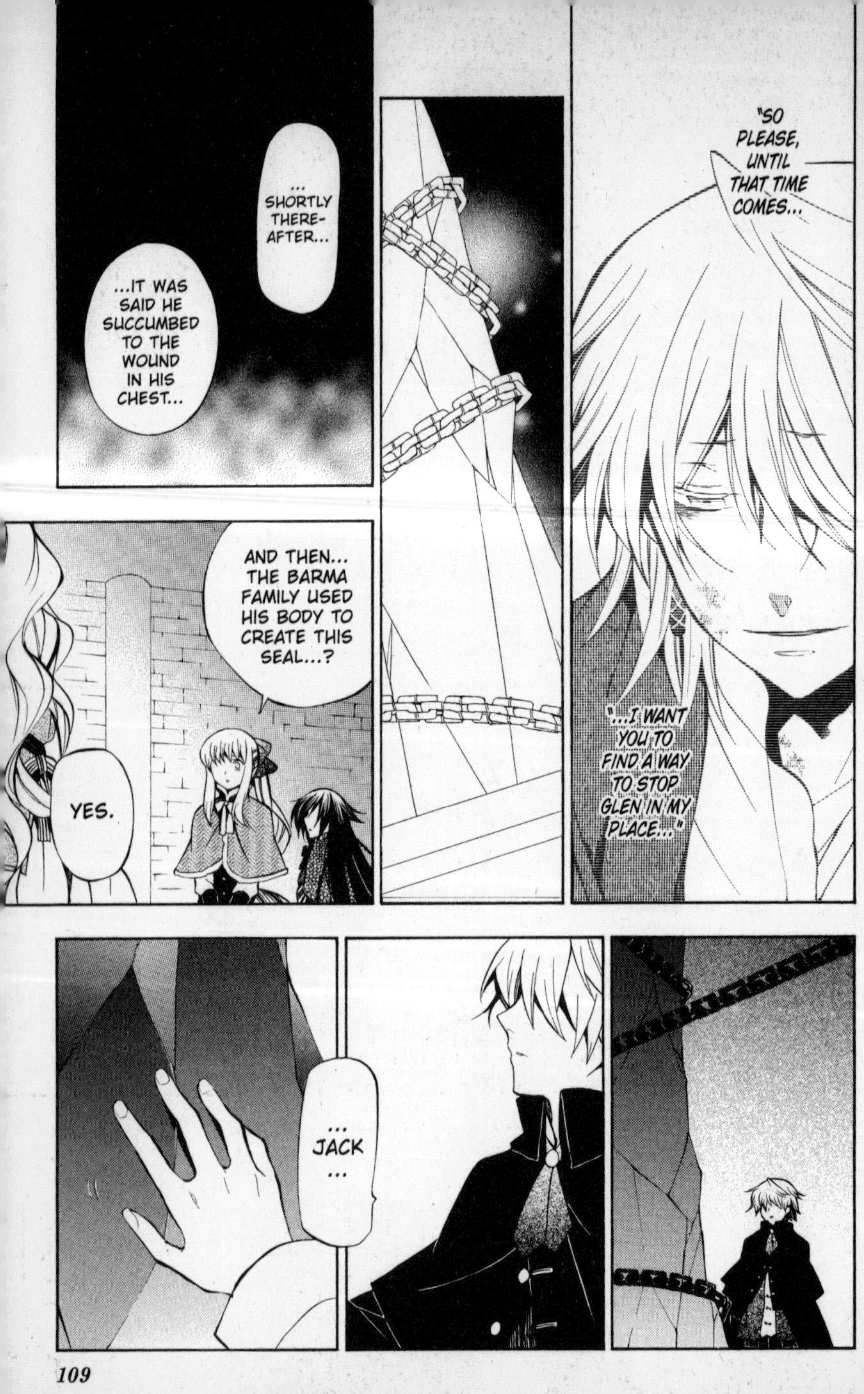
"SO PLEASE, UNTIL THAT TIME COMES...
"...I WANT YOU TO FIND A WAY TO STOP GLEN IN MY PLACE..."
...SHORTLY THERE-AFTER...
...IT WAS SAID HE SUCCUMBED TO THE WOUND IN HIS CHEST...
AND THEN... THE BARMA FAMILY USED HIS BODY TO CREATE THIS SEAL...?
YES.
...JACK...

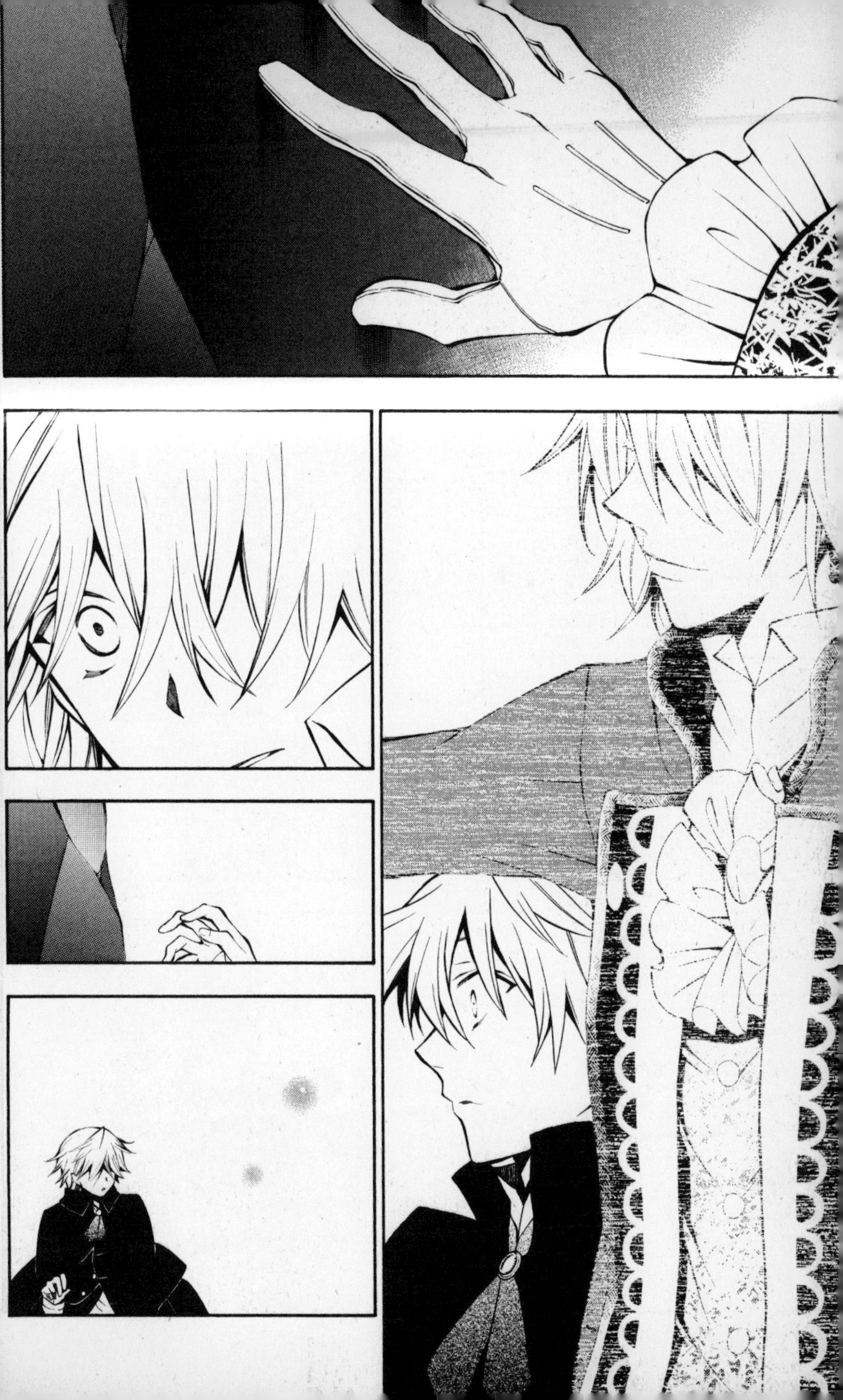

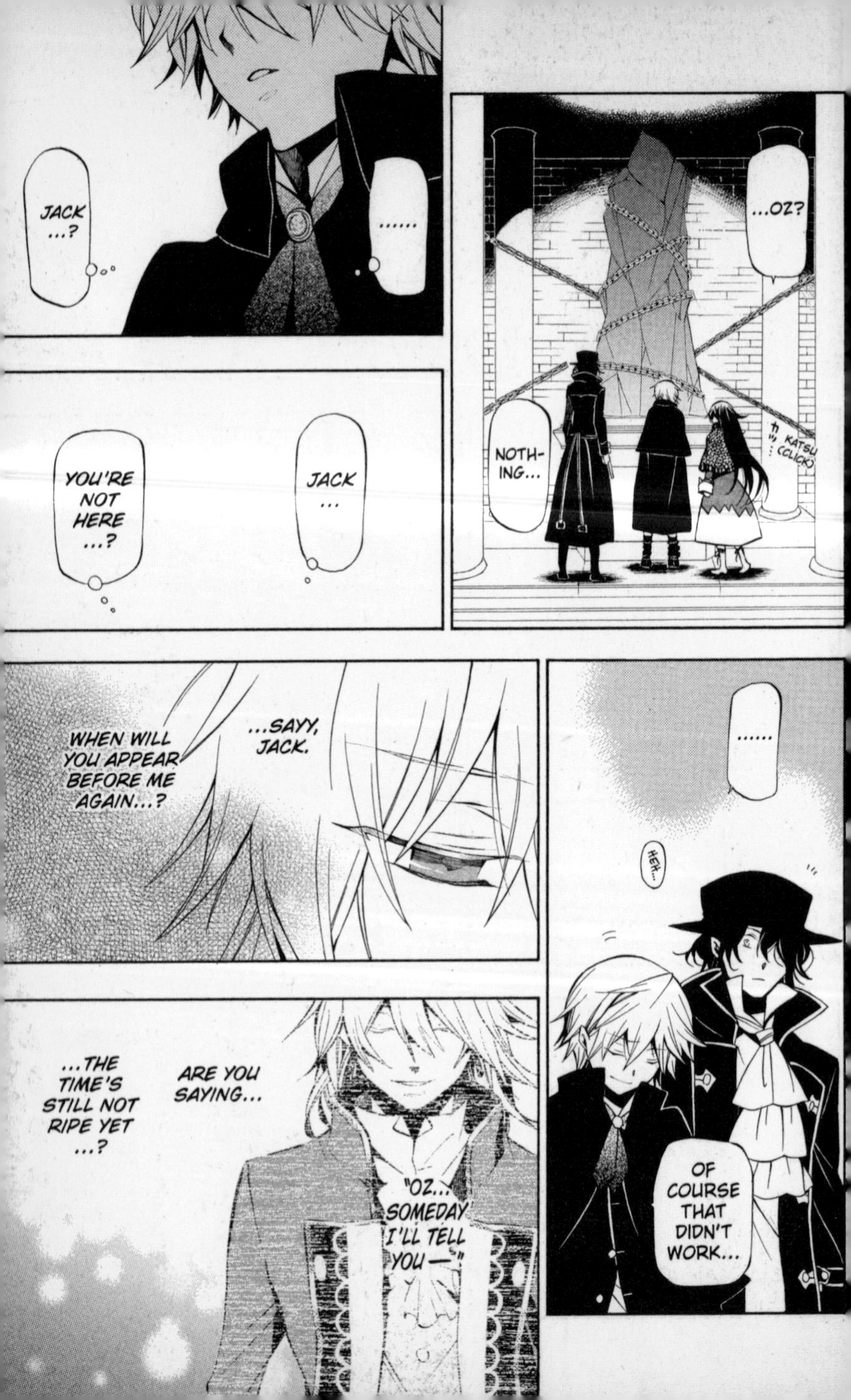
...OZ?
NOTHING...
KATSU (CLICK)
......
JACK ...?
JACK ...
YOU'RE NOT HERE ...?
......
HEH...
OF COURSE THAT DIDN'T WORK...
...SAYY, JACK.
WHEN WILL YOU APPEAR BEFORE ME AGAIN...?
ARE YOU SAYING...
...THE TIME'S STILL NOT RIPE YET ...?
"OZ... SOMEDAY I'LL TELL YOU—"

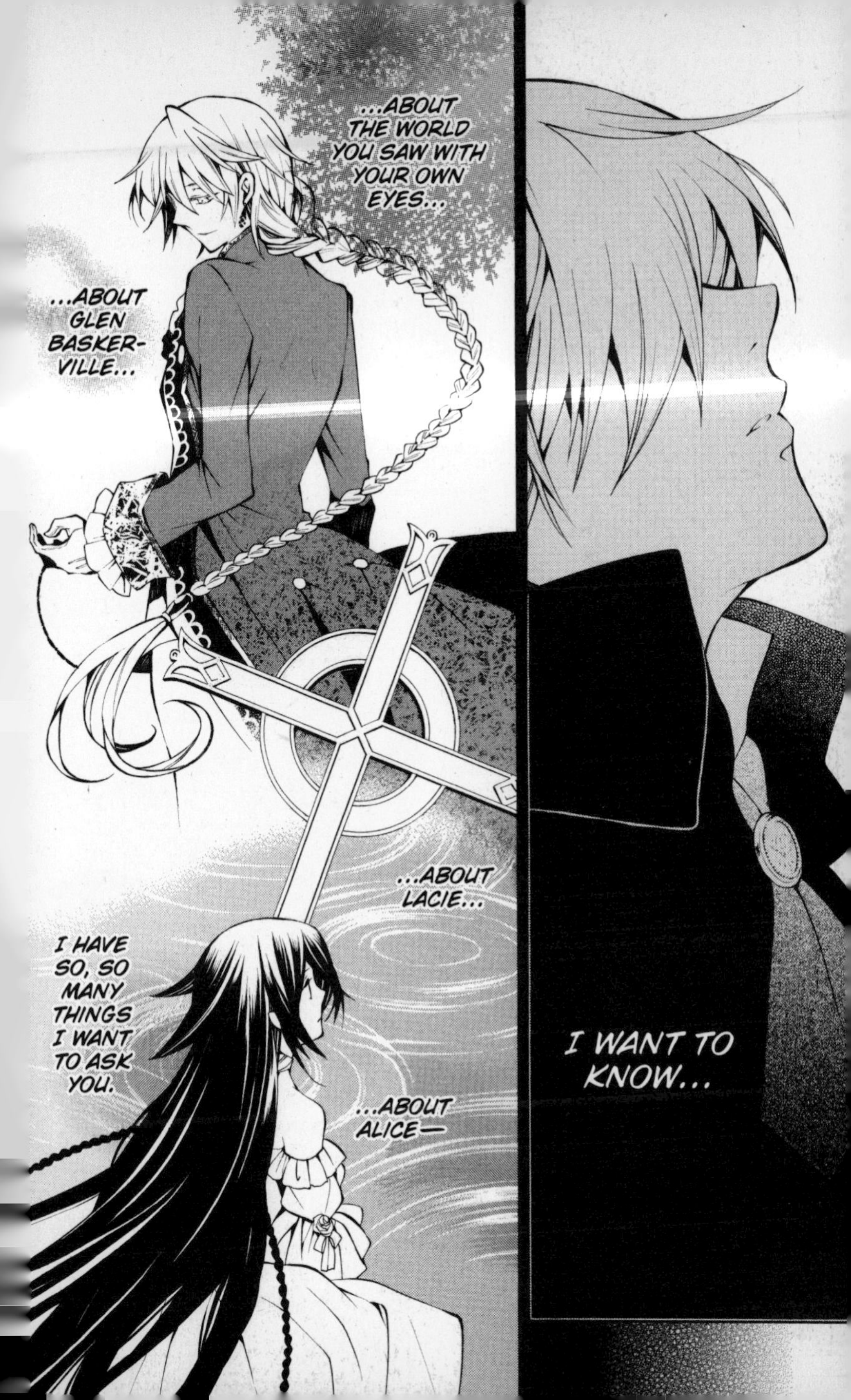
I WANT TO KNOW...
...ABOUT THE WORLD YOU SAW WITH YOUR OWN EYES...
...ABOUT GLEN BASKER-VILLE...
...ABOUT LACIE...
I HAVE SO, SO MANY THINGS I WANT TO ASK YOU.
...ABOUT ALICE—

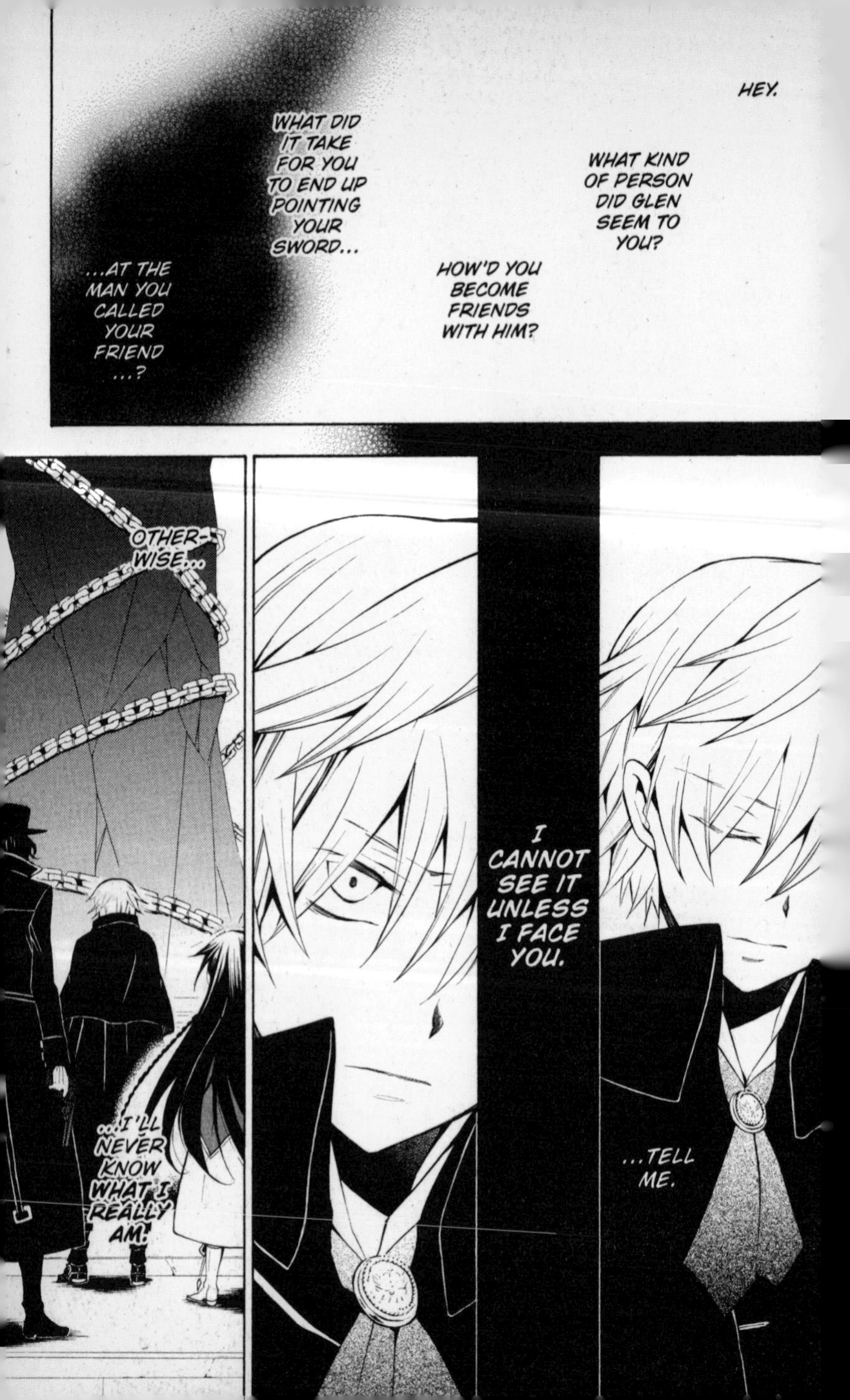
HEY.
WHAT KIND OF PERSON DID GLEN SEEM TO YOU?
HOW'D YOU BECOME FRIENDS WITH HIM?
WHAT DID IT TAKE FOR YOU TO END UP POINTING YOUR SWORD...
...AT THE MAN YOU CALLED YOUR FRIEND...?
...TELL ME.
I CANNOT SEE IT UNLESS I FACE YOU.
OTHER-WISE...
...I'LL NEVER KNOW WHAT I REALLY AM!

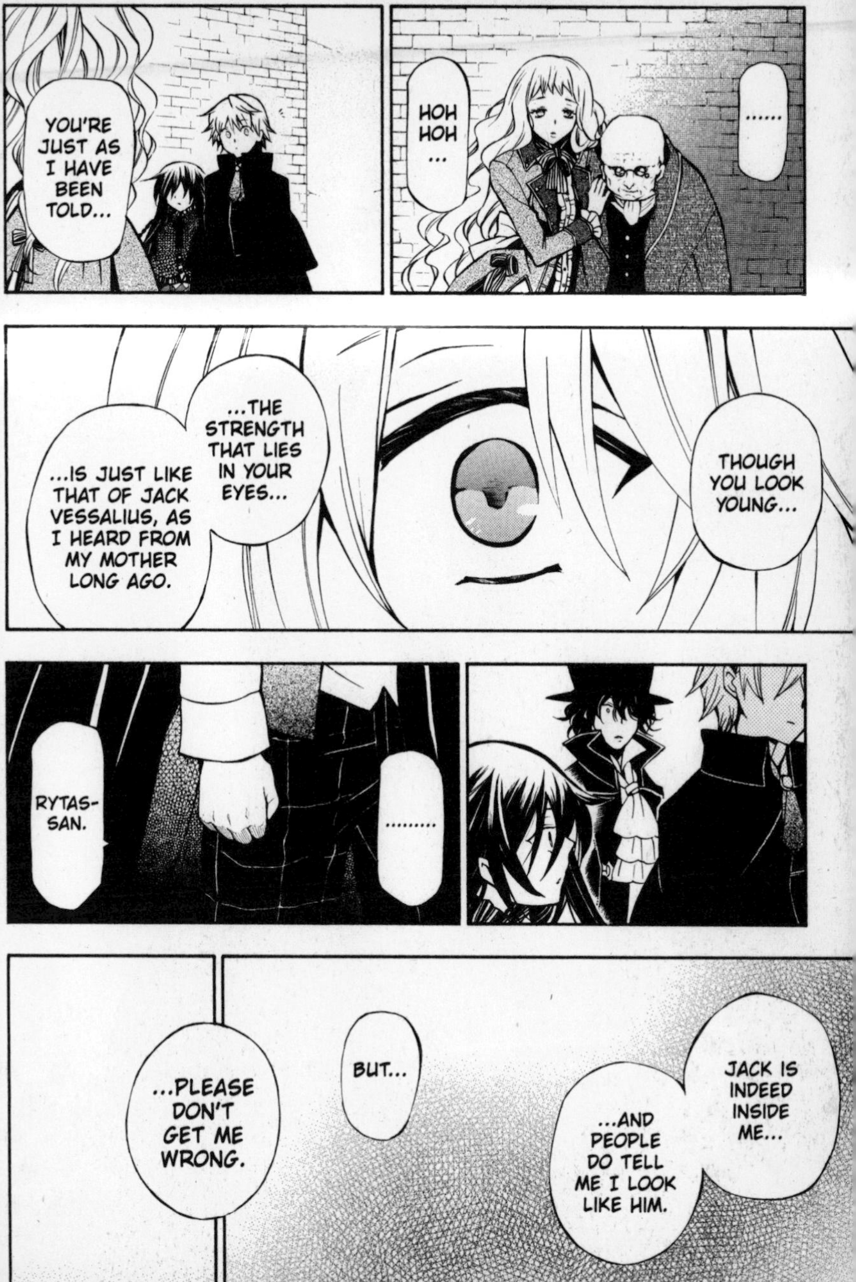
......
HOH HOH ...
YOU'RE JUST AS I HAVE BEEN TOLD...
THOUGH YOU LOOK YOUNG...
...THE STRENGTH THAT LIES IN YOUR EYES...
...IS JUST LIKE THAT OF JACK VESSALIUS, AS I HEARD FROM MY MOTHER LONG AGO.
....
RYTAS-SAN.
JACK IS INDEED INSIDE ME...
...AND PEOPLE DO TELL ME I LOOK LIKE HIM.
BUT...
...PLEASE DON'T GET ME WRONG.

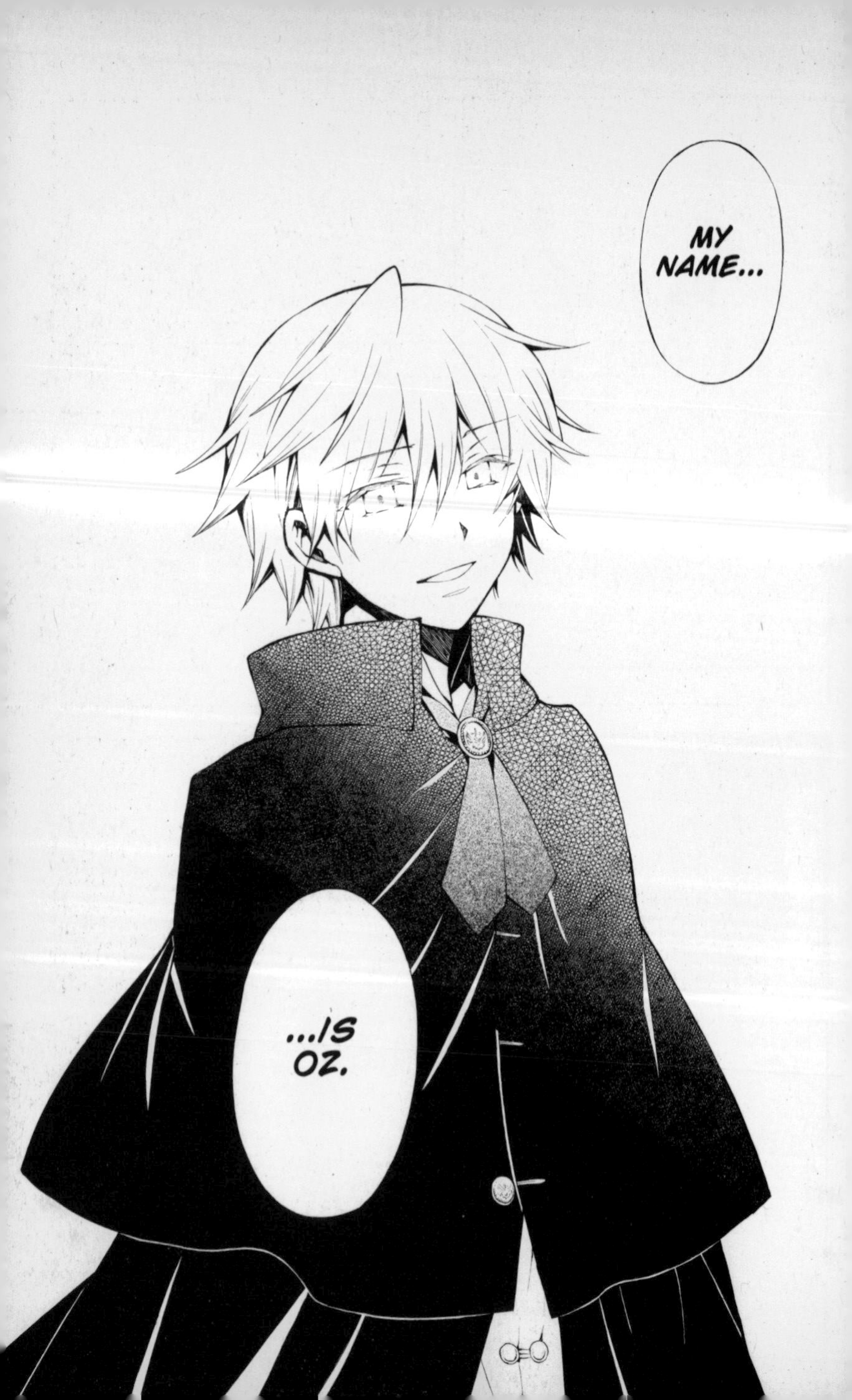
MY NAME...
...IS OZ.

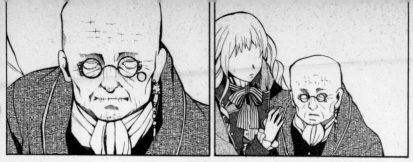

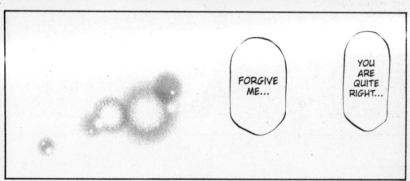

FORGIVE ME...

YOU ARE QUITE RIGHT...

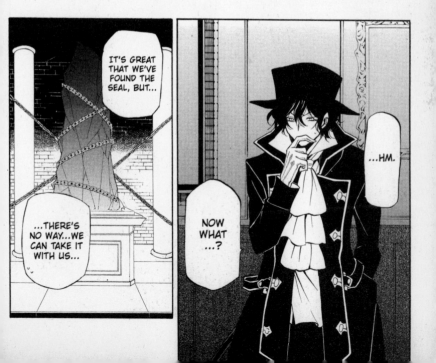

IT'S GREAT THAT WE'VE FOUND THE SEAL, BUT...

...THERE'S NO WAY...WE CAN TAKE IT WITH US...

NOW WHAT...?

...HM.

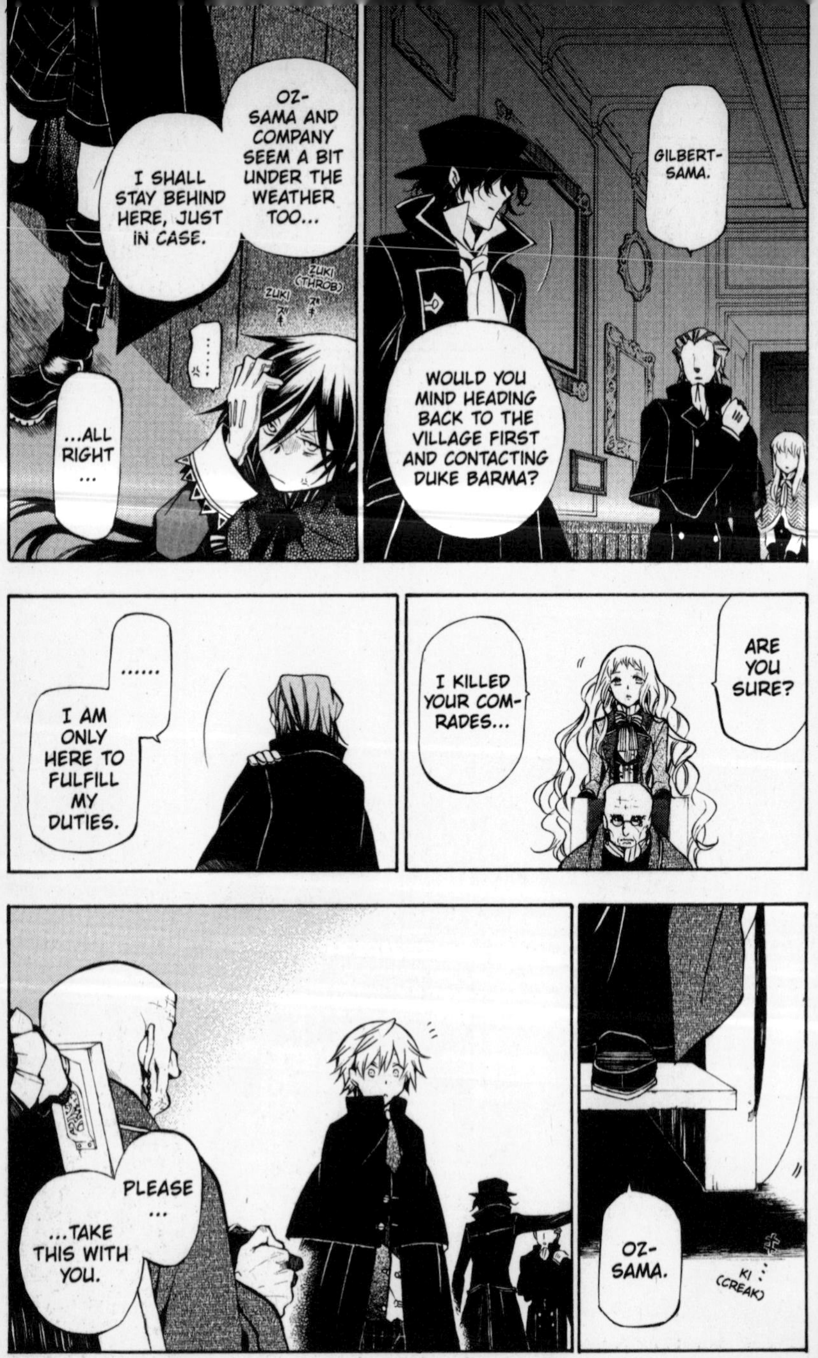
GILBERT-SAMA.
WOULD YOU MIND HEADING BACK TO THE VILLAGE FIRST AND CONTACTING DUKE BARMA?
OZ-SAMA AND COMPANY SEEM A BIT UNDER THE WEATHER TOO...
I SHALL STAY BEHIND HERE, JUST IN CASE.
ZUKI (THROB)
ZUKI
......
...ALL RIGHT...
ARE YOU SURE?
I KILLED YOUR COMRADES...
......
I AM ONLY HERE TO FULFILL MY DUTIES.
OZ-SAMA.
KI... (CREAK)
PLEASE...
...TAKE THIS WITH YOU.

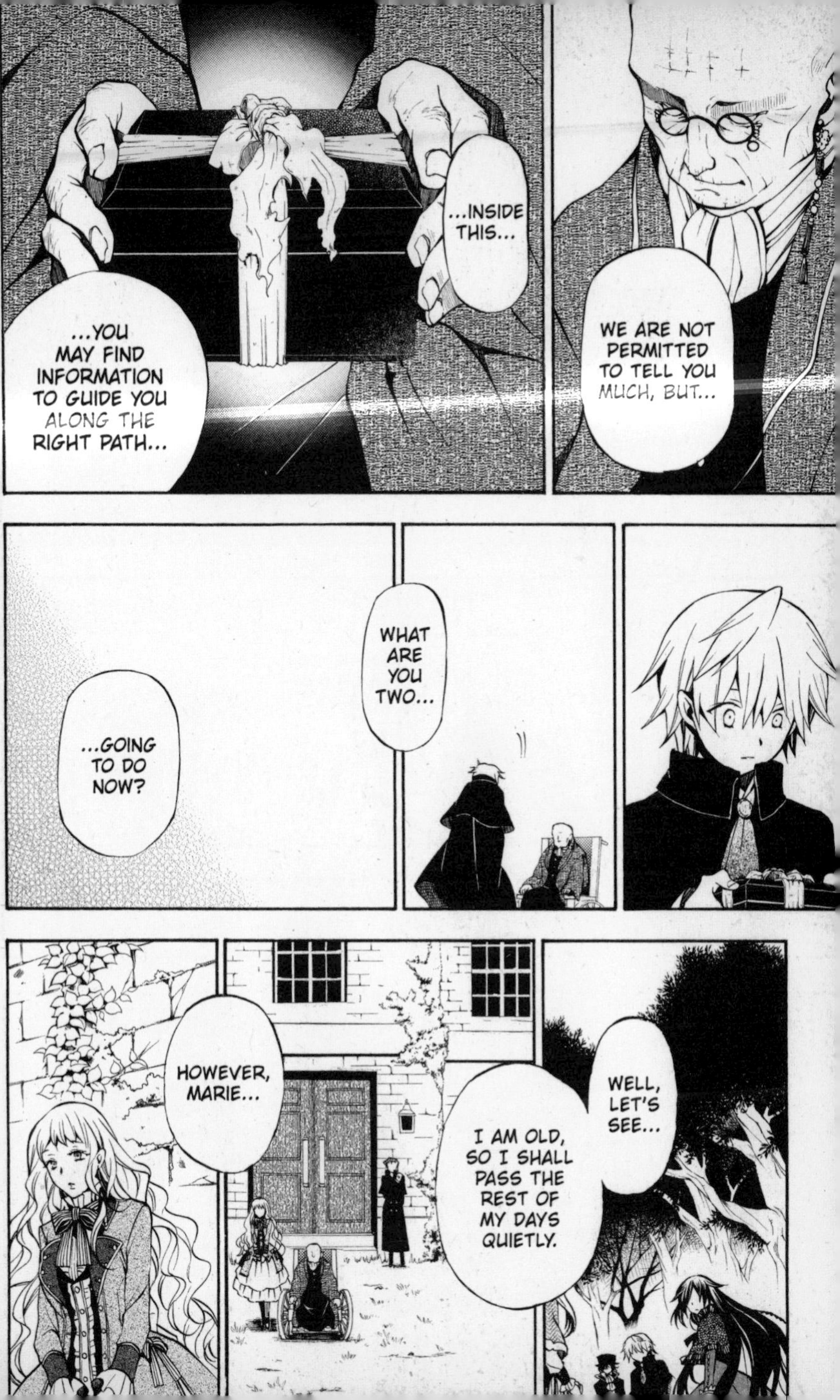
WE ARE NOT PERMITTED TO TELL YOU MUCH, BUT...
...INSIDE THIS...
...YOU MAY FIND INFORMATION TO GUIDE YOU ALONG THE RIGHT PATH...
WHAT ARE YOU TWO...
...GOING TO DO NOW?
WELL, LET'S SEE...
I AM OLD, SO I SHALL PASS THE REST OF MY DAYS QUIETLY.
HOWEVER, MARIE...

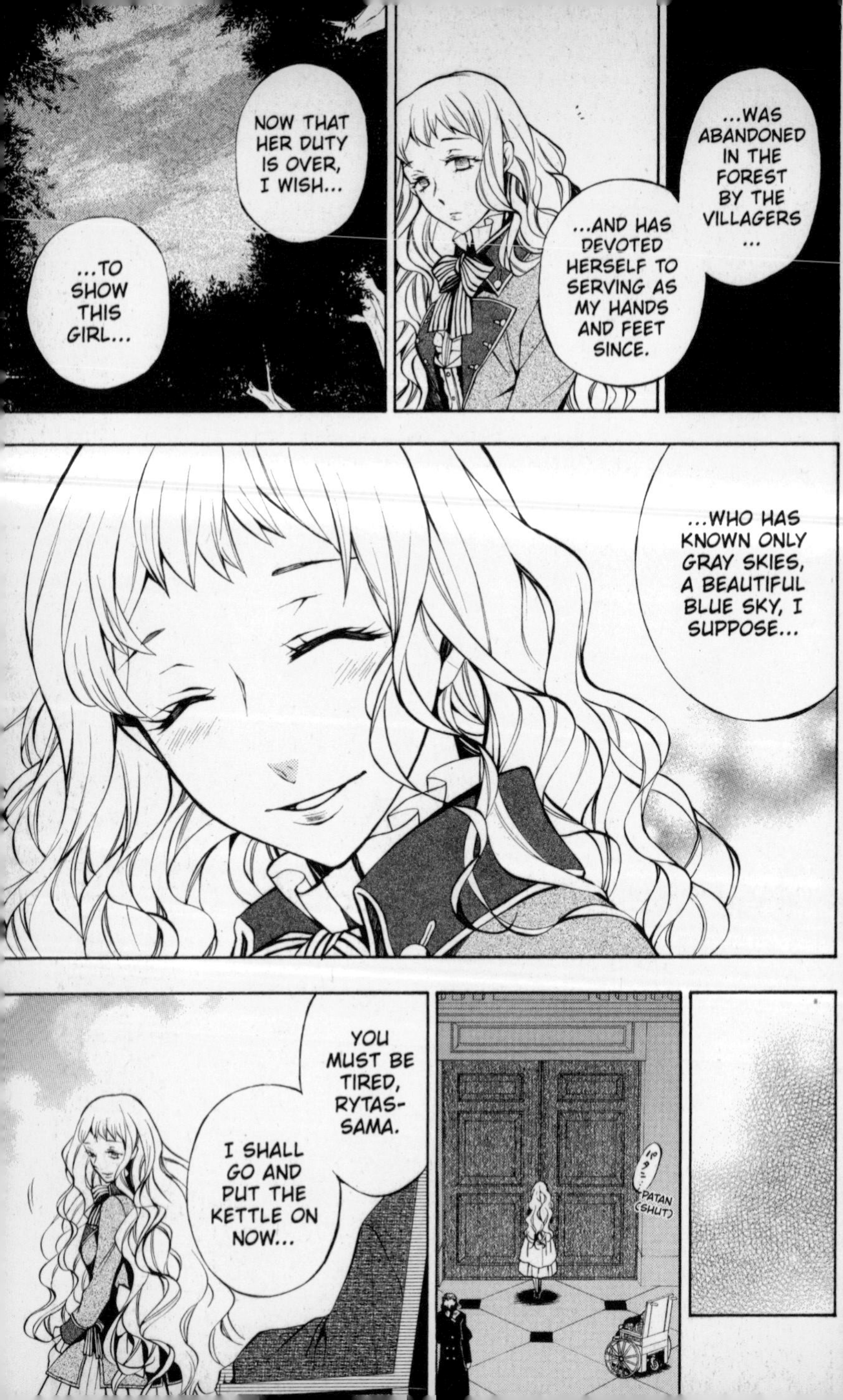
...WAS ABANDONED IN THE FOREST BY THE VILLAGERS ...
...AND HAS DEVOTED HERSELF TO SERVING AS MY HANDS AND FEET SINCE.
NOW THAT HER DUTY IS OVER, I WISH...
...TO SHOW THIS GIRL...
...WHO HAS KNOWN ONLY GRAY SKIES, A BEAUTIFUL BLUE SKY, I SUPPOSE...
パタン
PATAN (SHUT)
YOU MUST BE TIRED, RYTAS-SAMA.
I SHALL GO AND PUT THE KETTLE ON NOW...

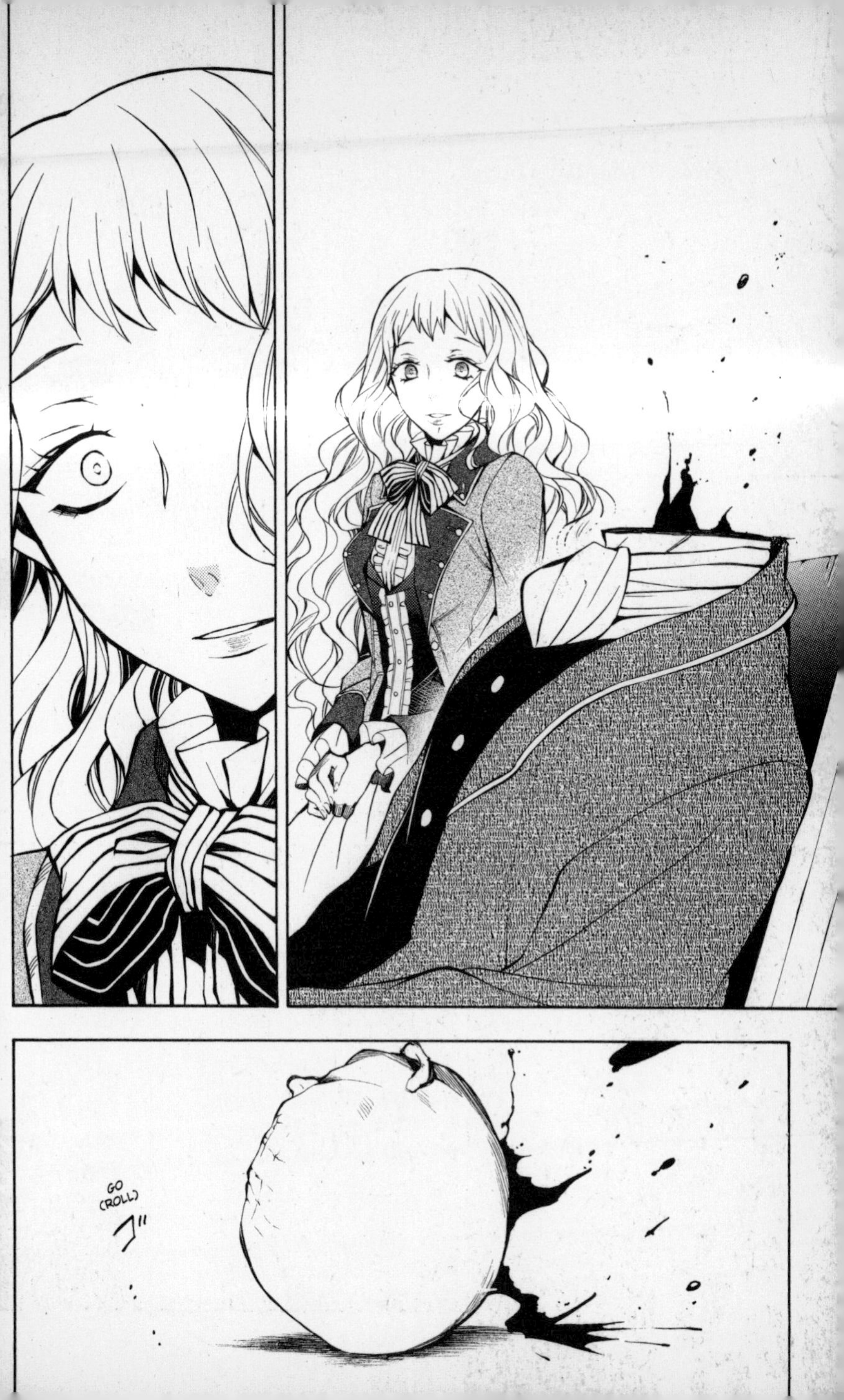
GO
(ROLL)
ゴ”

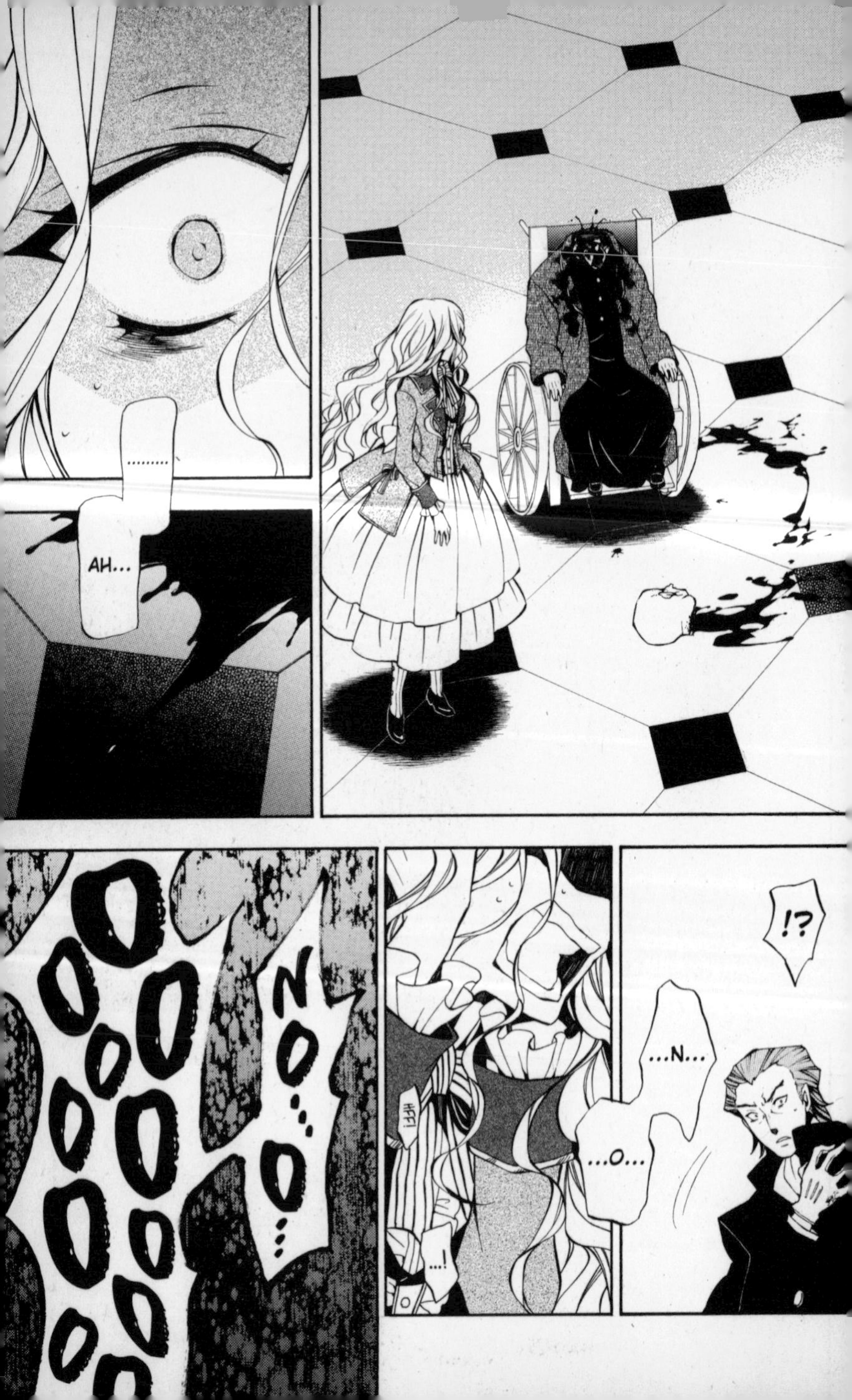
....
AH...
!?
...N...
...O...
HFF!
...!
NO......

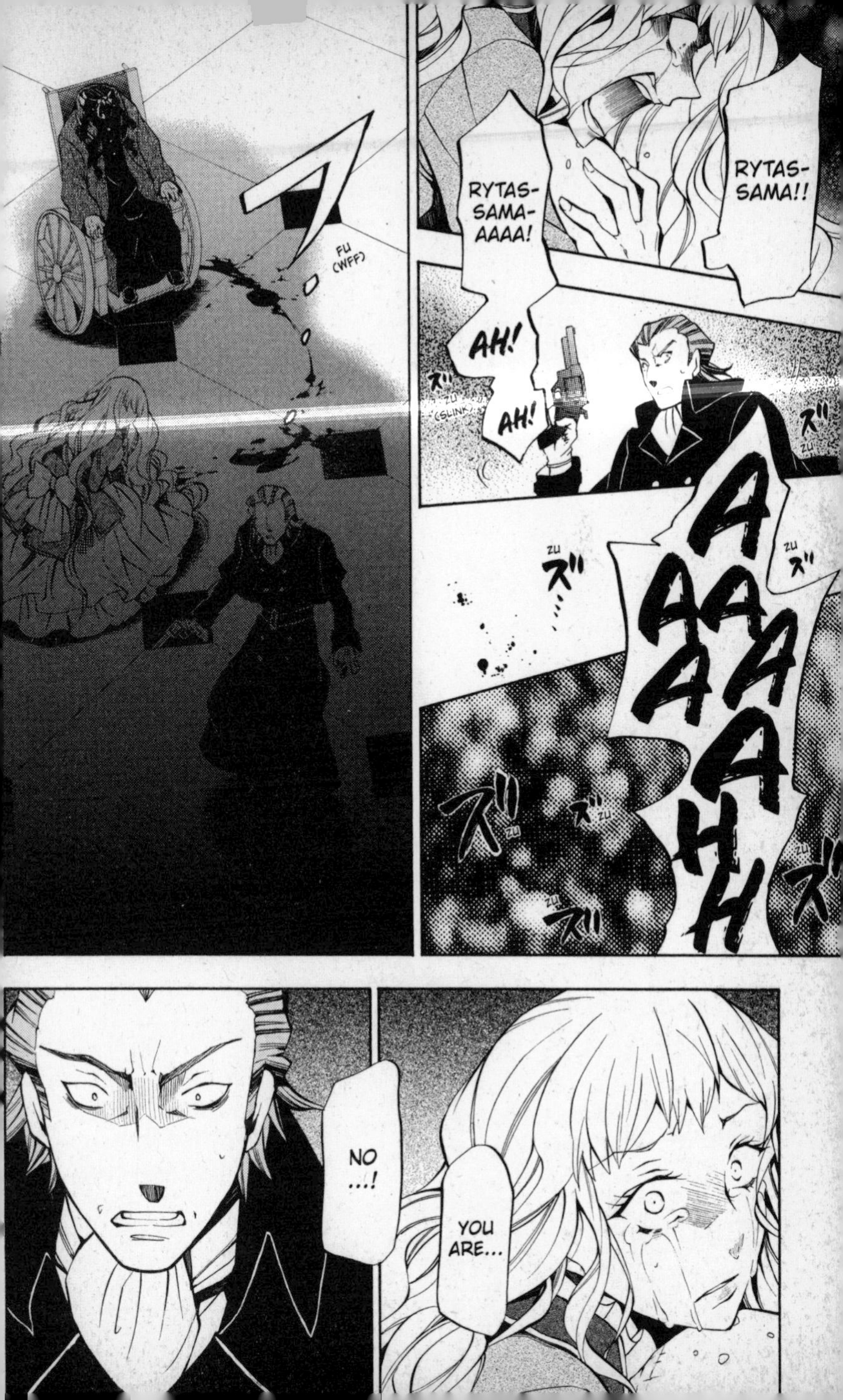
RYTAS-SAMA!!
RYTAS-SAMA-AAAAA!
AH!
ズ ZU (SLINK)
AH!
ズ ZU
AAAAAAAAH
ズ ZU
ズ ZU
ズ ZU
ズ ZU
ズ ZU
ズ ZU
FU (WFF)
YOU ARE...
NO ...!

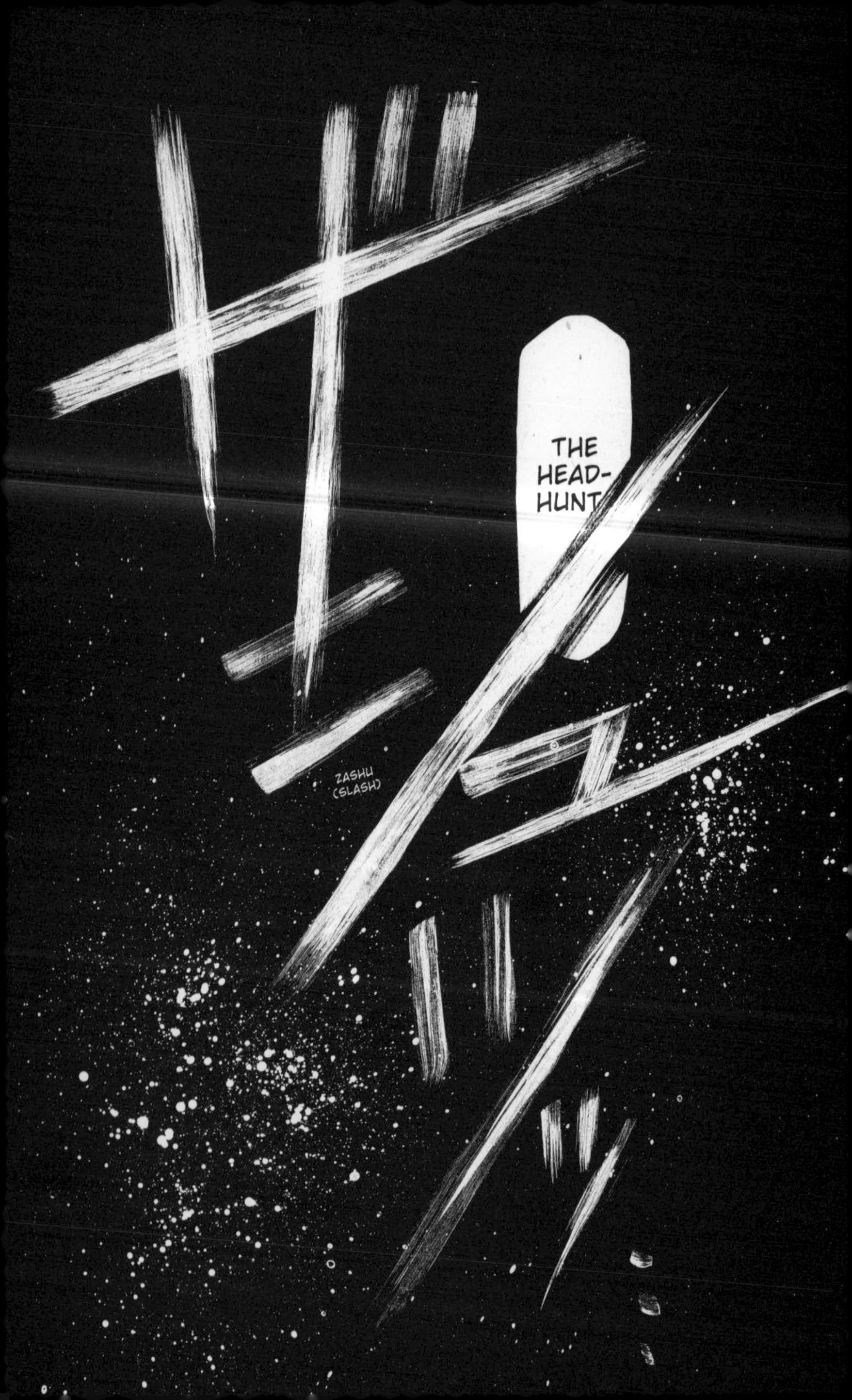
THE HEAD-HUNT
ZASHU (SLASH)

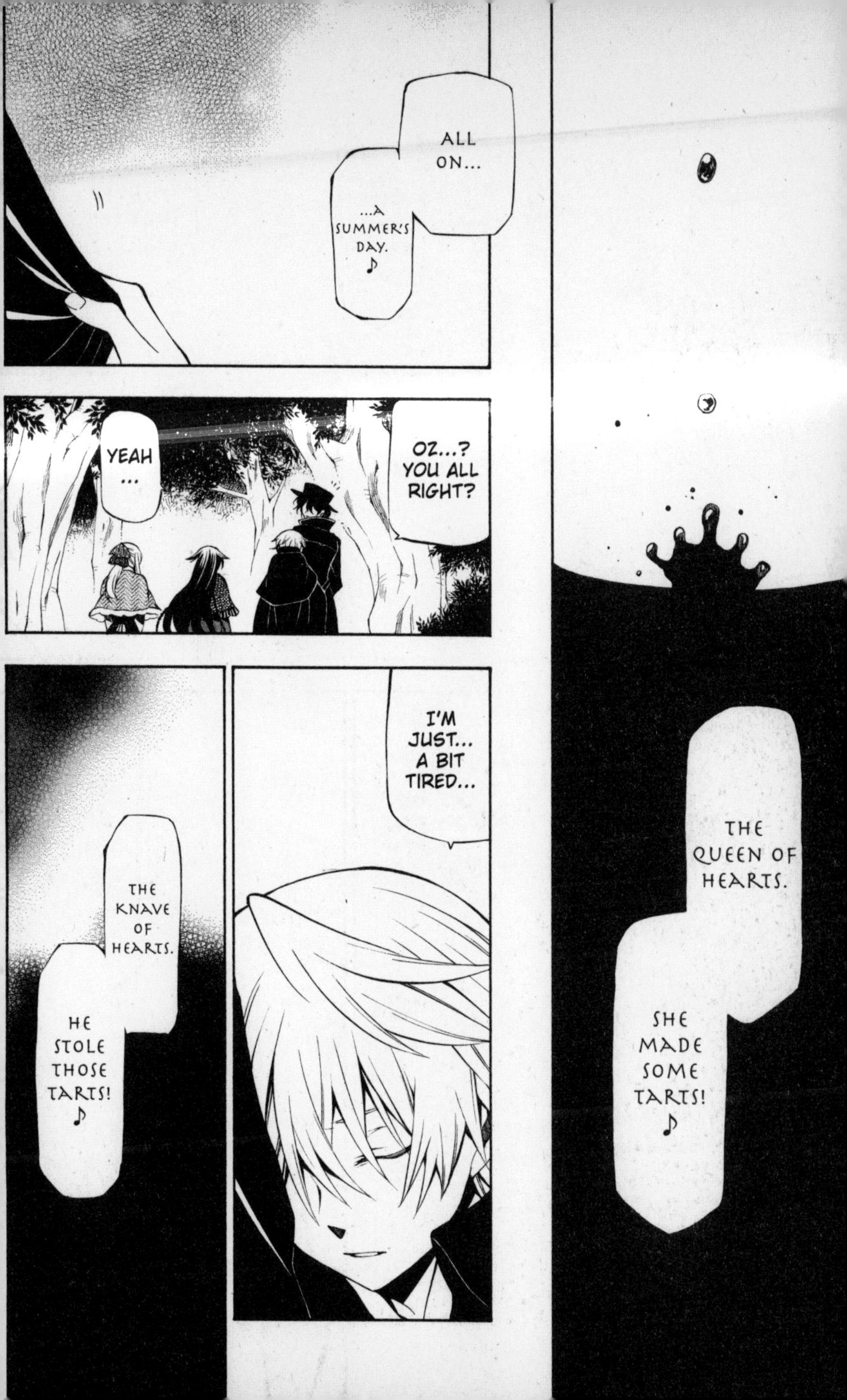
THE QUEEN OF HEARTS.
SHE MADE SOME TARTS! ♪
ALL ON...
...A SUMMER'S DAY. ♪
OZ...? YOU ALL RIGHT?
YEAH ...
I'M JUST... A BIT TIRED...
THE KNAVE OF HEARTS.
HE STOLE THOSE TARTS! ♪

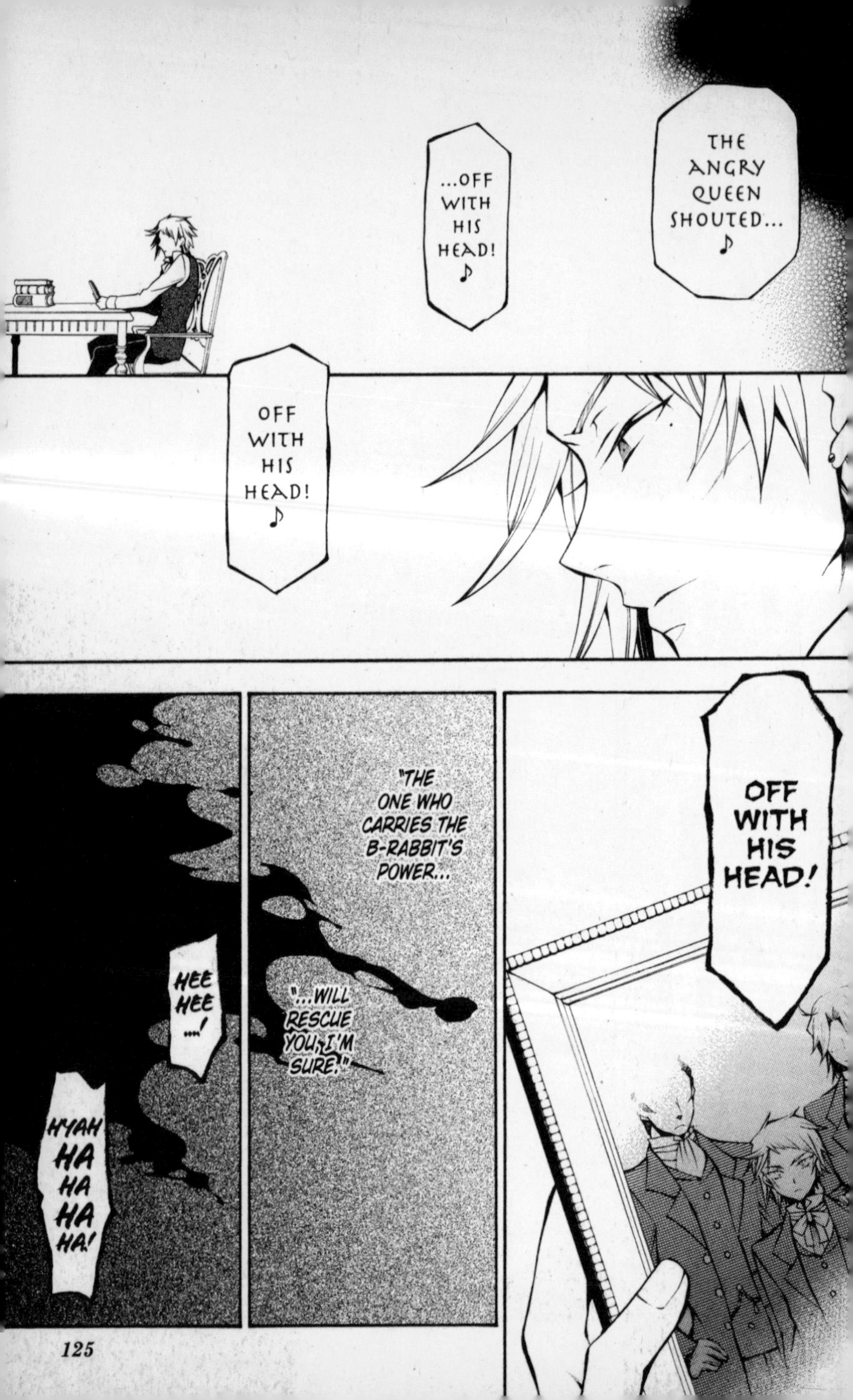
THE ANGRY QUEEN SHOUTED... ♪
...OFF WITH HIS HEAD! ♪
OFF WITH HIS HEAD! ♪
OFF WITH HIS HEAD!
"THE ONE WHO CARRIES THE B-RABBIT'S POWER...
"...WILL RESCUE YOU, I'M SURE."
HEE HEE...!
HYAH HA HA HA HA!

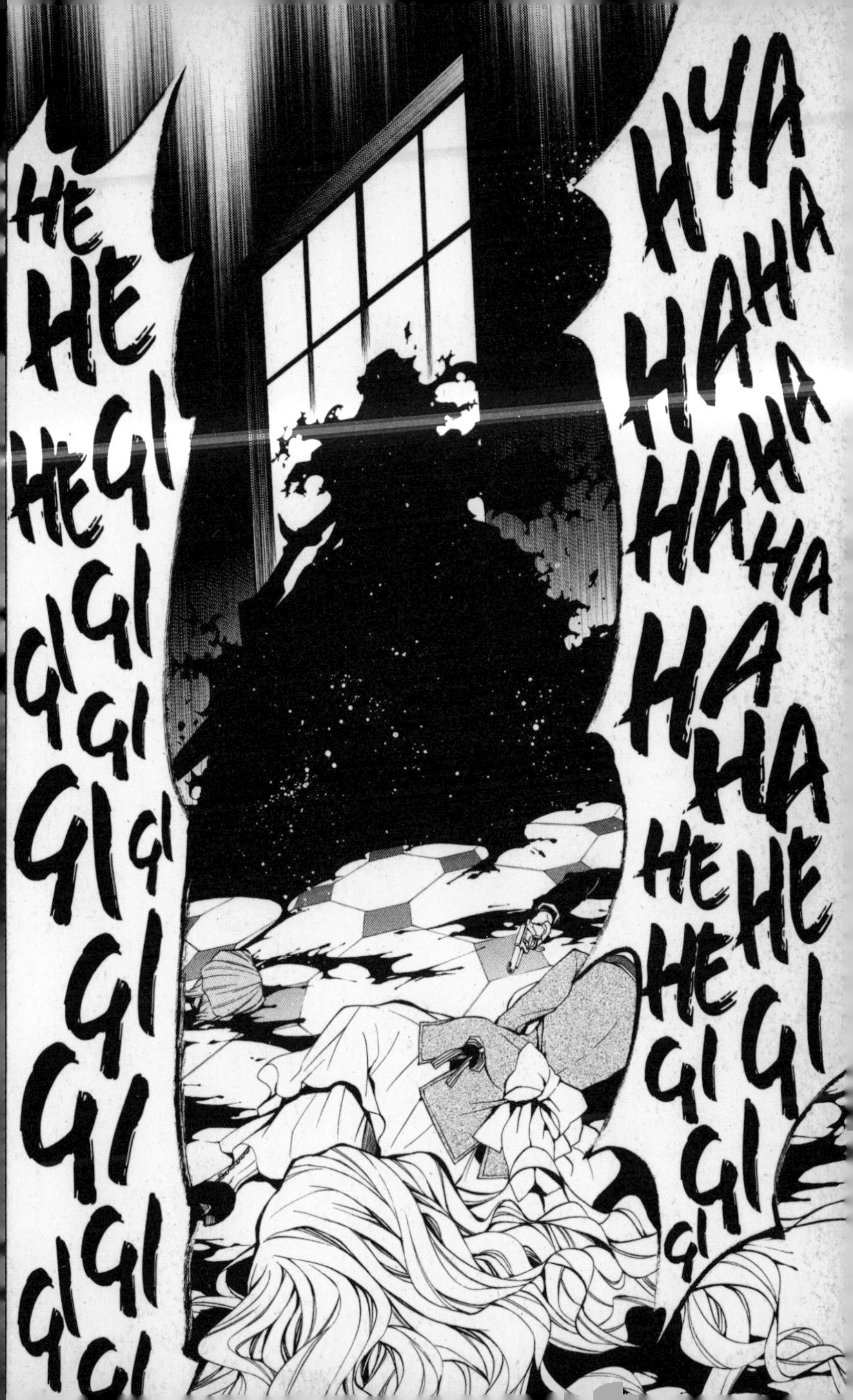
HYAHAHAHAHAHAHAHAHAHEHEHEHEGIGIGIGIGI
HEHEHEGIGIGIGIGIGIGIGIGIGIGIGIGIGIGI

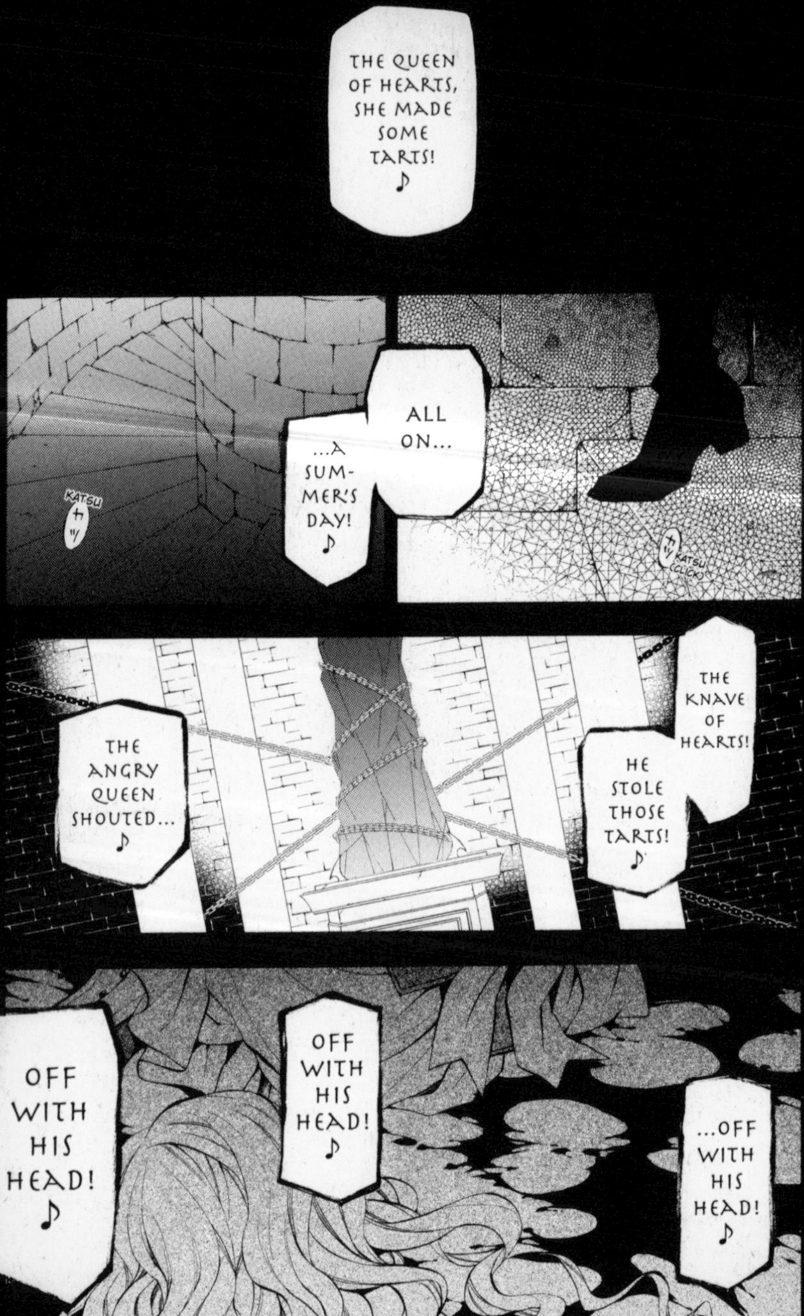
THE QUEEN OF HEARTS, SHE MADE SOME TARTS! ♪
KATSU (CLICK)
ALL ON...
...A SUMMER'S DAY! ♪
KATSU
THE KNAVE OF HEARTS!
HE STOLE THOSE TARTS! ♪
THE ANGRY QUEEN SHOUTED... ♪
...OFF WITH HIS HEAD! ♪
OFF WITH HIS HEAD! ♪
OFF WITH HIS HEAD! ♪

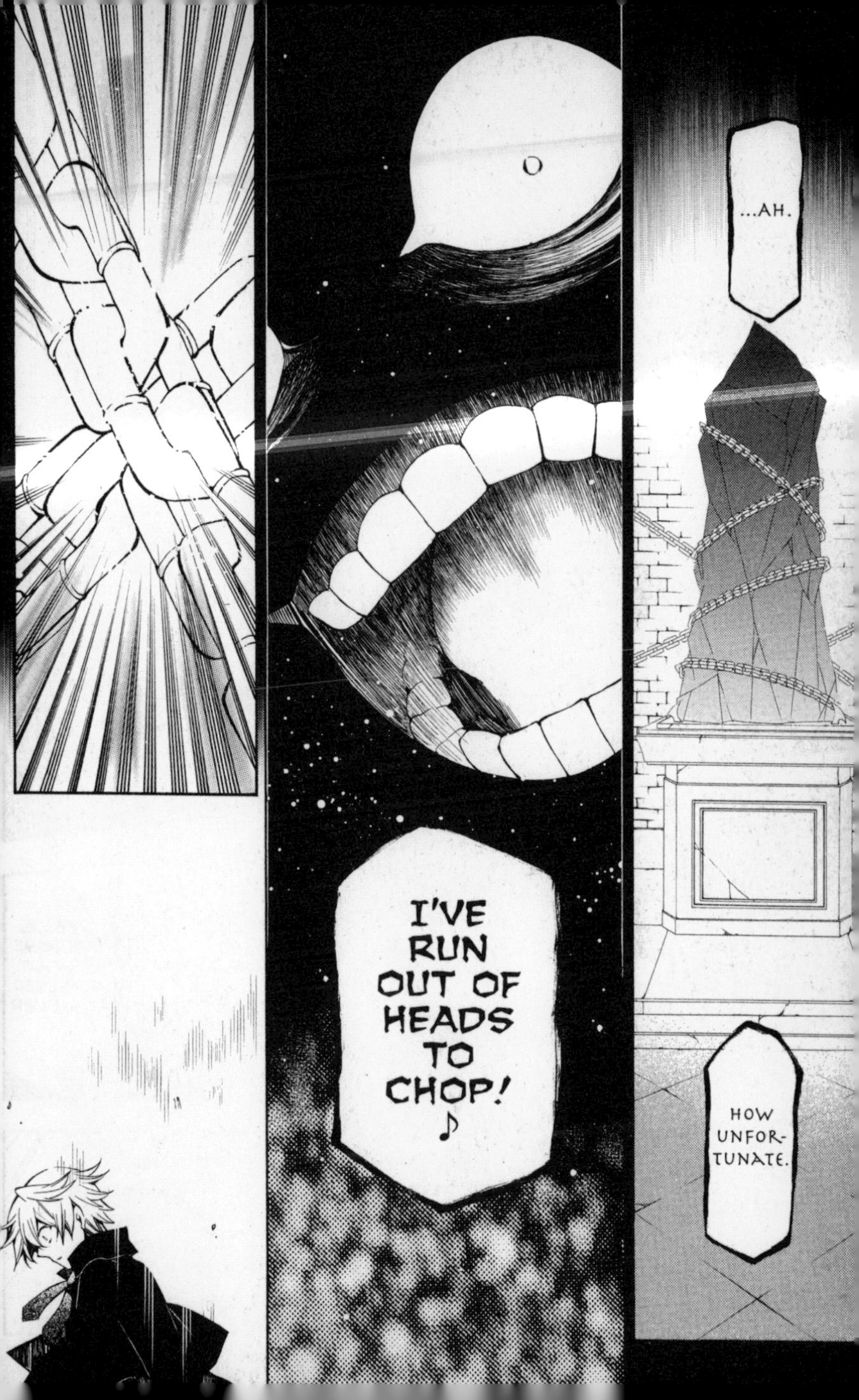
...AH.
HOW UNFORTUNATE.
O
I'VE RUN OUT OF HEADS TO CHOP! ♪

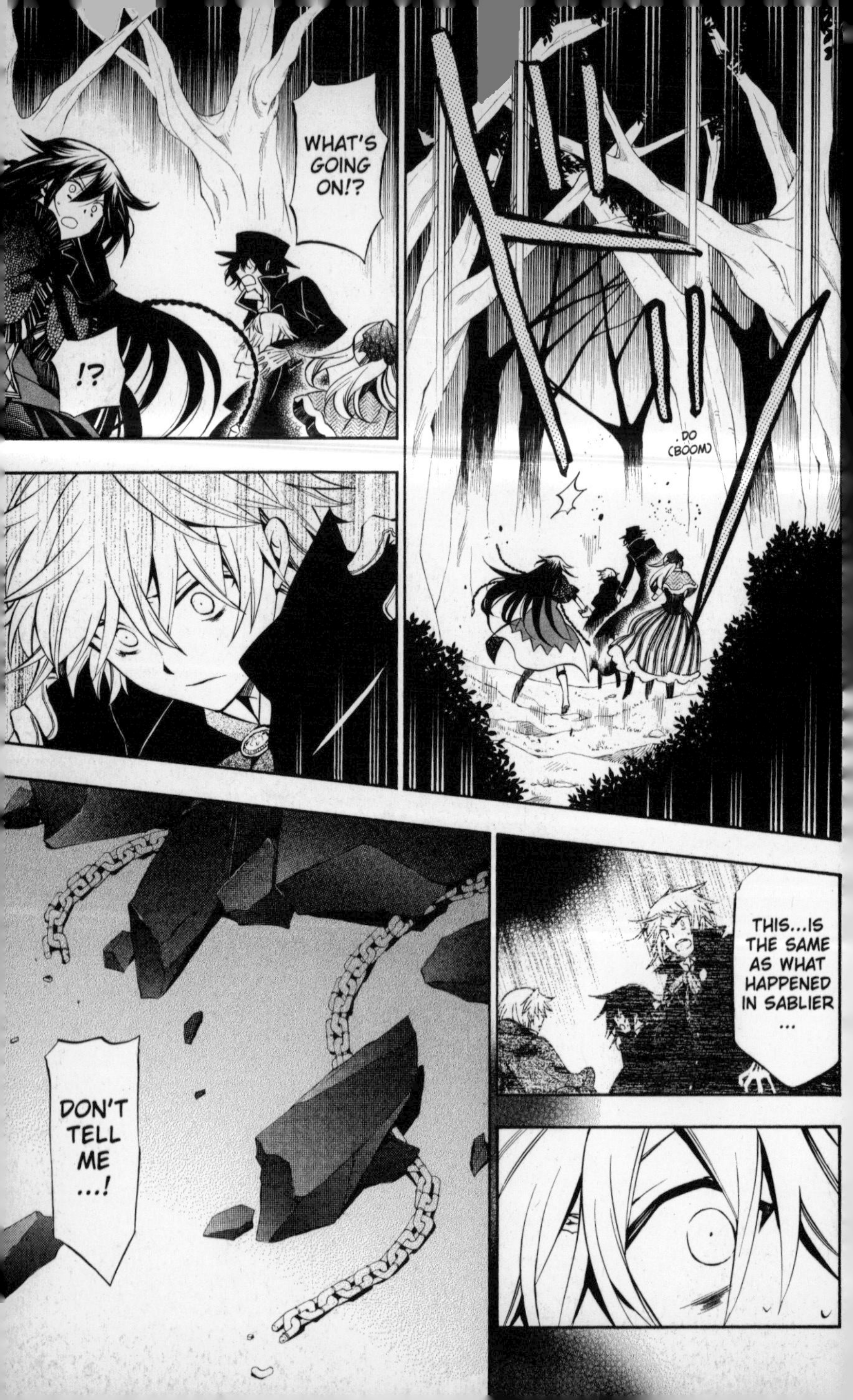
DO
(BOOM)
WHAT'S GOING ON!?
!?
THIS...IS THE SAME AS WHAT HAPPENED IN SABLIER ...
DON'T TELL ME ...!

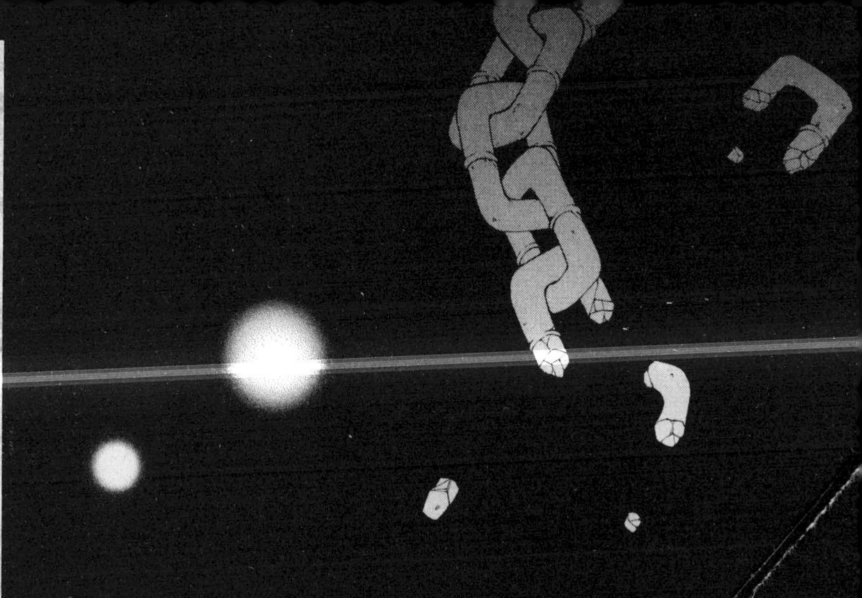

Retrace:XLV Queen of Hurts

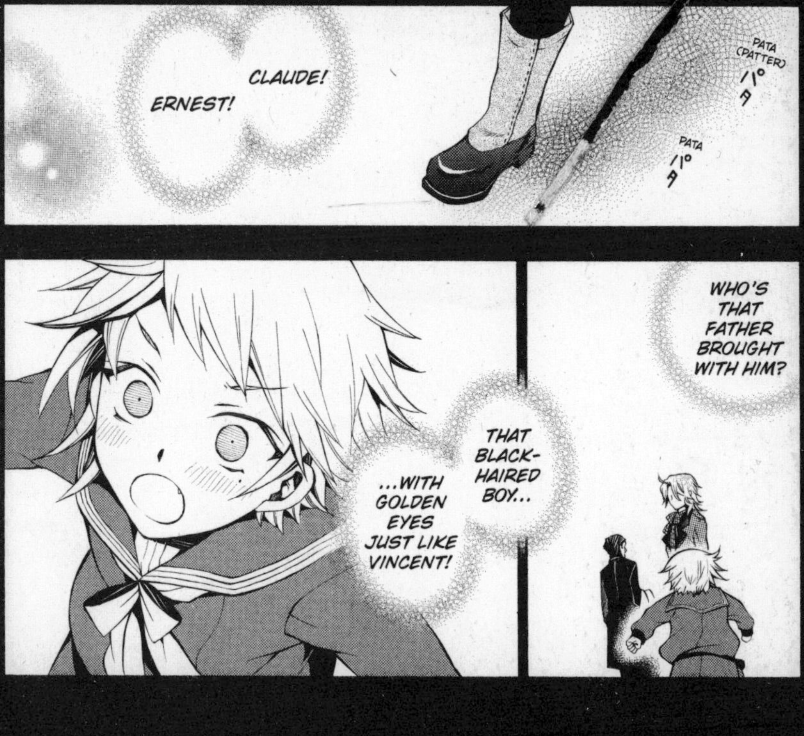
PATA (PATTER)
PATA
CLAUDE!
ERNEST!
WHO'S THAT FATHER BROUGHT WITH HIM?
THAT BLACK-HAIRED BOY...
...WITH GOLDEN EYES JUST LIKE VINCENT!

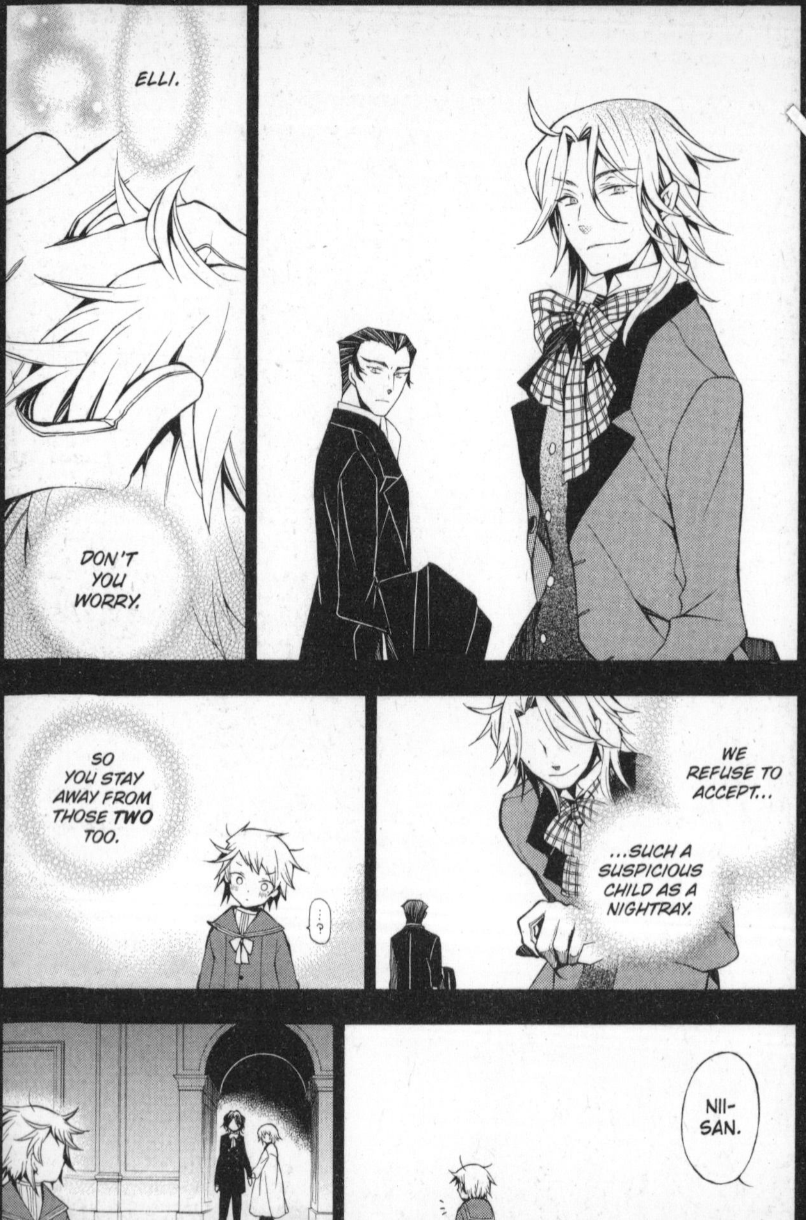
ELLI.
DON'T YOU WORRY.
WE REFUSE TO ACCEPT...
...SUCH A SUSPICIOUS CHILD AS A NIGHTRAY.
SO YOU STAY AWAY FROM THOSE TWO TOO.
...?
NII-SAN.

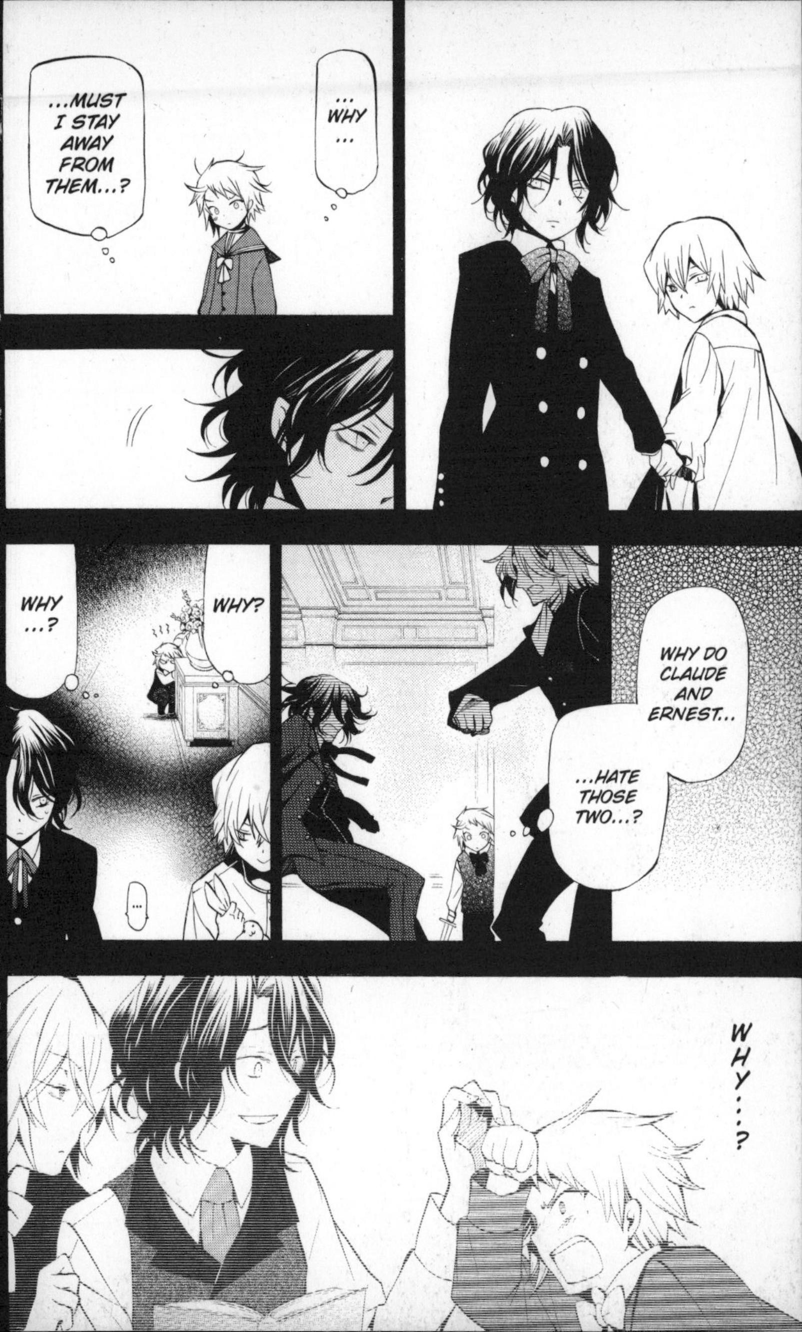
...WHY...
...MUST I STAY AWAY FROM THEM...?
WHY DO CLAUDE AND ERNEST...
...HATE THOSE TWO...?
WHY?
WHY...?
...
WHY...?

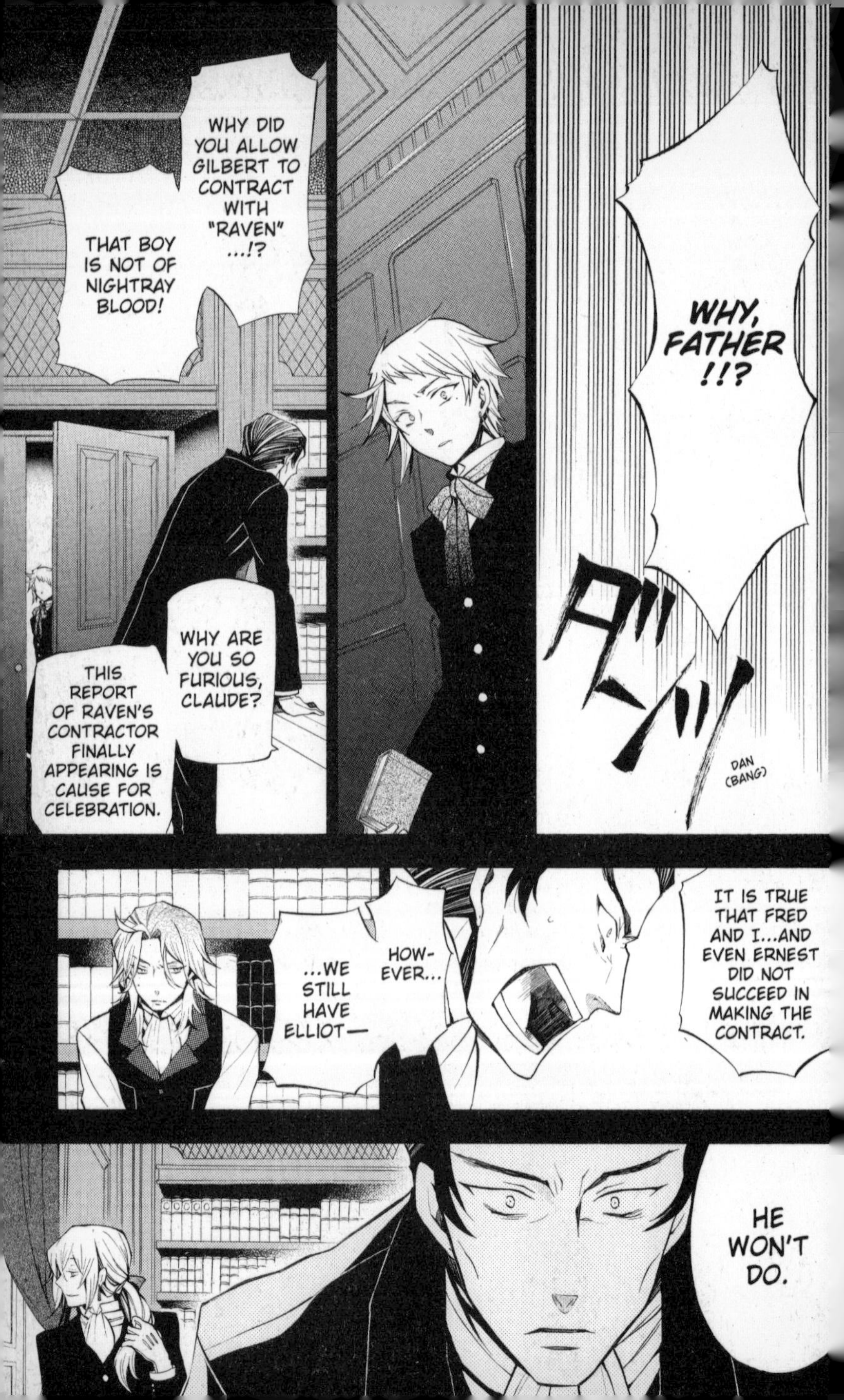
WHY, FATHER!!?
DAN (BANG)
WHY DID YOU ALLOW GILBERT TO CONTRACT WITH "RAVEN"...!?
THAT BOY IS NOT OF NIGHTRAY BLOOD!
WHY ARE YOU SO FURIOUS, CLAUDE?
THIS REPORT OF RAVEN'S CONTRACTOR FINALLY APPEARING IS CAUSE FOR CELEBRATION.
IT IS TRUE THAT FRED AND I...AND EVEN ERNEST DID NOT SUCCEED IN MAKING THE CONTRACT.
HOW-EVER...
...WE STILL HAVE ELLIOT—
HE WON'T DO.

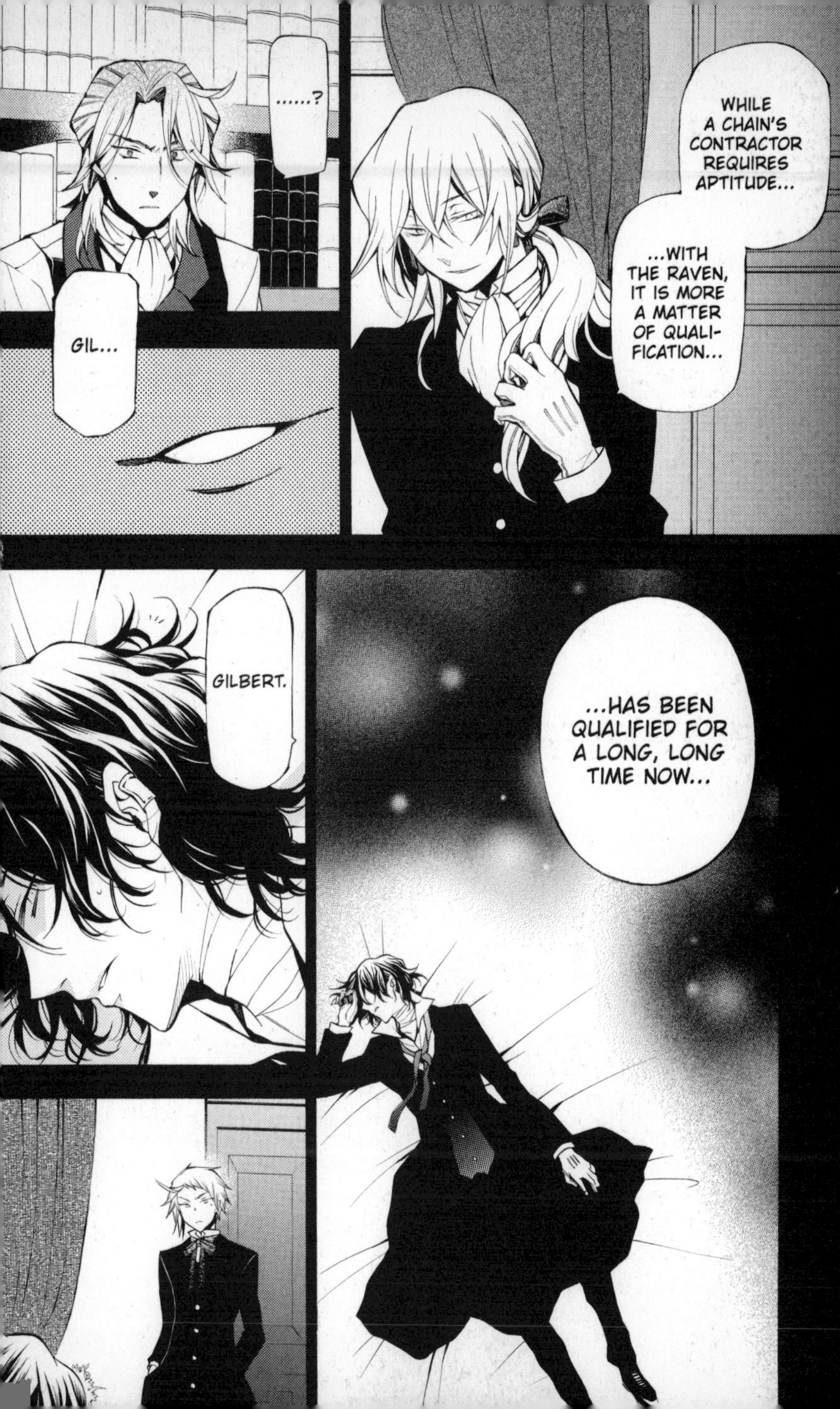
WHILE A CHAIN'S CONTRACTOR REQUIRES APTITUDE...
...WITH THE RAVEN, IT IS MORE A MATTER OF QUALI-FICATION...
......?
GIL...
...HAS BEEN QUALIFIED FOR A LONG, LONG TIME NOW...
GILBERT.

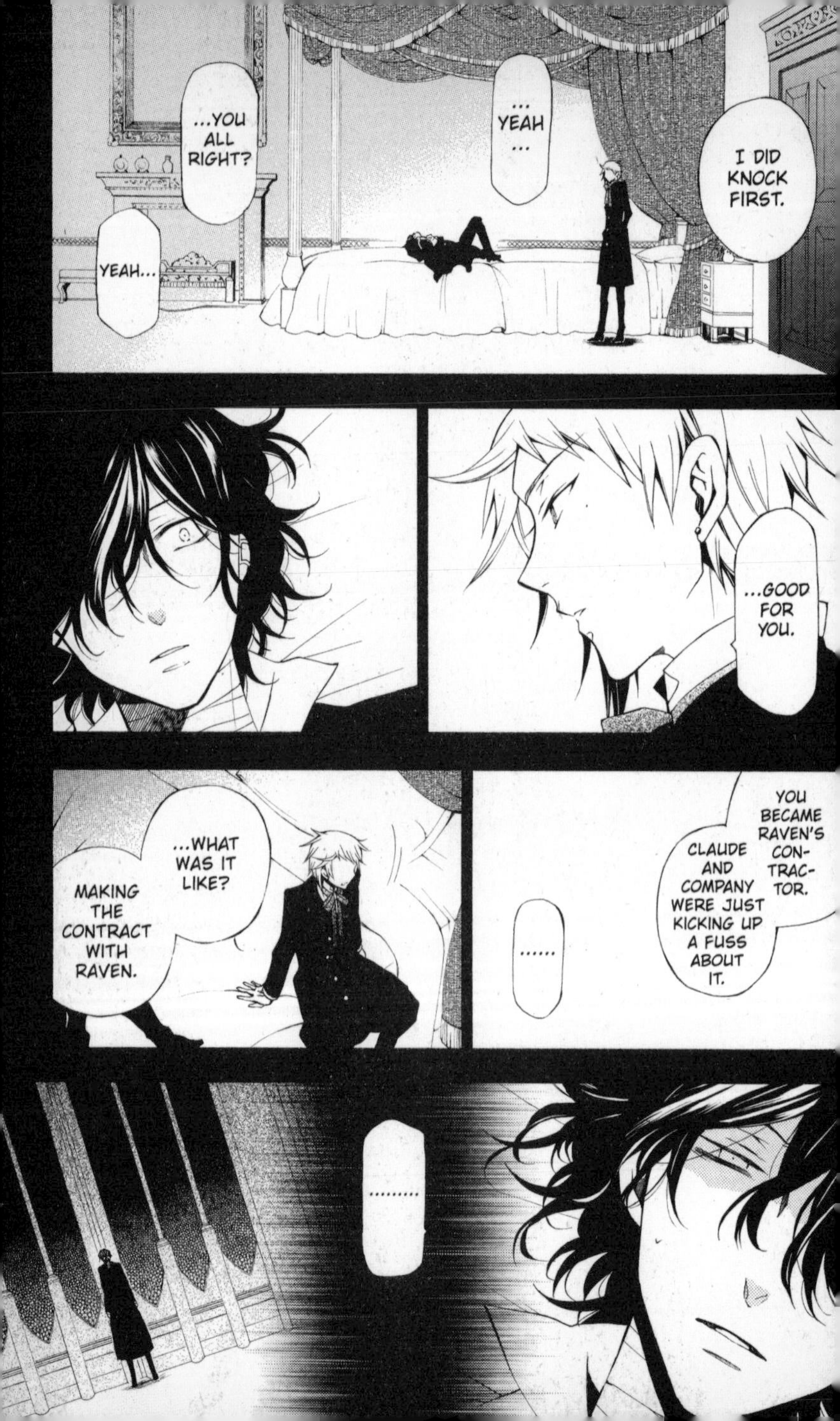
I DID KNOCK FIRST.
... YEAH ...
...YOU ALL RIGHT?
YEAH...
...GOOD FOR YOU.
YOU BECAME RAVEN'S CONTRACTOR.
CLAUDE AND COMPANY WERE JUST KICKING UP A FUSS ABOUT IT.
......
...WHAT WAS IT LIKE?
MAKING THE CONTRACT WITH RAVEN.
....

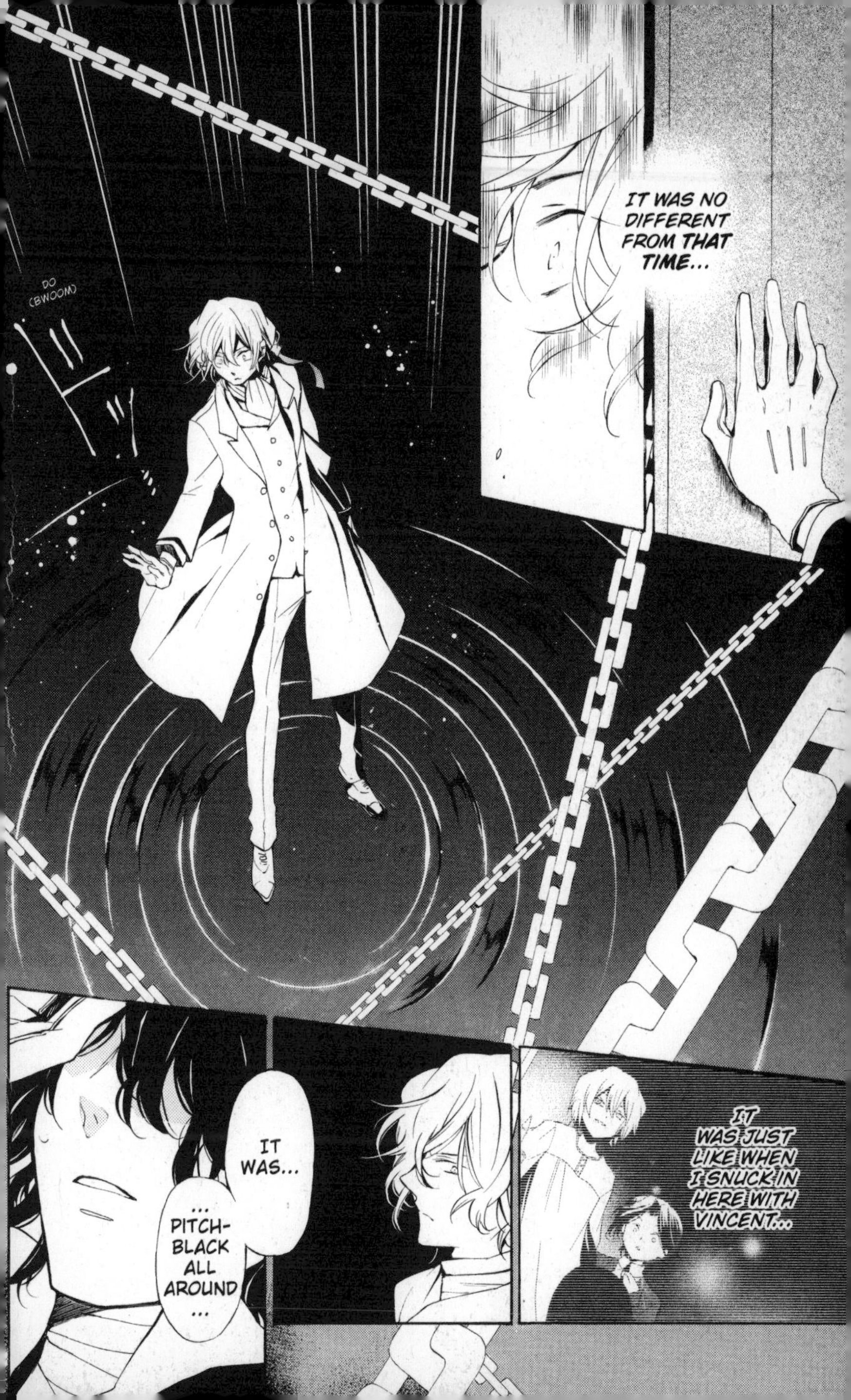
IT WAS NO DIFFERENT FROM THAT TIME...
DO (BWOOM)
IT WAS JUST LIKE WHEN I SNUCK IN HERE WITH VINCENT...
IT WAS...
...PITCH-BLACK ALL AROUND...

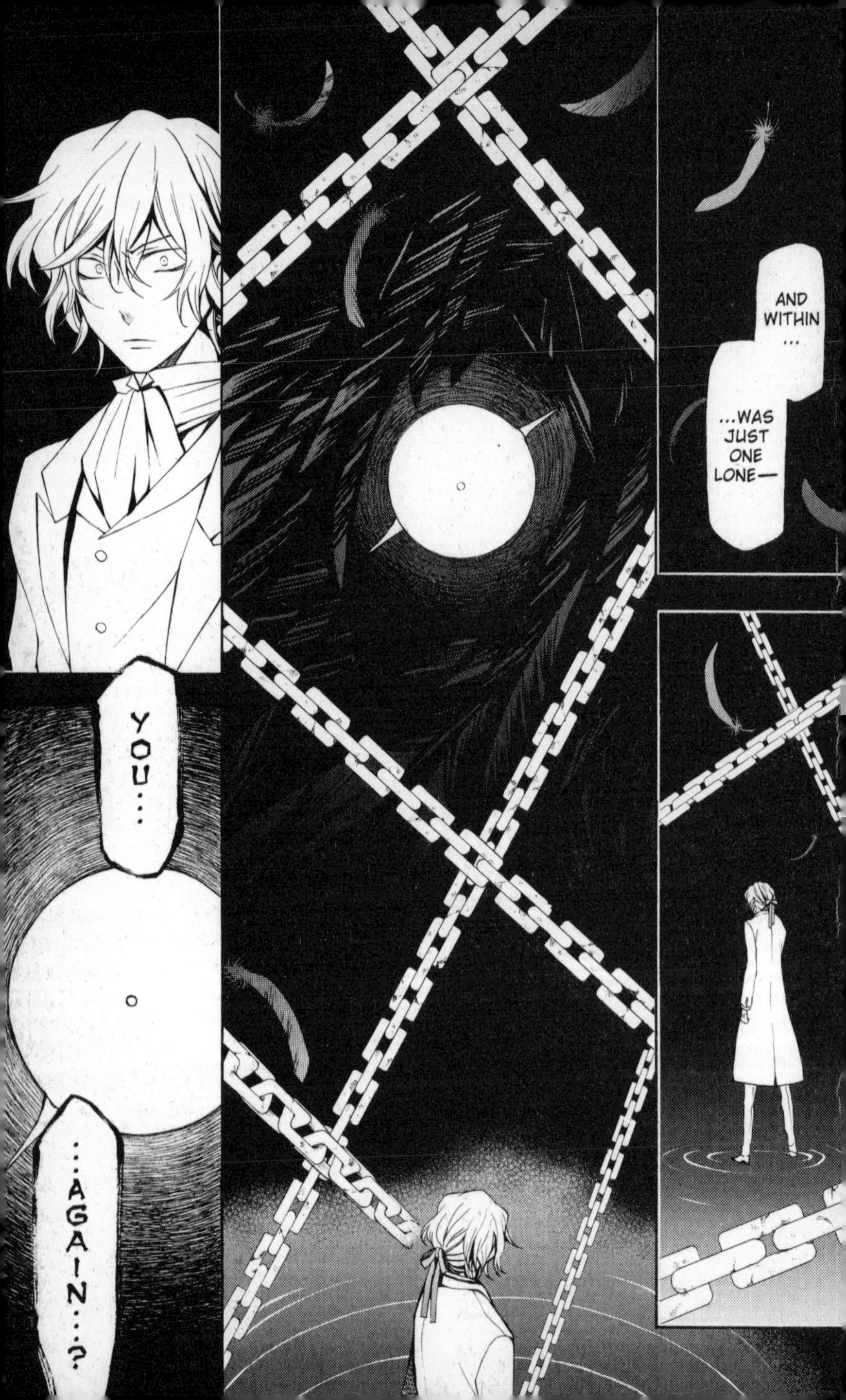
AND WITHIN...
...WAS JUST ONE LONE—
YOU...
...AGAIN...?

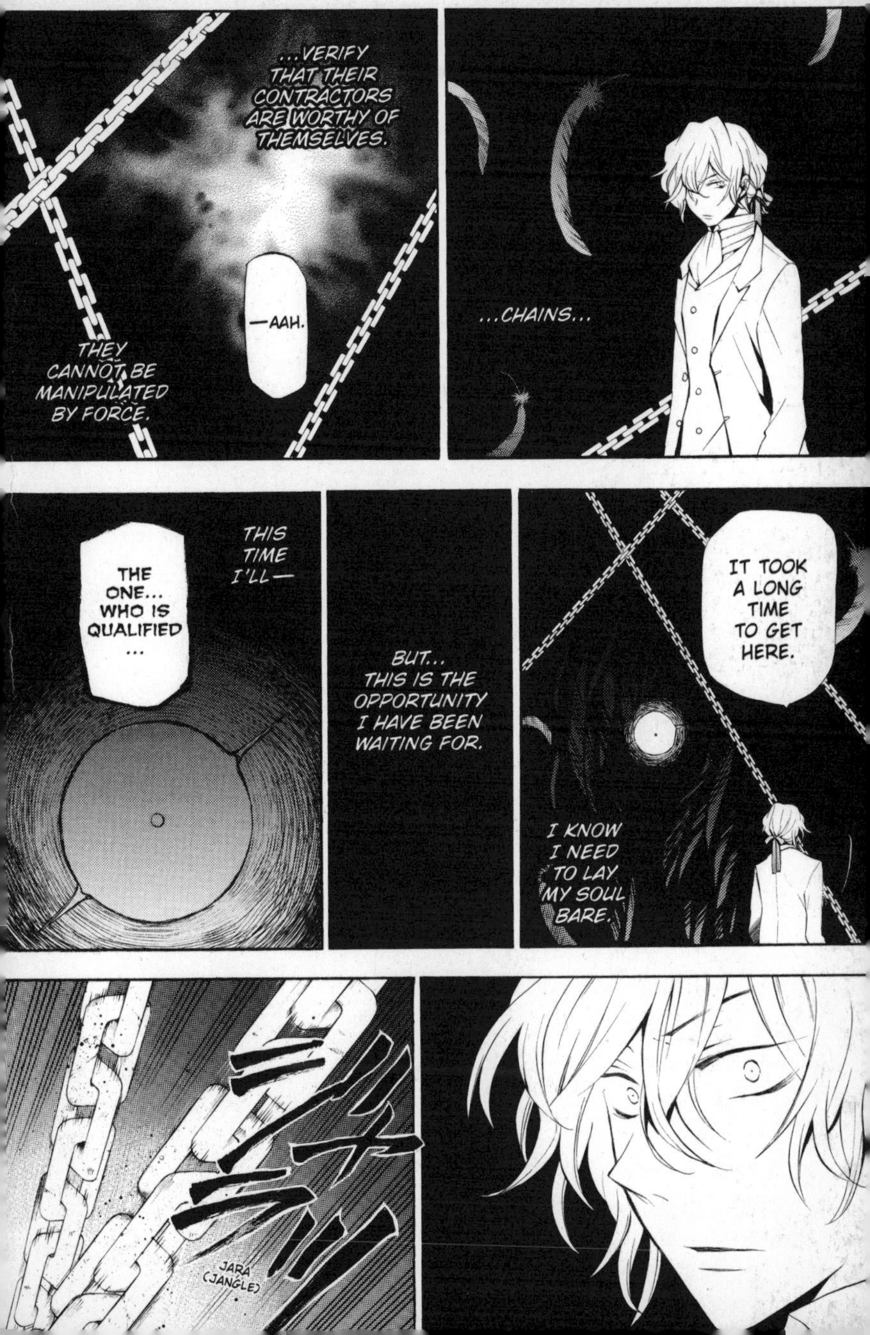
...CHAINS...
...VERIFY THAT THEIR CONTRACTORS ARE WORTHY OF THEMSELVES.
—AAH.
THEY CANNOT BE MANIPULATED BY FORCE.
IT TOOK A LONG TIME TO GET HERE.
I KNOW I NEED TO LAY MY SOUL BARE.
BUT... THIS IS THE OPPORTUNITY I HAVE BEEN WAITING FOR.
THIS TIME I'LL—
THE ONE... WHO IS QUALIFIED ...
JARA (JANGLE)

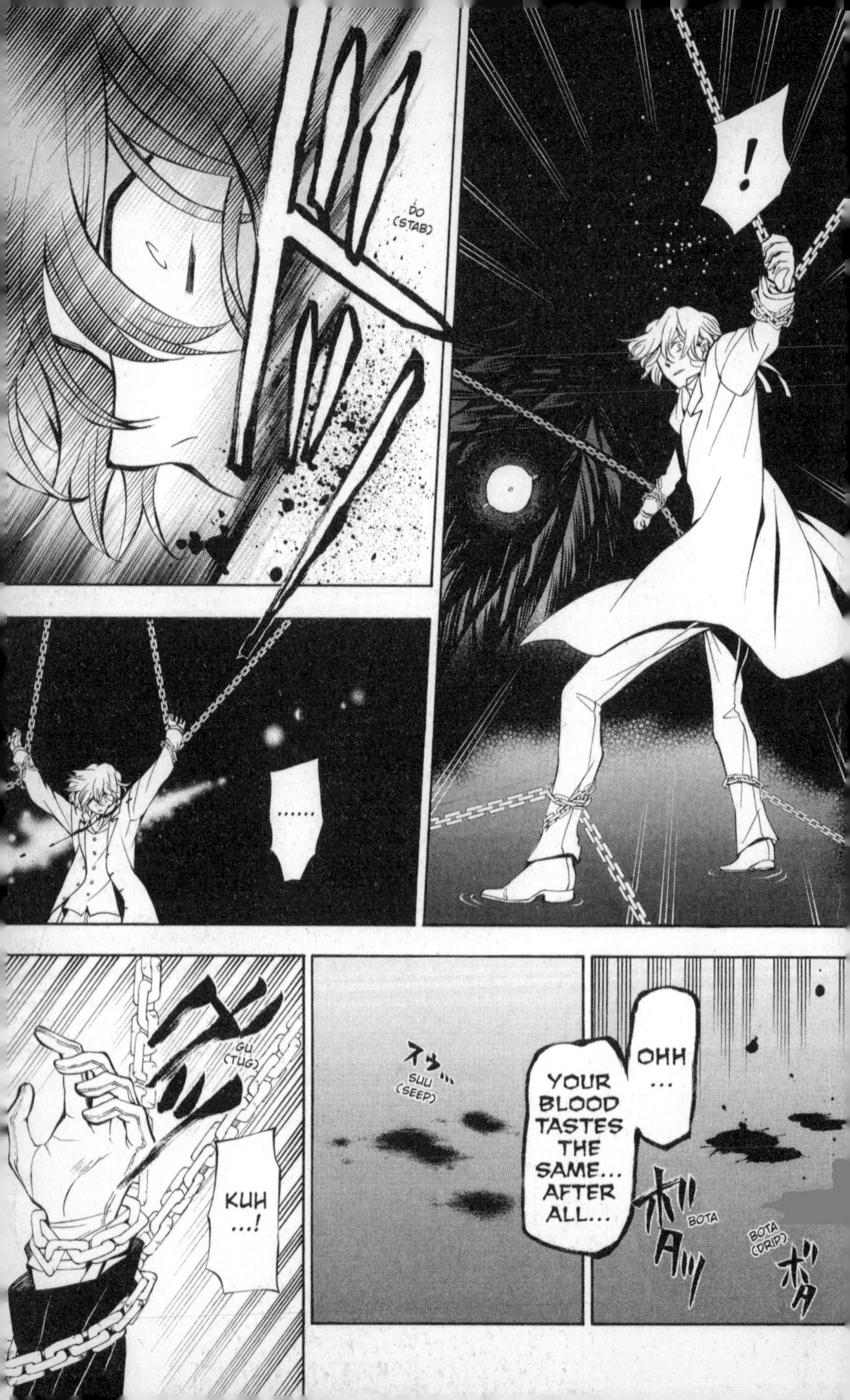
!
DO (STAB)
......
OHH...
YOUR BLOOD TASTES THE SAME... AFTER ALL...
BOTA
BOTA (DRIP)
SUU (SEEP)
GU (TUG)
KUH...!

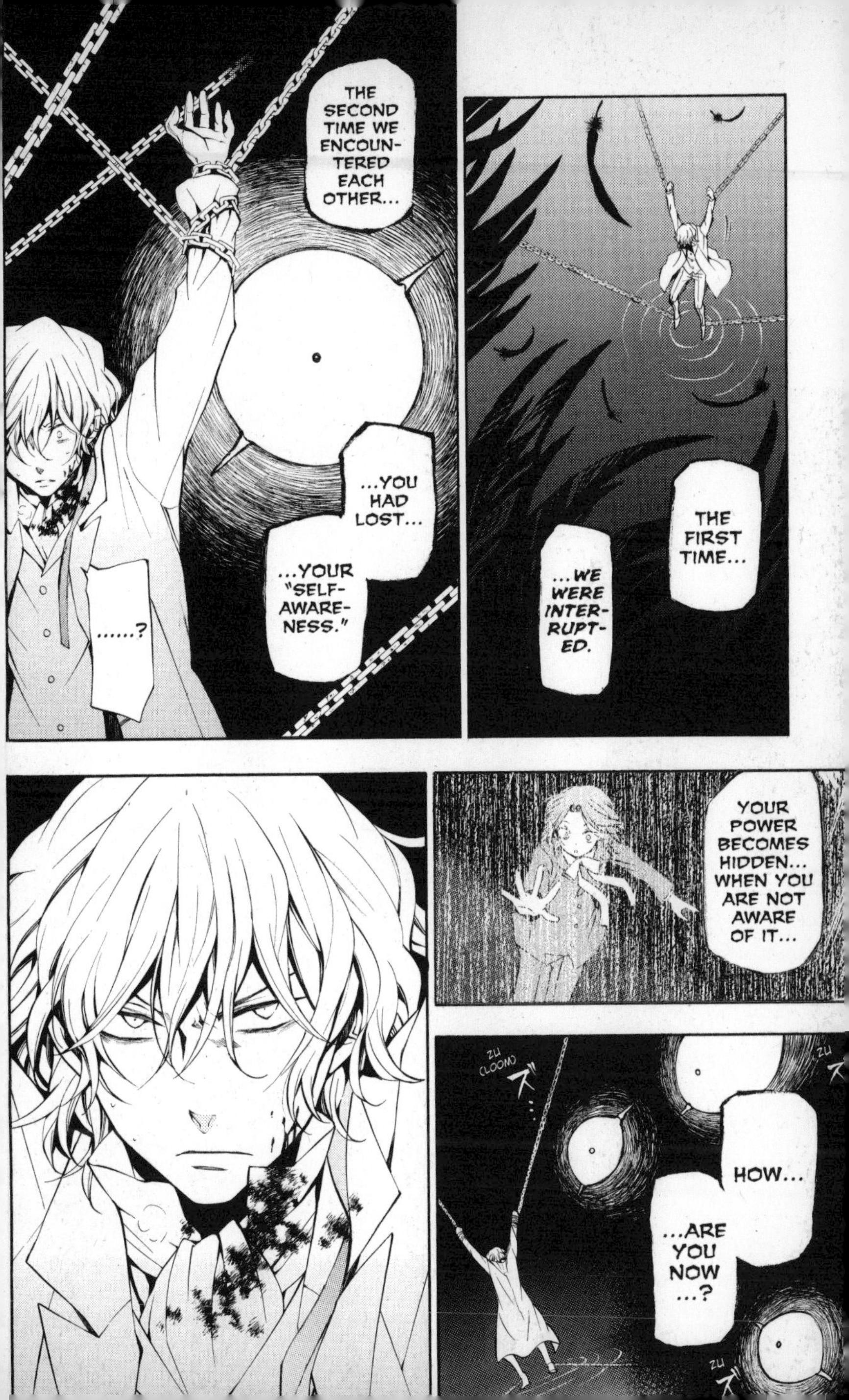
THE FIRST TIME...
...WE WERE INTERRUPTED.
THE SECOND TIME WE ENCOUNTERED EACH OTHER...
...YOU HAD LOST...
...YOUR "SELF-AWARENESS."
......?
YOUR POWER BECOMES HIDDEN... WHEN YOU ARE NOT AWARE OF IT...
ZU
ZU (LOOM)
HOW...
...ARE YOU NOW ...?
ZU

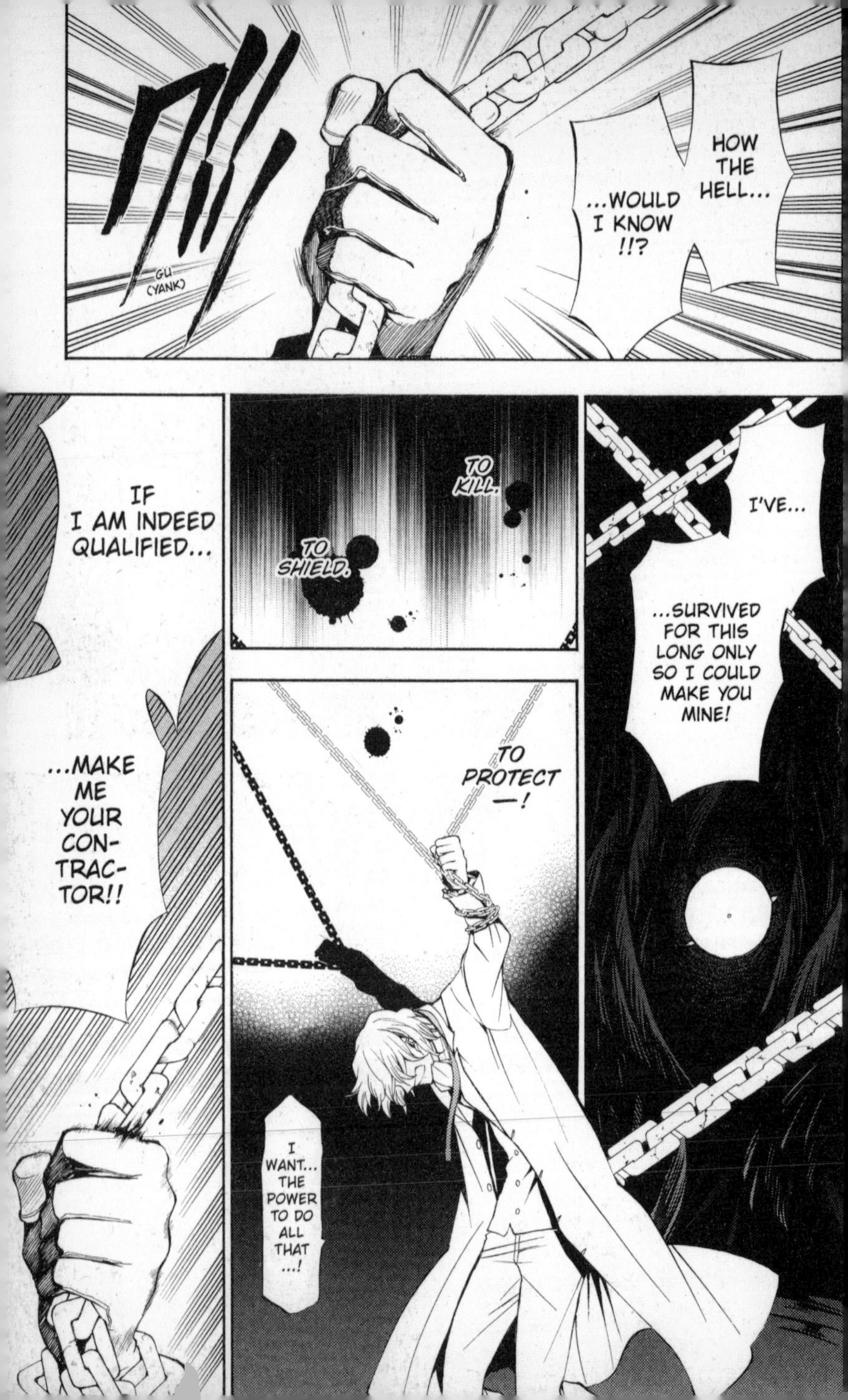
HOW THE HELL...
...WOULD I KNOW !!?
GU (YANK)
I'VE...
...SURVIVED FOR THIS LONG ONLY SO I COULD MAKE YOU MINE!
TO KILL.
TO SHIELD.
TO PROTECT—!
I WANT... THE POWER TO DO ALL THAT...!
IF I AM INDEED QUALIFIED...
...MAKE ME YOUR CON-TRAC-TOR!!

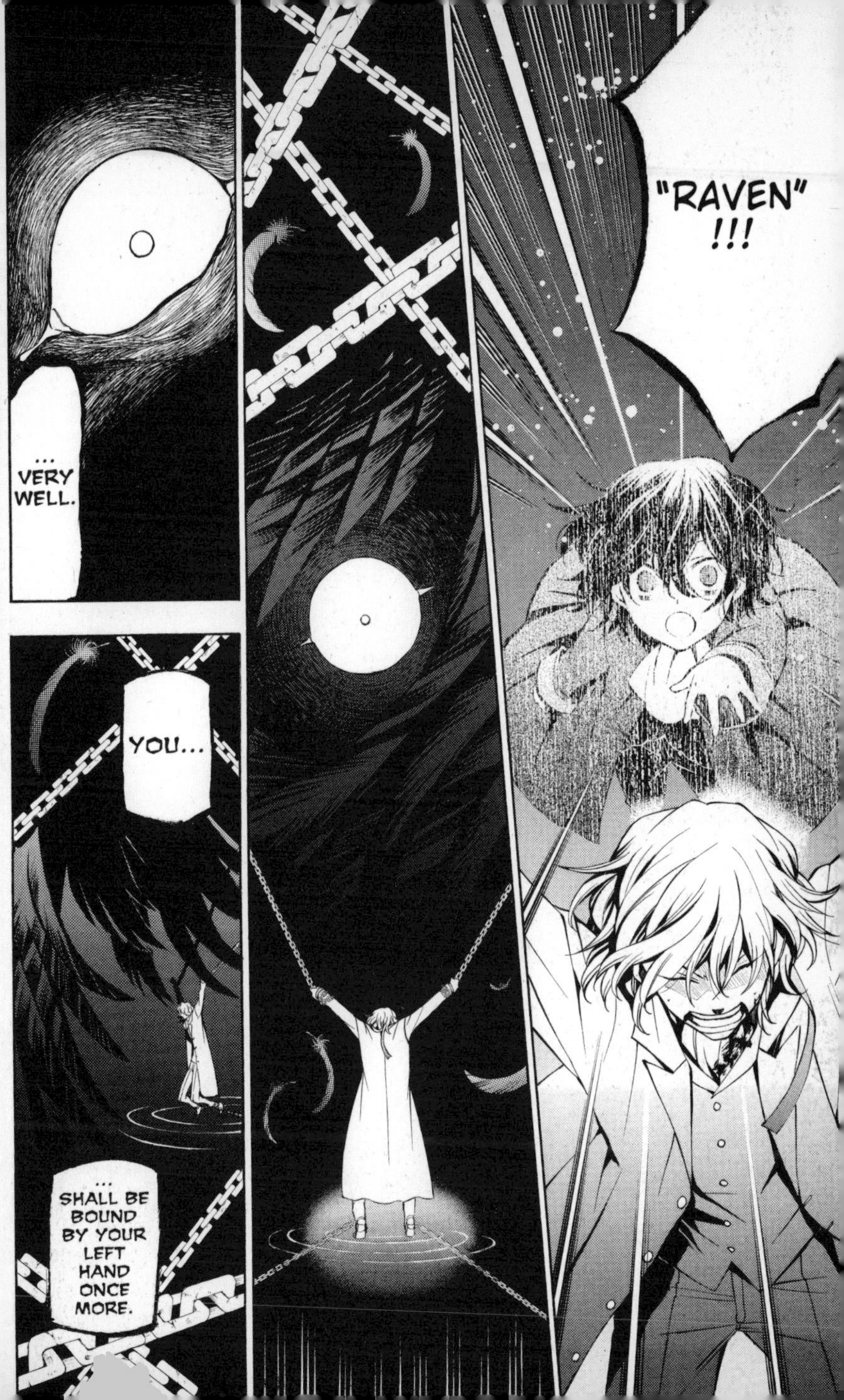
"RAVEN" !!!
... VERY WELL.
YOU...
... SHALL BE BOUND BY YOUR LEFT HAND ONCE MORE.

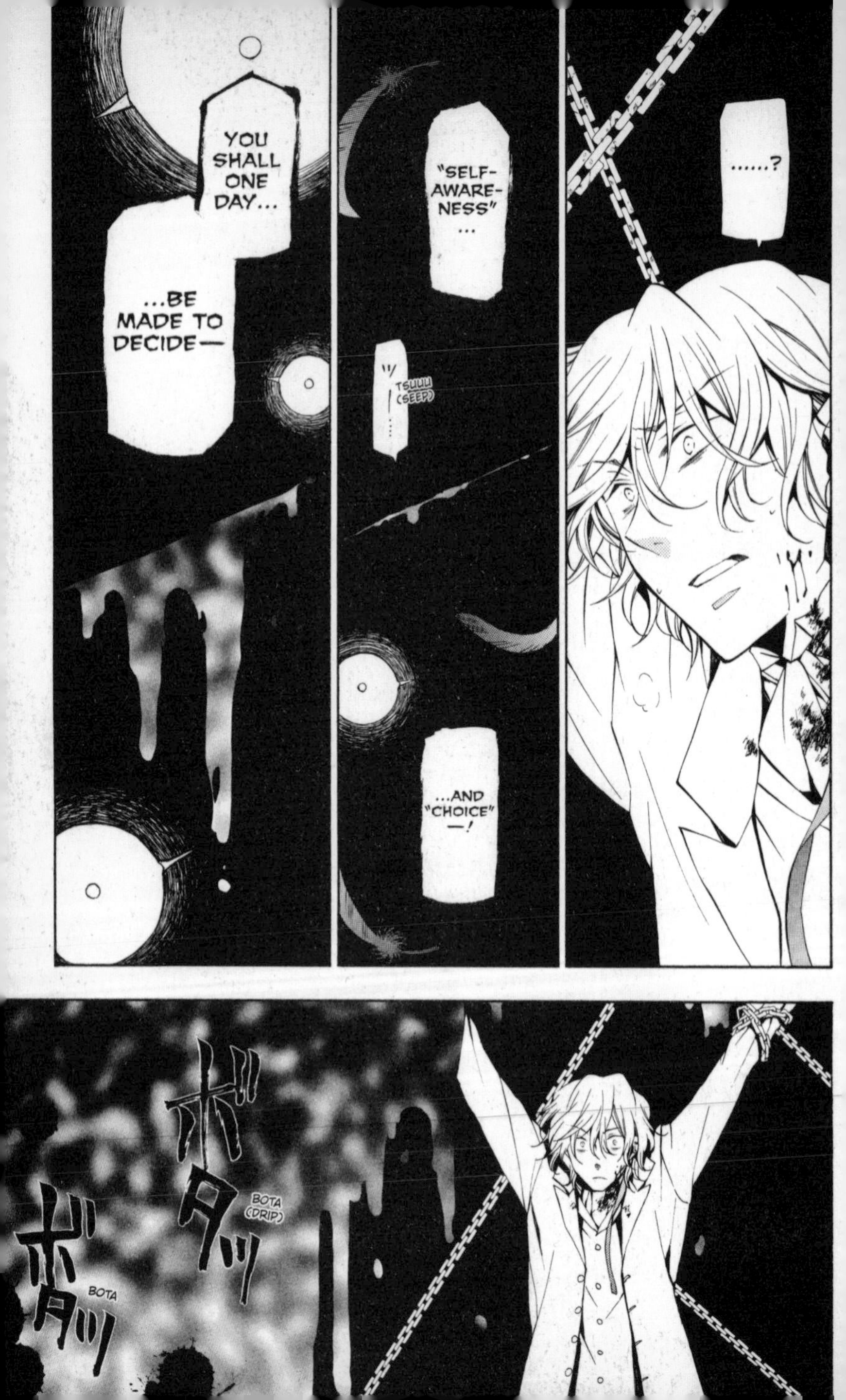
......?
"SELF-AWARENESS"...
TSUUU (SEEP)
...AND "CHOICE"—!
YOU SHALL ONE DAY...
...BE MADE TO DECIDE—
BOTA (DRIP)
BOTA

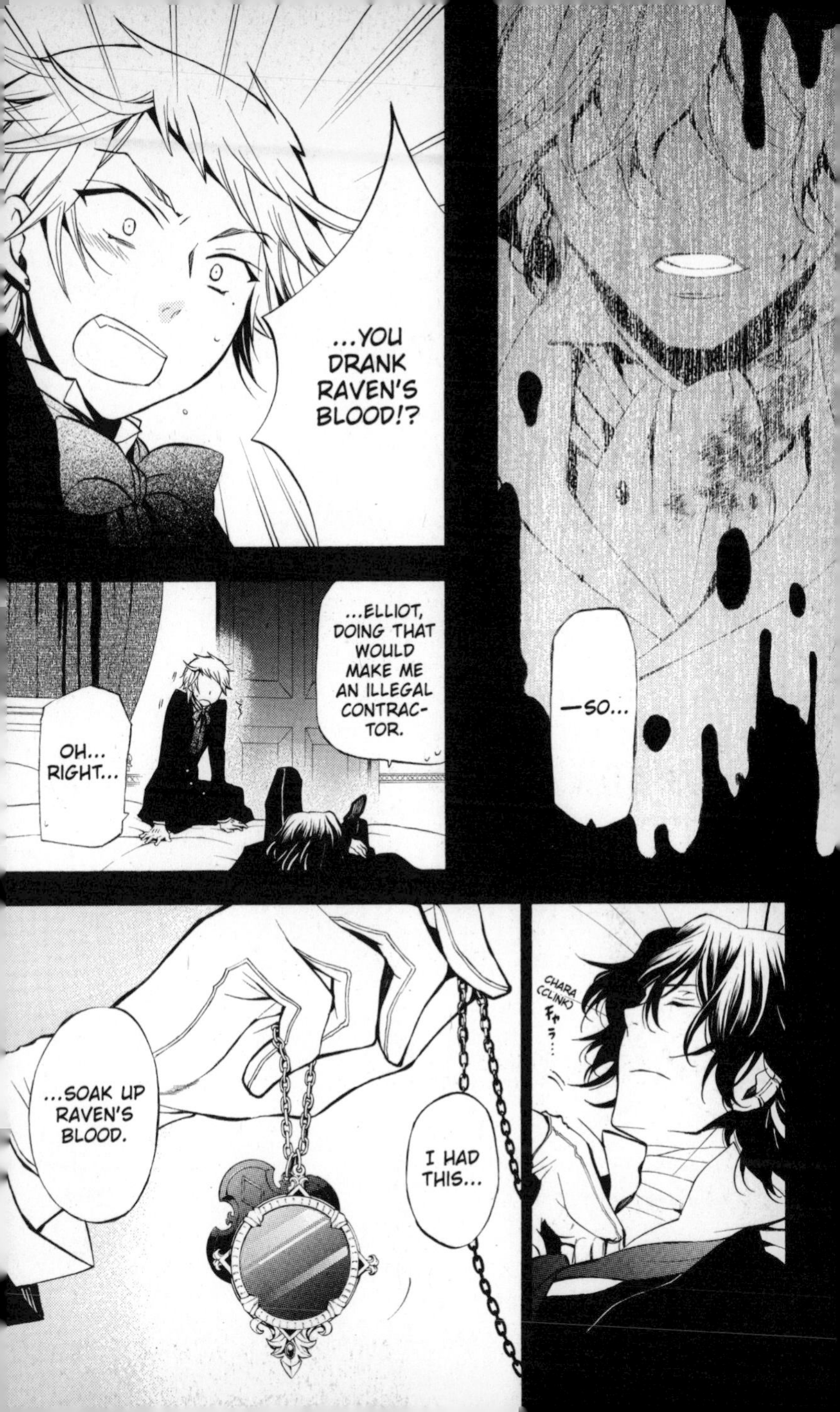
—SO...
...YOU DRANK RAVEN'S BLOOD!?
...ELLIOT, DOING THAT WOULD MAKE ME AN ILLEGAL CONTRACTOR.
OH... RIGHT...
CHARA (CLINK)
I HAD THIS...
...SOAK UP RAVEN'S BLOOD.

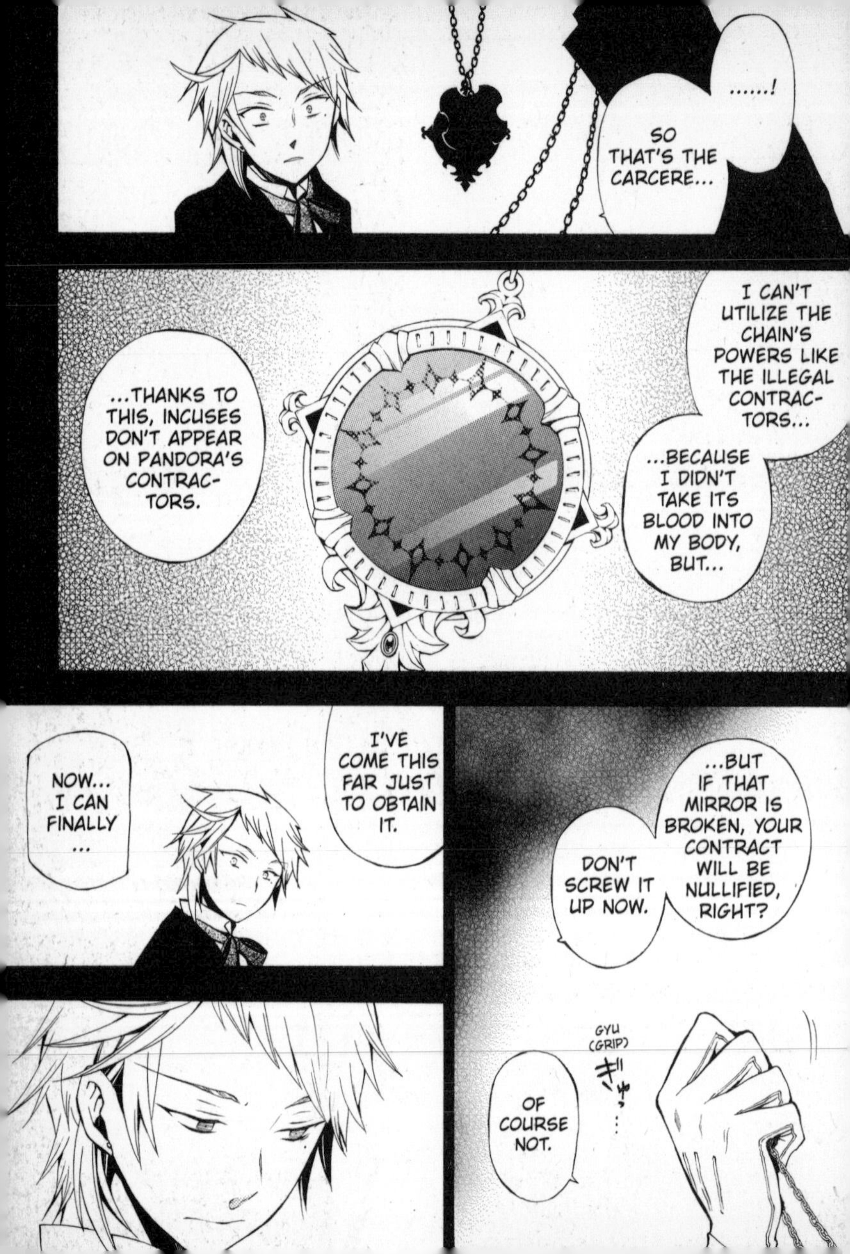
......!
SO THAT'S THE CARCERE...
I CAN'T UTILIZE THE CHAIN'S POWERS LIKE THE ILLEGAL CONTRAC-TORS...
...BECAUSE I DIDN'T TAKE ITS BLOOD INTO MY BODY, BUT...
...THANKS TO THIS, INCUSES DON'T APPEAR ON PANDORA'S CONTRAC-TORS.
...BUT IF THAT MIRROR IS BROKEN, YOUR CONTRACT WILL BE NULLIFIED, RIGHT?
DON'T SCREW IT UP NOW.
GYU (GRIP)
OF COURSE NOT.
I'VE COME THIS FAR JUST TO OBTAIN IT.
NOW... I CAN FINALLY ...

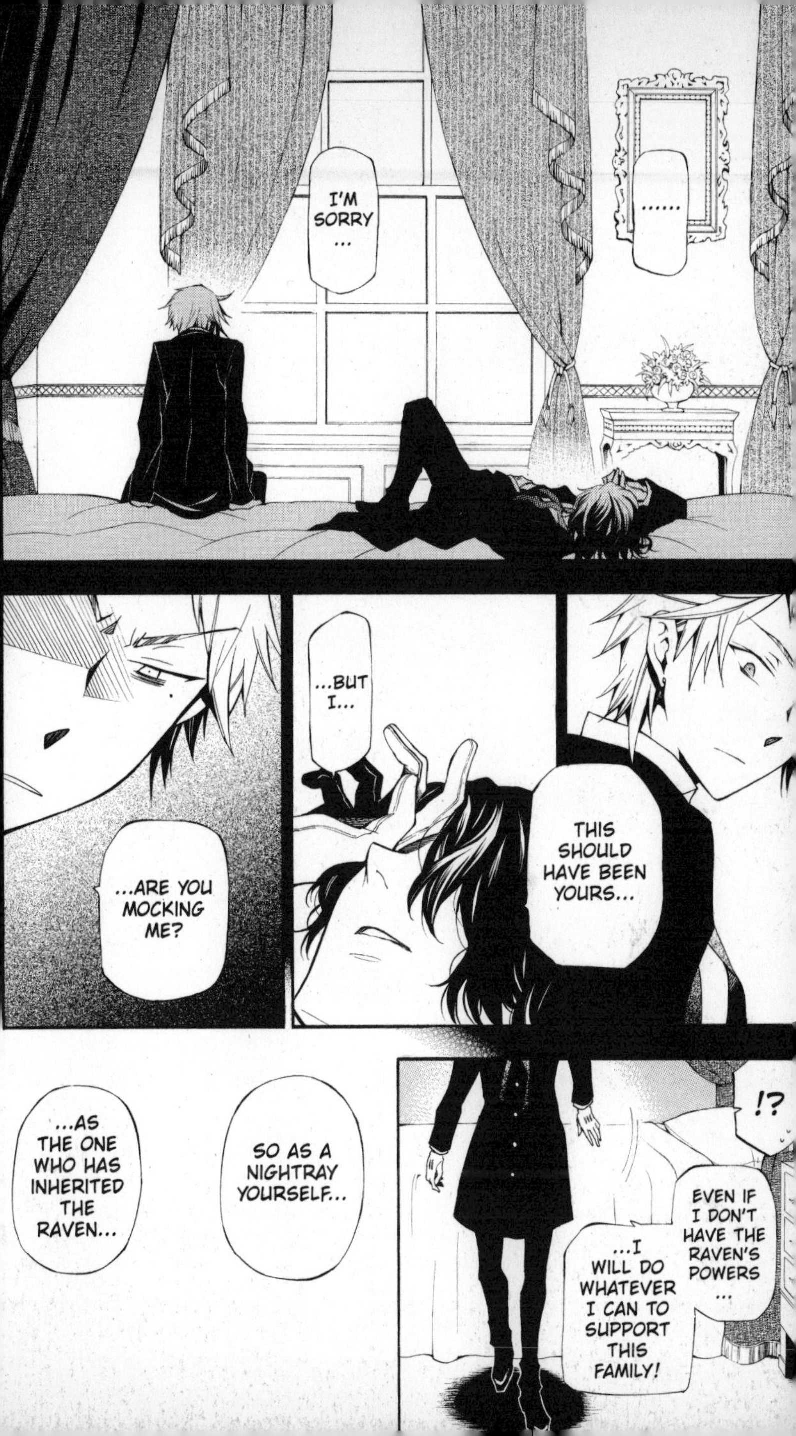
......
I'M SORRY ...
THIS SHOULD HAVE BEEN YOURS...
...BUT I...
...ARE YOU MOCKING ME?
!?
EVEN IF I DON'T HAVE THE RAVEN'S POWERS ...
...I WILL DO WHATEVER I CAN TO SUPPORT THIS FAMILY!
SO AS A NIGHTRAY YOURSELF...
...AS THE ONE WHO HAS INHERITED THE RAVEN...

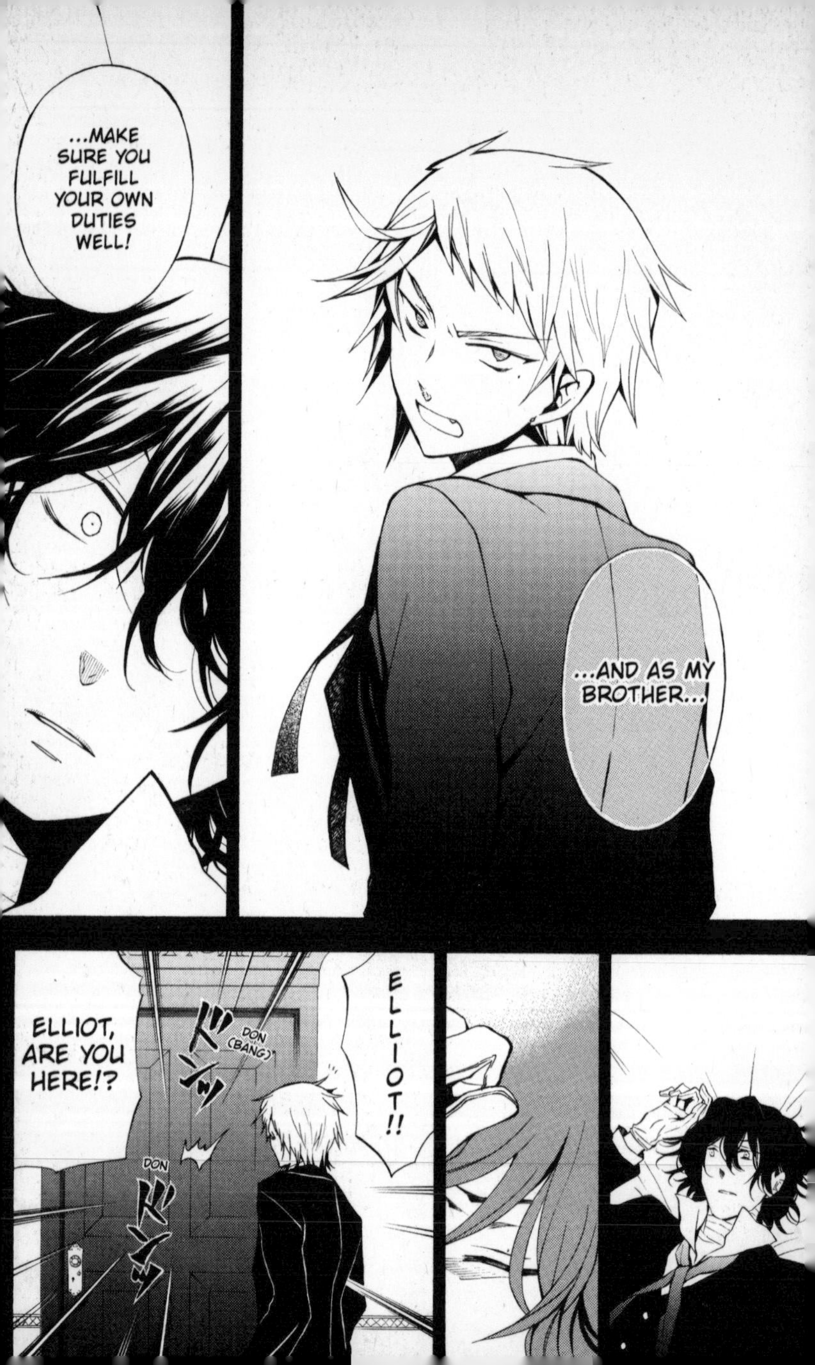
...AND AS MY BROTHER...
...MAKE SURE YOU FULFILL YOUR OWN DUTIES WELL!
ELLIOT!!
DON (BANG)
ELLIOT, ARE YOU HERE!?
DON

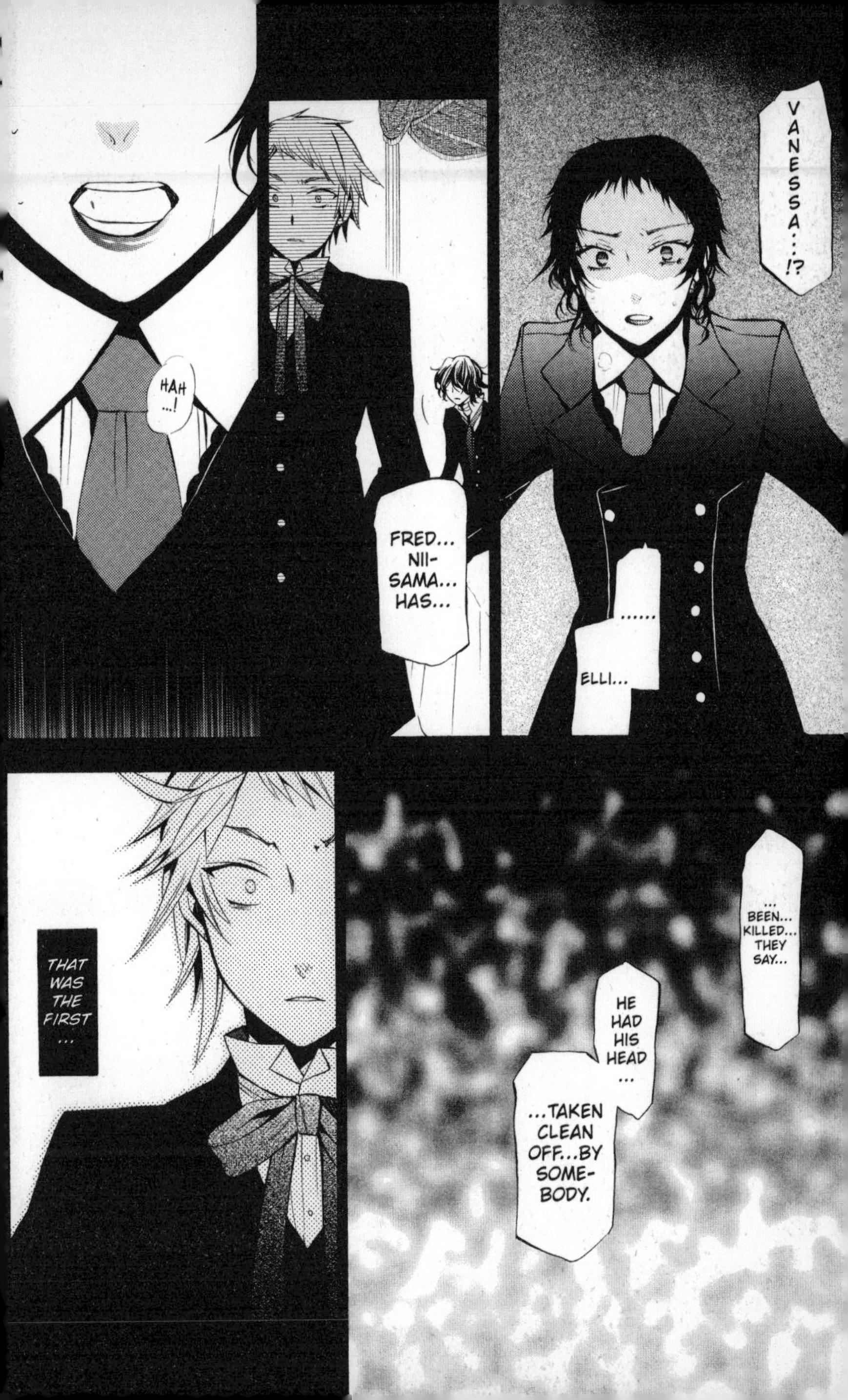

VANESSA...!?
......
ELLI...
FRED... NII-SAMA... HAS...
HAH ...!
... BEEN... KILLED... THEY SAY...
HE HAD HIS HEAD ...
...TAKEN CLEAN OFF...BY SOME-BODY.
THAT WAS THE FIRST ...

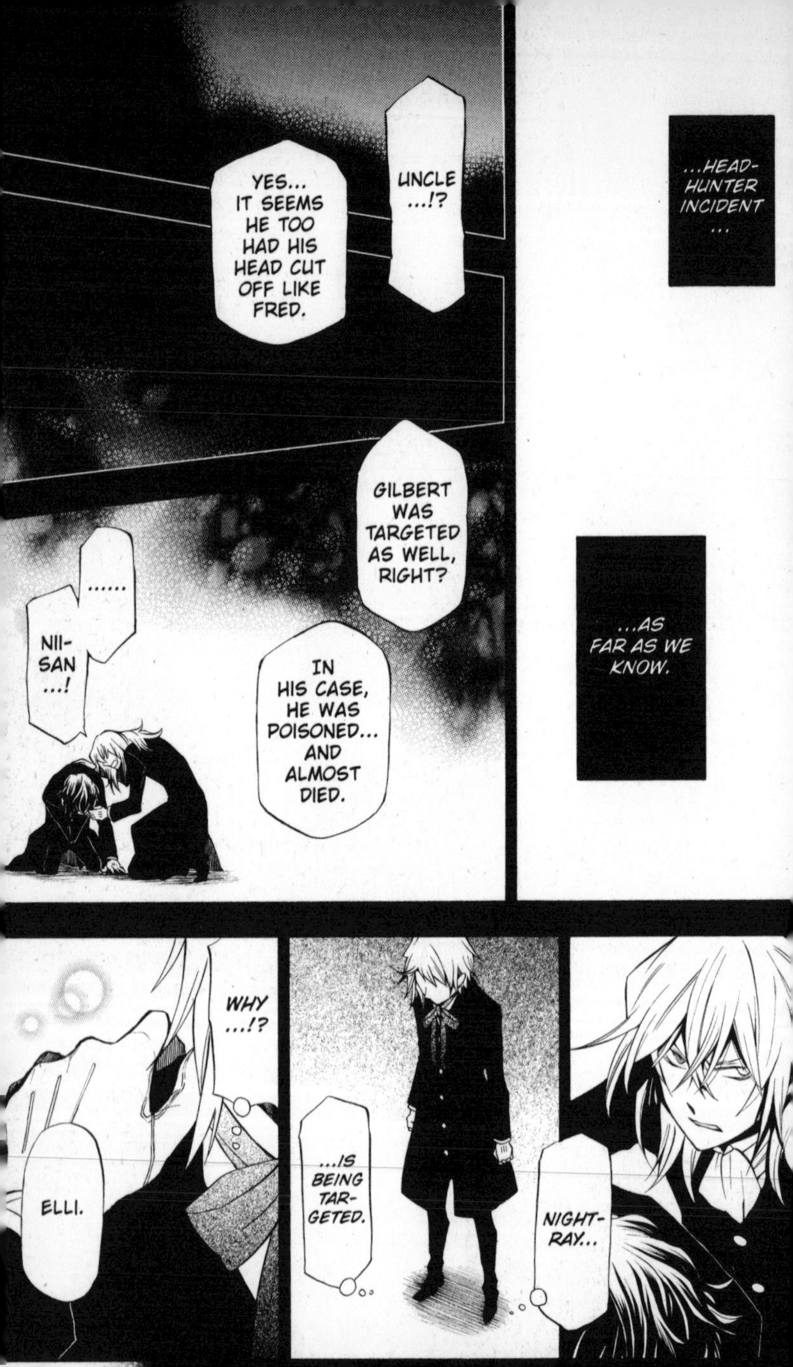
...HEAD-HUNTER INCIDENT ...
...AS FAR AS WE KNOW.
UNCLE ...!?
YES... IT SEEMS HE TOO HAD HIS HEAD CUT OFF LIKE FRED.
GILBERT WAS TARGETED AS WELL, RIGHT?
......
IN HIS CASE, HE WAS POISONED... AND ALMOST DIED.
NII-SAN ...!
NIGHT-RAY...
...IS BEING TAR-GETED.
WHY ...!?
ELLI.

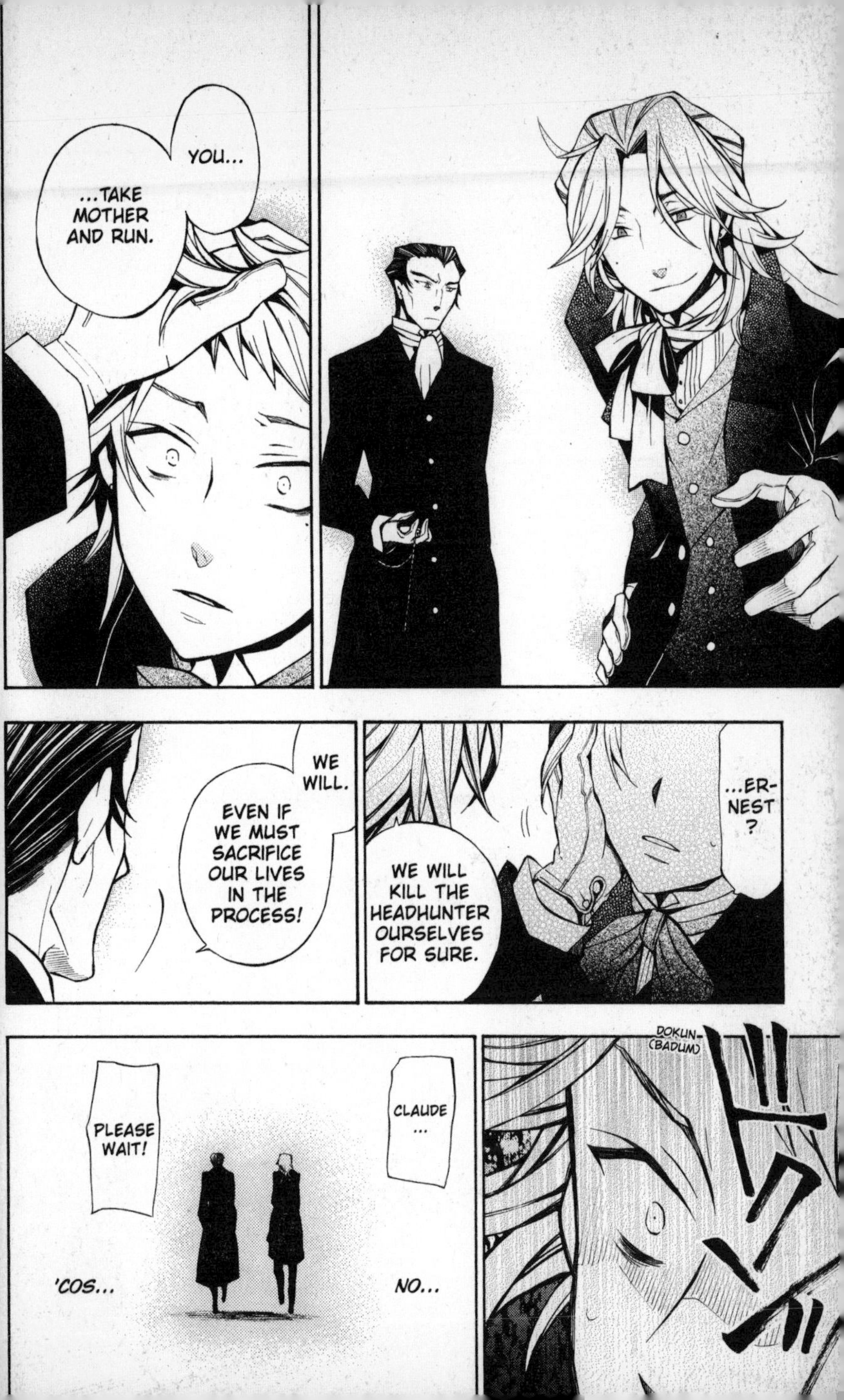
YOU...
...TAKE MOTHER AND RUN.
...ER-NEST?
WE WILL KILL THE HEADHUNTER OURSELVES FOR SURE.
WE WILL.
EVEN IF WE MUST SACRIFICE OUR LIVES IN THE PROCESS!
DOKUN-(BADUM)
CLAUDE...
PLEASE WAIT!
NO...
'COS...

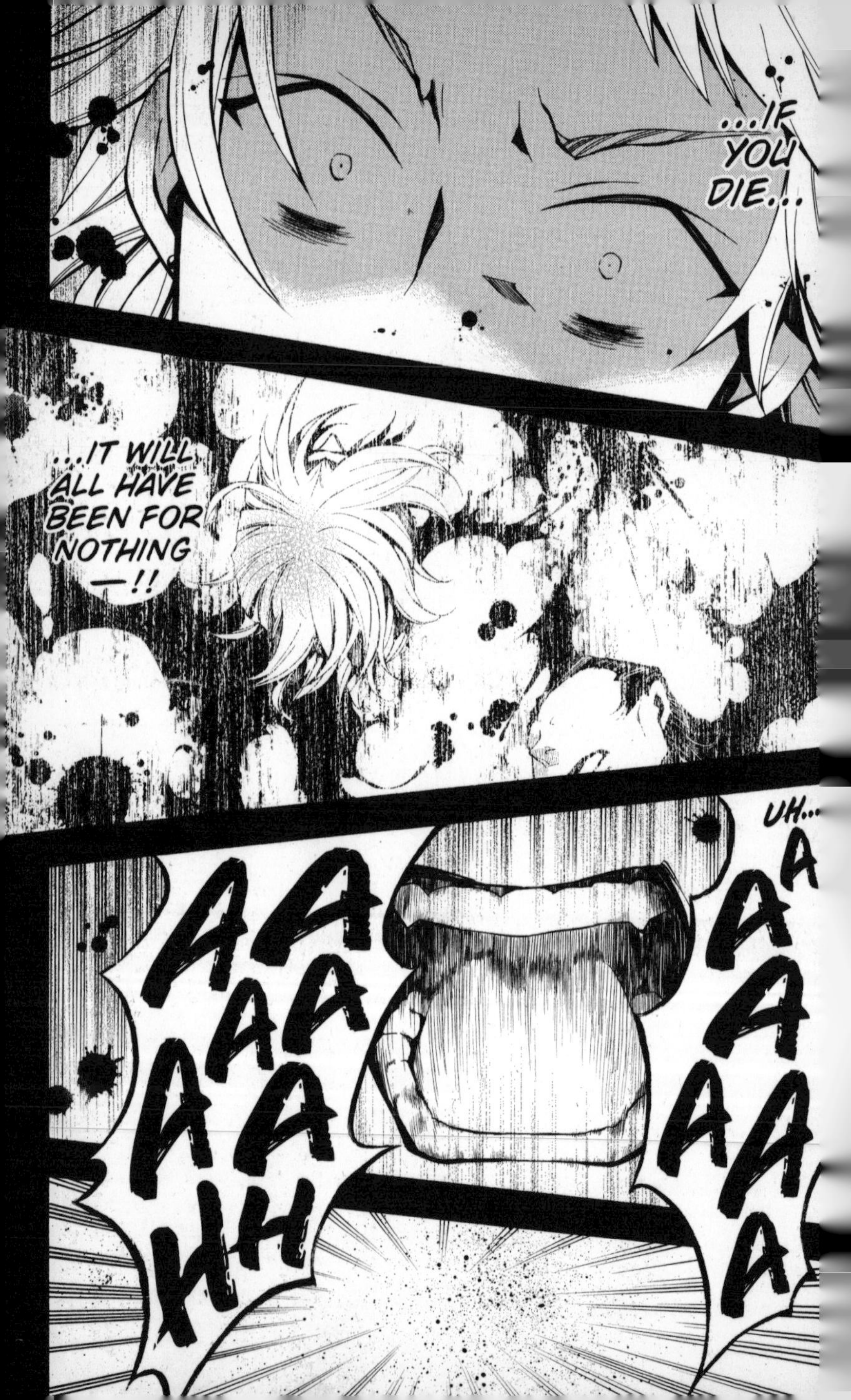
...IF YOU DIE...
...IT WILL ALL HAVE BEEN FOR NOTHING—!!
UH...
AAAAAAAAAAAA
AAAAAAAAAKHH

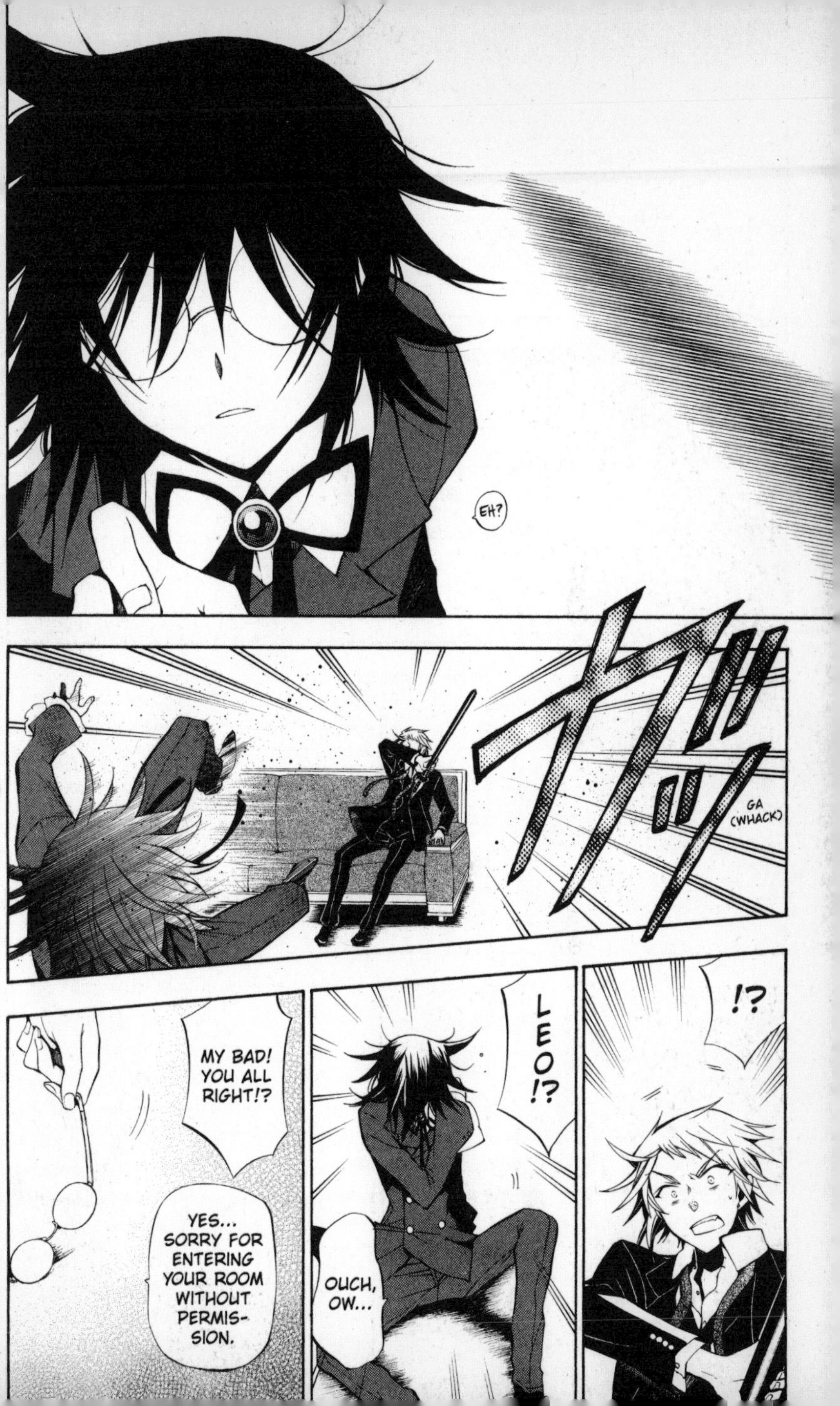
EH?
GA (WHACK)
!?
LEO!?
MY BAD! YOU ALL RIGHT!?
OUCH, OW...
YES... SORRY FOR ENTERING YOUR ROOM WITHOUT PERMIS-SION.

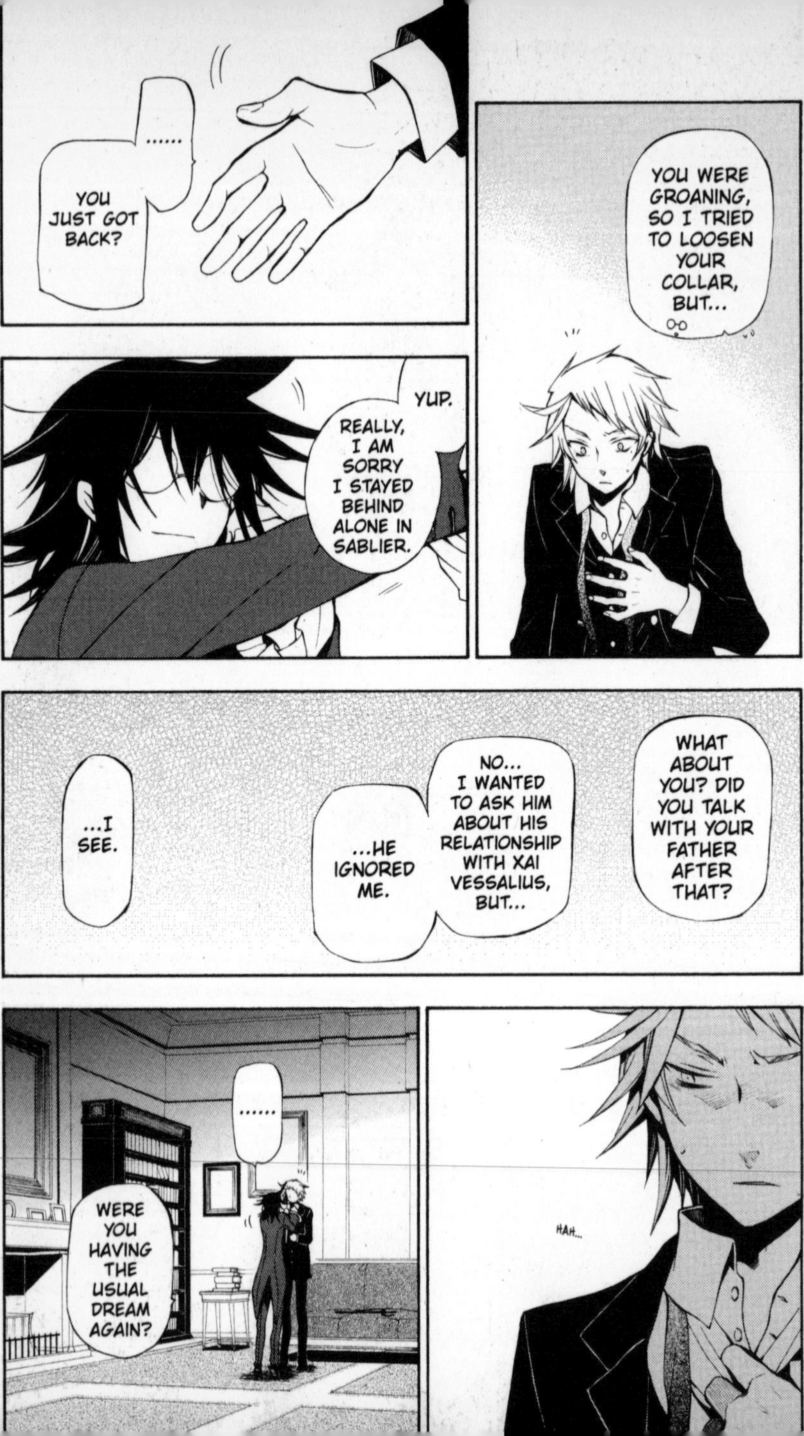
YOU WERE GROANING, SO I TRIED TO LOOSEN YOUR COLLAR, BUT...
......
YOU JUST GOT BACK?
YUP.
REALLY, I AM SORRY I STAYED BEHIND ALONE IN SABLIER.
WHAT ABOUT YOU? DID YOU TALK WITH YOUR FATHER AFTER THAT?
NO... I WANTED TO ASK HIM ABOUT HIS RELATIONSHIP WITH XAI VESSALIUS, BUT...
...HE IGNORED ME.
...I SEE.
HAH...
......
WERE YOU HAVING THE USUAL DREAM AGAIN?

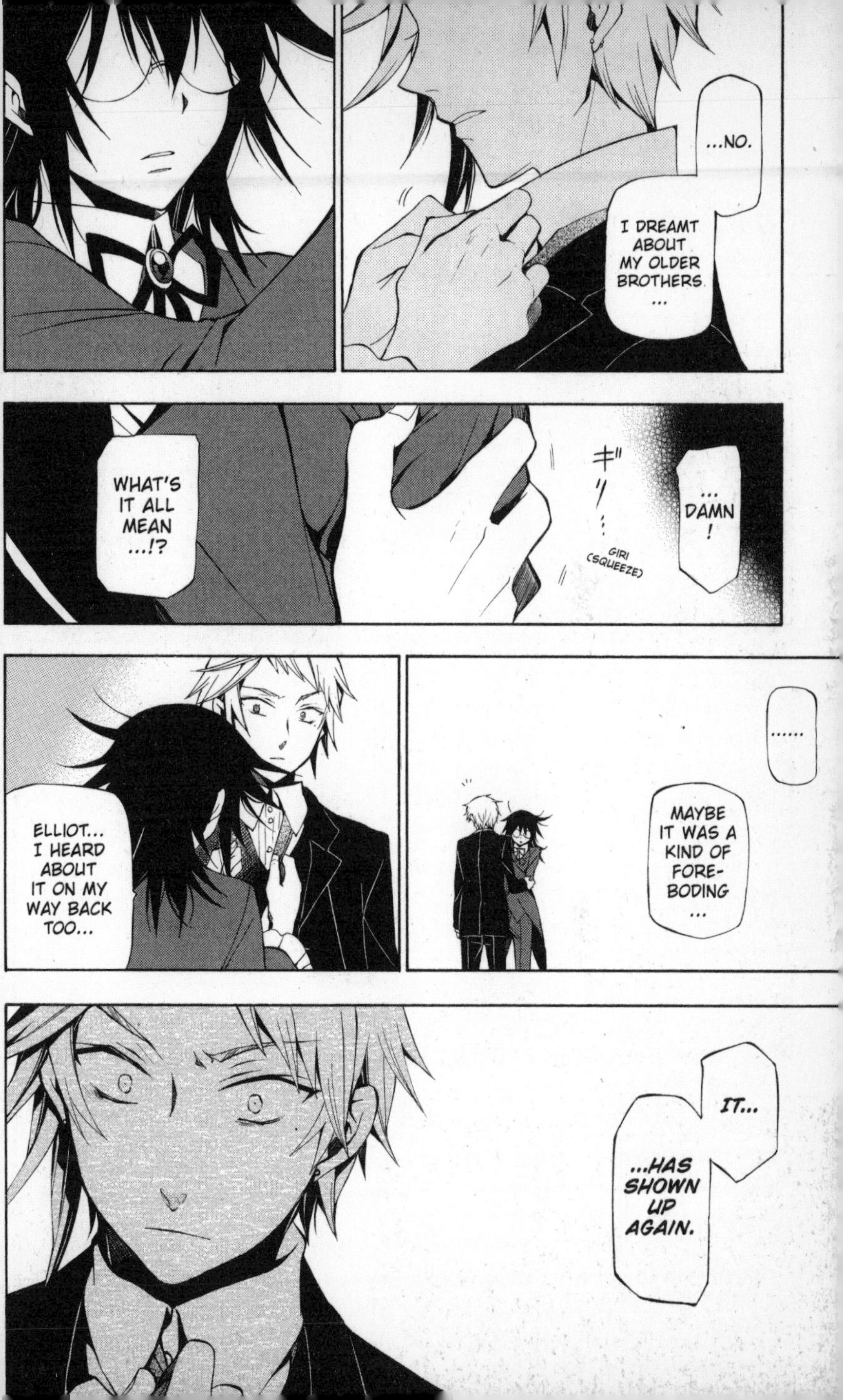
...NO.
I DREAMT ABOUT MY OLDER BROTHERS. ...
... DAMN !
ギリ
GIRI (SQUEEZE)
WHAT'S IT ALL MEAN ...!?
......
MAYBE IT WAS A KIND OF FORE-BODING ...
ELLIOT... I HEARD ABOUT IT ON MY WAY BACK TOO...
IT...
...HAS SHOWN UP AGAIN.

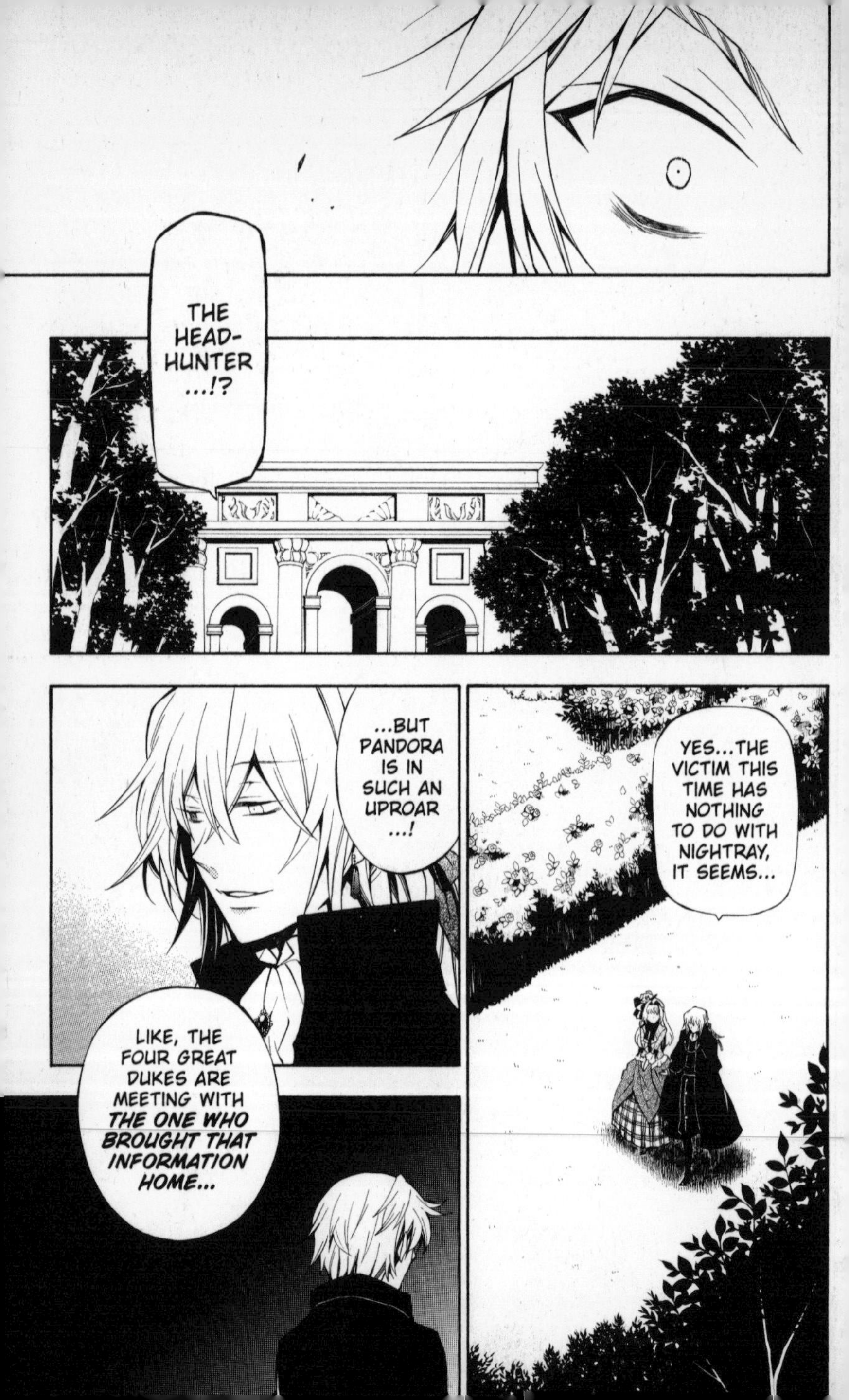
THE HEAD-HUNTER ...!?
YES...THE VICTIM THIS TIME HAS NOTHING TO DO WITH NIGHTRAY, IT SEEMS...
...BUT PANDORA IS IN SUCH AN UPROAR ...!
LIKE, THE FOUR GREAT DUKES ARE MEETING WITH *THE ONE WHO BROUGHT THAT INFORMATION HOME...*

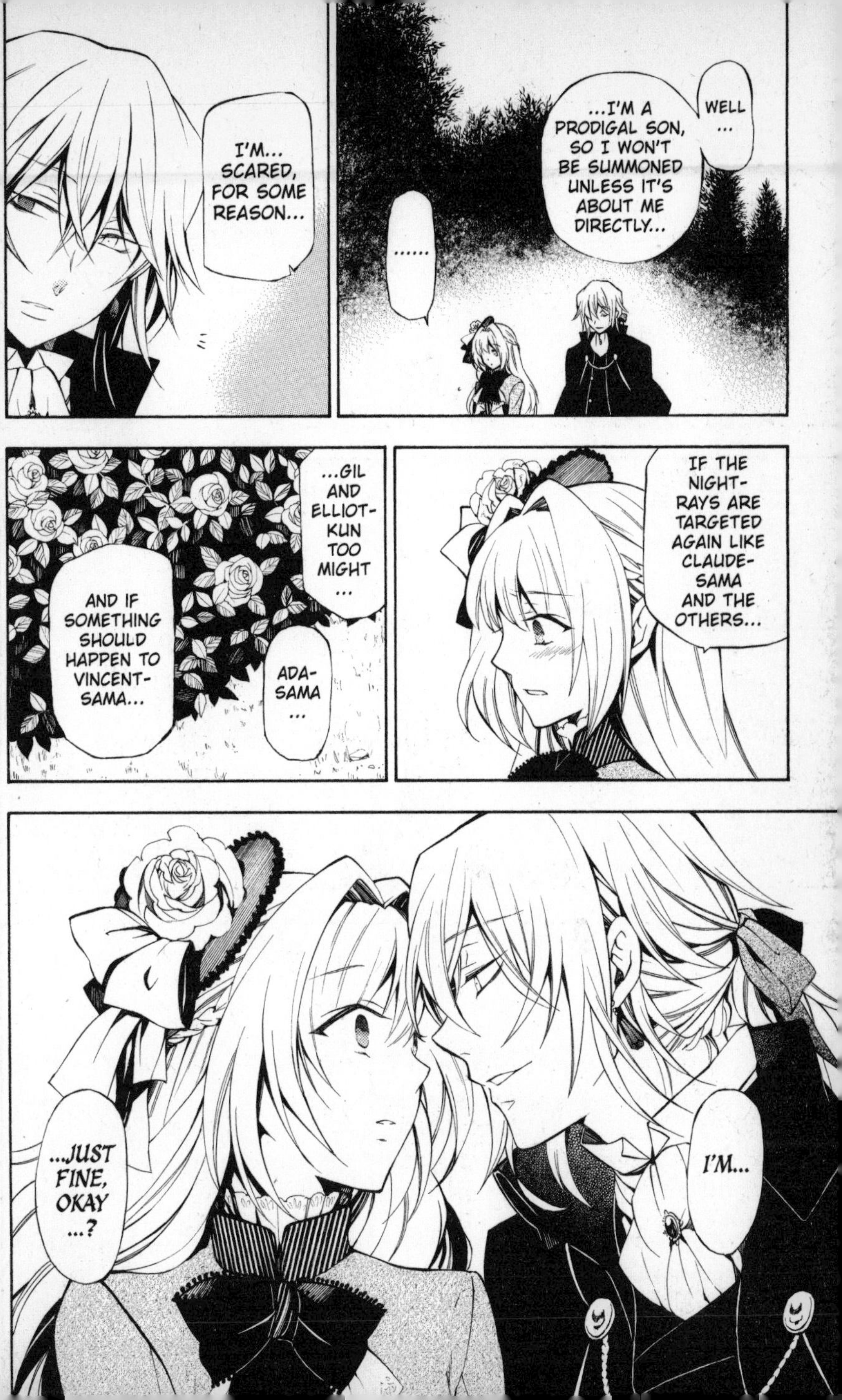
WELL ...
...I'M A PRODIGAL SON, SO I WON'T BE SUMMONED UNLESS IT'S ABOUT ME DIRECTLY...
......
I'M... SCARED, FOR SOME REASON...
IF THE NIGHT-RAYS ARE TARGETED AGAIN LIKE CLAUDE-SAMA AND THE OTHERS...
...GIL AND ELLIOT-KUN TOO MIGHT ...
AND IF SOMETHING SHOULD HAPPEN TO VINCENT-SAMA...
ADA-SAMA ...
I'M...
...JUST FINE, OKAY ...?

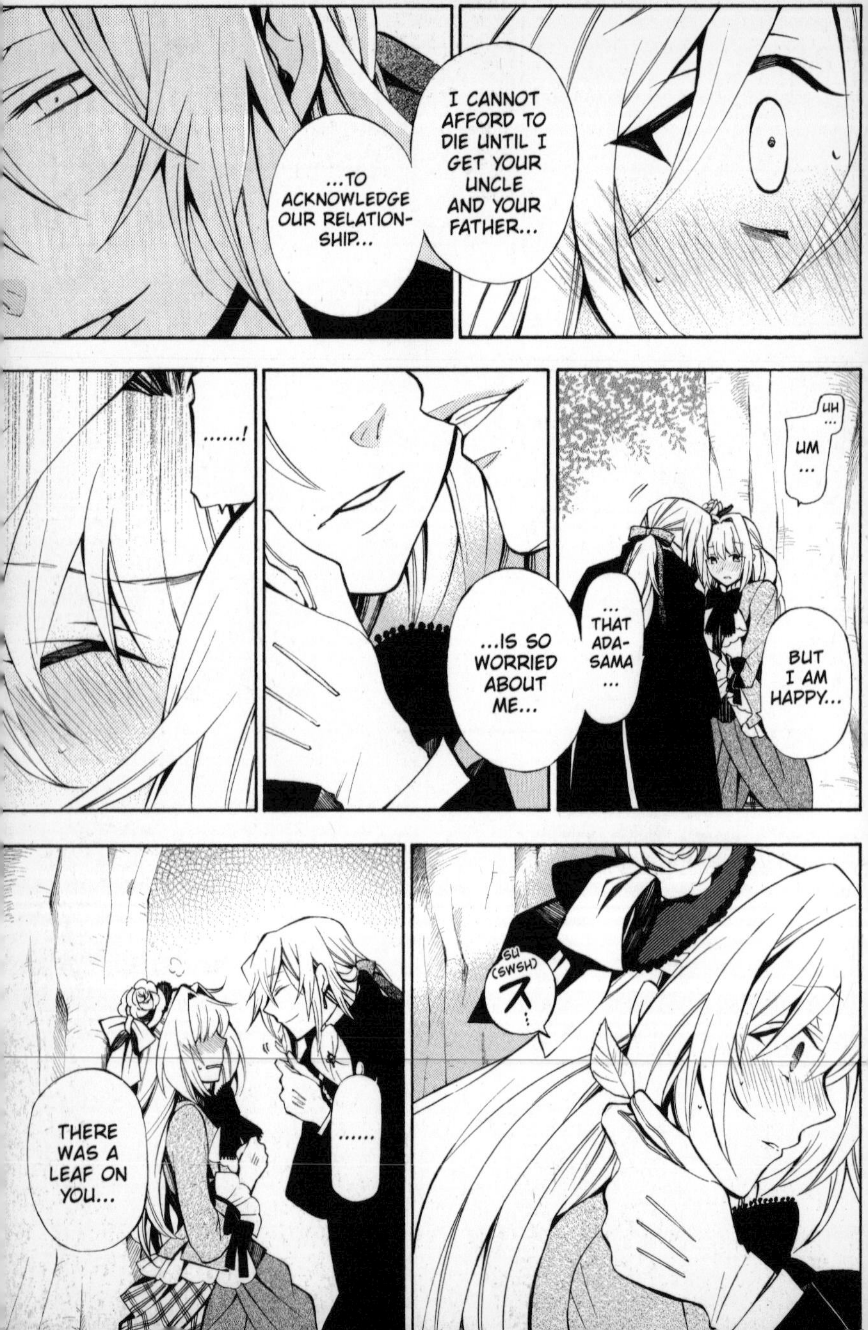
I CANNOT AFFORD TO DIE UNTIL I GET YOUR UNCLE AND YOUR FATHER...
...TO ACKNOWLEDGE OUR RELATIONSHIP...
UH... UM...
BUT I AM HAPPY...
...THAT ADA-SAMA...
...IS SO WORRIED ABOUT ME...
......!
SU (SWSH)
ス...
......
THERE WAS A LEAF ON YOU...

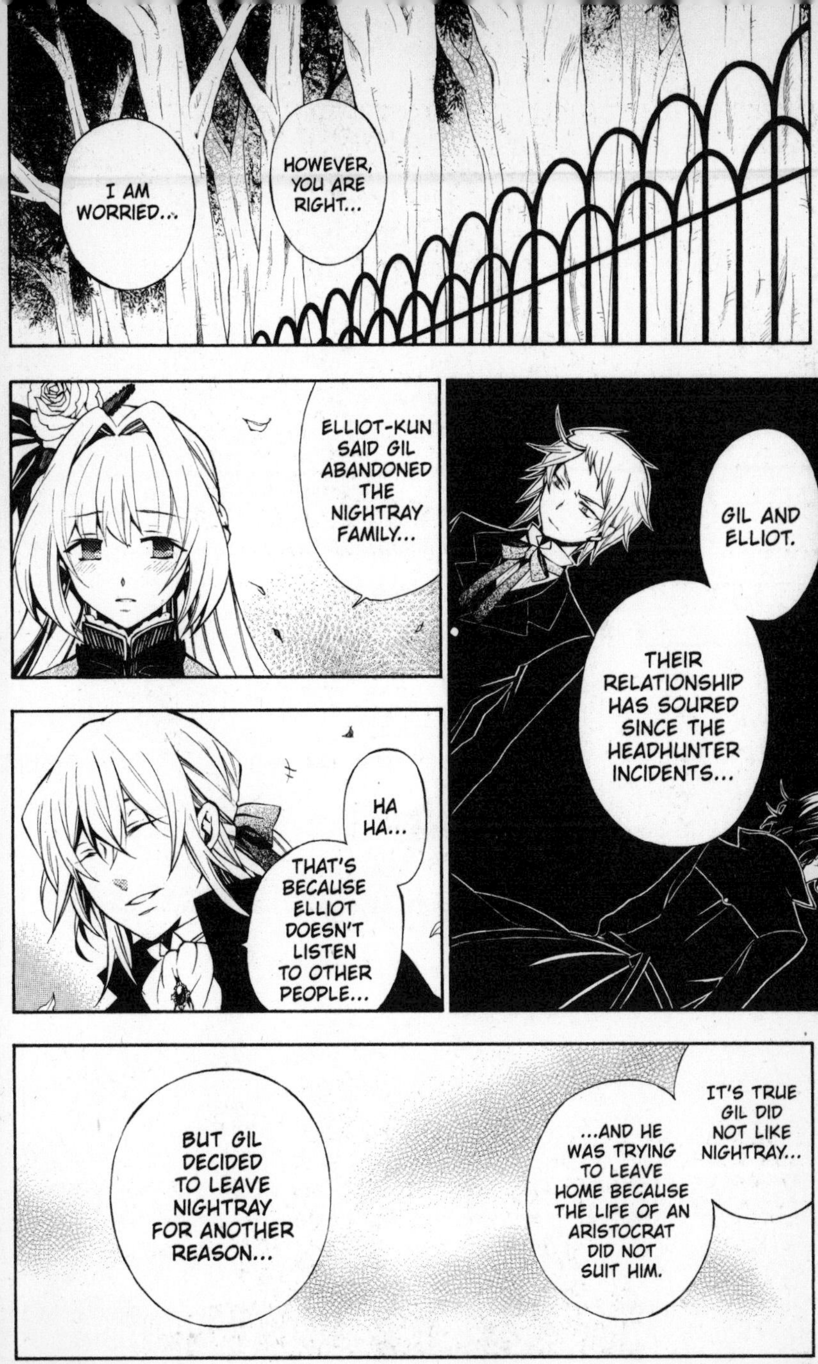
HOWEVER, YOU ARE RIGHT...
I AM WORRIED...
GIL AND ELLIOT.
THEIR RELATIONSHIP HAS SOURED SINCE THE HEADHUNTER INCIDENTS...
ELLIOT-KUN SAID GIL ABANDONED THE NIGHTRAY FAMILY...
HA HA...
THAT'S BECAUSE ELLIOT DOESN'T LISTEN TO OTHER PEOPLE...
IT'S TRUE GIL DID NOT LIKE NIGHTRAY...
...AND HE WAS TRYING TO LEAVE HOME BECAUSE THE LIFE OF AN ARISTOCRAT DID NOT SUIT HIM.
BUT GIL DECIDED TO LEAVE NIGHTRAY FOR ANOTHER REASON...

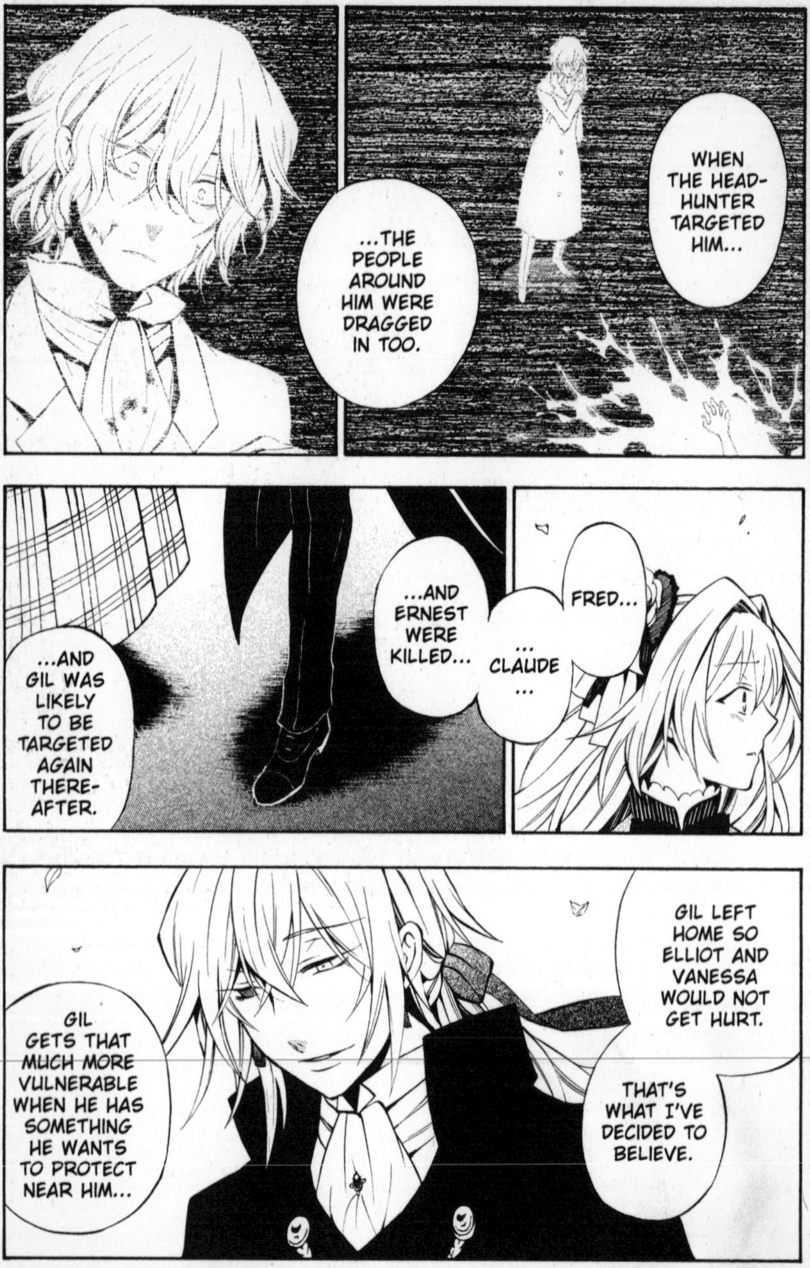
WHEN THE HEAD-HUNTER TARGETED HIM...
...THE PEOPLE AROUND HIM WERE DRAGGED IN TOO.
FRED...
...CLAUDE...
...AND ERNEST WERE KILLED...
...AND GIL WAS LIKELY TO BE TARGETED AGAIN THERE-AFTER.
GIL LEFT HOME SO ELLIOT AND VANESSA WOULD NOT GET HURT.
THAT'S WHAT I'VE DECIDED TO BELIEVE.
GIL GETS THAT MUCH MORE VULNERABLE WHEN HE HAS SOMETHING HE WANTS TO PROTECT NEAR HIM...

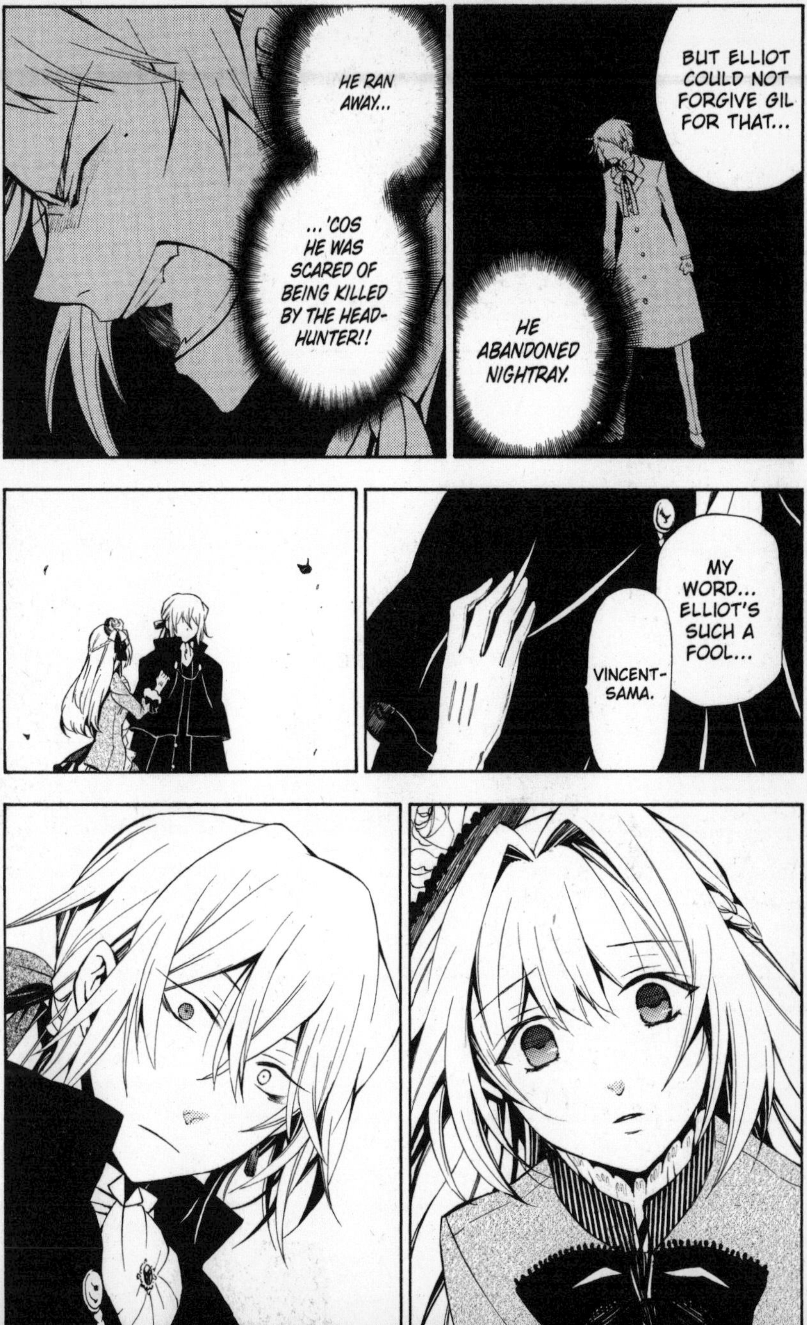
BUT ELLIOT COULD NOT FORGIVE GIL FOR THAT...
HE ABANDONED NIGHTRAY.
HE RAN AWAY...
...'COS HE WAS SCARED OF BEING KILLED BY THE HEAD-HUNTER!!
MY WORD... ELLIOT'S SUCH A FOOL...
VINCENT-SAMA.

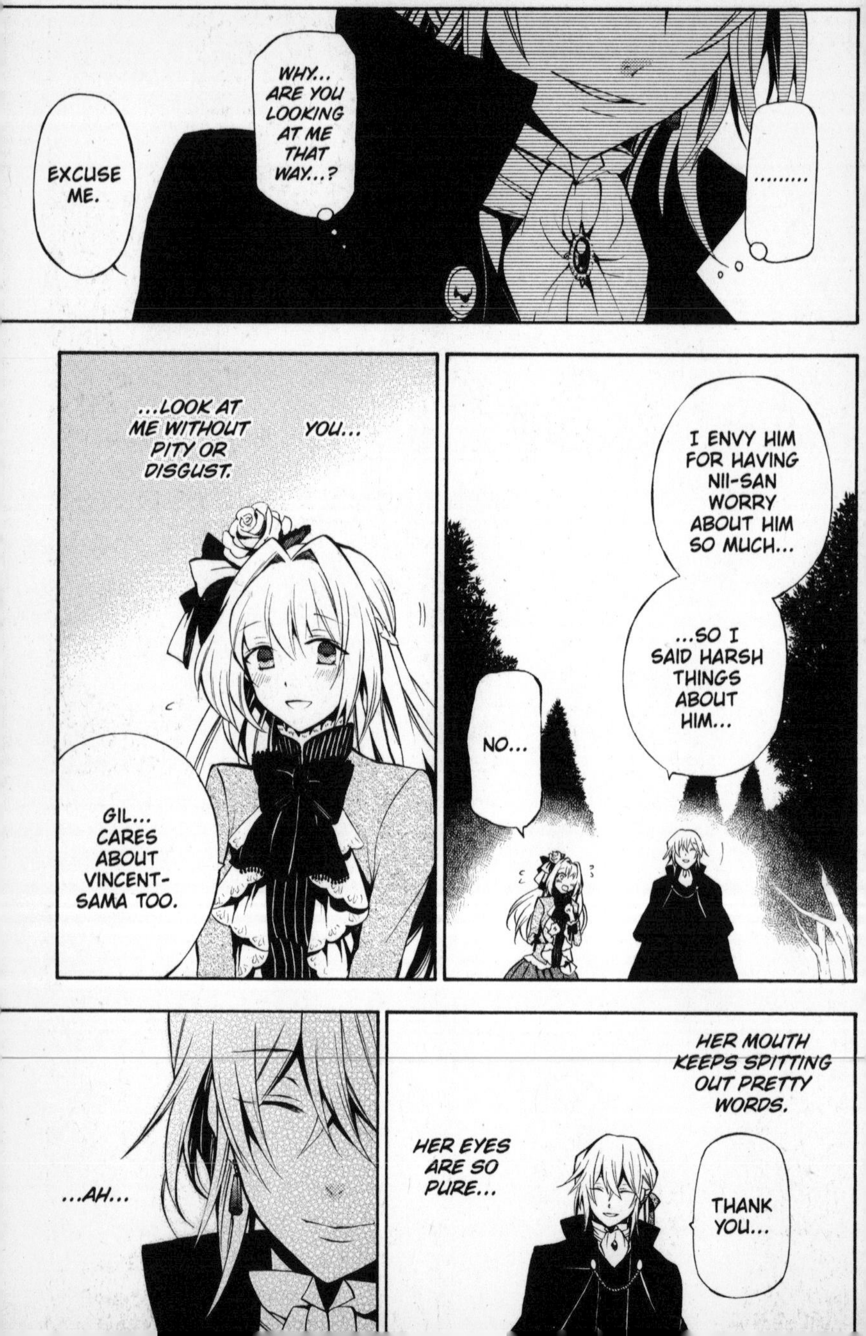
....
WHY... ARE YOU LOOKING AT ME THAT WAY...?
EXCUSE ME.
I ENVY HIM FOR HAVING NII-SAN WORRY ABOUT HIM SO MUCH...
...SO I SAID HARSH THINGS ABOUT HIM...
NO...
YOU...
...LOOK AT ME WITHOUT PITY OR DISGUST.
GIL... CARES ABOUT VINCENT-SAMA TOO.
HER MOUTH KEEPS SPITTING OUT PRETTY WORDS.
THANK YOU...
HER EYES ARE SO PURE...
...AH...

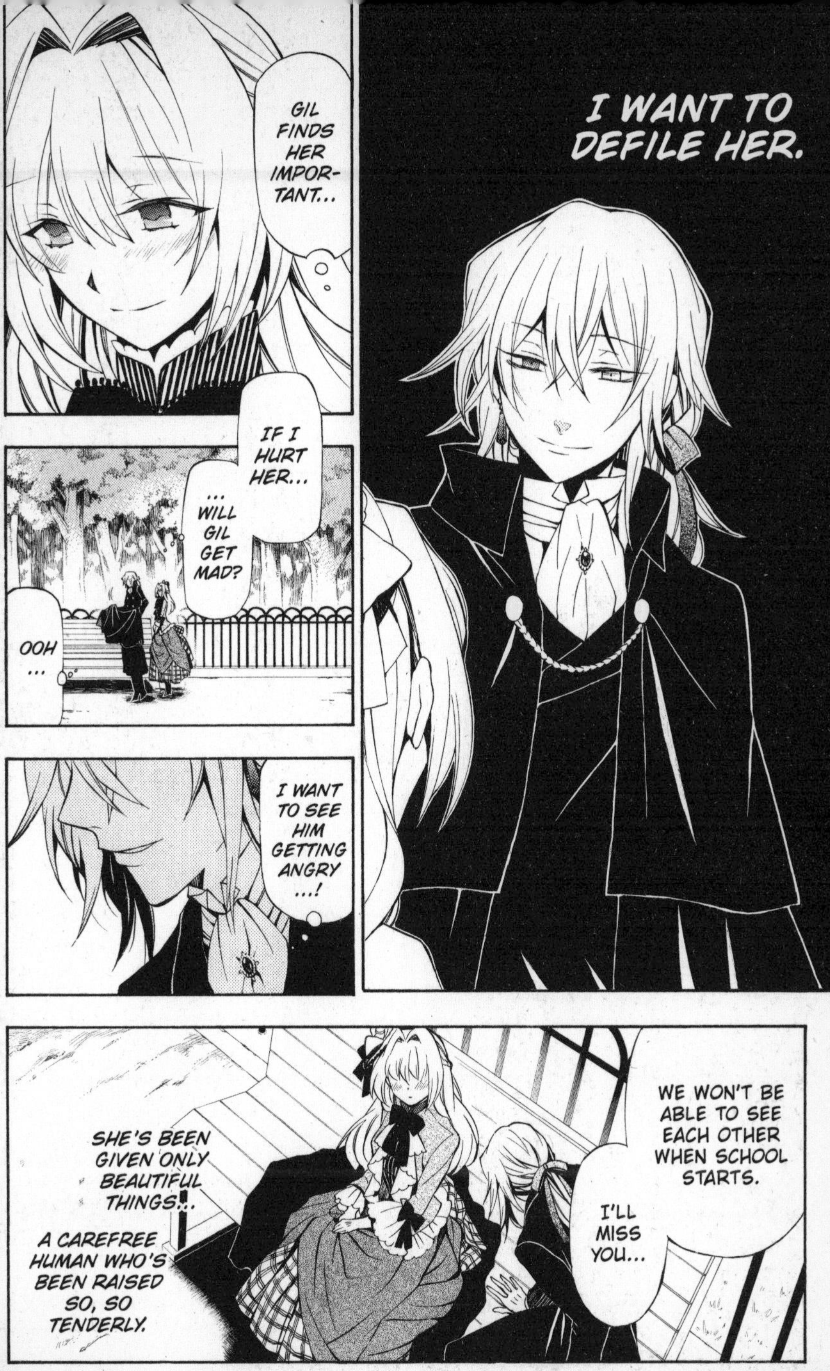
I WANT TO DEFILE HER.
GIL FINDS HER IMPORTANT...
IF I HURT HER...
...WILL GIL GET MAD?
OOH...
I WANT TO SEE HIM GETTING ANGRY ...!
WE WON'T BE ABLE TO SEE EACH OTHER WHEN SCHOOL STARTS.
I'LL MISS YOU...
SHE'S BEEN GIVEN ONLY BEAUTIFUL THINGS...
A CAREFREE HUMAN WHO'S BEEN RAISED SO, SO TENDERLY.

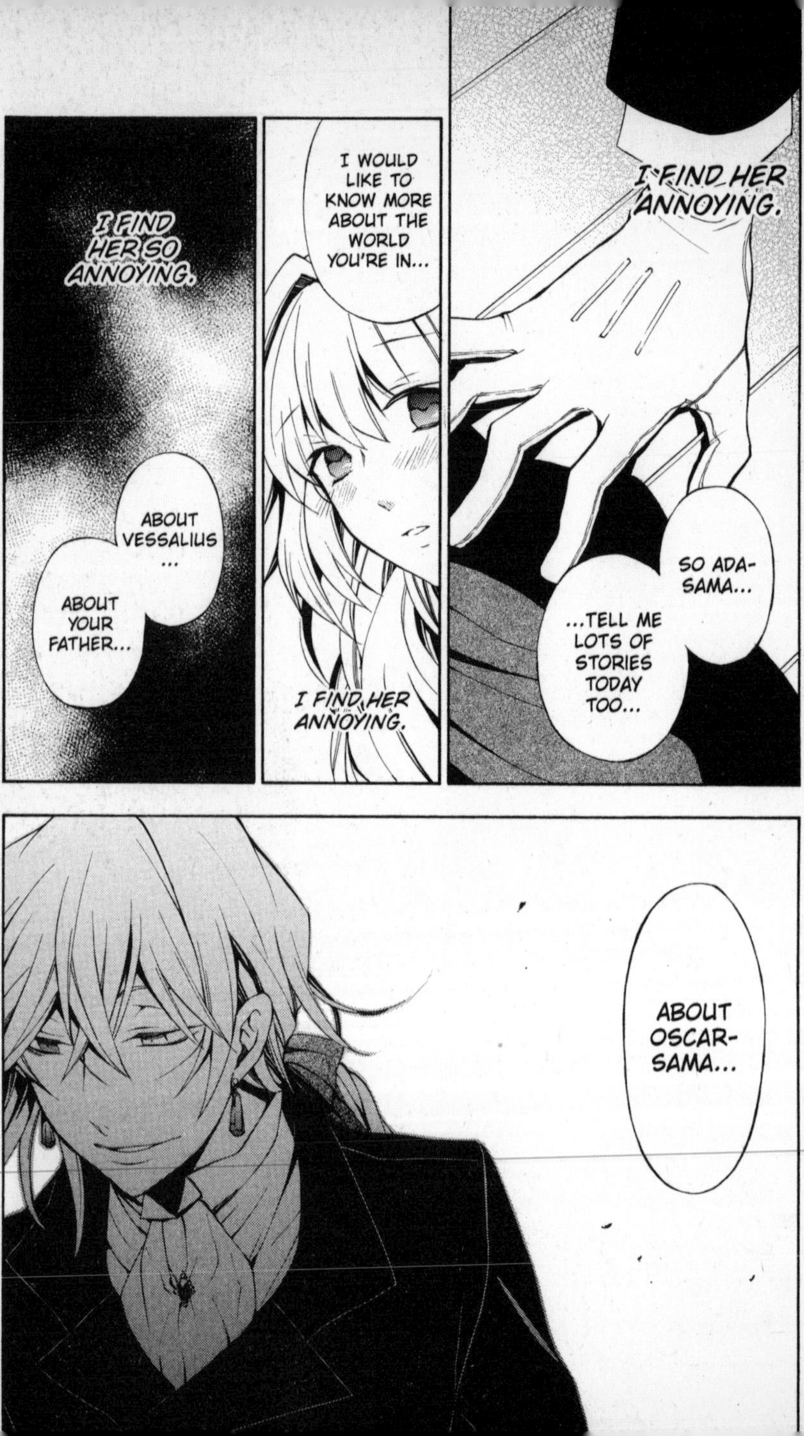
I FIND HER ANNOYING.
SO ADA-SAMA...
...TELL ME LOTS OF STORIES TODAY TOO...
I WOULD LIKE TO KNOW MORE ABOUT THE WORLD YOU'RE IN...
I FIND HER ANNOYING.
I FIND HER SO ANNOYING.
ABOUT VESSALIUS...
ABOUT YOUR FATHER...
ABOUT OSCAR-SAMA...

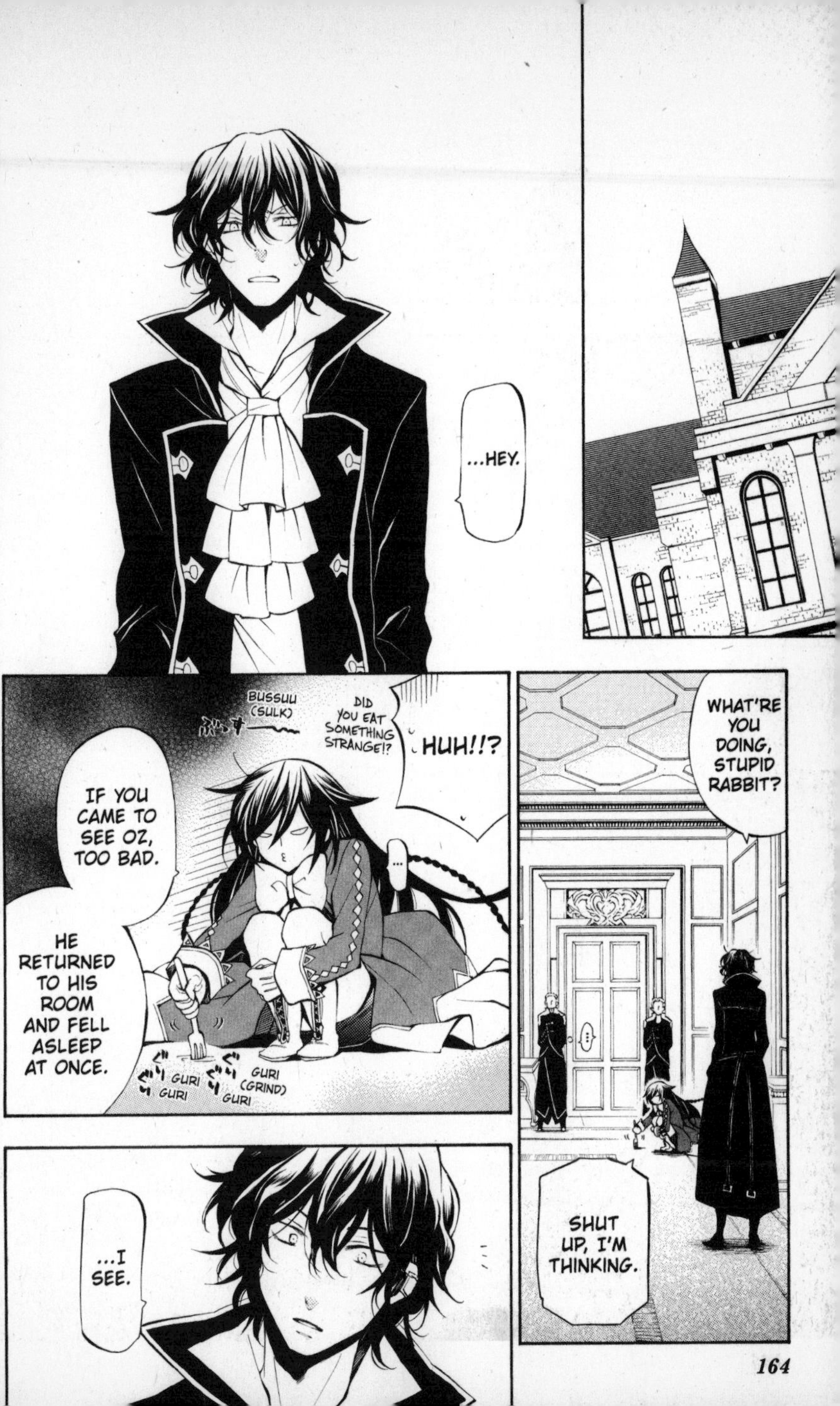
...HEY.
WHAT'RE YOU DOING, STUPID RABBIT?
...
SHUT UP, I'M THINKING.
HUH!!?
DID YOU EAT SOMETHING STRANGE!?
BUSSUU (SULK)
...
IF YOU CAME TO SEE OZ, TOO BAD.
HE RETURNED TO HIS ROOM AND FELL ASLEEP AT ONCE.
GURI (GRIND) GURI GURI GURI
...I SEE.

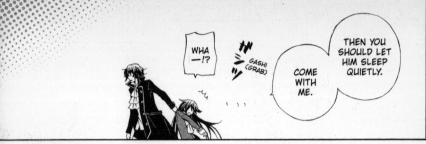

WHA—!?

GASHI (GRAB)

COME WITH ME.

THEN YOU SHOULD LET HIM SLEEP QUIETLY.

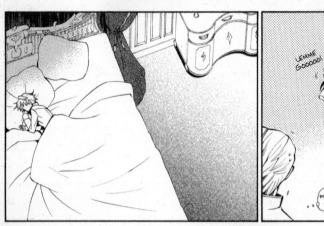

LEMME GOOOOO!

UNOH!

ZURU (DRAG)

ZURU

ZURU

ZURU

PHEW

MY BODY FEELS HEAVY...

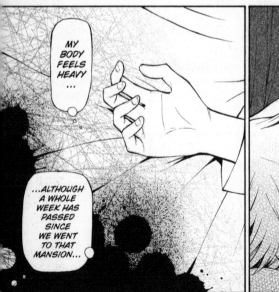

...ALTHOUGH A WHOLE WEEK HAS PASSED SINCE WE WENT TO THAT MANSION...

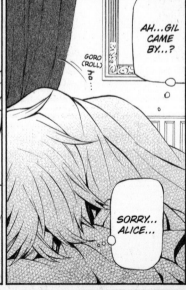

GORO (ROLL)

AH...GIL CAME BY...?

SORRY... ALICE...

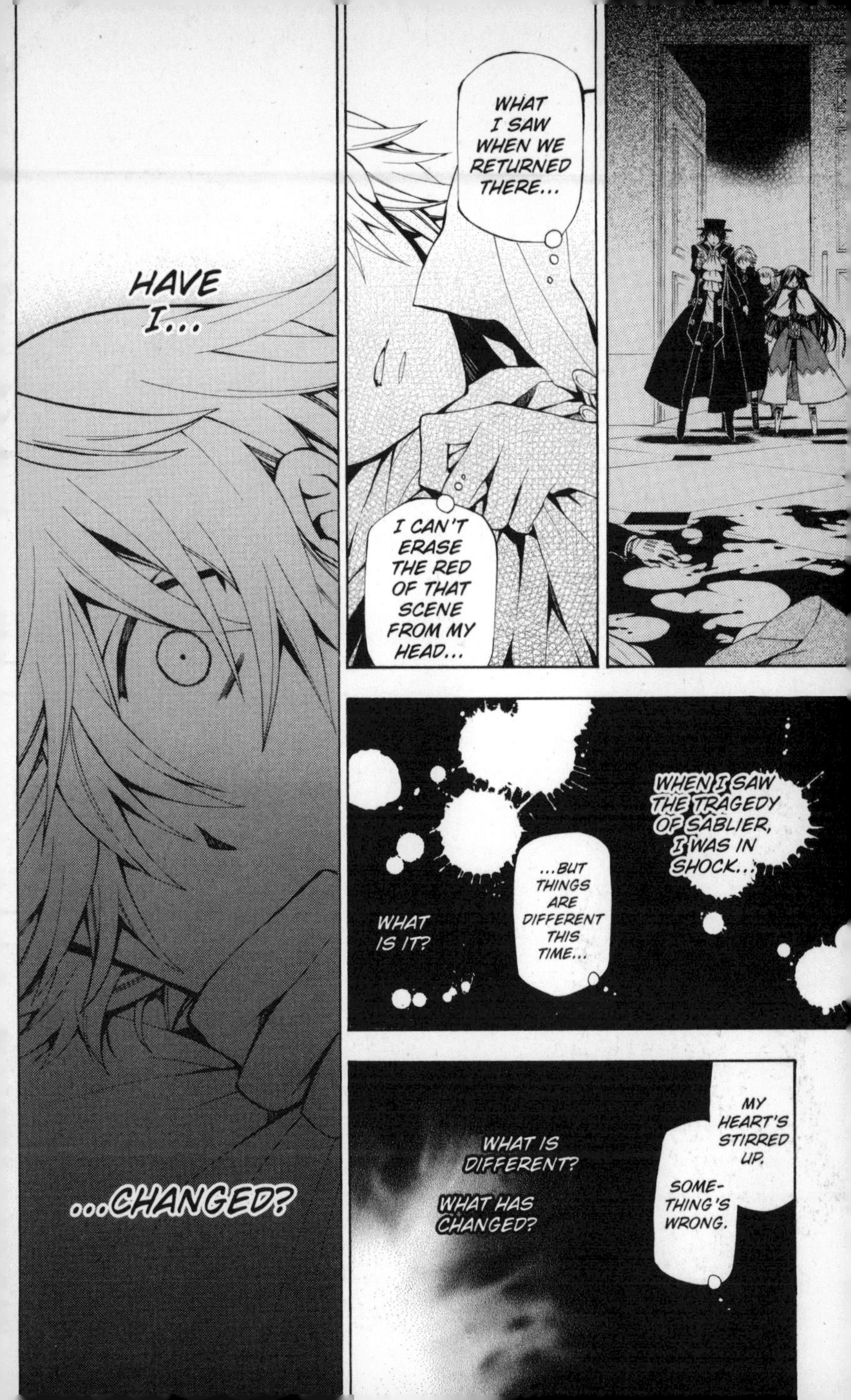
WHAT I SAW WHEN WE RETURNED THERE...
I CAN'T ERASE THE RED OF THAT SCENE FROM MY HEAD...
WHEN I SAW THE TRAGEDY OF SABLIER, I WAS IN SHOCK...
...BUT THINGS ARE DIFFERENT THIS TIME...
WHAT IS IT?
MY HEART'S STIRRED UP.
SOME-THING'S WRONG.
WHAT IS DIFFERENT?
WHAT HAS CHANGED?
HAVE I...
...CHANGED?

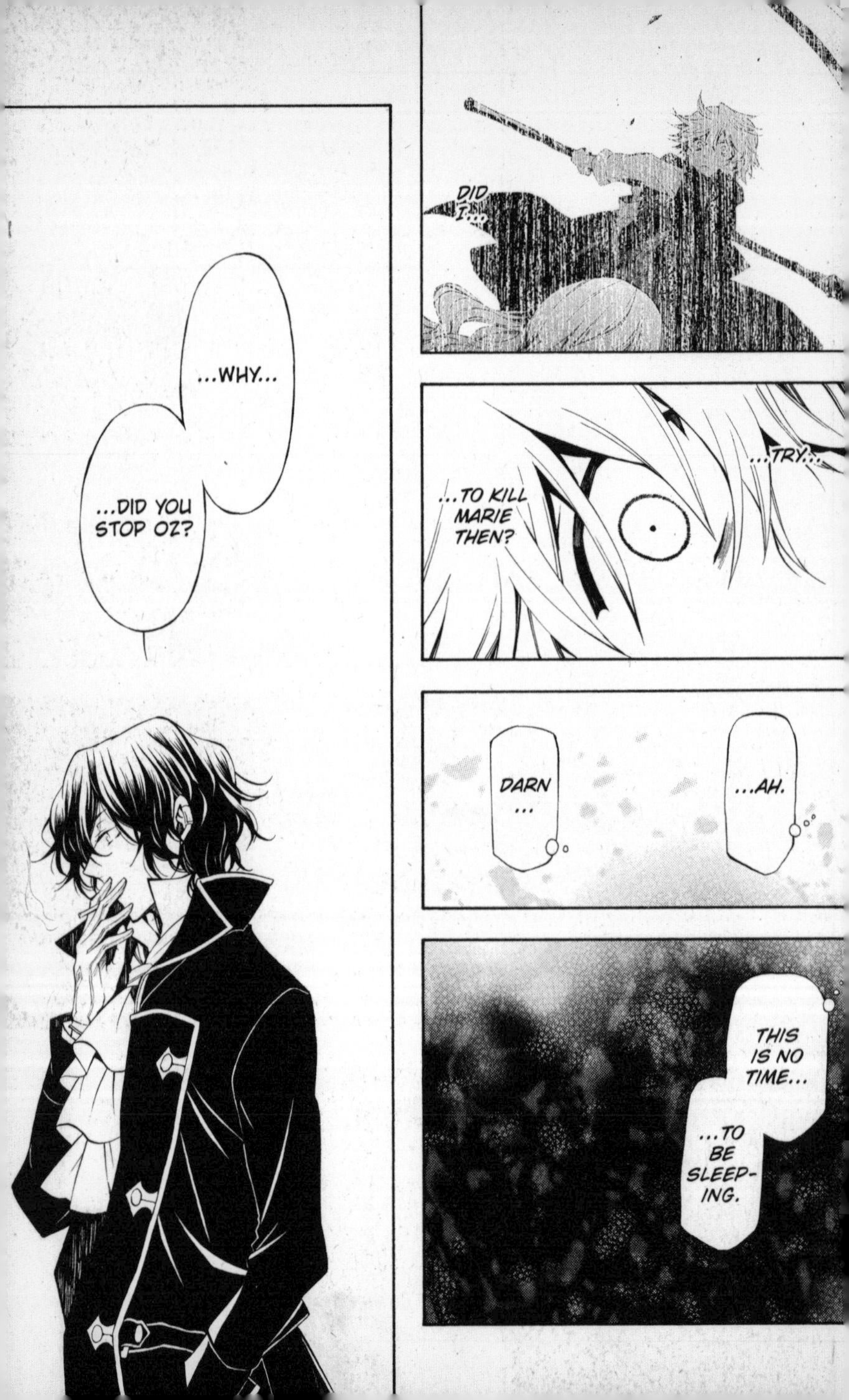
DID I...
...TRY...
...TO KILL MARIE THEN?
...AH.
DARN...
THIS IS NO TIME...
...TO BE SLEEPING.
...WHY...
...DID YOU STOP OZ?

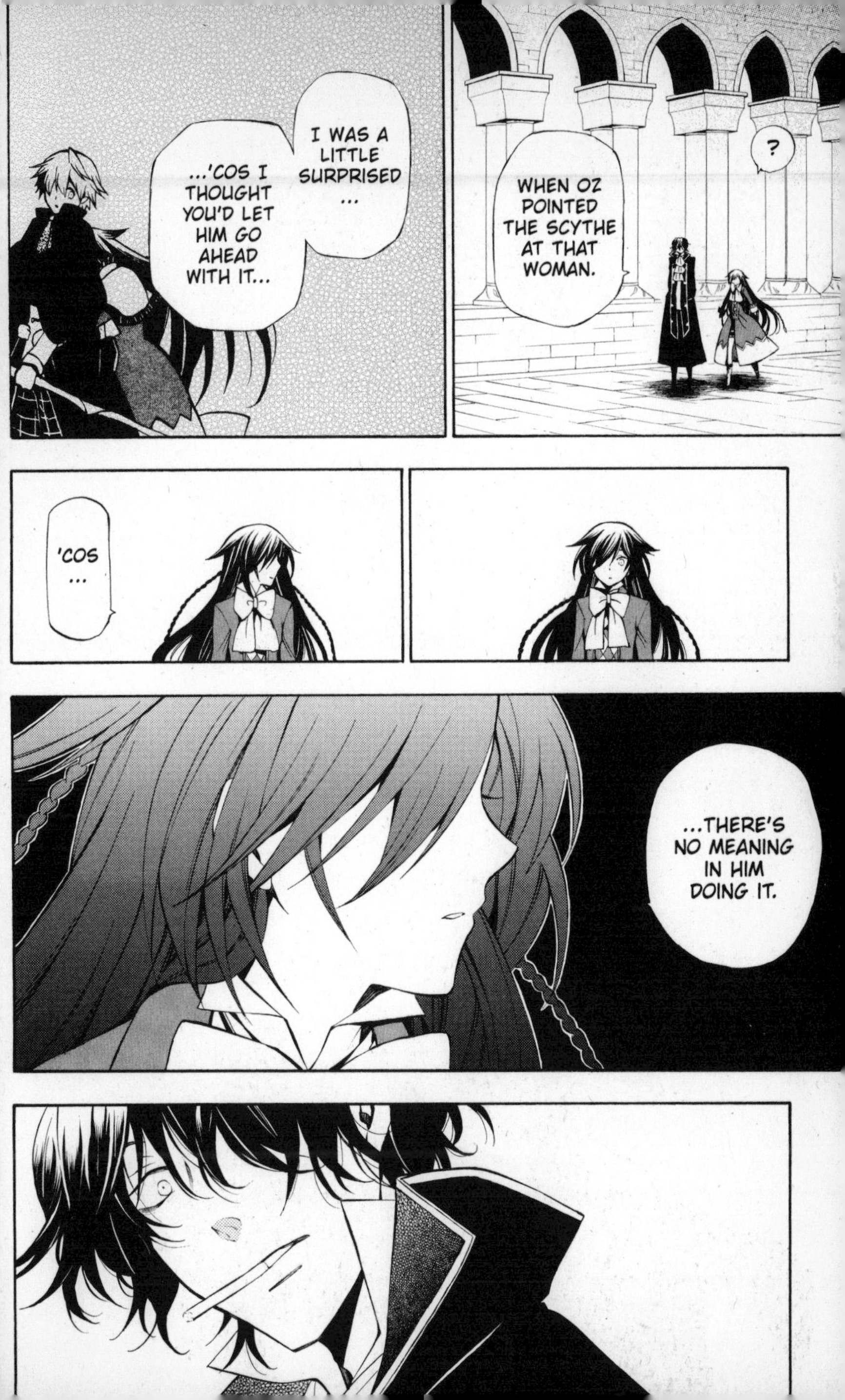
WHEN OZ POINTED THE SCYTHE AT THAT WOMAN.
?
I WAS A LITTLE SURPRISED ...
...'COS I THOUGHT YOU'D LET HIM GO AHEAD WITH IT...
'COS ...
...THERE'S NO MEANING IN HIM DOING IT.

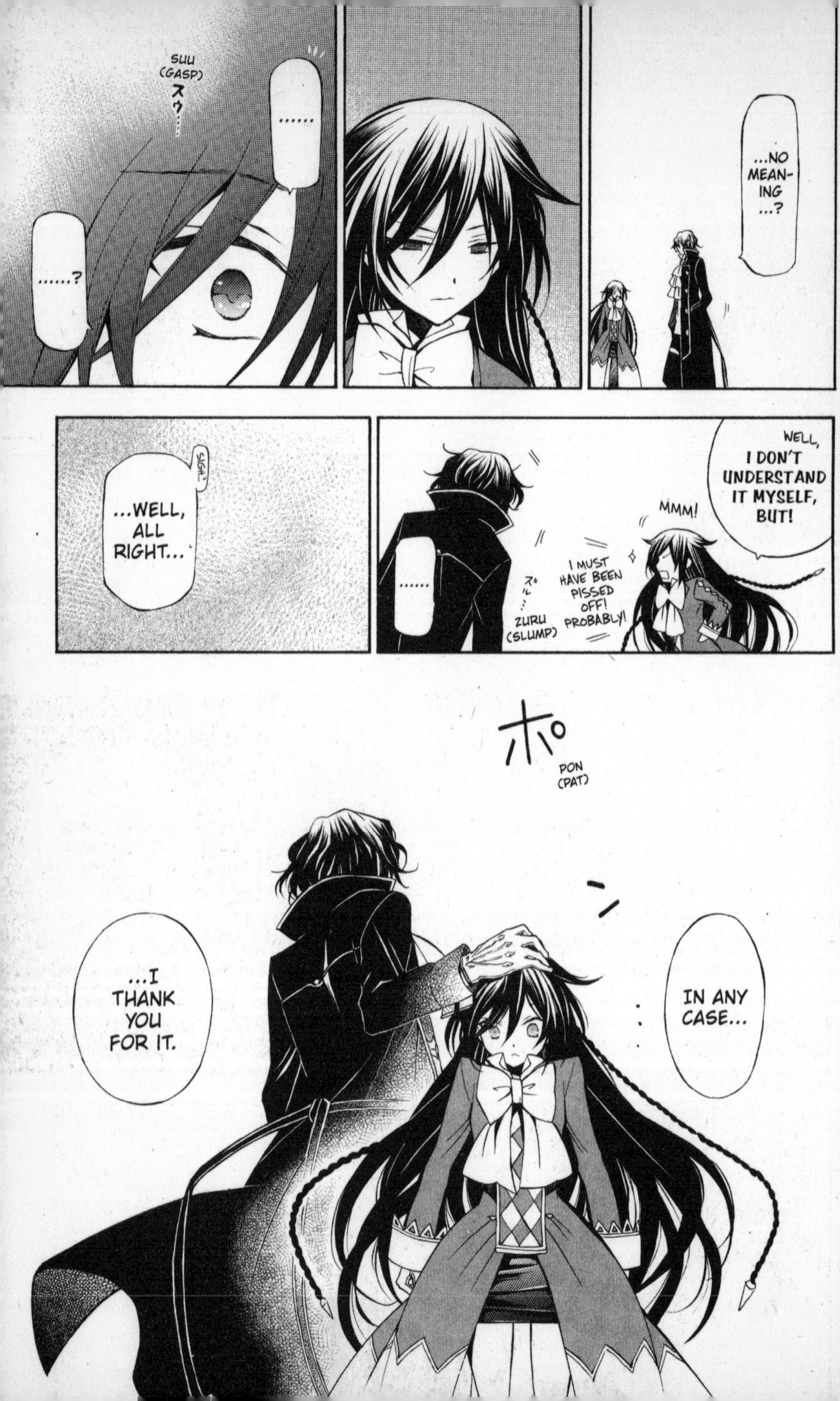
...NO MEAN-ING...?
SUU (GASP)
スウ…
......
......?
WELL, I DON'T UNDERSTAND IT MYSELF, BUT!
MMM!
I MUST HAVE BEEN PISSED OFF! PROBABLY!
ズル…
ZURU (SLUMP)
......
SIGH...
...WELL, ALL RIGHT...
ポ
PON (PAT)
IN ANY CASE...
...I THANK YOU FOR IT.

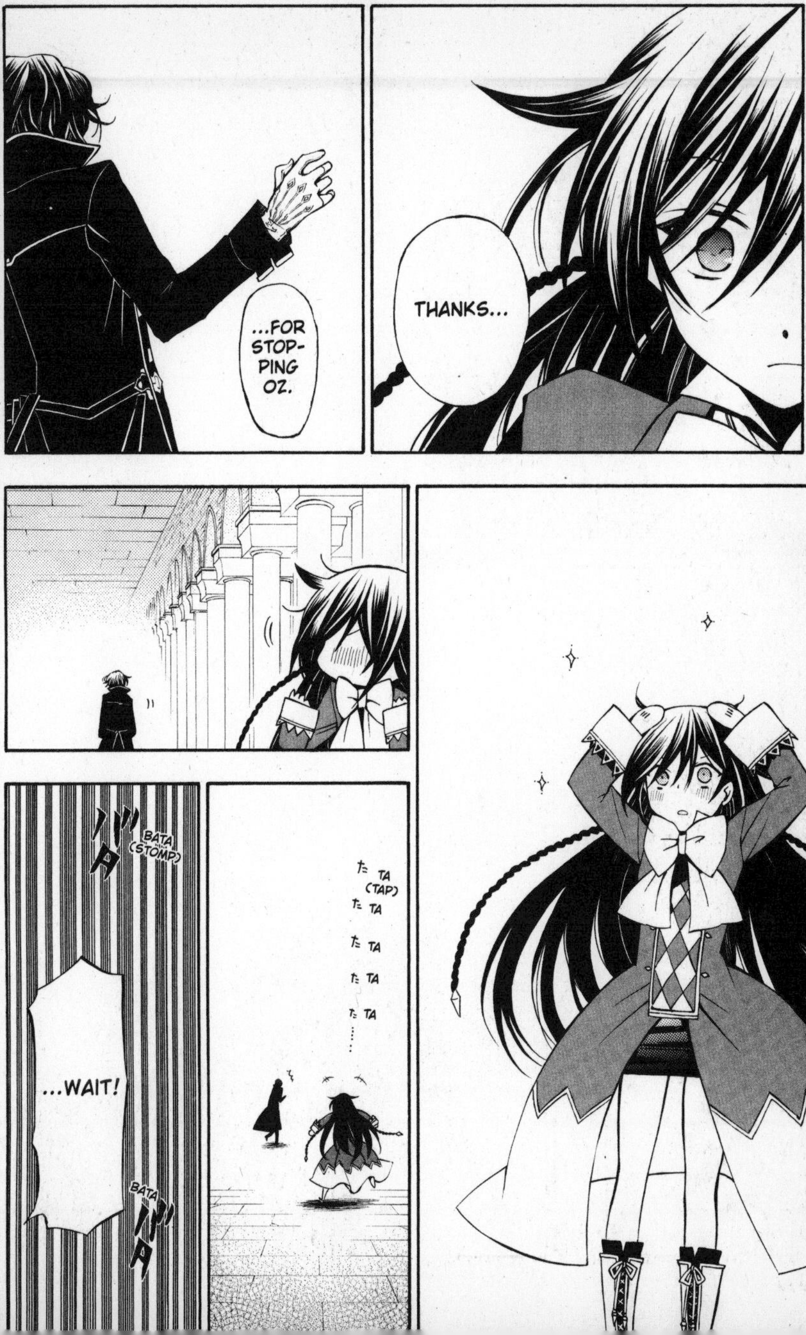
THANKS...
...FOR STOPPING OZ.
た TA (TAP)
た TA
た TA
た TA
た TA
......
バタ BATA (STOMP)
...WAIT!
BATA バタ

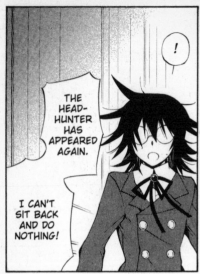

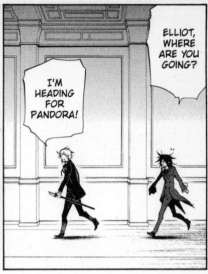

ELLIOT, WHERE ARE YOU GOING?
I'M HEADING FOR PANDORA!
!
THE HEAD-HUNTER HAS APPEARED AGAIN.
I CAN'T SIT BACK AND DO NOTHING!
FRED.
CLAUDE.
ERNEST...
I...
...WILL NEVER FORGIVE THAT THING...!

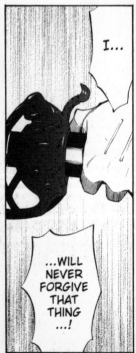

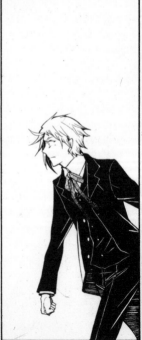

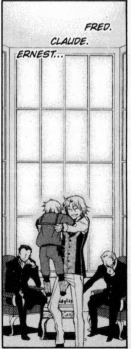

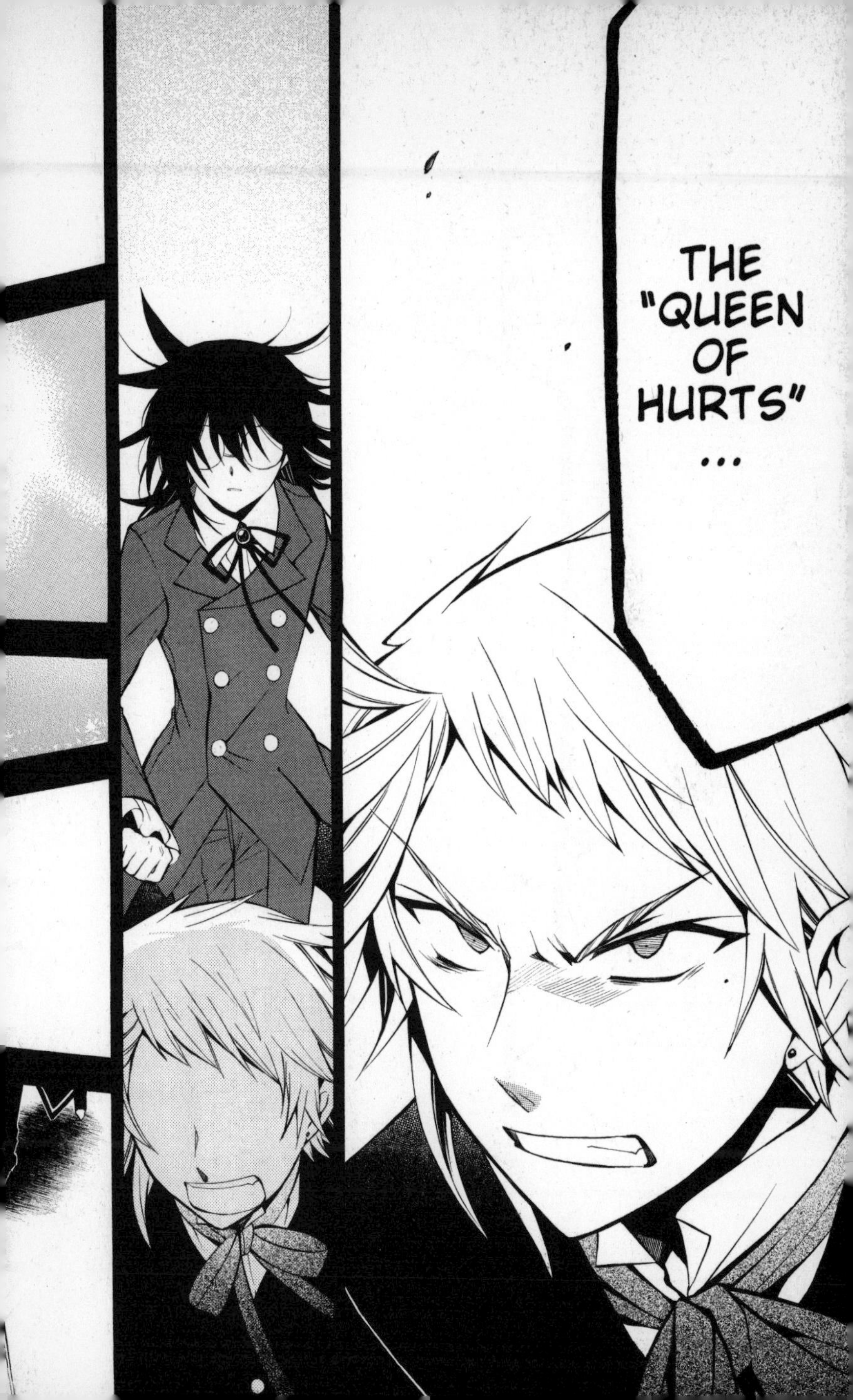
THE "QUEEN OF HURTS" ...

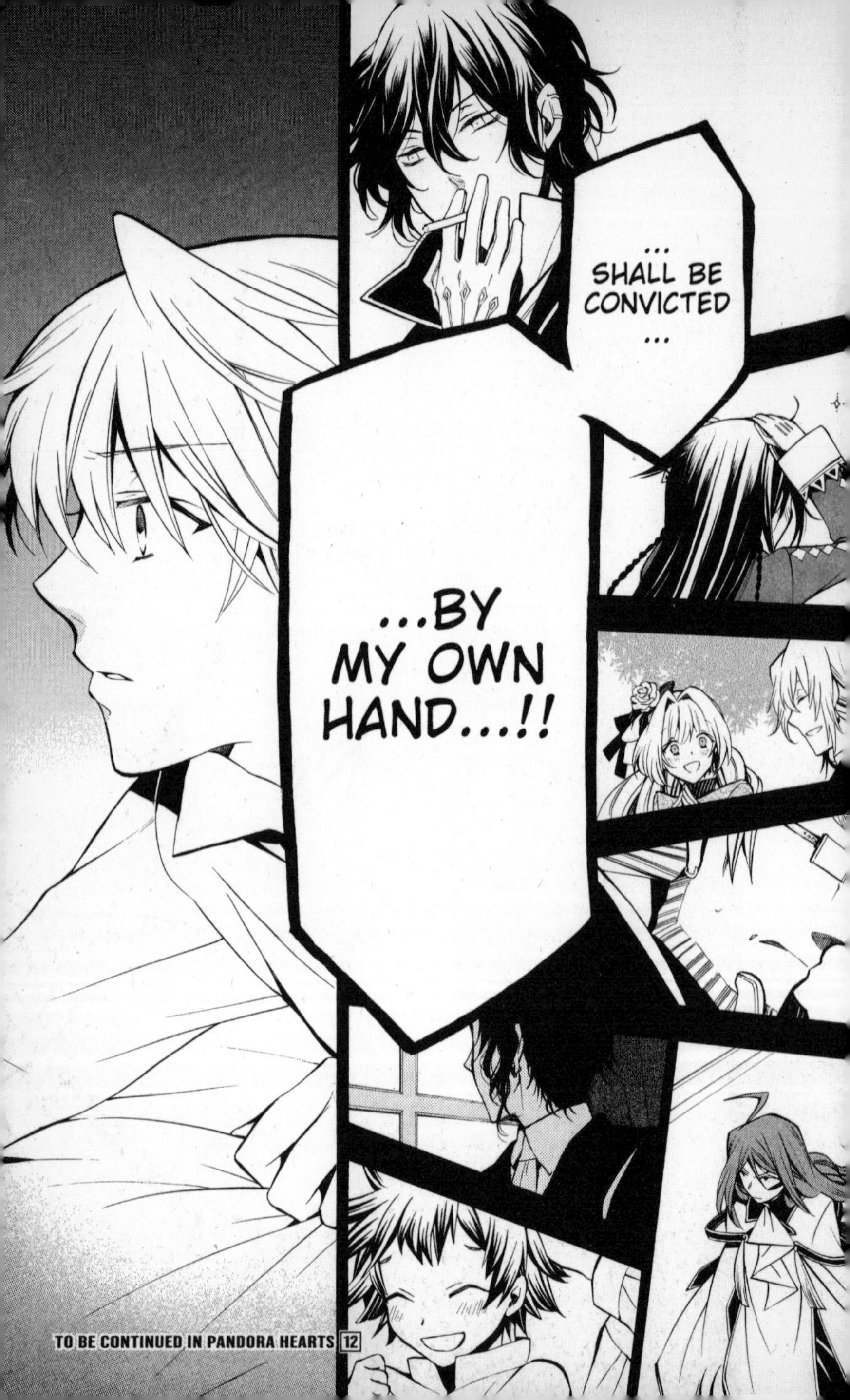
... SHALL BE CONVICTED ...
...BY MY OWN HAND...!!

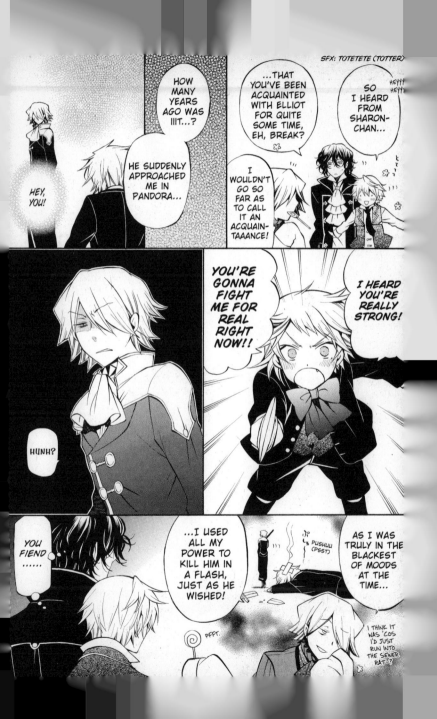

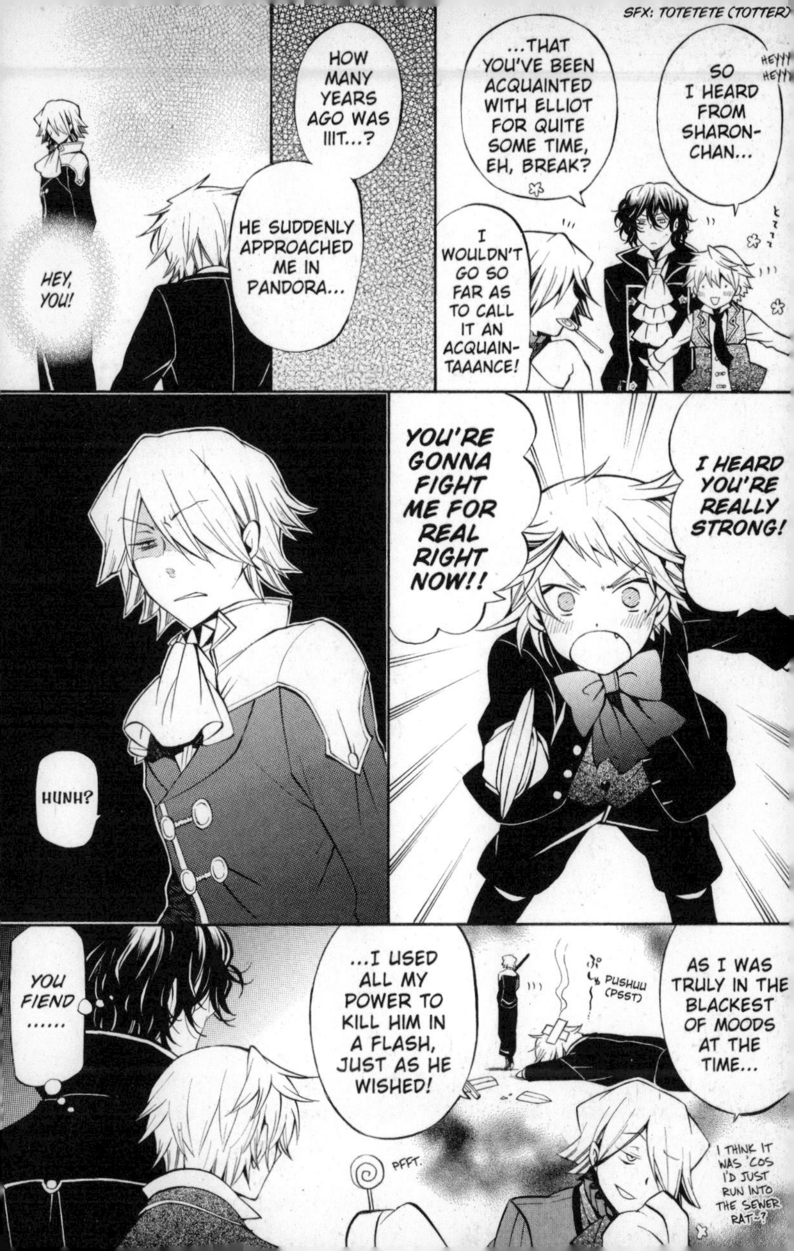
SFX: TOTETETE (TOTTER)
SO I HEARD FROM SHARON-CHAN...
HEYYY HEYYY
...THAT YOU'VE BEEN ACQUAINTED WITH ELLIOT FOR QUITE SOME TIME, EH, BREAK?
I WOULDN'T GO SO FAR AS TO CALL IT AN ACQUAIN-TAAANCE!
HOW MANY YEARS AGO WAS IIIT...?
HE SUDDENLY APPROACHED ME IN PANDORA...
HEY, YOU!
I HEARD YOU'RE REALLY STRONG!
YOU'RE GONNA FIGHT ME FOR REAL RIGHT NOW!!
HUNH?
AS I WAS TRULY IN THE BLACKEST OF MOODS AT THE TIME...
I THINK IT WAS 'COS I'D JUST RUN INTO THE SEWER RAT~?
PUSHUU (PSST)
...I USED ALL MY POWER TO KILL HIM IN A FLASH, JUST AS HE WISHED!
PFFT.
YOU FIEND ......

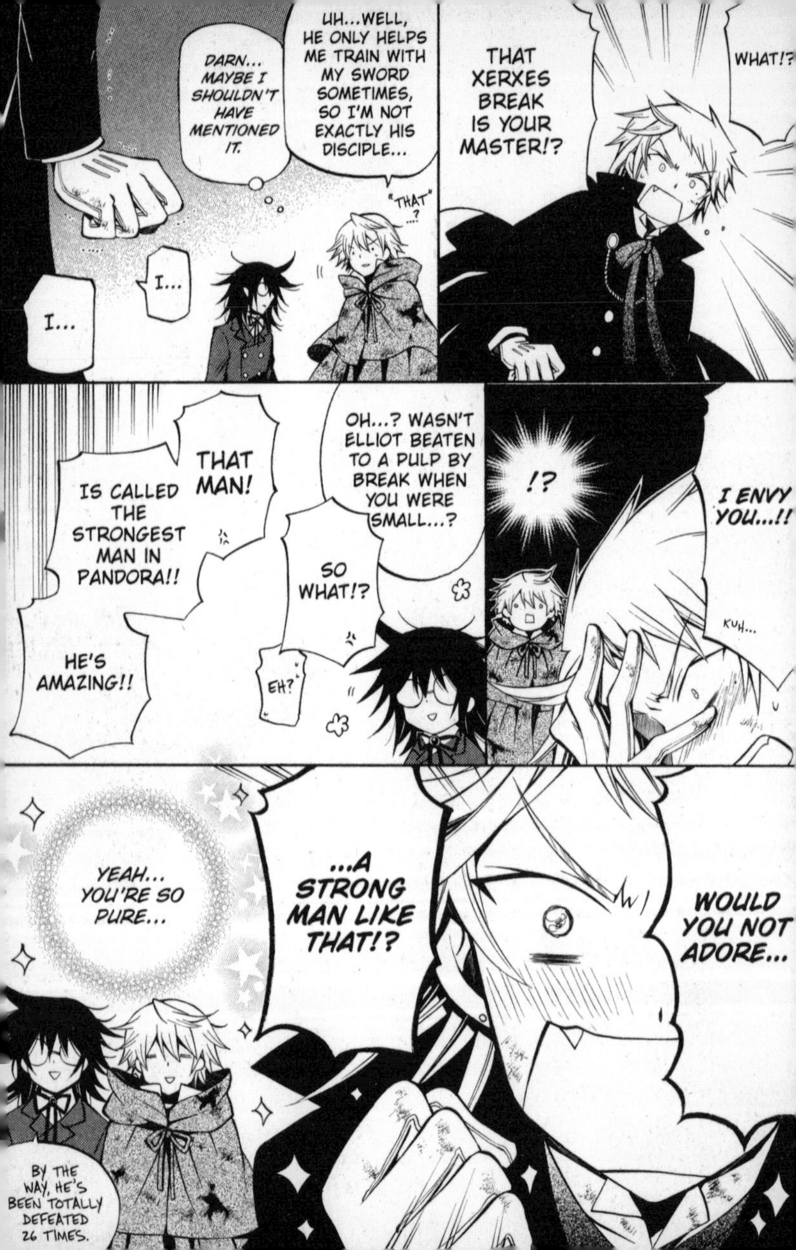
WHAT!?
THAT XERXES BREAK IS YOUR MASTER!?
UH...WELL, HE ONLY HELPS ME TRAIN WITH MY SWORD SOMETIMES, SO I'M NOT EXACTLY HIS DISCIPLE...
DARN... MAYBE I SHOULDN'T HAVE MENTIONED IT.
"THAT" ...?
I...
I...
!?
I ENVY YOU...!!
KUH...
THAT MAN!
IS CALLED THE STRONGEST MAN IN PANDORA!!
OH...? WASN'T ELLIOT BEATEN TO A PULP BY BREAK WHEN YOU WERE SMALL...?
SO WHAT!?
EH?
HE'S AMAZING!!
WOULD YOU NOT ADORE...
...A STRONG MAN LIKE THAT!?
YEAH... YOU'RE SO PURE...
BY THE WAY, HE'S BEEN TOTALLY DEFEATED 26 TIMES.

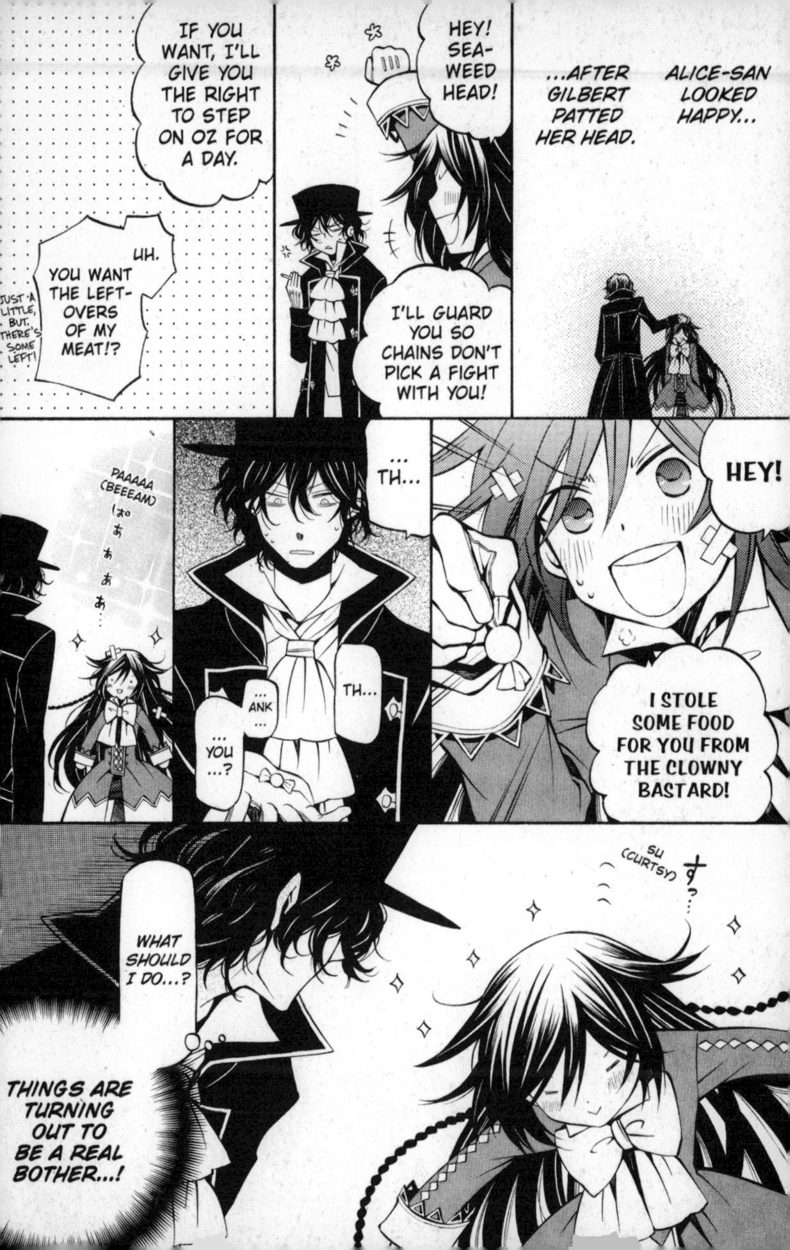
ALICE-SAN LOOKED HAPPY...
...AFTER GILBERT PATTED HER HEAD.
HEY! SEA-WEED HEAD!
I'LL GUARD YOU SO CHAINS DON'T PICK A FIGHT WITH YOU!
IF YOU WANT, I'LL GIVE YOU THE RIGHT TO STEP ON OZ FOR A DAY.
UH. YOU WANT THE LEFT-OVERS OF MY MEAT!?
JUST A LITTLE, BUT, THERE'S SOME LEFT!
HEY!
I STOLE SOME FOOD FOR YOU FROM THE CLOWNY BASTARD!
...TH...
TH...
...ANK...
...YOU...?
PAAAAA (BEEEAM)
ぱぁあああ…
SU (CURTSY)
す…
WHAT SHOULD I DO...?
THINGS ARE TURNING OUT TO BE A REAL BOTHER...!

Special Thanks !!

FUMITO YAMAZAKI
YOUR GATEAU CHOCOLAT
IS DELICIOUS.

SEIRA MINAMI-SAN
A CAPYBARA IN HER PREVIOUS LIFE.

SAEKO TAKIGAWA-SAN
HER CHEEKS ARE SOFT.

SOU MINAZUKI-SAN
I CAN SEXUALLY HARASS YOU...!?

YUKINO-SAN
I WANNA POKE YOU.

RYO-CHAN
SURPRISINGLY SHARP-TONGUED

YAJI-SAMA
EUROPEAN AMERICAAAAN

AKKII-SAN
I WANT YOUR CHARACTER
TO COLLAPSE.

YUMI NASHIGASA-SAN
A FIRST RACE THAT
I'VE ENCOUNTERED.

MIDORI ENDO-SAN
I WANT TO SLAP YOU.
NO, I ALREADY AM.

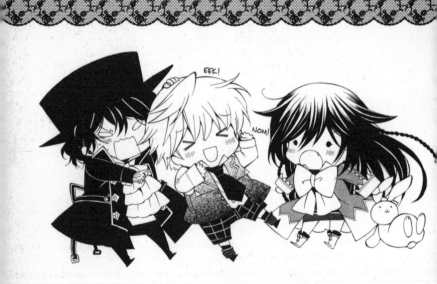

BIG BROTHER   A STARBUCKS REGULAR

MY EDITOR TAKEGASA-SAMA
HEY YOU, GYAH GYAH

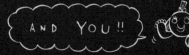

AND YOU !!

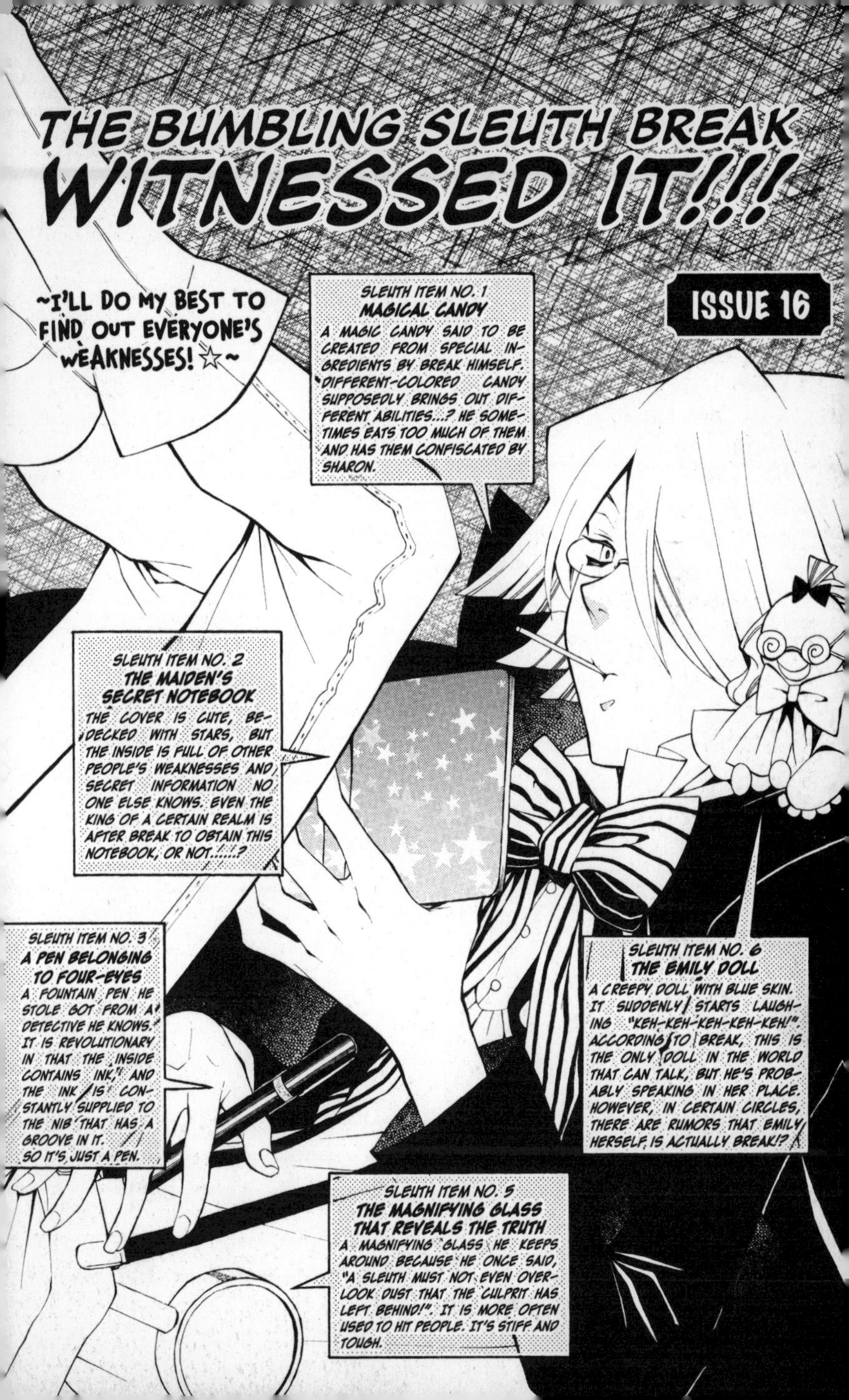

THE BUMBLING SLEUTH BREAK
WITNESSED IT!!!
ISSUE 16
SLEUTH ITEM NO. 1 MAGICAL CANDY A MAGIC CANDY SAID TO BE CREATED FROM SPECIAL INGREDIENTS BY BREAK HIMSELF. DIFFERENT-COLORED CANDY SUPPOSEDLY BRINGS OUT DIFFERENT ABILITIES...? HE SOMETIMES EATS TOO MUCH OF THEM AND HAS THEM CONFISCATED BY SHARON.
~I'LL DO MY BEST TO FIND OUT EVERYONE'S WEAKNESSES! ☆~
SLEUTH ITEM NO. 2 THE MAIDEN'S SECRET NOTEBOOK THE COVER IS CUTE, BEDECKED WITH STARS, BUT THE INSIDE IS FULL OF OTHER PEOPLE'S WEAKNESSES AND SECRET INFORMATION NO ONE ELSE KNOWS. EVEN THE KING OF A CERTAIN REALM IS AFTER BREAK TO OBTAIN THIS NOTEBOOK, OR NOT.....?
SLEUTH ITEM NO. 6 THE EMILY DOLL A CREEPY DOLL WITH BLUE SKIN. IT SUDDENLY STARTS LAUGHING "KEH-KEH-KEH-KEH-KEH!". ACCORDING TO BREAK, THIS IS THE ONLY DOLL IN THE WORLD THAT CAN TALK, BUT HE'S PROBABLY SPEAKING IN HER PLACE. HOWEVER, IN CERTAIN CIRCLES, THERE ARE RUMORS THAT EMILY HERSELF IS ACTUALLY BREAK!?
SLEUTH ITEM NO. 3 A PEN BELONGING TO FOUR-EYES A FOUNTAIN PEN HE STOLE GOT FROM A DETECTIVE HE KNOWS. IT IS REVOLUTIONARY IN THAT THE INSIDE CONTAINS INK, AND THE INK IS CONSTANTLY SUPPLIED TO THE NIB THAT HAS A GROOVE IN IT. SO IT'S JUST A PEN.
SLEUTH ITEM NO. 5 THE MAGNIFYING GLASS THAT REVEALS THE TRUTH A MAGNIFYING GLASS HE KEEPS AROUND BECAUSE HE ONCE SAID, "A SLEUTH MUST NOT EVEN OVERLOOK DUST THAT THE CULPRIT HAS LEFT BEHIND!". IT IS MORE OFTEN USED TO HIT PEOPLE. IT'S STIFF AND TOUGH.

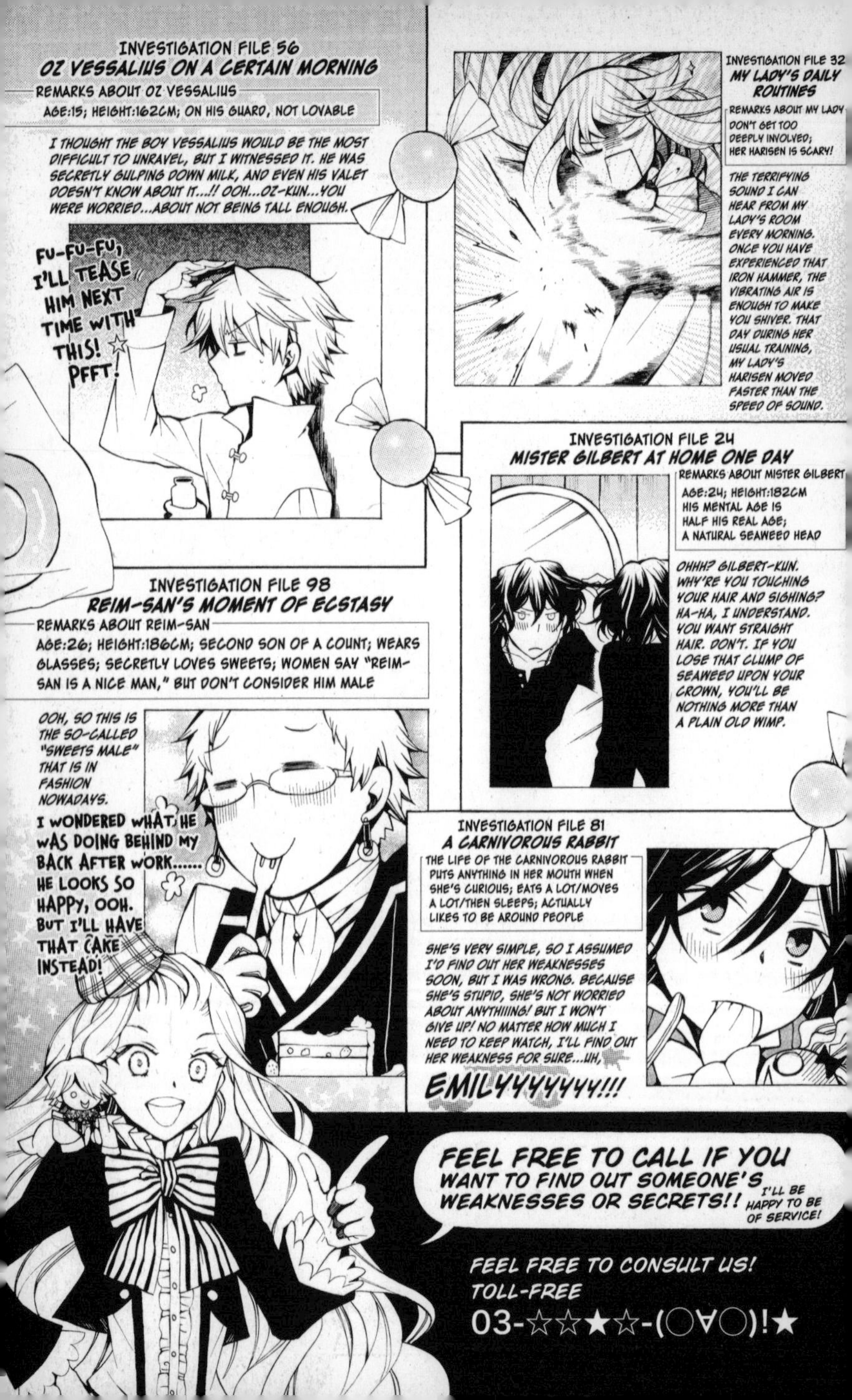

INVESTIGATION FILE 32
MY LADY'S DAILY ROUTINES
REMARKS ABOUT MY LADY
DON'T GET TOO DEEPLY INVOLVED; HER HARISEN IS SCARY!
THE TERRIFYING SOUND I CAN HEAR FROM MY LADY'S ROOM EVERY MORNING. ONCE YOU HAVE EXPERIENCED THAT IRON HAMMER, THE VIBRATING AIR IS ENOUGH TO MAKE YOU SHIVER. THAT DAY DURING HER USUAL TRAINING, MY LADY'S HARISEN MOVED FASTER THAN THE SPEED OF SOUND.
INVESTIGATION FILE 56
OZ VESSALIUS ON A CERTAIN MORNING
REMARKS ABOUT OZ VESSALIUS
AGE:15; HEIGHT:162CM; ON HIS GUARD, NOT LOVABLE
I THOUGHT THE BOY VESSALIUS WOULD BE THE MOST DIFFICULT TO UNRAVEL, BUT I WITNESSED IT. HE WAS SECRETLY GULPING DOWN MILK, AND EVEN HIS VALET DOESN'T KNOW ABOUT IT...!! OOH...OZ-KUN...YOU WERE WORRIED...ABOUT NOT BEING TALL ENOUGH.
FU-FU-FU, I'LL TEASE HIM NEXT TIME WITH THIS! ☆ PFFT!
INVESTIGATION FILE 24
MISTER GILBERT AT HOME ONE DAY
REMARKS ABOUT MISTER GILBERT
AGE:24; HEIGHT:182CM
HIS MENTAL AGE IS HALF HIS REAL AGE; A NATURAL SEAWEED HEAD
OHHH? GILBERT-KUN. WHY'RE YOU TOUCHING YOUR HAIR AND SIGHING? HA-HA, I UNDERSTAND. YOU WANT STRAIGHT HAIR. DON'T. IF YOU LOSE THAT CLUMP OF SEAWEED UPON YOUR CROWN, YOU'LL BE NOTHING MORE THAN A PLAIN OLD WIMP.
INVESTIGATION FILE 98
REIM-SAN'S MOMENT OF ECSTASY
REMARKS ABOUT REIM-SAN
AGE:26; HEIGHT:186CM; SECOND SON OF A COUNT; WEARS GLASSES; SECRETLY LOVES SWEETS; WOMEN SAY "REIM-SAN IS A NICE MAN," BUT DON'T CONSIDER HIM MALE
OOH, SO THIS IS THE SO-CALLED "SWEETS MALE" THAT IS IN FASHION NOWADAYS.
I WONDERED WHAT HE WAS DOING BEHIND MY BACK AFTER WORK...... HE LOOKS SO HAPPY, OOH. BUT I'LL HAVE THAT CAKE INSTEAD!
INVESTIGATION FILE 81
A CARNIVOROUS RABBIT
THE LIFE OF THE CARNIVOROUS RABBIT PUTS ANYTHING IN HER MOUTH WHEN SHE'S CURIOUS; EATS A LOT/MOVES A LOT/THEN SLEEPS; ACTUALLY LIKES TO BE AROUND PEOPLE
SHE'S VERY SIMPLE, SO I ASSUMED I'D FIND OUT HER WEAKNESSES SOON, BUT I WAS WRONG. BECAUSE SHE'S STUPID, SHE'S NOT WORRIED ABOUT ANYTHIIING! BUT I WON'T GIVE UP! NO MATTER HOW MUCH I NEED TO KEEP WATCH, I'LL FIND OUT HER WEAKNESS FOR SURE...UH,
EMILYYYYYYY!!!
FEEL FREE TO CALL IF YOU WANT TO FIND OUT SOMEONE'S WEAKNESSES OR SECRETS!!
I'LL BE HAPPY TO BE OF SERVICE!
FEEL FREE TO CONSULT US!
TOLL-FREE
03-☆☆★☆-(○∀○)!★

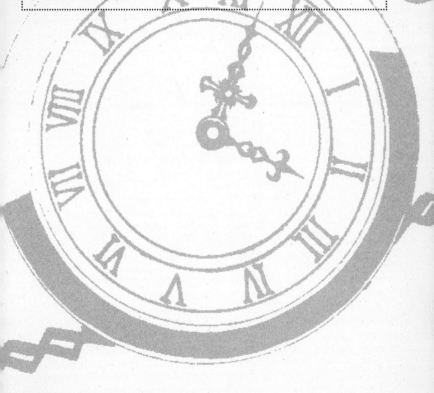

COMMON HONORIFICS

no honorific: Indicates familiarity or closeness; if used without permission or reason, addressing someone in this manner would constitute an insult.

-san: The Japanese equivalent of Mr./Mrs./Miss. If a situation calls for politeness, this is the fail-safe honorific.

-sama: Conveys great respect; may also indicate that the social status of the speaker is lower than that of the addressee.

-kun: Used most often when referring to boys (though it can be applied to girls as well), this indicates affection or familiarity. Occasionally used by older men among their peers, but it may also be used by anyone referring to a person of lower standing.

-chan: An affectionate honorific indicating familiarity used mostly in reference to girls; also used in reference to cute persons or animals of either gender.

PandoraHearts

MOCHIZUKI'S MUSINGS

VOLUME 11

I received e-mails from people who were seriously fooled for a moment by my comments here in Volume 10. I'm sorry, it looks like I won't be able to leave Japan for quite some time.

But this year I will go abroad! Yes, I shall!

I-I'm not declaring that I won't be able to go... again...

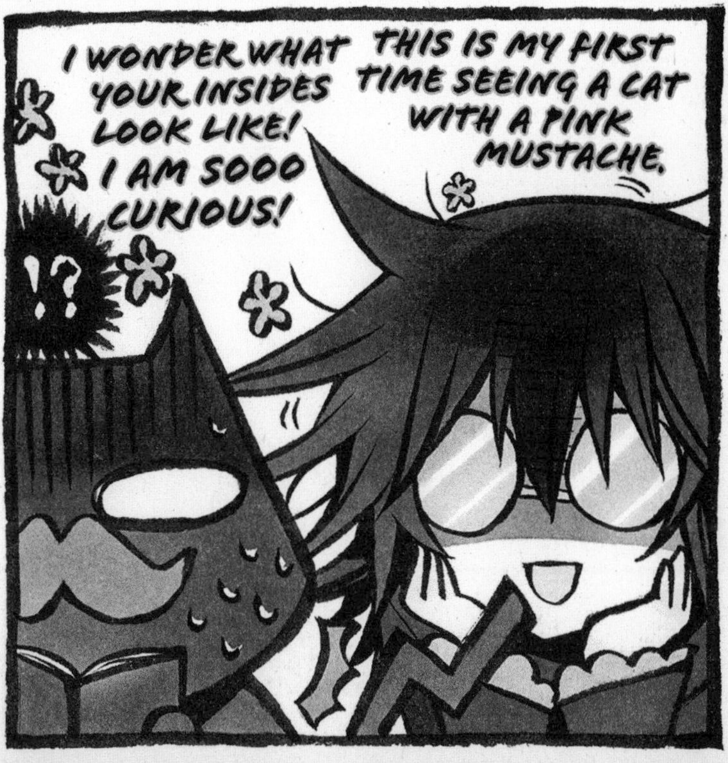
THIS IS MY FIRST TIME SEEING A CAT WITH A PINK MUSTACHE.
I WONDER WHAT YOUR INSIDES LOOK LIKE! I AM SOOO CURIOUS!
!?

PandoraHearts

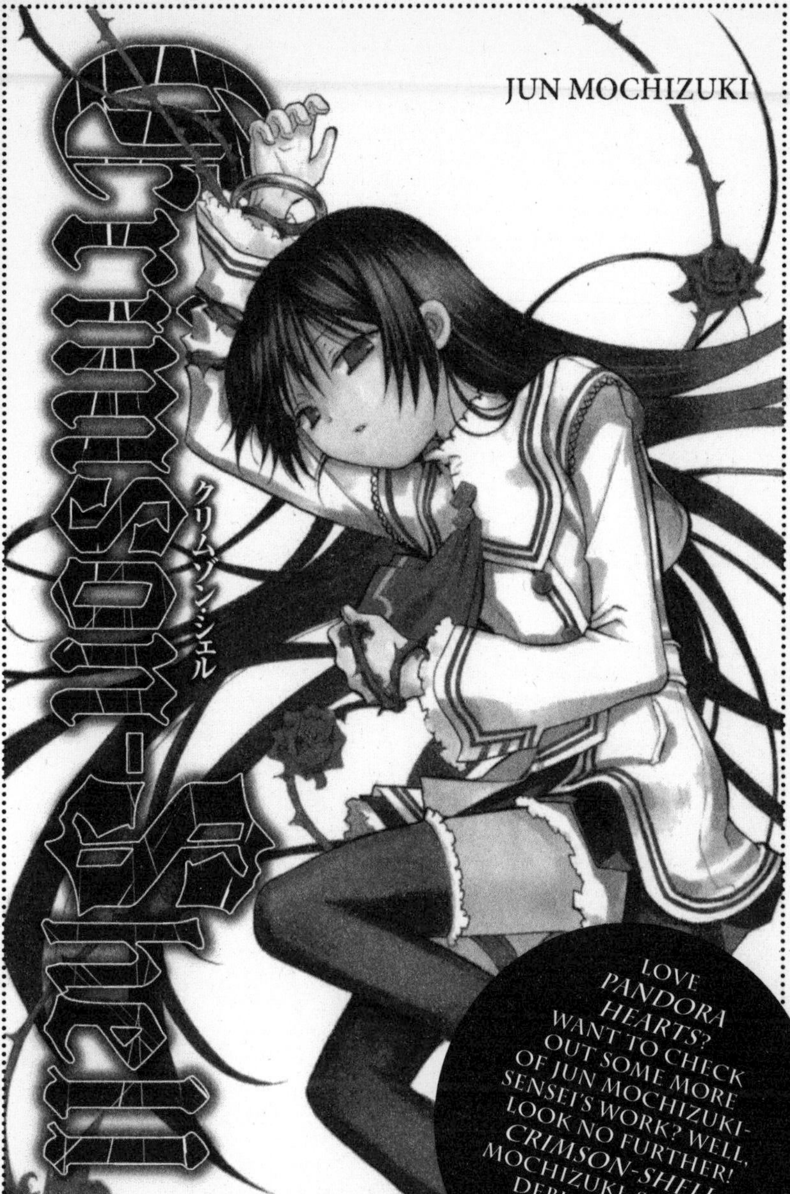
Crimson-Shell
クリムゾン・シェル
JUN MOCHIZUKI
LOVE *PANDORA HEARTS*? WANT TO CHECK OUT SOME MORE OF JUN MOCHIZUKI-SENSEI'S WORK? WELL, LOOK NO FURTHER! *CRIMSON-SHELL*, MOCHIZUKI-SENSEI'S DEBUT, IS NOW AVAILABLE FROM YEN PRESS!

PandoraHearts

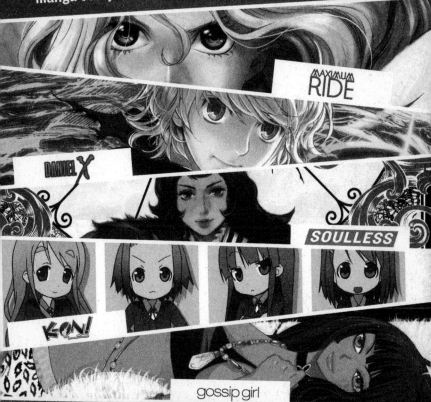
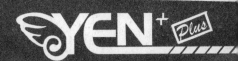

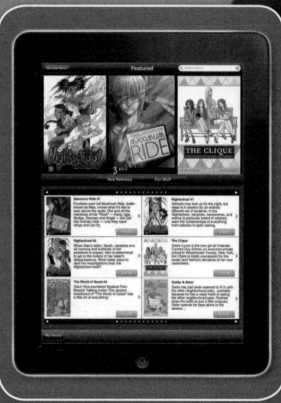
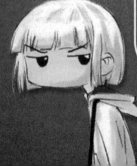

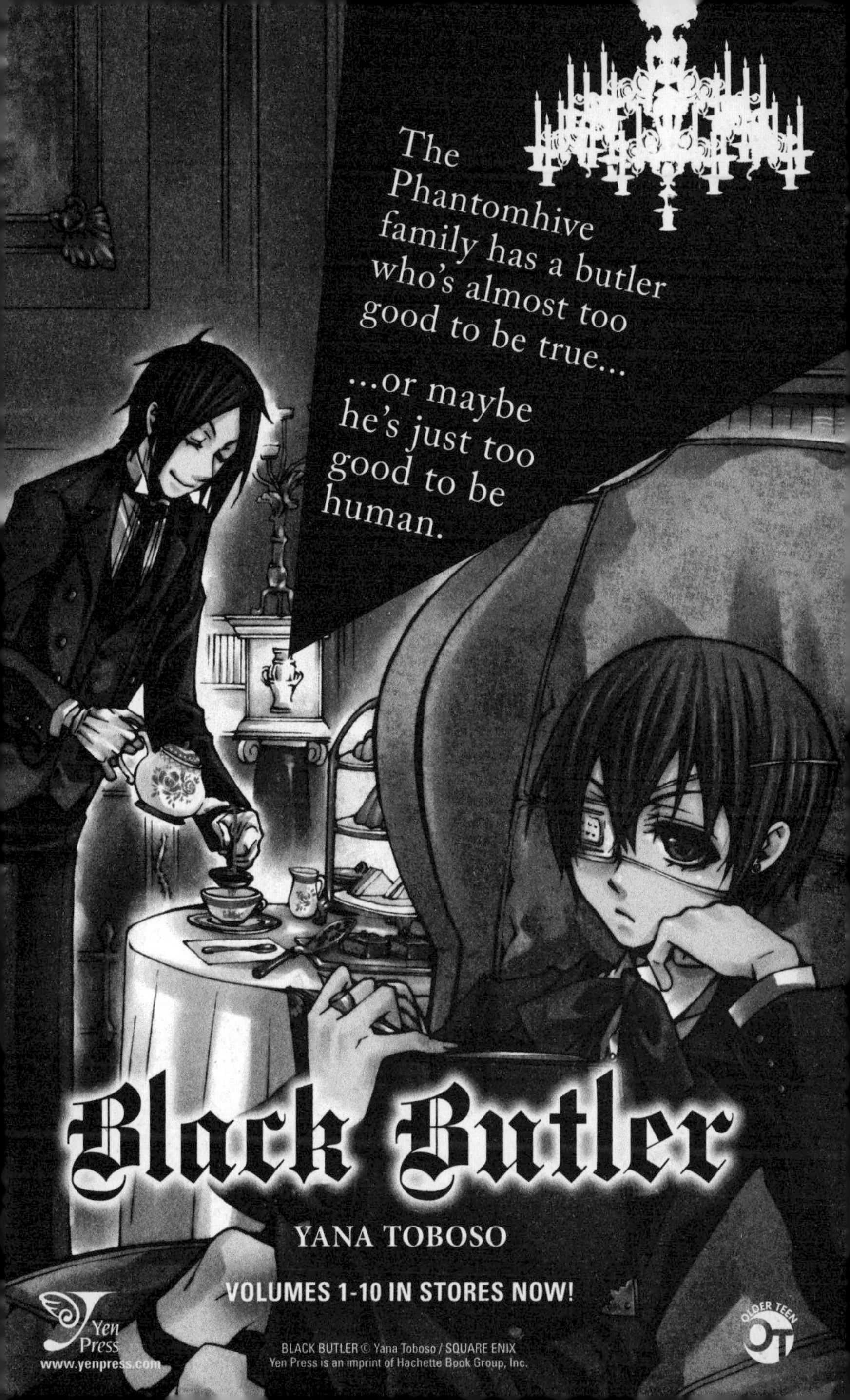
The Phantomhive family has a butler who's almost too good to be true...
...or maybe he's just too good to be human.
Black Butler
YANA TOBOSO
VOLUMES 1-10 IN STORES NOW!
Yen Press
www.yenpress.com
BLACK BUTLER © Yana Toboso / SQUARE ENIX
Yen Press is an imprint of Hachette Book Group, Inc.
OLDER TEEN
OT

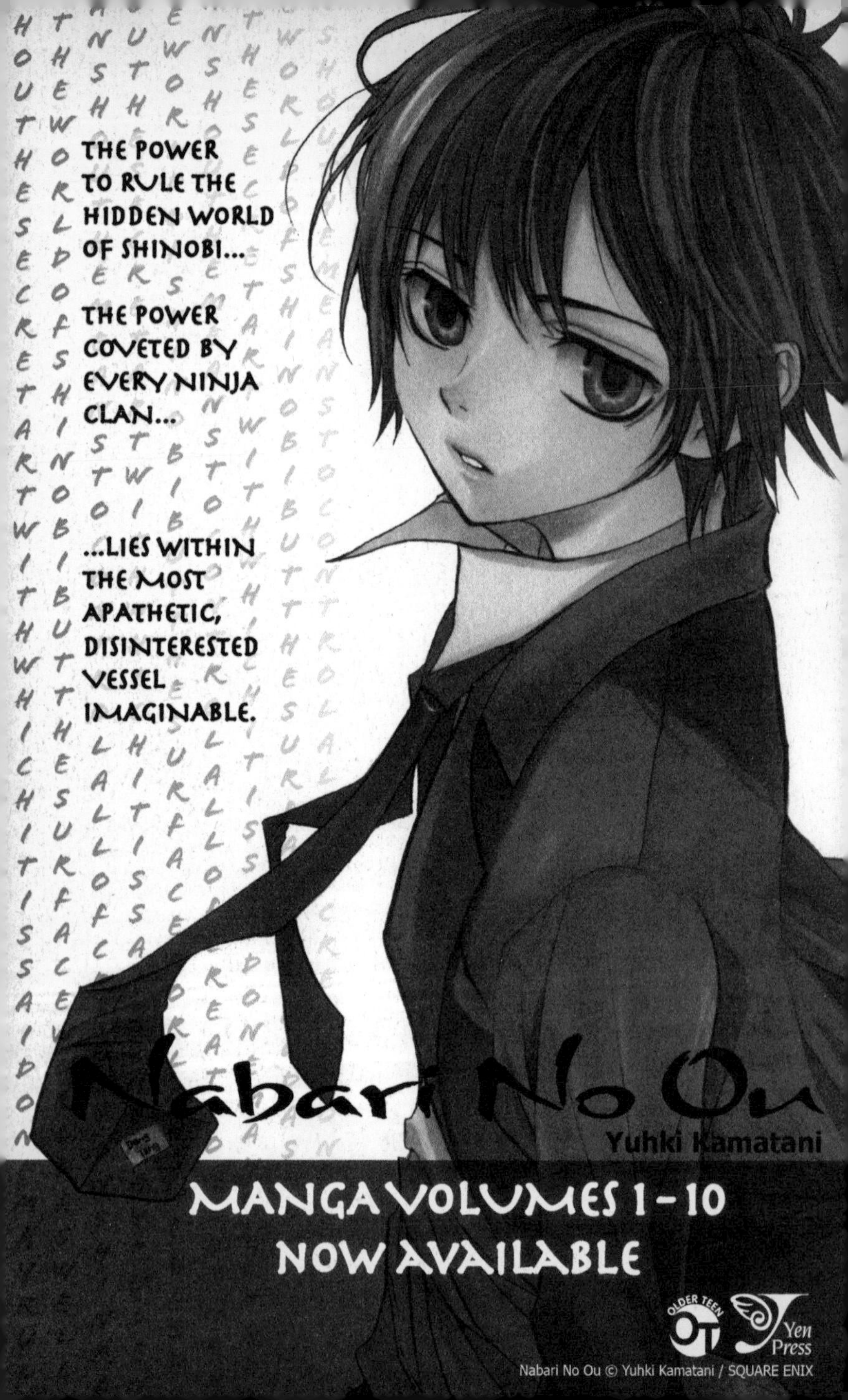
THE POWER TO RULE THE HIDDEN WORLD OF SHINOBI...
THE POWER COVETED BY EVERY NINJA CLAN...
...LIES WITHIN THE MOST APATHETIC, DISINTERESTED VESSEL IMAGINABLE.
Nabari No Ou
Yuhki Kamatani
MANGA VOLUMES 1-10
NOW AVAILABLE
OLDER TEEN OT
Yen Press
Nabari No Ou © Yuhki Kamatani / SQUARE ENIX

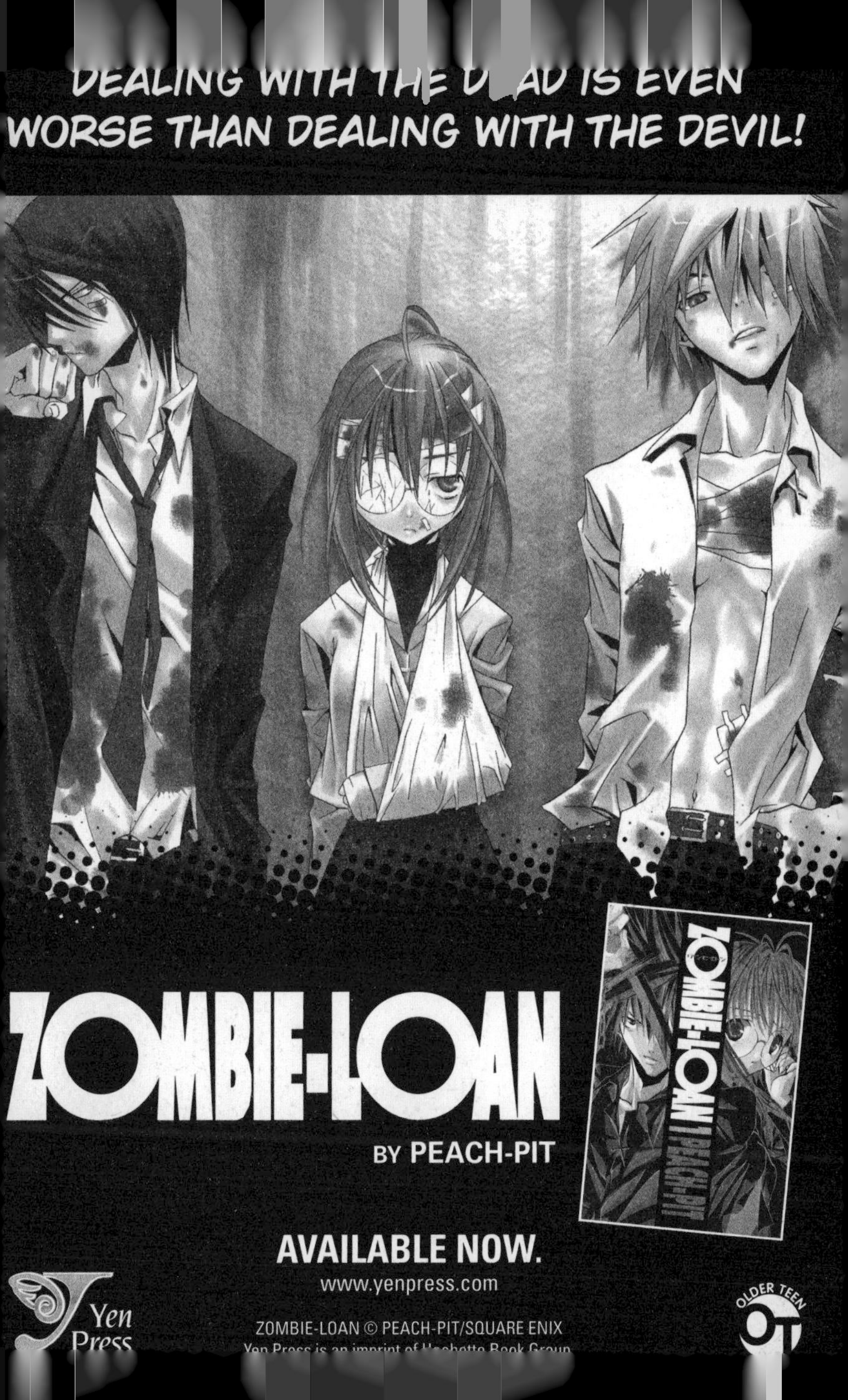
DEALING WITH THE DEAD IS EVEN WORSE THAN DEALING WITH THE DEVIL!
ZOMBIE-LOAN
BY PEACH-PIT
ZOMBIE-LOAN 1 PEACH-PIT
AVAILABLE NOW.
www.yenpress.com
Yen Press
OLDER TEEN OT
ZOMBIE-LOAN © PEACH-PIT/SQUARE ENIX
Yen Press is an imprint of Hachette Book Group

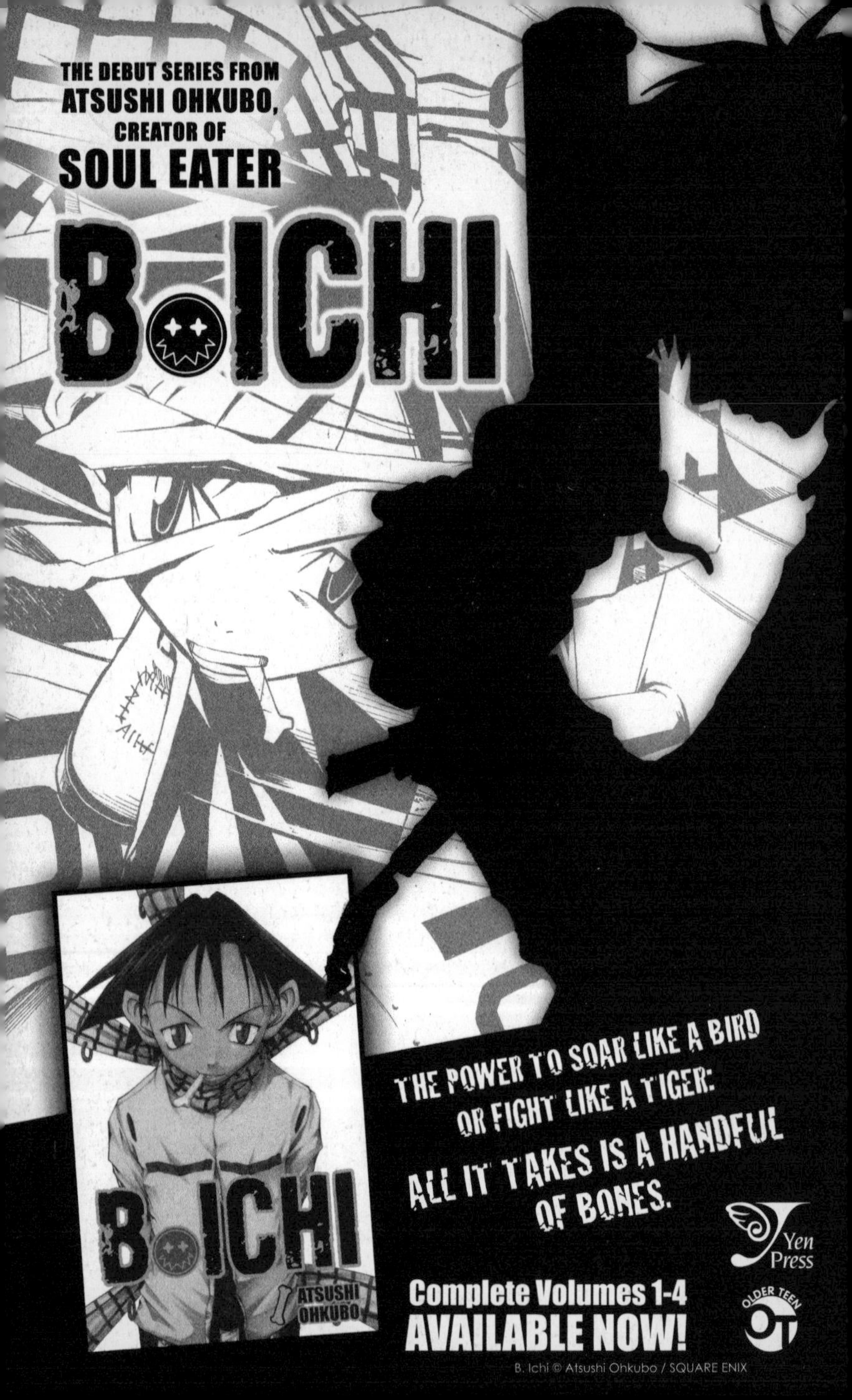
THE DEBUT SERIES FROM ATSUSHI OHKUBO, CREATOR OF SOUL EATER
B. ICHI
B. ICHI
ATSUSHI OHKUBO
THE POWER TO SOAR LIKE A BIRD OR FIGHT LIKE A TIGER:
ALL IT TAKES IS A HANDFUL OF BONES.
Yen Press
OLDER TEEN OT
Complete Volumes 1-4
AVAILABLE NOW!
B. Ichi © Atsushi Ohkubo / SQUARE ENIX

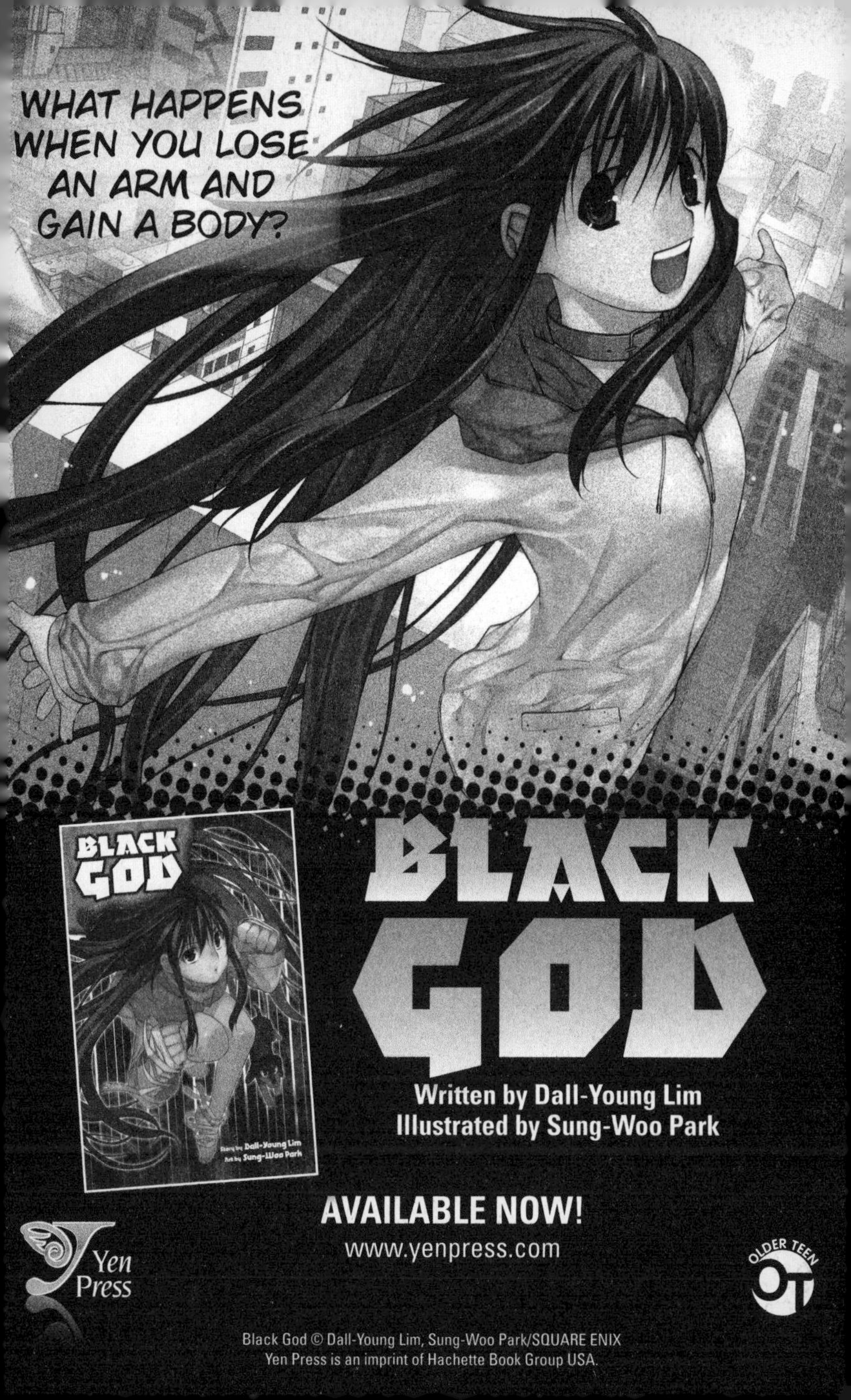
WHAT HAPPENS WHEN YOU LOSE AN ARM AND GAIN A BODY?
BLACK GOD
Story by Dall-Young Lim
Art by Sung-Woo Park
BLACK GOD
Written by Dall-Young Lim
Illustrated by Sung-Woo Park
AVAILABLE NOW!
www.yenpress.com
Yen Press
OLDER TEEN
OT
Black God © Dall-Young Lim, Sung-Woo Park/SQUARE ENIX
Yen Press is an imprint of Hachette Book Group USA.

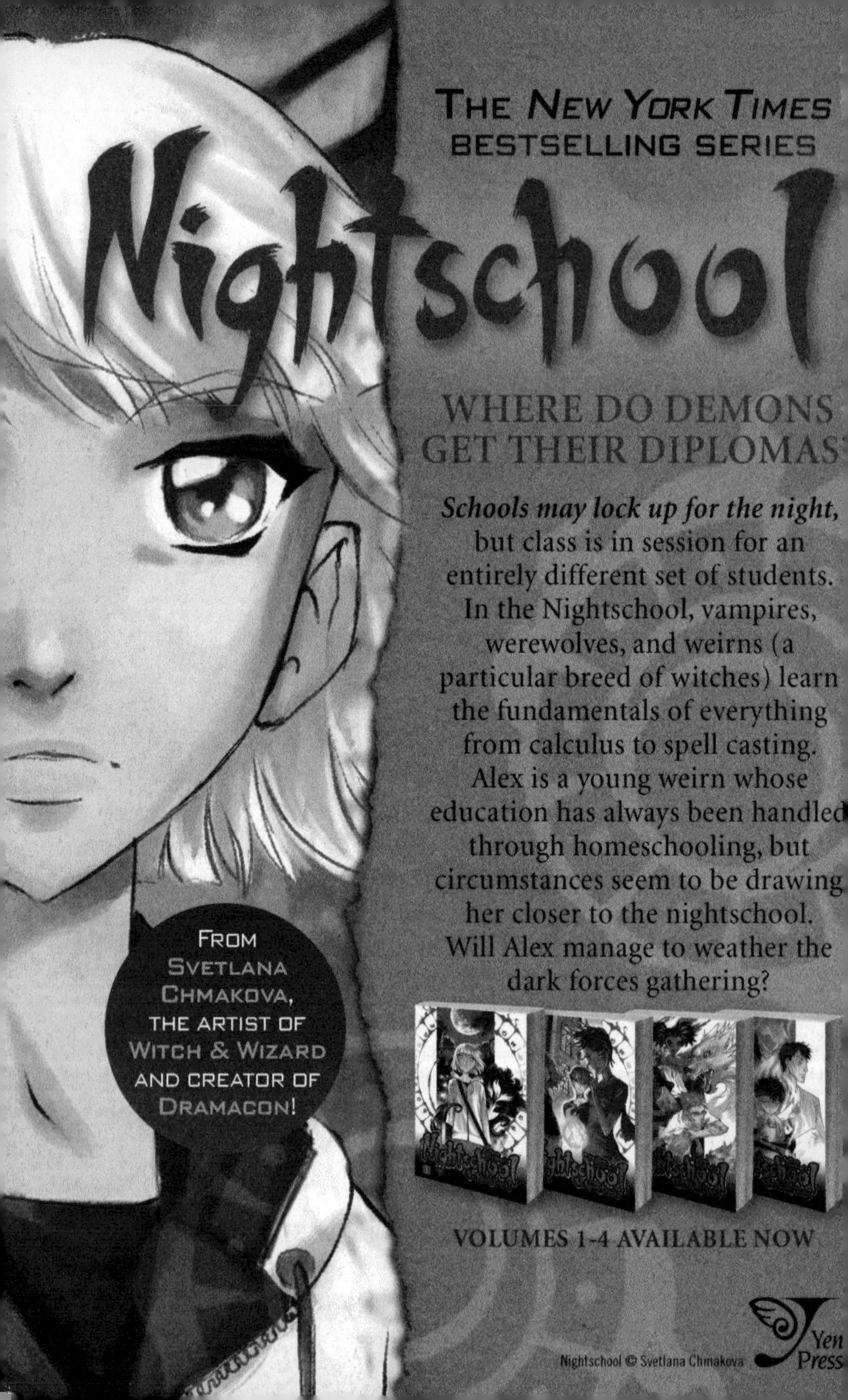
THE NEW YORK TIMES BESTSELLING SERIES
Nightschool
WHERE DO DEMONS GET THEIR DIPLOMAS?
Schools may lock up for the night, but class is in session for an entirely different set of students. In the Nightschool, vampires, werewolves, and weirns (a particular breed of witches) learn the fundamentals of everything from calculus to spell casting. Alex is a young weirn whose education has always been handled through homeschooling, but circumstances seem to be drawing her closer to the nightschool. Will Alex manage to weather the dark forces gathering?
FROM SVETLANA CHMAKOVA, THE ARTIST OF WITCH & WIZARD AND CREATOR OF DRAMACON!
VOLUMES 1-4 AVAILABLE NOW
Nightschool © Svetlana Chmakova
Yen Press

PANDORA HEARTS ⑪

JUN MOCHIZUKI

Translation: Tomo Kimura • Lettering: Alexis Eckerman

PANDORA HEARTS Vol. 11 © 2010 Jun Mochizuki / SQUARE ENIX CO., LTD. All rights reserved. First published Japan in 2010 by SQUARE ENIX CO., LTD. English translation rights arranged with SQUARE ENIX CO., LTD. and Hachette Book Group through Tuttle-Mori Agency, Inc.

Translation © 2012 by SQUARE ENIX CO., LTD.

Yen Press
Hachette Book Group
237 Park Avenue, New York, NY 10017

www.HachetteBookGroup.com
www.YenPress.com

Yen Press is an imprint of Hachette Book Group, Inc. The Yen Press name and logo are trademarks of Hachette Book Group, Inc.

First Yen Press Edition: July 2012

ISBN: 978-0-316-19729-8

10 9 8 7 6 5 4 3 2 1

BVG

Printed in the United States of America